Tourism and Development in Mountain Regions

Tourism and Development in
Mountain Regions

Edited by

Pamela M. Godde
The Mountain Institute
Franklin, West Virginia
USA

Martin F. Price
Mountain Regions and Conservation Programme
Environmental Change Unit
University of Oxford
UK

and

Friedrich M. Zimmermann
Department of Geography
University of Graz
Austria

CABI *Publishing*

CABI *Publishing* is a division of CAB *International*

CABI Publishing
CAB International
Wallingford
Oxon OX10 8DE
UK

CABI Publishing
10 E. 40th Street
Suite 3203
New York, NY 10016
USA

Tel: +44 (0)1491 832111
Fax: +44 (0)1491 833508
Email: cabi@cabi.org

Tel: +1 212 481 7018
Fax: +1 212 686 7993
Email: cabi-nao@cabi.org

A catalogue record for this book is available from the British Library, London, UK.

Library of Congress Cataloging-in-Publication Data
Tourism and development in mountain regions / edited by P. Godde, M. Price, and F.M. Zimmerman.
    p. cm.
  Includes bibliographical references and index.
  ISBN 0-85199-391-5 (alk. paper)
  1. Tourism.   2. Mountains--Recreational use.   3. Mountain ecology.
 I. Godde, P. (Pam)   II. Price, Martin F.   III. Zimmerman, F.M. (Friedrich M.)
G155.A1T589348   1999
338 . . . 4'77965--dc21   99-27724
                                                             CIP

ISBN 0 85199 391 5

Typeset by AMA DataSet Ltd, UK.
Printed and bound in the UK by Biddles Ltd, Guildford and King's Lynn.

Contents

v

Contributors

David Barkin, *Department of Economics, Universidad Autónoma Metropolitana, Apartado 23-181, 16000 Xochimilco, Mexico City, Mexico*

Michael Bartoš, *Institute of Landscape Ecology, Academy of Sciences of the Czech Republic, Na Sádkách 7, České Budějovice, Czech Republic*

Wendy Brewer Lama, *The Mountain Institute, PO Box 2785, Kathmandu, Nepal*

Ralf C. Buckley, *International Centre for Ecotourism Research, School of Environmental and Applied Science, Griffith University, Parklands Drive, Gold Coast, Queensland 9726, Australia*

Janet Cochrane, *Centre for South-East Asian Studies, University of Hull, Hull HU6 7RX, UK*

Maureen A. DeCoursey, *PO Box 879, Woodacre, CA 94973, USA*

Peter U.C. Dieke, *The Scottish Hotel School, University of Strathclyde, Curran Building, 94 Cathedral Street, Glasgow G4 0LG, UK*

Helen Farr, *Department of Agriculture, University of Aberdeen, 581 King Street, Aberdeen AB24 5UA, UK*

Romella S. Glorioso, *Laurence Moss & Associates, 2442 Cerrillos Road, PMB 422, Santa Fe, NM 87505, USA*

Pamela M. Godde, *The Mountain Institute, PO Box 907, Franklin, WV 26807, USA*

Chandra P. Gurung, *WWF Nepal Program, PO Box 7660, Lal Durbar, Kathmandu, Nepal*

Michael Herman, *Laurence Moss & Associates, 2442 Cerrillos Road, PMB 422, Santa Fe, NM 87505, USA*

Drahomíra Kušová, *Laurence Moss & Associates, 2442 Cerrillos Road, PMB 422, Santa Fe, NM 87505, USA*

L. Rory MacLellan, *Institute of Landscape Ecology, Academy of Sciences of the Czech Republic, Na Sádkách 7, České Budějovice, Czech Republic*

Christopher Monz, *National Outdoor Leadership School, 288 Main Street, Lander, WY 82520, USA*

Laurence A.G. Moss, *Laurence Moss & Associates, 2442 Cerrillos Road, PMB 422, Santa Fe, NM 87505, USA*

Robert E. Pfister, *Resource Recreation and Tourism, University of Northern British Columbia, 3333 University Way, Prince George, British Columbia, V2N 4Z9, Canada*

Catherine M. Pickering, *International Center for Ecotourism Research, School of Environmental and Applied Science, Griffith University, Parklands Drive, Gold Coast, Queensland 9726, Australia*

Martin F. Price, *Mountain Regions and Conservation Programme, Environmental Change Unit, University of Oxford, 11 Bevington Road, Oxford OX2 6NB, UK*

Alan Saffery, *Mongolian National Tourism Center, Chinggis Avenue 11, Ulaanbaatar, Mongolia*

Bill Slee, *Department of Agriculture, University of Aberdeen, 581 King Street, Aberdeen AB24 5UA, UK*

Patrick Snowdon, *Department of Agriculture, University of Aberdeen, 581 King Street, Aberdeen AB24 5UA, UK*

Jan Těšitel, *Institute of Landscape Ecology, Academy of Sciences of the Czech Republic, Na Sádkách 7, České Budějovice, Czech Republic*

Bhim Kumari Thapa, *The Scottish Hotel School, University of Strathclyde, Curran Building, 94 Cathedral Street, Glasgow G4 0LG, UK*

Desideria Tonderayi, *University of Calgary, Calgary, Alberta, T2N 0V1, Canada*

Georgia Valaoras, *Asklepiou 14, GR-10680 Athens, Greece*

Jan Warnken, *International Center for Ecotourism Research, School of Environmental and Applied Science, Griffith University, Parklands Drive, Gold Coast, Queensland 9726, Australia*

František Zemek, *Institute of Landscape Ecology, Academy of Sciences of the Czech Republic, Na Sádkách 7, České Budějovice, Czech Republic*

Friedrich M. Zimmermann, *Department of Geography, University of Graz, Heinrichstraße 36, A-8010 Graz, Austria*

Erratum

Tourism and Development in Mountain Regions
Edited by P.M. Godde, M.F. Price and F.M. Zimmermann

The addresses for Michael Heřman, Drahormíra Kušová and L. Rory MacLellan on pages vii and viii are incorrect. The details given at the head of the appropriate chapters are the correct addresses.

Tourism and Development in Mountain Regions: Moving Forward into the New Millennium

1

Pamela M. Godde,[1] Martin F. Price[2] and Friedrich M. Zimmermann[3]

[1]The Mountain Institute, PO Box 907, Franklin, WV 26807, USA; [2]Mountain Regions and Conservation Programme, Environmental Change Unit, University of Oxford, 11 Bevington Road, Oxford OX2 6NB, UK; [3]Department of Geography, University of Graz, Heinrichstraße 36, A-8010 Graz, Austria

Introduction

Agenda 21 and increasing awareness

Perhaps no other activity has grown over the past decades with the same speed and global dispersal as tourism. Such growth has inspired increasing dialogue among practitioners, policy-makers, academics and other tourism stakeholders about the form and function of tourism in the next millennium. In a sense, this dialogue heralds an age of increasing consciousness. Not only are we seriously questioning the impacts of tourism on the biosphere as well as on people and their cultures and societies, but we are starting to take more directed action toward the sustainable maintenance of precious resources.

The various types of tourism that have arisen over the past few decades, such as ecotourism, nature-based tourism, alternative tourism, and small-scale tourism (Cater and Lowman, 1994; Bramwell et al., 1996; Weaver, 1998; Fennell, 1999) are indicative of this higher level of awareness. It is further linked to increasing interest in various ecosystems considered to be 'fragile', or to have a greater propensity to be affected by human activities, including tourism. The international community formally began to recognize the global importance of sustaining various 'fragile ecosystems' at the United Nations Conference on Environment and Development (UNCED) in

Rio de Janeiro in 1992. Two chapters in 'Agenda 21', the plan for action into the 21st century endorsed at UNCED by the heads of state or government of almost all of the world's nations, addressed the management of such eco-systems: Chapter 12 on dryland ecosystems, and Chapter 13 on mountain ecosystems. The concept of 'fragile environments' applies to 'areas that are particularly susceptible to damage by human activities, with relatively slow rates of recovery' (Harrison and Price, 1997: 5). It also applies, however, to the human communities that depend on these environments and are suscep-tible to change 'by external human forces, whose magnitude and potential impacts are not always predictable' (Harrison and Price, 1997).

Chapter 13 of Agenda 21 – 'Managing fragile ecosystems: sustainable mountain development' – indicates the vital importance of mountain eco-systems to the global community and emphasizes the needs for the protec-tion of these ecosystems and the sustainable development of mountain regions. The chapter stresses the importance of mountains to global survival and urges 'the proper management of mountain resources and socio-economic development of the people'. It includes two programme areas: (i) 'generating and strengthening knowledge about the ecology and sustainable development of mountain ecosystem' and (ii) 'promoting integrated water-shed development and alternative livelihood opportunities' (Price, 1999).

Since UNCED, several governmental and non-governmental institutions at both national and international levels, as well as research institutions and concerned people, have worked to advance the agenda put forth in Chapter 13 of Agenda 21 (Price, 1999). Not surprisingly, tourism and recreation have featured prominently, as a number of examples can attest. In 1995, the Inter-national NGO Consultation on the Mountain Agenda identified tourism as one of the nine key issues of importance to mountain regions (The Mountain Institute, 1995). In 1996, the European NGO Consultation on Sustainable Mountain Development also recognized the need for clear policies for tour-ism (ARPE/CIAPP, 1996), which has been a primary source of income in the European mountains, particularly the Alps (Zimmermann, 1998a). In 1997, the state-of-knowledge report, *Mountains of the World: a Global Priority* (Messerli and Ives, 1997) was published. One of the chapters (Price *et al.*, 1997) is devoted to tourism and its related phenomenon, amenity migration, while several other chapters include discussion of tourism. In 1998, the Mountain Forum hosted an electronic conference entitled 'Community-based Mountain Tourism: Practices for Linking Conservation with Enterprise'. From this conference came a report in 1999 in which various practices for achieving sustainable and equitable community-based tourism and development in mountain areas are outlined (Godde, 1999). Such practies include the encouragement and reinforcement of holistic manage-ment strategies, local ownership and control of resources, external know-ledge and technology, and organizational capacity building, to list only a few. At the same time, a document on Mountains and Tourism, prepared by Mountain Agenda (1999), identified multi-stakeholder roles and multi-level approaches as cornerstones of successful tourism within the context of sustainable mountain development. Both these reports were submitted to the seventh session of the UN Commission on Sustainable Development in April 1999, at which tourism was the economic sector given special attention.

Mountains on global agendas

In the 1990s, a growing number of projects and programmes have addressed mountain tourism. These have included the regional project of the International Centre for Integrated Mountain Development (ICIMOD), summarized by Sharma (1998) in one of a number of recent books specifically on mountain tourism (Debarbieux, 1995; Luger and Inmann, 1995; East *et al.*, 1998). Each of the many recent publications on mountain tourism will contribute to two key future events. First, the Seventh Conference of the Parties to the Convention on Biological Diversity will focus on the biological diversity of mountain ecosystems in the year 2001. Given the importance of biodiversity as a factor in attracting tourists, this event should consider the linkages between these two issues of global importance. Second, the United Nations General Assembly has declared that 2002 will be both the International Year of Mountains and the International Year of Ecotourism, which will offer particular opportunities to address the roles of tourism in relation to the needs of mountain people and the environments on which they depend.

Mountains are prominent on global agendas not only because of their importance for tourism – though the experience of visitors to mountain regions has undoubtedly been one factor in increasing global awareness – but also because they cover one-fifth of the earth's land surface and supply important resources to over half of the world's population (Ives, 1992). Among these, water may be the most important (Bandyopadhyay *et al.*, 1997; Mountain Agenda, 1998). Also, the unique biophysical characteristics of mountains – significant changes in altitude and dramatic variations in climate over short distances – have led to rich and diverse reservoirs of species and ecosystems, which supply some of the world's most valuable natural sources of food and medicine (National Research Council, 1989; Zimmerer, 1996; Jenik, 1997; Sterly, 1997). The gene banks of mountain species, both natural and cultivated, represent important resources for human health and survival in the present and in the future. Mountains also supply other important resources, from agriculture, forestry and mining.

However, the importance of mountain regions does not stop at environmental resources; mountains also hold valuable human resources. About one-tenth of the global population inhabits mountains, including a variety of diverse cultures and the largest number of ethnic groups (Grötzbach and Stadel, 1997) with a wealth of local knowledge. Isolation coupled with limited communication and diverse migration patterns have allowed mountain communities to keep many of their traditional ways of life for generations.

Thus, these communities generally have experienced relatively slower rates of cultural change than their counterparts in lowland regions; though rates of change have been accelerating in recent years due to rapid growth in

Fig. 1.1.   On Mount Penulisan (1740 m), the village of Sukawana, Bali, perform a ceremony to bid farewell to the gods who will rise from the mountain tops (photo by Thomas Reuter).

Fig. 1.2.   As spiritual centres, mountains often provide a place of meditation and worship Prabhupada's Palace of Gold, Moundsville, West Virginia (photo by James Kelly).

accessibility and increasing incorporation into regional and global markets. In many regions worldwide, mountain people have been able to maintain important local folk knowledge and ways of life, including language, folk-lore, craft, religion, healing methods and natural resource management practices. The highlands of Thailand provide one example of the wealth of mountain areas. For centuries these mountains and upland regions have been home to a number of marginalized indigenous groups, who had been pushed to these regions in earlier times. Making their homes here, the diverse linguistic groups inhabiting the upland regions of Thailand maintain their rich oral and handicraft traditions, many of which have become resources for the tourist trade (Akin Rabibhadana, 1992). The Kingdom of Bhutan offers another example, where various architectural structures that reflect the art of traditional Bhutanese building techniques and craftsman-ship can be found. The importance of these buildings lies in their integral connection between the practical and the symbolic, between environment and culture (Semple, 1998). They also reflect a sense of place so important to many mountain peoples (Benbaum, 1997).

The wealth of cultural diversity found in the mountains can only broaden human understanding and practices. Yet, mountains are cultural receptacles in other ways. As Bernbaum (1997) describes well, mountains are also spiritual centres; places of power; abodes of deities; places of worship, paradises, divine ancestors and of the dead; and sources of blessings, inspiration, revelation and transformation. They evoke the highest values and most sacred of beliefs of many people and cultures worldwide, and have brought pilgrims from far and wide to congregate on their peaks for millennia. In fact, a form of mountain tourism has existed as long as mountains have included religious sites and hence have been destinations of religious pilgrimages, and such sites are found in a large number of the world's mountain ranges. Yet the religious and the secular sojourner alike experience spiritual awakenings brought forth by the power of mountains; the experience of transcendence that mountains bring, in other words, is not limited to the religious. The Judeo-Christian pilgrim to Mount Sinai, or the Hindu pilgrim to Gunung Agung on Bali, may attach a religious meaning to their experience not shared by the secular visitor to the same places. But both the religious and non-religious traveller may experience the same sense of awe and spiritual renewal that these places evoke (Cooper, 1997). For many people, this is a fundamental draw to mountain environments.

Tourism in Mountain Regions

The tourist's motivations

Whether a traveller's motivations are religious or secular, mountains are significant destinations. After coastal regions, mountains may be second in

global popularity as tourist destinations (Mieczkowski, 1995). Tourists flock
to the mountains for a number of reasons. In addition to the wish to gain a
sense of renewal and spiritual well-being, another contributing factor to the
popularity of mountain tourism is the explosion of lowland populations and
over-crowding in urban centres. In wanting to escape urban pollution,
noise, crime and other related stresses, people look to mountain environments for their serenity and relative calm. This is particularly true for domestic tourism, which dominates over international tourism in most mountain
regions. One example of this global phenomenon are the hill stations of the
Indian Himalaya, which were first developed by the colonial British, and are
now visited in the summer by middle-class Indians seeking to escape the
heat and congestion of the plains (Aditya and Singh, 1997). The development of tourism in the European Alps had already begun in the 18th century,
when artists, writers, poets and members of the aristocracy travelled for
educational, religious and health reasons. Around the beginning of the 19th
century, climbers began to explore the peaks of the Alps. Tourism as a mass
phenomenon started in the second half of the 19th century, with the first
railroads crossing the Alps. In 1863, Thomas Cook led the first package tour
to Switzerland. Reacting to the increasing number of tourists, cableways
were established, the first one on to Rigi in 1873 (Zimmermann, 1995).
Similar trends also occurred in North America, where the expansion of the
railways made the Rocky Mountains accessible to tourists and mountain
climbers in the late 19th century, and a cog railway was built to take tourists
to the summit of Pike's Peak in Colorado in 1891 (Price, 1990).

Undoubtedly, mountain tourism derives partly from the romantic ideal-
ism of people jaded by urban living for, as MacCannell (1976) noted some
years ago, travel has a romantic aspect. This is perhaps particularly relevant
to mountain areas, where the pristine and 'untouched' beauty remains both
a reality and an image of mountain areas. Even before the Romanticism of
Shelley, Byron and Keats, mountains carried a desirable image, inspiring
many to try to regain lost values believed to be a result of industrialization
and technology. Much of this relates to the current environmental movement, in which a return to simplicity and wholesome living are stressed.

Another motivation is to seek adventure and to participate in recreational sports. Snow-shoeing, downhill and cross-country skiing, and hiking
each bring a sense of adventure and have been practised for enjoyment for
over a century. Heli-skiing, snowboarding, and snowmobiling have more
recently been added to the winter attractions that mountains offer, while
trekking, camping, climbing, rafting, kayaking, canoeing, and mountain
biking fill tourists' time in other seasons. The degree to which mountain
sports are diversifying, combined with innovative advances in sports
technology, contribute to the number of tourists to mountain regions (see
Buckley *et al.*, Chapter 2, this volume). In addition, while opportunities for
these recreational sports have long attracted people to locations within their
own regions, they now comprise an element within a global market for

people who have the advantages of more leisure time, greater economic security and more efficient travel to a growing diversity of destinations. Some skiers and snow-boarders, for example, ski year round, travelling from one hemisphere to the next, a phenomenon made possible by lower airfares and an increasing number of airports near and in mountain regions.

Mountain tourism – a multi-faceted phenomenon

The title of this book, *Tourism and Development in Mountain Regions*, may give the reader the impression that it will consider only the question of attracting income from tourists to satisfy the economic goals of a nation, region, or mountain community. Indeed, the financial facet of tourism has been central to people interested in raising the economic status of mountain communities and people, and cannot be quickly overlooked, for mountain communities include some of the poorest and most marginalized in the world (Ives, 1997). The danger of this approach, however, is that it ignores the fact that tourism is a multi-faceted phenomenon that encompasses economic as well as political, social, cultural, historical and psychological dimensions. Understanding tourism entails looking at it as 'a massive and complex interaction of people, who demand a wide range of services, facilities, and inputs' (Price *et al.*, 1997: 251). Working from this definition of tourism, we may realize that tourism comprises social networks with the purpose of achieving a number of goals, including individual, social, cultural, political and economic aspirations. Within the range of groups of people involved, those of host communities and the tourists are most important, for tourism as a whole hinges on the mutual benefits created and exchanged between these groups (Smith, 1989).

　　To a large extent, mountain people who pursue tourism do so for economic benefits. For the Tenggerese people of Indonesia (Cochrane, Chapter 10, this volume), tourism offers the attraction of relatively high wage incomes at rapid return, versus the alternative of subsistence agriculture. Yet economic advantages are not the only reason why hosts take up tourism enterprises. In her study of tourism based on teaching traditional weaving skills in the alps of Japan, Creighton (1995) shows that a primary motivation for hosts taking up this mountain tourism activity is to escape the hectic pace of corporate life in the urban areas below. Another example comes from the Sierra Madres of southern Mexico, where community members are creating a cooperative of cultural museums to strengthen indigenous traditions and culture (Morales, 1998). This in turn can serve political and social purposes through the granting of a shared sense of cultural legitimacy. It is also worth noting that, in many mountain regions, the provision of services to tourists builds on old traditions of providing hospitality to travellers; one example being 'tea-house trekking' in Nepal (Odell and Lama, 1998).

   Thus the reasons why people in mountain regions decide to pursue tourism enterprises can be numerous, encompassing many values and alternatives. This is also true for tourists, whose reasons for selecting a given destination are varied and complex. Most important, however, is the understanding that the guest motivations may not always match those of host communities. Tourist interests tend to be short-term, centring on ideas of receiving the most service and the best experience within a given time frame and for a given price. In contrast, hosts often hope that the efforts they put into developing a tourism enterprise will have a long-term payback, which in part depends upon the sustained prevalence of a suitable environment, a reasonable level of economic gain, and a sustained level of host community well-being. Yet, tourists' interests rarely meet the demands of long-term viability, and there are many examples of tourist enterprises and regions that have fallen victim to changing trends, new sources of competition, new means of access or merely economic downturn. Even in the European Alps, for instance, which are now one of the global centres of tourism, it is often forgotten that, after a period of rapid growth before the First World War, the period between the two World Wars was one in which many settlements reverted to traditional agriculture because of decreased demands for tourism and increasing competition from other destinations (Kroener, 1968; Direction du Projet MAB Pays d'Enhaut, 1985). Summer tourism in the European Alps, with all its long traditions, has been characterized by strong fluctuations since the beginning of the 1970s. During recent years there have been dramatic recessions. 'Summer in the Alps', in its traditional form, no longer seems to be sufficiently attractive given prevailing socio-economic, demographic and social changes; moreover it is subject to considerable international competition. Additionally a loss of attractive countryside for summer activities due to the building of infra- and superstructures for winter sports, and a decreasing interest of the local population for tourism entrepreneurship led to significant decreases in numbers of overnight stays in the 1990s (Zimmermann, 1998b).

   Given the number of wars and similar conflicts that take place in mountain areas, perceived or actual risks to personal safety can also be important factors in a rapid decrease in tourist visits, as seen in Afghanistan, Bosnia, Kashmir, Nicaragua, Rwanda, Yemen, Ethiopia and Peru in recent years. Such problems of image are often hard to change – though, with a return of political stability, numbers of visitors to the mountains of the last two countries have begun to rise again. With regard to the prerequisite for another type of tourism, there are many examples of ski areas that have received few visitors in years when little snow fell early in the season, so that a 'low snow' year was perceived, in spite of good snowfalls later on. On the other hand extreme snowfalls and recent avalanche catastrophes in the Alps have shown diverse negative effects. Those who see a future in tourism need to consider that tourists are not attracted by uncertainty, and that tourism is a comparatively uncertain business.

Beyond the basic socio-economic component of host–guest inter-actions, others come into play. As MacLellan, Dieke and Thapa (Chapter 9) and Tonderayi (Chapter 15) point out, government policies can play a major role in determining the scope of tourism in an area. These might include a restrictive tourism policy, as in Bhutan, policies determining the amount of funding available to a community for developing the appropriate infra-structure, or policies that limit the number of tourists visiting an area, as Gurung and DeCoursey (Chapter 12) discuss with regard to Upper Mustang. Non-governmental organizations (NGOs) also play a role in tourism, largely through their direct involvement with communities, as described by a number of authors in this publication and for various parts of the Indian and Nepalese Himalaya by Goldsmith (1998), Inmann (1998), Inmann and Luger (1998), and Kohli (1998). Finally, the private sector and entrepreneurs are involved in mountain tourism through the development of enterprises in a region, including hotels, restaurants and tour services. While private sector involvement is often generated by the interest to earn a quick profit, it can also be generated by genuine interest in and concern for the region (see Fletcher, 1998).

Concepts in Tourism Development

Like 'tourism', the term 'development' is complex, embodying a number of ideas accumulated and revised in recent decades. In its very essence, development implies change: 'a process that improves the living conditions of people . . . (relating) to non-material wants as well as to physical require-ments. Development goals that call for the increase in social welfare or the improvement of the quality of life reflect this agreement' (Bartlemus, 1994: 1). Yet, one set of 'improvements' may lead to decreases in other aspects of quality of life. A number of examples may be cited from mountain regions. In the Kathmandu Valley of Nepal, rapid population growth, fuelled by significant in-migration and the introduction of motorized transport, have resulted in a highly polluted environment (Shah and Nagpal, 1997). In the Star Mountains of Papua New Guinea, mining waste from the Ok Tedi Mine flowed into the Fly River, killing tens of thousands of fish and polluting local gardens, destroying the traditional livelihood of many mountain communities (Banks and Ballard, 1997).

Such development not only affects the well-being of local communities forced to live in a degraded environment, but also the environment of the global community through the processes of cumulative and systemic global environmental change (Turner *et al.*, 1990). The raised awareness of the destructive effects of development on the environment in the latter half of this century has led to the now generally inseparable adjective in the concept of 'sustainable development'. With its roots particularly at the 1972 United Nations Conference on the Human Environment, the concept was

Fig. 1.3. Thousands of tourists visit Yosemite National Park in the US Sierra Nevada annually. The issue of limiting the number of vehicles allowed to enter the park has been much debated (photo by Jerry M. Gasser).

explored in considerable detail at the International Institute for Applied Systems Analysis in the mid-1980s (Clark and Munn, 1986), and then popularized by the World Commission on Environment and Development in 1987, which defined it as 'development that meets the needs of the present without compromising the ability of future generations to meet their own needs' (WCED, 1987: 43). However, this definition is rather vague, as it specifies neither a time horizon nor the types of human needs, and does not even mention the complex interactions of environment and development (Bartlemus, 1994). It also can be perceived as including a significant internal contradiction: the long-term continuation of an existing condition and, at the same time, change. Thus, increasingly, sustainable development is seen as a process that aims at ensuring that current needs are satisfied while retaining the capacity of natural resources to provide long-term needs, and meeting goals of social equity and environmental quality. A simple, consistent definition is not possible, as the process will be defined differently by each culture (Roe, 1996).

The related concept of 'sustainable tourism' is also interpreted in different ways. From a global political point of view, it is worth noting the economic approach taken by the World Travel and Tourism Council, the World Tourism Organization, and the Earth Council (1995), which implies that sustainable tourism can be achieved through forms of economic development that involve large numbers of tourists. A broader approach is to recognize that three sets of interrelated factors – ecological, economic and socio-cultural – must be considered together (FNNPE, 1993; Bisaz and Lutz, 1998, in Godde, 1999: 11), and that, perhaps, political aspects need to be specifically added (Bramwell *et al.*, 1996). Banskota and Sharma (1998) have suggested that this should be done in the context of carrying capacity, though this is in itself a very difficult concept to operationalize, as it relies principally on quantitative indicators and the assumption that thresholds can be identified. More recently, issues of whether and how sustainable tourism can work have emerged from a broader geographic perspective (see Hall and Lew, 1998), in which analysis proceeds largely from environmental, regional, spatial and evolutionary considerations (Hall and Lew, 1998: 5). Principles, partnerships and best practice for sustainable tourism development has been a main issue raised by the European Partners for the Environment, based on research by an international expert group. A hierarchy of initiatives in the European Alps was discussed from the supra-regional (Alpine Convention) to the very local level, like agrotourism or the concept of 'Green Villages in Austria' (Williams and Shaw, 1996).

People are also starting to contest the concept of sustainable tourism when it appears to conflict with traditional beliefs and/or values. For example, among many indigenous groups, the idea of linking conservation with enterprise in the form of tourism does not fit well with indigenous ways of thinking (Mallari and Enote, 1996; McLaren *et al.*, 1998). Generally speaking, the argument is based on the widely held belief that sustainability is largely devoid of considerations to the symbolic and symbiotic relation humans have with the environment. Nevertheless, if it is accepted that sustainability is culturally defined, as suggested by Roe (1996), and that 'land takes care of the people and people take care of the land', then the fact that the relationship between people and their environment is not unidirectional can be recognized.

Burdens in Mountain Development

Poverty and environmental degradation remain a fact in many mountain areas. Mountain communities are generally poorer than their counterparts in the lowland regions and often bear the burden of mountain development – whether mining, logging, hydroelectric plants, transport lines or tourism. These communities bear this burden not only with regard to the natural environment, but also with regard to the impacts on their economy and social and cultural life. With this in mind, sustainable development becomes a key concept, particularly when understood in the triangle of sustainability laid out in the 1992 Rio Declaration on Environment and Development. According to Rieder and Wyder (1997: 89), sustainability is achieved when all three components of the triangle – the ecology, the economy and the society – improve simultaneously: 'If one attempts continually to influence the three components in a positive way, a progressive improvement of the overall sustainability evolves'. As with any balance, an increase in attention to one part of the system leads to a disruption in equilibrium. For example, attention primarily to economic measures can result in a decrease in other measures, such as the ecological and/or social conditions of local communities. With traditional forms of tourism development, one component – usually the economic aspect – has generally been emphasized more than the others. Similarly, ideas of sustainable tourism often tend to centre on aspects of the environment, leaving issues of social well-being aside. Frequently, it is believed that if the environment and economy of an area are sustained, the community attached to that environment and economy will also prosper. This, however, is not always the case, for development can easily disrupt the social order, and tourism is certainly no exception – as, for instance, in the many places where the growth of tourism has led to excessive costs for housing or food supplies for long-term residents, as well as immigrants working in the tourism industry (Price *et al.*, 1997). Thus, efforts toward sustainability must include all components – social, environmental and economic.

For better or for worse, the age of mountain remoteness is passing. While mountains have long been the desired destination of tourism and pilgrims seeking scenic beauty, wilderness, solitude, spiritual well-being or recreation, these once secluded areas are now becoming open to a variety of interests. With the advent of technology and travel, mountain frontiers that once equated to biophysical and cultural survival are being exposed to human intervention. Even the greatest pessimist cannot simply 'wish tourism away'. Yet even the greatest optimist cannot overlook the challenges of making tourism sustainable.

Effects of tourism and development in mountain regions

Even before practitioners, policy-makers and academics began applying the concept of 'sustainability' to mountain tourism, problems of environmental degradation, overcrowding and cultural exploitation had clearly presented themselves. Perhaps the most important question facing those involved in tourism development relates to the extent to which tourism affects the local host communities and the surrounding environment. With regard to the physical environment, Monz in Chapter 3 shows that even the seemingly harmless human activity of trekking results in far-reaching impacts on mountain environments. The development of trails leads to the loss of some species and the introduction of others, and also to soil erosion, and trekkers often bring and leave considerable amounts of waste. The more extreme forms of mountain tourism development, such as downhill skiing and the expansion of resorts at high altitudes, can have significant impacts not only on the surrounding mountain environments but also on downstream water supply (Bandyopadhyay *et al.*, 1997; Buckley *et al.*, Chapter 2, this volume).

The socio-cultural environment also can be strongly affected by tourism. Built heritage, for example, tends to be one of the more tangible features of a cultural environment that can be destroyed through the demolition of buildings, the adoption of simpler, faster building techniques or the adoption of different structural forms and/or functions. Yet, even the less visible aspects of a society, such as its internal structure, may be altered through new patterns of social relations that derive from the power or influence that newer enterprises, such as tourism, bring. In general, writers on tourism have viewed change within affected societies as adverse and have emphasized the negative effects of tourism – yet societies and cultures everywhere change and adapt to new and different circumstances. No culture is static. Furthermore, the effects of tourism on socio-cultural environments and the changes that it brings are not necessarily negative. Mountain tourism has brought higher standards of living to many places. Ives (1997), for example, notes that mass tourism, particularly in the form of alpine skiing from the 1960s, has contributed to the affluence of select areas of Switzerland, areas which, prior to the introduction of tourism, were economically marginal. Nevertheless, tourism is a very unevenly distributed phenomenon, even in the Alps, and only those communities which have seen a growth in tourism in recent decades have experienced stable or growing populations (Bätzing *et al.*, 1996). Similarly, tourism only occurs in a relatively small number of Himalayan valleys (Sharma, 1998). One group that has benefited greatly are the Sherpas of the Khumbu of Nepal (Stevens, 1993; Rogers and Aitchison, 1998).

Tourism can also bring about positive changes to marginalized groups within mountain communities, perhaps most notably women and children. Women's issues are important to recognize in the context of mountains and development for two major reasons. First, women typically have close relationships with mountain environments through their roles as family care-givers (Byers and Sainju, 1994: 219). In the mountains of developing countries, they are generally the ones responsible for supplying the family with food, medicine and water from the surrounding area. As such, actions toward sustainable development of land management practices hinge on the full participation and integration of women. More importantly, however, women tend to bear the greatest burdens in times of increased stress, particularly in under-developed regions. When women suffer, children are more likely to also suffer. Lama (this volume) highlights some of the advantages of tourism for mountain women in Nepal, including economic independence. This argument corresponds with other similar studies (Gurung, 1995; Valaoras, 1998; Walker, 1998 in Godde, 1999: 25–26). At the same time, however, and as Lama states, tourism may not change the overall status of women, but instead only add to their traditional responsibilities.

The potentials that micro-enterprises within tourism offer for improvements in the quality of life of mountain communities are also important to consider when weighing the advantages and disadvantages of tourism in a mountain area. Sales of locally produced vegetables or crafts in mountain areas, for example, can provide significant income for some community members and can empower marginalized people (Cone, 1995; Inmann, 1998). Sales of arts can also increase pride in a group's heritage and increase opportunities for self-determination (McGee, 1998). Some writers even speculate that such sales can also provide the supplementary income necessary for the development of local infrastructures in small mountain regions, including education, communication and health care (Huse *et al.*, 1998: 736). Yates (1998) discusses how the production and sales of traditional crafts in mountain regions in the USA lends to a sense of personal satisfaction and substantially higher quality of life. However, while tourism can bring such benefits to mountain regions, it can never be the sole means of economic gain in a community.

Another advantage of tourism is that it can deter other, more damaging forms of development that strip mountains of their resources. In the larger scheme of things, tourism may contribute less than other economic activities to the sum of negative environmental impacts. Grazing, logging and unsustainable practices in agriculture are generally greater sources of environmental degradation, leaving tourism accountable for only a small portion of deterioration. In areas where levels of grazing or timber harvesting are excessive, for example, the erosion of already poor soils may occur. Catastrophic events often follow unsustainable practices, underscoring the importance of mountain forests and landscapes in the livelihood and security of mountain and lowland areas alike (Hewitt, 1997). Often forms of 'soft' tourism can provide viable alternatives to these other forms of development. In the case of Mount Koroyanitu in Fiji, for example, local highland communities have been working with Fiji Pine to develop tourism as an alternative to logging and to save endemic species of flora (Baba, 1997). Tourism can also be changed from a cause of environmental degradation to a source of environmental restoration, as exemplified by the planting of trees by pilgrims to the Hindu shrine of Badrinath, and their subsequent maintenance by beggars (Bernbaum, 1997).

Thus, at the same time that tourism compromises the sustainability of mountain resources, it may also encourage it by bringing people to these places and giving them an awareness of the beauty and environmental and cultural resources of mountains. In general, the extent to which tourism affects the physical and cultural features of a place depends largely on how tourism is managed and the form it takes. Mass tourism, for example, tends to lead not only to the degradation of the environmental features of a mountain area, but also to significant losses of mountain community values and ways of life. The development of tourist attractions in sacred sites spurred by mass tourism interest disrupts one's relationship with the land and can lead to a weakened sense of one's identity with a site or a mountain. At the same time and if carefully managed, mountain sacredness can carry tourist appeal

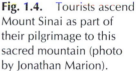

Fig. 1.4. Tourists ascend Mount Sinai as part of their pilgrimage to this sacred mountain (photo by Jonathan Marion).

and transform a site known for climbing or trekking into an area of viewing (Bernbaum, 1997; Kelly, 1998).

Overall, the effects of tourism on mountain communities and the environments on which they depend can vary; in some places, tourism enhances quality of life and environmental sustainability, while in others it poses more problems than benefits. Despite the negative effects tourism might have on the environment and local cultures, the potential for positive effects leaves us with a certain degree of optimism. If designed in a sustainable manner and carefully regulated, tourism has the potential to provide a primary and/or supplementary means of development. However, as each mountain region or community has specific attributes, a specific approach to the development of tourism will be needed. In many instances, development projects have been short-lived due to their inappropriateness for unique mountain conditions, but these have also taught us that greater sensitivity is required and that challenges specific to mountain regions must be recognized.

Potentials of Tourism in Mountain Regions for the Third Millennium

The case studies in this book address the diverse aspects of mountain tourism as an issue of growing concern around the world. They draw on work achieved in the field of mountain and upland region tourism in the last decade of the second millennium and provide a basis for defining the work that will be needed in the third millennium. They also convey important messages in the spheres of natural science, culture, economics, community participation, planning and governance.

Both separately and together, these papers bring a focus on mountains into the literature of tourism, especially sustainable tourism. As individual chapters, they refer to different cases specific to their respective geographic, political and economic contexts. They also derive from the authors' variety of professions. While these might appear individual in their specific aims, style of research and language, together they work to promote the common interest of providing a more sustainable future for mountain environments and communities, as well as people downstream and further afield who receive the benefits of mountains. Each paper differs in the area of interest represented, but they are connected through their emphasis on the creation of better practices, policies and legal mechanisms.

The chapters in the initial part of the book tend to focus on the impacts that various tourism activities have had and continue to have on the biophysical environments, and their human inhabitants, of mountain areas around the globe in order to identify solutions for better tourism practice. From the impacts of walking and camping on mountain flora and fauna to those of ski resorts on climate change, the first part of the book presents several and varied scenarios of challenges and potential solutions that mountain tourism faces. Drawing from their fieldwork in Australia, Buckley, Pickering and Warnken explore the impacts of both summer and winter recreation on mountain environments, and of climate change on tourism (Chapter 2). Through their analysis of environmental impact studies on mountain resorts in Australia over the past several decades, they confirm that tourism has major implications for land management in mountain regions. Along parallel lines, Monz's analytical work explores specific systems to monitor impacts of hiking and trail use. While his study is based on the specific findings of monitoring systems in Phantom Canyon, Colorado, USA, the study may have broader implications for mountain regions around the globe. Together, these two papers contribute thorough research on the variety of environmental effects caused by various human activities, and they underscore the importance of using monitoring and assessment tools for a wide range of mountain tourism and recreation activities. Equally, these writers, along with others in this publication, demonstrate that issues of mountain tourism and development are not limited to developing countries. Generally speaking, the term 'development' is applied to those countries or regions that are less capable of providing a certain standard of living to their population. But if we are speaking of *development toward sustainability* in the areas of social well-being and ecological conservation, as well as economic stability, then few regions fall outside the need for such a change. For this reason, this book comprises case studies from mountain regions in industrialized, non-industrialized and post-industrializing countries alike.

Moving around the globe to Greece, Valaoras (Chapter 4) discusses environmental features unique to the region and describes the potential for ecotourism as a model for sustainable development in the Prespa region. She argues that the conservation of mountain environments through tourism relies on: the involvement of the local community, who tend to maintain an appropriate scale and the ecological integrity of the region; existing basic infrastructure (e.g. food, accommodation, services); funding and policy that encourage the strengthening of the local economy and appropriate development; and the use of mountain tourism in conjunction with other economic activities. Valaoras' chapter offers positive implications for tourism in mountain regions, so long as the appropriate mechanisms are in place.

Moss, Tesitel, Zemek, Bartos, Kusova and Herman in Chapter 5 offer an innovative approach to looking at tourism and its impacts, focusing on its application in the Sumava Bioregion in south-west Bohemia, Czech Republic. These authors detail the findings of their work in progress on an inter-disciplinary bioregional ecosystemic approach to sustaining the ecological integrity of a mountain region while enhancing the well-being of its inhabitants. The implications of this approach are tremendous, and thus it is taken up in the concluding chapter as the direction for the future for planning and managing for tourism in particular and change in general in mountain regions.

The emphasis in Chapter 6 is on the cultural dimension of tourism in mountain regions, with particular attention to cultural identity and change, cultural autonomy and self-determination. In this chapter, Pfister examines the role that storytelling plays in maintaining indigenous culture and the implication this has for tourism in mountain areas. While the chapter specifically speaks of the Nisga'a people of northern British Columbia, Canada, it draws from the experiences of indigenous people worldwide. The fact that this chapter is the sole contribution that deals specifically with culture speaks of the need to attend more greatly to the cultural aspects of tourism in mountain areas. It also speaks of the need to involve those people who have an understanding of this dimension, academic and non-academic alike, in the dissemination of this knowledge.

From here, the book moves into an exploration of the economic basis and policy development of tourism in mountain regions through the eyes of several authors. Considering six mountain and upland regions in France, Portugal and the UK together, Snowdon, Slee and Farr offer an analytical comparison of the various economic impacts of both hard and soft tourism, and the implications this has for rural development policy (Chapter 7). Specifically, they question the degree to which soft tourism can deliver the same economic benefits as hard tourism in all mountain regions. They recognize that, on the one hand, soft tourism fits the model of 'development' with regard to local community empowerment and economic benefits. Yet, on the other hand, the long-term profitability, demand and local linkages of tourism are highly variable and dependent on specific political and economic contexts already in place.

This view of the potentials of soft tourism in mountain regions is complemented by Barkin, who in Chapter 8 focuses specifically on the challenges that a particular local development project within the Monarch butterfly region in west-central Mexico has faced with regard to economic betterment. The issue raised by Barkin of restrictions on local, often indigenous, people from accessing traditional resources and the implications that such restrictions bring, is hard-felt in many mountain regions. The emphasis placed on the need to approach tourism as one component of a larger economic fabric has relevant application to other areas. In the case of Mexico, as in the case of Greece, Barkin suggests the use of agroforestry as a primary supplement to tourism.

In Chapter 9, MacLellan, Dieke and Thapa look at the relationship between the supply and demand as well as costs and benefits of tourism in Nepal. The authors conclude that existing policies and institutional structures within Nepal do not effectively address the disjunction between mountain tourism, mountain economic activities and resource exploitation. Existing policies do not carefully balance issues of economic gain – and distribution – and environmental degradation. Their call for a clear, long-term policy for mountain tourism is echoed in a later chapter by Gurung and DeCoursey (Chapter 12).

The idea of community participation introduced by Valaoras in Chapter 4 is revisited by a number of authors, who examine the role that community participation may or may not play in mountain tourism, and in the broader scheme of sustainable development. These writers explore the relationship between sustainable tourism, community control and a strong alliance of the numerous stakeholders, and offer various views on the potentials for community participation. Cochrane (Chapter 10), for example, explores the effects of tourism on local communities within and in the proximity of Bromo Tengger Semeru National Park in Indonesia. Her findings show that tourism can directly and indirectly benefit people's economic, social and cultural welfare, yet at the same time, she questions the extent to which participatory tourism can be sustainable to all levels at all times. The question she poses is, in fact, a salient one, particularly when applied to the diversity of mountain regions worldwide.

In Chapter 11, Lama takes up a different issue with regard to community-based mountain tourism, focusing on the involvement of women in tourism, particularly as it relates to the pronounced gender imbalance in tourism decision-making in villages in Nepal. Despite their participation in caring for tourists as guests to their villages, women are often excluded from community meetings and policy development relating to tourism because of their lack of education and lower social status. The author describes what she terms a participatory appreciative approach to community-based tourism, and details how this approach can bring positive change to women's lives in villages as well as to the cultural and natural environment. Although Lama's piece is specific to Nepal, there are many implications for women's participation in tourism in other mountain regions.

Gurung and DeCoursey offer a similar view of community-based mountain tourism in Nepal, yet focus on the entire community as opposed to a single sector within the community. These authors explore the Upper Mustang Conservation and Development Project in Lo-Manthang, or Upper Mustang region, of the Himalayas and the governmental policies that affect this project. Looking at environmental education programmes for the local people, lodge management training, sanitation and hygiene development, and conservation efforts, the authors argue that ecotourism has potential to bring positive change. At the same time, however, they argue that lack of proper planning and preparation, as reflected in tourism policy, may lead to unsustainable practices.

Saffery's paper on Gurvansaikhan National Park in the Gobi region of Mongolia (Chapter 13) offers an example of the difficulties in involving local communities. Saffery's analogy of tourism as a race is appropriate for Mongolia and confirms Gurung and DeCoursey's warning that problems can occur where tourism is implemented too quickly and without proper planning. All societies discussed in this book are stakeholders in tourism, whether now or in the future, yet the degree to which they participate in local tourism ventures varies. A number of reasons account for this variation. In Mongolia, tourism has only recently been introduced into national policy. This contrasts sharply with the case studies from the Himalayan region, where the countries of Nepal, Bhutan and India have included tourism as a part of national policy for some time (Sharma, 1998). In these instances, the sophistication of tourism policy is reflected in the extent to which the government and/or managing NGOs support local involvement and provide the necessary tools.

The final two case studies presented in this publication are equally relevant to sustaining cultural and natural resources in mountain regions. These chapters deal with amenity migration, a phenomenon with historical roots, but now emerging as a significant societal force and beginning to be drawn into policy and research circles. Amenity migration refers to the movement of people to a particular region for the vision of life in a quieter, more pristine environment and/or distinct cultural attributes (Moss, 1994). Glorioso and Tonderayi's papers contribute to the literature on mountain amenity migration by focusing on issues specific to the Czech Republic and Zimbabwe. As Price *et al.* (1997) have argued, the distinction between tourism and amenity migration is not always clear, and Glorioso in Chapter 14 and Tonderayi in Chapter 15 support this. Through their discussion of amenity migration, wider issues related to tourism become apparent. Thus, while tourists may initially visit mountain areas for the common reasons of rest, rejuvenation, recreation and adventure, they may later return with the intention of remaining for a longer term. Some may purchase a second home to be used as a sanctuary away from the congestion of urban life. In a sense, the inclusion of amenity migration in a study of tourism can shed light on future issues, particularly those related to how people identify themselves as a community, and how their well-being and that of their ecosystems are linked to an association with place.

Each of these chapters addresses particular issues and situations in particular mountain regions, regions that are unique with regard to local cultures, steeped with beliefs, values and traditional ways of life, with regard to political structures, and economic systems, with regard to environments. Because of the uniqueness that each mountain region, and micro-region, has, it would be naïve to assume that the individual experiences, whether positive or negative, can or might be replicated in other mountain regions. At the same time, however, in the effort to address the growing concerns of mountain change, including tourism, it is essential to consider these chapters for what they might bring to the experiences of tourism in other mountain regions.

The central challenge with tourism as a form of development is the inherent difficulty of predicting the impacts of such a multi-faceted uncertain industry and resolving debates about the best way to avoid such impacts while taking advantage of potentials. Case studies serve as the most valuable tool for guiding the future of tourism; they offer us foresight into the possible peaks and pitfalls of tourism and help work out current issues of debate. The case studies presented in this publication are no exception. Through their diverse voices and perspectives, they bring light to the range of concerns and potentials for mountain tourism now and in the future.

References

Aditya, K.D. and Singh, H. (1997) Morphology and infrastructural development in Himalayan gateway towns – a case study of Haldwani-cum-Kathgodam. *The Geographer* 44, 61–82.

Akin Rabibhadana, M.R. (1992) Tourism and culture: Bang-Fai Festival. Background report. Thailand Development Research Institute Foundation, Chon Buri, Thailand.

ARPE/CIAPP (1996) Recommendations of NGOs and mountain populations to governments and to the European Union. ARPE, Toulouse.

Baba, J. (1997) Towards sustainable livelihoods: the Koroyanitu Development Programme. In: Bornemeier, J., Victor, M. and Durst, P. (eds) *Ecotourism for Forest Conservation and Community Development: Proceedings of an International Seminar held in Chiang Mai, Thailand, 28–31 January 1997.* RECOFTC/FAO, pp. 103–116.

Bandyopadhyay, J., Rodda, J.C., Kattelmann, R., Kundzewicz, Z.W. and Kraemer, D. (1997) Highland waters – a resource of global significance. In: Messerli, B. and

Ives, J.D. (eds) *Mountains of the World: a Global Priority.* Parthenon Press, London and New York, pp. 131–156.

Banks, G. and Ballard, C. (1997) The Ok Tedi settlement: issues, outcomes and implications. National Centre for Development Studies, Australian National University, Canberra.

Banskota, K. and Sharma, P. (1998) Mountain tourism for local community development in Nepal: a case study of Upper Mustang. ICIMOD Discussion Paper Series No. MEI 98/1. International Centre for Integrated Mountain Development, Kathmandu.

Bartlemus, P. (1994) *Environment, Growth and Development: the Concepts and Strategies of Sustainability.* Routledge, London and New York.

Bätzing, W., Perlik, M. and Dekleva, M. (1996) Urbanization and depopulation in the Alps. *Mountain Research and Development* 16, 335–350.

Bernbaum, E. (1997) The spiritual and cultural significance of mountains. In: Messerli, B. and Ives, J.D. (eds) *Mountains of the World: a Global Priority.* Parthenon Press, New York, pp. 39–60.

Bramwell, B., Henry, I., Jackson, G. and van der Straaten, J. (1996) A framework for understanding sustainable tourism management. In: Bramwell, B., Henry, I., Jackson, G., Prat, A.G., Richards, G. and van der Straaten, J. (eds) *Sustainable Tourism Management: Principles and Practice.* Tilburg University Press, Tilburg, pp. 23–71.

Byers, E. and Sainju, M. (1994) Mountain ecosystems and women: opportunities for sustainable development and conservation. *Mountain Research and Development* 14, 213–228.

Cater, G. and Lowman, G. (eds) (1994) *Ecotourism: a Sustainable Option?* John Wiley & Sons, Chichester.

Clark, W.C. and Munn, R.E. (eds) (1986) *Sustainable Development of the Biosphere.* Cambridge University Press, Cambridge.

Cooper, A. (1997) *Sacred Mountains: Ancient Wisdom and Modern Meanings.* Floris, Edinburgh.

Cone, C.A. (1995) Crafting Selves: The lives of two Mayan women. *Annals of Tourism Research* 20, 314–327.

Creighton, M.R. (1995) Japanese craft tourism: liberating the crane wife. *Annals of Tourism Research* 20, 463–478.

Debarbieux, B. (1995) *Tourism et Montagne.* Economica, Paris.

Direction du projet MAB Pays d'Enhaut (1985) Tourisme Pays d'Enhaut: synthese partielle. Schlussbericht Schweizerisches MAB-Programme No. 15. Bundesamt für Umweltschutz, Bern.

East, P., Luger, K. and Inmann, K. (eds) (1998) *Sustainability in Mountain Tourism: Perspectives for the Himalayan Countries.* Book Faith India, Delhi and Studienverlag, Innsbruck.

Federation of Nature and National Parks of Europe (1993) *Loving Them to Death? Sustainable Tourism in Europe's Nature and National Parks.* FNNPE, Grafenau.

Fennell, D. A. (1999) *Ecotourism: an Introduction.* Routledge, London

Fletcher, T. (1998) CBMT: a cultural ecotourism in Canada. Contribution to Community-Based Mountain Tourism Electronic Conference, Mountain Forum.

Godde, P. (ed.) (1999) Community-based mountain tourism: practices for linking conservation with enterprise. Summary report of the Mountain Forum e-conference, April, May 1998. The Mountain Institute, Franklin, West Virginia.

Goldsmith, Z. (1998) Ecotourism – old wine, new bottles? Experience from Ladakh. In: East, P., Luger, K. and Inmann, K. (eds) *Sustainability in Mountain Tourism: Perspectives for the Himalayan Countries.* Book Faith India, Delhi and Studienverlag, Innsbruck, pp. 255–267.

Grötzbach, E. and Stadel, C. (1997) Mountain peoples and culture. In: Messerli, B. and Ives, J.D. (eds) *Mountains of the World: a Global Priority.* Parthenon Press, London and New York, pp. 17–38.

Gurung, D. (1995) Tourism and gender: impact and implications of tourism on Nepalese women. ICIMOD Discussion Paper Series No. MEI 95/3. International Centre for Integrated Mountain Development, Kathmandu.

Hall, C.M. and Lew, A.A. (1998) *Sustainable Tourism: a Geographical Perspective.* Longman, Harlow, Essex.

Harrison, D. and Price, M.F. (1997) Fragile environments, fragile communities? An introduction. In: Price, M.F. (ed.) *People and Tourism in Fragile Environments.* John Wiley & Sons, Chichester, pp. 1–18.

Hewitt, K. (1997) Risks and disasters in mountain lands. In: Messerli, B. and Ives, J.D. (eds) *Mountains of the World: a Global Priority.* Parthenon Press, London and New York, pp. 371–408.

Huse, M., Gustavsen, T. and Almedal, S. (1998) Tourism impact comparisons among Norwegian towns. *Annals of Tourism Research* 25, 721–738.

Inmann, K. (1998) Small steps into the future: CCODER's community development and tourism projects. In: East, P., Luger, K. and Inmann, K. (eds) *Sustainability in Mountain Tourism: Perspectives for the Himalayan Countries.* Book Faith India, Delhi and Studienverlag, Innsbruck, pp. 281–288.

Inmann, K. and Luger, K. (1998) Tourism and village development: the Oeko Himal Strategy for sustainable tourism. In: East, P., Luger, K. and Inmann, K. (eds) *Sustainability in Mountain Tourism: Perspectives for the Himalayan Countries.* Book Faith India, Delhi and Studienverlag, Innsbruck, pp. 289–312.

Ives, J.D. (1992) Preface. In: Stone, P.B. (ed.) *The State of the World's Mountains: a Global Report.* Zed Books, London.

Ives, J.D. (1997) Comparative inequalities – mountain communities and mountain families. In: Messerli, B. and Ives, J.D. (eds) *Mountains of the World: a Global Priority.* Parthenon Press, London and New York, pp. 61–84.

Jenik, J. (1997) The diversity of mountain life. In: Messerli, B. and Ives, J.D. (eds) *Mountains of the World: a Global Priority.* Parthenon Press, London and New York, pp. 199–236.

Kelly, J.B. (1998) CBMT: responsible tourism. Contribution to Community-Based Mountain Tourism Electronic Conference, Mountain Forum.

Kohli, M.S. (1998) An action plan for mountain tourism in India: the Gangotri Conservation Project. In: East, P., Luger, K. and Inmann, K. (eds) *Sustainability in Mountain Tourism: Perspectives for the Himalayan Countries.* Book Faith India, Delhi and Studienverlag, Innsbruck, pp. 269–279.

Kroener, A. (1968) *Grindelwald: Die Entwicklung eines Bergbauerndorfes zu einem internationalen Tourismuszentrum.* Geographisches Institut, Universität Stuttgart.

Luger, K. and Inmann, K. (eds) (1995) *Verreiste Berge.* Studienverlag, Innsbruck.

MacCannell, D. (1976) *The Tourist: a New Theory of the Leisure Class.* Schocken Books, New York.

Mallari, A.A. and Enote, J.E. (1996) Maintaining control: culture and tourism in the Pueblo of Zuni, New Mexico. In: Price, M.F. (ed.) *People and Tourism in Fragile Environments*. John Wiley & Sons, Chichester, pp. 19–31.

McGee, C. (1998) CBMT: traditional art of the Huicholes and tourism. Contribution to Community-Based Mountain Tourism Electronic Conference, Mountain Forum.

McLaren, D., Taylor, R. and Lacey, D. (1998) CBMT: Local knowledge and rethinking tourism. Contribution to Community-Based Mountain Tourism Electronic Conference, Mountain Forum.

Messerli, B. and Ives, J.D. (eds) (1997) *Mountains of the World: a Global Priority*. Parthenon Press, London and New York.

Mieczkowski, Z. (1995) *Environmental Issues of Tourism and Recreation*. University Press of America, Lanham, Maryland.

Morales, T. (1998) CBMT: A case of community-based tourism in Oaxaca. Contribution to Community-Based Mountain Tourism Electronic Conference, Mountain Forum.

Moss, L.A. (1994) Beyond tourism: the amenity migrants. In: Mannermaa, M., Inayatullah, S. and Slaughter, R. (eds) *Coherence and Chaos in Our Uncommon Futures: Visions, Means, Actions*. Finland Futures Research Centre, Turku School of Economics and Business Administration, Turku, Finland, pp. 121–127.

Mountain Agenda (1998) Mountains of the world: water towers for the 21st Century. Mountain Agenda, Bern.

Mountain Agenda (1999) Mountains of the world: tourism and sustainable mountain development. Mountain Agenda, Bern.

National Research Council (1989) *Lost Crops of the Incas: Little Known Plants of the Andes with Promise for Worldwide Cultivation*. National Academy Press, Washington DC.

Odell, M.J. and Lama, W.B. (1998) Tea house trekking in Nepal: the case for environmentally friendly indigenous tourism. In: East, P., Luger, K. and Inmann, K. (eds) *Sustainability in Mountain Tourism: Perspectives for the Himalayan Countries*. Book Faith India, Delhi and Studienverlag, Innsbruck, pp. 191–205.

Price, M.F. (1990) Mountain forests as common-property resources: management policies and their outcomes in the Colorado Rockies and Swiss Alps. *ETH-Zürich Forstwissenschaftliche Beiträge*, No. 9.

Price, M.F. (1999) Chapter 13 in Action 1992–97 – a task manager's report. Food and Agriculture Organization of the United Nations, Rome.

Price, M.F., Moss, L.A.G. and Williams, P.W. (1997) Tourism and amenity migration. In: Messerli, B. and Ives, J.D. (eds) *Mountains of the World: a Global Priority*. Parthenon Press, London and New York, pp. 249–280.

Rieder, P. and Wyder, J. (1997) Economic and political framework for sustainability of mountain areas. In: Messerli, B. and Ives, J.D. (eds) *Mountains of the World: a Global Priority*. Parthenon Press, London and New York, pp. 85–102.

Roe, E.M. (1996) Sustainable development and cultural theory. *The International Journal of Sustainable Development and World Ecology* 3, 1–14.

Rogers, R. and Aitchison, J. (1998) Towards sustainable tourism in the Everest region of Nepal. IUCN Nepal, Kathmandu.

Semple, B. (1998) CBMT: traditional architecture, culture, and environment. Contribution to Community-Based Mountain Tourism Electronic Conference, Mountain Forum.

Shah, J. and Nagpal, T. (1997) Urban air quality management strategy in Asia: Kathmandu Valley Report World Bank Technical Paper, No. 378.

Sharma, P. (1998) Sustainable tourism in the Hindukush-Himalaya: issues and approaches. In: East, P., Luger, K. and Inmann, K. (eds) *Sustainability in Mountain Tourism: Perspectives for the Himalayan Countries.* Book Faith India, Delhi and Studienverlag, Innsbruck, pp. 47–69.

Smith, V. (ed.) (1989) *Hosts and Guests: the Anthropology of Tourism,* 2nd edn. University of Pennsylvania Press, Philadelphia.

Sterly, J. (1997) *Simbu Plant-Lore. Plants used by the People in the Central Highlands of New Guinea.* Dietrich Reimer Verlag, Berlin.

Stevens, S.F. (1993) *Claiming the High Ground: Sherpas, Subsistence and Environmental Change in the Highest Himalaya.* University of California Press, Berkeley.

The Mountain Institute (1995) International NGO Consultation on the Mountain Agenda: Summary Report and Recommendations to the United Nations Commission on Sustainable Development. The Mountain Institute, Franklin, West Virginia, USA.

Turner, B.L., Kasperson, R.E., Meyer, W.B., Dow, K.M., Golding, D., Kasperson, X., Mitchell, R.C. and Ratick, S.J. (1990) Two types of global environmental change: definition and spatial-scale issues in their human dimension. *Global Environmental Change: Human and Policy Dimensions* 1, 14–22.

Valaoras, G. (1998) Alternative development and biodiversity conservation: two case studies from Greece. Contribution to the Mountain Forum Website Library.

Weaver, D.B. (1998) *Ecotourism in the Less Developed World.* CAB International, Wallingford and New York.

Williams, A.M. and Shaw, G. (1996) Tourism, leisure, nature protection and agritourism: principles, partnerships and practice. The EPE (European Partners for the Environment) Workbook Series for Implementing Sustainability in Europe, Tourism Research Group, Exeter, Brussels.

World Commission on Environment and Development (1987) *Our Common Future.* Oxford University Press, Oxford and New York.

World Travel and Tourism Council, World Tourism Organization, and Earth Council (1995) Agenda 21 for the Travel and Tourism Industry: Towards Environmentally Sustainable Development. WTTC, London.

Yates, K. (1998) CBMT: Local knowledge: linking tradition with enterprise. Contribution to Community-Based Mountain Tourism Electronic Conference, Mountain Forum.

Zimmerer, K.S. (1996) *Changing Fortunes: Biodiversity and Peasant Livelihood in the Peruvian Andes.* University of California Press, Berkeley.

Zimmermann, F.M. (1995) The Alpine region: regional restructuring opportunities and constraints in a fragile environment. In: Montanari, A. and Williams, A.M. (eds) *European Tourism Regions, Spaces and Restructuring.* John Wiley & Sons, Chichester, New York, pp. 19–40.

Zimmermann, F.M. (1998a) Nature, society and the economy in partnership: European perspectives in mountain tourism. In: East, P., Luger, K. and Inmann, K.

(eds) *Sustainability in Mountain Tourism: Perspectives for the Himalayan Countries*. Book Faith India, Delhi and Studienverlag, Innsbruck, pp. 71–91.

Zimmermann, F.M. (1998b) Austria: contrasting tourist seasons and contrasting regions. In: Williams, A.M. and Shaw, G. (eds) *Tourism and Economic Development. European Experiences*, 3rd edn. John Wiley & Sons, Chichester, New York, pp. 175–197.

Environmental Management for Alpine Tourism and Resorts in Australia

Ralf C. Buckley, Catherine M. Pickering and Jan Warnken

International Center for Ecotourism Research, School of Environmental and Applied Science and Cooperative Research Centre for Sustainable Tourism, Griffith University, Parklands Drive, Gold Coast, Queensland 9726, Australia

Introduction

Ski resorts are one of the most intensive forms of tourism development in mountain areas. They have large capital and operating costs, and significant environmental impacts, many of which are unavoidable. As resort owners and operators compete for clients by expanding facilities, they are increasingly seeking to expand revenues by broadening the range of activities from 'ski resorts' to 'winter resorts', and lengthening their operating season from 'winter resorts' to 'mountain resorts'.

Some such resorts are now medium-sized towns in their own right. The aggregate value of real estate at Vail, Colorado, for example, is reported at over US$3 billion. As well as lifts, gear hire, food and accommodation, these large towns include year-round residential housing, supermarkets, upmarket art and clothing stores, and large convention centres, together with associated municipal infrastructure. Helicopters, snowcats and snowmobiles extend their activities in winter; and golf courses, fishing, horse riding and parapenting in summer.

Alpine tourism is not all mega-resorts. In winter it also includes minimal-impact wilderness touring on cross-country or telemark skis, or snowboards and snowshoes; guided commercial backcountry tours; huts; rope tows; small club skifields; larger commercial skifields without accommodation; and skifields with lodge accommodation only, as well as resorts with full hotel accommodation and restaurant services. Alpine tourism in summer includes fishing, golf, mountain biking, coach tours, car tours, off-road tours, guided walks, horse riding, camping in organized campsites, backcountry camping, hiking on trails, hiking off trails, sightseeing, wild-flower viewing, rock climbing and abseiling, and paragliding. Some of these activities make use of resorts and associated facilities; others use facilities such as roads, trails and organized campsites separate from resorts. A grow-ing number of these activities, however, do not use any fixed facilities, but are carried out entirely in backcountry and remote wilderness areas.

Environmental impacts and management for mountain tourism have been studied much more extensively in Europe and North America than in Asia or South America. Resort developments or expansions in the USA and Canada routinely require large-scale environmental impact statements (EISs), for example, such as those produced recently for a number of resorts in Colorado. The impacts of backcountry recreation, both summer and winter, are also relatively well-studied for the mountains of North America (e.g. Willard and Marr, 1970; Price, 1985), the UK (Wood, 1987a, b; Bayfield, 1994), and the Alps (Meyer, 1993; Zimmermann, 1998) and to a lesser extent Japan (Tsuyuzaki, 1990). The types of impacts studied include trampling of vegetation (e.g. Cole, 1992) and introduction of weeds (Marion et al., 1986); compaction by snowmobiles (Greller et al., 1974); barriers to movement of wildlife; and changes to water quality and flow.

Environmental management for tourism in the Australian alpine and associated high-country has also been studied to some degree, though none of the EISs for mountain resorts are as recent (Table 2.1). Environmental management issues for alpine tourism and resorts in Australia are signifi-cantly different from those in other continents, for two main reasons. Firstly, the area of Australia that receives significant snowfall is very small, and the snow cover does not last long. Secondly, many of the Australian alpine plant and animal species are endemic, not just to the Australian continent but to the alpine region alone, and many of their life histories are rather different from those of their counterparts in other continents.

The Australian Alpine

Mountain tourism in Australia involves high-intensity use of a very small area. Snow cover in Australia is limited both temporally and spatially as compared to Europe, Asia and the Americas. Only around 11,500 km^2 of the continent receives regular winter snowfall, 0.15% of Australia (Costin et al., 1979). The largest and most extensive area to receive snow, around Mt Kosciuszko in the Snowy Mountains in New South Wales, covers only 2500 km^2. Only 1200 km^2 of the Snowy Mountains receive 60 or more days of snow cover, and only 250 km^2 or 0.001% of Australia is true alpine (Costin et al., 1979; Green and Osborne, 1994). Other much smaller alpine regions occur as relatively isolated areas centred on the higher peaks between Mt Hotham and Mt Bogong in Victoria (1000 km^2 with 60 or more days of snow cover); in the Brindabella Ranges in the Australian Capital

Territory (150 km²); and in the central Highlands and higher peaks in Tasmania (Costin, 1989; Green and Osborne, 1994).

Besides being small in area, the alpine regions in Australia have a very limited altitudinal range. The maximum range from snowline to the peak is only 800 m; the highest peak in Australia, Mt Kosciuszko, reaches only 2228 m; and snow cover is variable and patchy, particularly in the smaller alpine areas in Victoria and Tasmania. Even in the true alpine around Mt Kosciuszko, snow banks that persist from year to year are very unusual, with the snow seasons usually lasting around 5 months (Galloway, 1988; Brown and Millner, 1989).

Each of the alpine regions in Australia has a distinctive and characteristic biota, and these are all of major biological significance. The main alpine region in southeastern Australia supports a large number of endemic animal species, including the endangered mountain pygmy possum (Good, 1992; Green and Osborne, 1994). The flora in the true alpine area around Mt Kosciuszko is particularly diverse, with 21 endemic and 33 rare species in a total assemblage of 190 species (Costin *et al.*, 1979; Smith, 1986; Good, 1992). Both plants and animals show a range of distinctive adaptations to the environment, similar to those of alpine species elsewhere (Green and Osborne, 1994; Pickering, 1997).

The alpine area around Mt Kosciuszko was declared a State Park in 1944, became a National Park in 1967, and was listed as an UNESCO-MAB Biosphere Reserve in 1977. In 1996 the governments of New South Wales, Victoria and ACT, together with the Australian Commonwealth Government, signed a Memorandum of Understanding for cooperative management of the Australian Alps National Parks, a group of five connected parks which together include most of mainland Australia's alpine and subalpine regions.

Tourism in the Australian Alpine

Although Australia is large and its alpine areas small, the Australian population is very heavily urbanized, and the largest cities are close to the mountains. Snow country is hence accessible to much of the population of Australia. The alpine regions in Victoria and New South Wales are within easy access for about 80% of the Australia population (Good, 1992). Over three million people per annum visit Kosciuszko National Park alone, from a total population of 18 million (Environment Science and Services, 1994). Ski tourism is now the principal economic activity in the Australian snow country, having outstripped other industries such as grazing, forestry and hydroelectric power generation. The ski industry contributed around A$110–140 million per annum to the local economy in the 1980s (Good, 1992) and approximately A$410 million per annum to the national economy (Konig, 1998).

Alpine tourism in Australia is much more than just ski tourism. Until the mid-1980s most visitors to the Snowy Mountains arrived during the winter months, with around 80% involved in alpine skiing (Mackay and Allcock, 1988; Good, 1992). More recently, however, the growth in winter activities has levelled off, through saturation of the limited skiable snowfields and resort facilities during peak periods. Other winter activities such as cross-country skiing, backcountry skiing and snowboarding have increased (Mackay and Nixon, 1995; Konig, 1998). In addition, there has been a pro-portionately larger increase in summer visitation rates, with around 50% of visits in summer (NSW NPWS, 1988). Most summer visitors (70%) are engaged in car touring and sightseeing, but increasing numbers go bushwalking and camping (40%), wildflower viewing, abseiling, mountain biking, paragliding, fishing, etc. (Mackay and Allcock, 1988). These changes are broadening the environmental impacts of tourism to include those associated with summer recreational activities, as well as winter resorts and skiing.

Environmental Impacts and Management Measures at Mountain Resorts

The precise types of impact associated with mountain resorts, and their ecological significance, depend heavily on location and environment. Clearing vegetation for ski runs, for example, is of much greater concern in countries or areas where the relevant vegetation type is of limited extent than where it is widespread. Infrastructure development is of greater concern if it occupies habitat areas of endangered plant or animal species. Discharge of treated sewage into rivers and water consumption for snowmaking are of greater concern in national parks than agricultural areas. In practice this means that ski resorts are of particular environmental concern in countries that have very small alpine and subalpine areas, small short-lived snowfields and high endemicity of plant and animal species, both terrestrial and aquatic, such as Australia.

The environmental impacts associated with ski resorts may be considered in two major categories: construction and operation. The former is a convenient term for impacts associated with the permanent features of the facility: not only those due to the construction process itself, but also those which are unavoidable once it is in place. The latter are those due to day-to-day operations, typically dependent in magnitude on visitor numbers.

Impacts associated with permanent structures can generally only be avoided or reduced at the design stage. Once the resort is built, these impacts are beyond the control of the operations manager except through reconstruction or retrofitting where relevant. Impacts associated with the actual construction process can generally be reduced to some degree by appropriate precautions, such as selecting the time of year and time of day that minimizes impacts, avoiding more easily damaged areas, and adopting measures to reduce soil and vegetation damage, runoff, noise, etc. Some measures may increase construction costs, however, and many construction impacts are unavoidable. Operational impacts are under more control through day-to-day management measures, but many can only be reduced by a relatively small proportion. In addition, many are directly related to the number of skiers, which resorts generally want to maximize.

The main components of ski fields and resorts that give rise to construction impacts include:

- major earthworks, terrain reshaping, landscaping
- roads, carparks, parking lots, bus interchanges
- firebreaks, firetrails, maintenance tracks
- water reservoirs, sewage treatment ponds, dams and bunds
- ski trails and tracks
- ski lifts and towers
- snowmaking equipment including hoses, pumps, etc.
- floodlights

Table 2.1.   Impacts associated with construction of mountain resorts.

Type of impact	Australian EISs which identified this impact (see footnote)									
	1	2	3	4	5	6	7	8	9	10
Soil compaction				*				*		
Topsoil disturbance				*		*		*		
Soil erosion				*				*		
Risk of mudslides and avalanches										
Slopewash and sediment runoff	*			*	*			*		*
Changed surface drainage	*			*		*		*		*
Groundwater depletion										*
Changed subsurface flows						*		*		
Rapid thaw on roads, buildings, etc.				*						
Increased stream turbidity	*			*				*		
Increased spring flooding	*									
Contaminated runoff to streams										
nutrients in slopewash	*									
fertilizer from revegetation	*		*							
oil wash from roads, etc.				*						*
Airborne dust										
Construction noise	*			*		*				
Vegetation clearance	*			*		*		*		
Loss of vegetation types or plant communities (e.g. through changed groundwater)								*		
Smaller populations of particular plant species										
Introduction of weeds										
in revegetation mulches, etc.	*	*		*				*		
colonizing bare areas		*								
Non-local native plants	*									
Plant pathogens										
Barriers to animal movement										*
Noise disturbance to animals	*			*						
Reduced animal habitat								*	*	
Increased habitat fragmentation										
Reduced tree cover	*	*						*		
Increased open areas						*				
Increased grassed areas						*				
Increased predation risk										

Notes: 1 = Corin Forest Ski Recreation Facilities EIS (1985); 2 = Mt Hotham Alpine Village EIS (1982); 3 = Mt Baw Baw Ski Lift EIS (1981); 4 = Mt Stirling Alpine Resort EIS (1983); 5 = The Stables Ski Lodge EIS (1988); 6 = Thredbo Village Master Plan EIS (1988); 7 = Augmentation of Sewage Treatment Works EIS (1984); 8 = Blue Cow Ski Resort EIS (1985); 9 = Perisher Access Loop PER (1984); 10 = Perisher Skitube EIS (1984).

- plant and machinery
- fences, barriers
- day shelters, ticket kiosks, restaurants
- vehicle, plant and maintenance sheds
- powerhouses or electricity substations
- buildings for gear rental, ski school, ski patrol, etc.
- staff housing
- visitor accommodation, hotels
- shops, retail outlets, etc.
- heliports, airstrips.

Some of the main potential environment impacts from these components are listed in Table 2.1. Also shown are the Australian skifields for which EISs identified the issues concerned. This does not necessarily imply, of course, that similar impacts did not occur for the other cases listed, but simply that their EISs did not consider them as issues of major concern. Nor does it necessarily imply that the impacts proved in practice to be of major ecological significance, but simply that they were identified with the potential to do so. Possible management measures to alleviate such impacts are summarized in Table 2.2, again with cases where they were identified in Australian EISs.

During day-to-day operations, ski resorts operate machinery, consume energy, water and resources, and generate wastes. Large numbers of people travel to, from and within the site, in vehicles and on skis and snowboards. Some of the main environmental management issues are summarized in Table 2.3. Operational impacts during summer use are outlined in Table 2.4, and potential management and mitigation measures in Table 2.5.

Comparison between Australia and North America

EISs for Australian ski resort development date mostly from the mid-1980s, when there was a period of expansion. This included the Thredbo Village Master Plan, which was required because accommodation development in the Thredbo area has exceeded the capacity of the infrastructure, such as sewage treatment facilities. It also included construction of the Skitube, a long rail tunnel through one of the ranges, which provided access to a group of New South Wales skifields from a parking area below the snowline. Since that date, growth in physical facilities and infrastructure has occurred largely outside the Alpine National Park, notably in Jindabyne, which became a major satellite and dormitory town for the New South Wales skifields. The growth of Jindabyne has occurred in a rapid but piecemeal way, with new development approved through local government planning processes, which have not required an EIS.

In North America, whilst there have been no major new ski resorts constructed from scratch in the past decade, there has been substantial expansion and refitting at a number of resorts, including construction of new

Table 2.2.   Management measures for construction impacts.

Measure	Australian EISs which identified this measure (see footnote to Table 2.1)									
	1	2	3	4	5	6	7	8	9	10
Identify and avoid critical plant and animal habitats										
Design to prevent soil saturation (e.g. use diagonal and gladed runs)										
Place towers away from sensitive plant communities								*		
Use helicopters to install towers								*		
Minimize area of disturbance	*	*						*		
especially in erosion-prone areas	*					*				
especially near groundwater-dependent plant communities	*							*		
Minimize degree of disturbance by machinery	*									
Comply with soil conservation guidelines					*					
Trap slopewash sediment										
with silt traps and settling ponds								*		*
with straw bales and fences						*				
Water exposed dry surfaces										*
Start revegetation as soon as possible			*					*		
Stabilize slopes with seeded bitumen–straw	*									
Use seedless straw for mulching	*									
Fence off areas of significant vegetation						*				
Apply fertilizer little and often only, during main growth season	*									

lifts and facilities and clearing of new runs in both US and Canadian resorts. In Colorado, which has the largest concentration of US ski resorts, most of this development has taken place in lands leased from the US Forest Service, and EISs have generally been required. Recent examples include EISs for Snowmass, Steamboat Springs, Telluride, Crested Butte and Aspen Highlands (USDAFS, 1994, 1995, 1996, 1997a, b).

These EISs, produced in the mid to late 1990s under US legislation, are substantially more detailed than their counterparts produced under Australian legislation in the early mid-1980s. These differences are demonstrated in Tables 2.1–2.5, where the categories of impacts and management measures are summarized from the Colorado EISs, expressed in relatively general terms and including only those relevant to Australia. The tables indicate which of these issues were considered in the Australian EISs.

Land, water, energy and other resource consumption and conservation issues, for example, listed in Table 2.3, were generally not addressed in any detail in the Australian EISs in the 1980s. Provision of adequate power, water and sewage treatment facilities was generally considered a technical rather than an environmental concern, except where construction of major new powerlines or pipelines was required.

It is not clear, however, whether this difference in detail is due to differences between countries, or the difference in date. Australian EIA legislation is largely derived from its US predecessors, and is generally quite similar in scope and requirements. There are, however, differences in institutional frameworks, which affect how stringently these legislative requirements are applied in practice. It is possible, therefore, that the greater detail of the US ski resort EISs is part of a broader pattern for EISs in general. Alternatively, it is possible that the difference reflects a general improvement in the technical quality of EISs over time, in both countries. A detailed study of all Australian tourism EISs, however, found that whilst their technical quality improved from the 1970s to the 1980s, it did not improve significantly from the 1980s to the 1990s (Warnken and Buckley, 1998). If ski resort EISs reflect this general trend, there would be no *a priori* reason to expect that if any had been written during the 1990s, they would be any more detailed than their predecessors in the 1980s.

Impacts of Backcountry Tourism

Impacts of alpine tourism in Australia and elsewhere are not limited to resorts. Backcountry activities and accommodation, in both winter and summer, can also cause impacts on alpine environments (Tables 2.6, 2.7 and 2.8).

Away from resorts, accommodation can range from caravan and camping sites with car access, to snow caves and small tents in wilderness areas (NSW NPWS, 1988; Good, 1992, Table 6). Permanent structures such as roadside camping areas and isolated huts in the high country all involve vegetation clearance and disturbance, and soil erosion and compaction during construction (NSW NPWS, 1988). Many of these impacts continue during use of the facilities, along with other impacts such as disturbance to wildlife, production of wastes, water pollution, noise, visual impacts and the introduction of weeds and pathogens (Table 2.6). Transitory accommodation such as tents and snow caves also has impacts, notably faecal contamination (Timms, 1980; NSW NPWS, 1988; Cullan and Norris, 1989; Marston and Yapp, 1991). For example, intensive camping in the fragile catchment areas around the glacial lakes in Kosciuszko National Park, including the construction and use of snow caves in winter, has led to erosion, soil compaction, loss of vegetation and faecal contamination of the glacial lakes.

For visitors who stay near roadheads, the recreational activities that bring people to the alpine region may be less damaging than the transport and accommodation that they use to arrive and stay (Tables 2.7 and 2.8). In backcountry areas, however, impacts are also caused by recreational

Table 2.3. Operational impacts of mountain resorts in winter.

Type of impact	Australian EISs which identified this impact (see footnote to Table 2.1)									
	1	2	3	4	5	6	7	8	9	10
Energy consumption										
lifts										
lights										
other										
offsite impacts										
Water consumption										
snowmaking	*									
commercial										
domestic										
firefighting										
Resource consumption										
consumables										
disposables (plates, cups, etc.)										
packaging										
recycling										
Land alienation due to:										
landfill										
garbage and compost from:										
liftsite restaurants										
local accommodation										
infrastructure corridors										
oil and fuel leaks, etc.										
Noise from:			*							
snowmaking	*						*			
lifts										
snowcats										
snowmobiles										
helicopters										*
access traffic	*									*
on-site vehicles										
generators										
maintenance										
avalanche bombing										
voices										
Reduced air quality from:										
vehicle exhausts										
cooking and heating										

Table 2.3. *Continued.*

Type of impact	Australian EISs which identified this impact (see footnote to Table 2.1)									
	1	2	3	4	5	6	7	8	9	10
Modified creek flows								*		
decreases in winter due to snowmaking	*							*		
increased flooding in spring	*									
increased runoff from cleared areas and extended snowpack	*			*				*		*
Reduced water quality in rivers downstream of resort, from:										
organic matter, particularly nutrients, bacteria and other microorganisms in treated sewage discharges	*	*				*	*	*		*
sediment, bacteria and nutrients in surface runoff from ski slopes (including snowmaking)	*						*			
oil, grease and trash in surface runoff from roads and base areas				*						*
salt from roads and roofs										
Changes to species composition and ecology of aquatic communities downstream of resort and sewage discharge points, including algae and invertebrates	*	*				*	*			*
Soil compaction from oversnow and maintenance vehicles										
Vegetation damage from:										
on-site vehicles										
snow compaction from oversnow vehicles										
extended snowpack, late thaw										
snow grooming vehicles										
skiers, when snow cover is thin				*				*		
Disturbance to native wildlife from										
noise (as above)										
floodlighting at night	*									
barriers to movement, including fences and cleared runs	*									*
compaction of subnivial space										
road kills	*									*
predation by feral animals and escaped pets										
scavenger species attracted to food scraps and garbage	*	*		*						

Data from authors' observations (RB) in Australia and internationally, and from Australian and US EISs.

Table 2.4. Operational impacts of mountain resorts in summer.

Type of impact	Australian EISs which identified this impact (see footnote to Table 2.1)									
	1	2	3	4	5	6	7	8	9	10
Skifield in summer										
landslides on cleared areas										
runoff from cleared areas										
vegetation damage from summer maintenance vehicles	*	*		*				*		
vegetation damage from feral animals	*									
increased fire frequency	*			*		*				
introduction of weed seed on people and vehicles	*	*		*				*		
wildlife predation from pets, etc.	*									
feral animals in cleared areas						*				
Golf										
clearance for fairways										
pollution of ground and surface water with pesticides and fertilizers										
bird kills from pesticides on grass										
water consumption for irrigation										
Fishing										
reduction of native fish and other aquatic fauna through predation and/or competition from stocked fish species										
contamination of lakes and streambeds with lead weights										
entanglement of birds in discarded monofilament line										
Horse riding										
track erosion from hooves										
horse manure deposited on tracks and camps										
introduction of weed seeds in fodder										
social impacts on other recreational users										

Data from author's observations (RB) and Australian and US EISs.

activities themselves (Tables 2.6 and 2.7). For example, hiking on unformed trails has caused extensive soil erosion and vegetation damage in alpine areas of New South Wales (Edwards, 1977; Keane *et al.*, 1979), Victoria (Preston *et al.*, 1986; Hardie, 1993) and Tasmania (Calais, 1986). Weeds have also been introduced in some areas (Mallan, 1986; Knutson, 1998).

The environmental significance of recreation and adventure tourism in areas away from resorts has long been recognized by Australia's alpine National Parks. In some instances, rather heavy-handed and less than successful management approaches have been employed. More generally,

Table 2.5. Management measures for operational impacts.

Measure	Australian EISs which identified this measure (see footnote to Table 2.1)									
	1	2	3	4	5	6	7	8	9	10
Seal and drain roads								*		
Maintain existing drainage patterns						*				
Keep vehicles on roads								*		
Use best-practice sewage treatment	*					*				
Use animal-proof rubbish bins	*	*								
Take all rubbish offsite daily	*									
Restrict visitor access areas in summer	*									
Ban open fires in summer; install electric barbeques, close site on fireban days	*									
Construct summer tracks and paths		*						*		
Visitor education programmes		*				*				

Table 2.6. Impacts of backcountry accommodation.

Type of impact	Huts	Camp sites	Tents	Snow caves
Vegetation clearance and disturbance	*	*	*	
Soil erosion and/compaction	*	*		
Disturbance to native wildlife from:				
noise and human activities	*	*	*	
snow compaction	*			*
Visual impacts	*	*	*	
Litter and human waste	*	*	*	*
Introduction of weeds				
in revegetation mulches	*	*		
on vehicles		*		
in socks, and on boots and tentpegs	*	*	*	
colonizing bare areas	*	*		
Fire damage	*	*		
Modified drainage patterns	*	*		

Data from author's observations (RB, CP) and from Knutson (1998), Hardie (1993), Buckley and Pannell (1990), Cullan and Norris (1989), NSW NPWS (1988), Calais (1986) Mallan (1986), Preston and Whitehead (1986), Timms (1980), Keane (1979), and Edwards (1977).

Table 2.7. Impacts of winter backcountry activities.

Type of impact	Nordic ski tracks	Snowcats, snow-mobiles	Off-track skiing and boarding	Ice climbing
Soil erosion and/or compaction from:				
groomed tracks, heavy use, access points	*	*		
Vegetation damage from:				
groomed tracks and snow compaction	*	*		
Disturbance to native wildlife from:				
compression of subnivial space	*	*		
noise, sight, olfactory disturbance	*	*	*	*
Litter	*	*	*	*
Human waste		*	*	*
Vehicle exhaust		*		

Data sources as in Table 2.6.

however, the alpine National Parks have relied principally on regulations and education. There is a series of seven minimal-impact posters and brochures intended to make users aware of their impacts and ways to minimize them. There are also bans on the use of wood fires and restrictions on camping in particularly fragile environments such as the catchments of alpine lakes (NSW NPWS, 1988; Hardie, 1993; Mackay and Nixon, 1995).

Overall, changes in alpine tourism today are expanding its impacts to include those associated with intensive short-term use in the backcountry, as well as those associated with fixed structures such as resorts. Management of these activities is particularly important, as many occur in areas with especially high conservation values.

Climate Change

Major changes to the climate of Australia's alpine areas are predicted within the next two decades. Likely changes include a reduction in snow cover, increased temperatures and possibly lower precipitation. Current models indicate both a substantial reduction in the total area covered by snow, and a substantial reduction in the duration of snow cover in many areas (Whetton, 1998). Such reductions in snow cover and duration are likely to have large effects on mountain tourism in the Australian alpine. Poor snow seasons in the past have resulted in dramatic declines in incomes for resorts and associated commercial activities (Keage, 1990; Konig, 1998). Surveys of people currently visiting resorts to ski or snowboard indicate that if snow cover declines the majority would either give up skiing, ski overseas, or ski in Australia less often (Konig, 1998).

Table 2.8. Impacts of summer backcountry activities.

Type of impact	Scenic car tours	Wildflower tours (car and walk)	Mountain biking	Abseiling and rock climbing	Trail hiking	Off-track hiking
Soil erosion and/or compaction, vegetation clearance and disturbance, modified drainage patterns and visual impacts:						
roads and tracks	*	*				
foot and bike trails		*	*	*	*	
off-track		*	*	*		*
Disturbance to native wildlife from:						
noise, sight and smell	*	*	*	*	*	*
road kills	*		*			
Reduced air quality from vehicle exhausts	*					
Introduction of weeds						
in straw or gravel		*	*		*	
on vehicles and bike tyres	*	*	*			
in socks and boots		*	*	*	*	*
colonizing bare areas		*	*	*	*	*
Waste production						
litter	*	*	*	*	*	
faecal material				*	*	*

Data sources as in Table 2.6.

Changes in climate are also likely to result in major changes in the conditions experienced by alpine plants and animals, whose distribution depends strongly on the duration of snow cover. Increased summer temperatures, shorter snow cover and reduced precipitation are likely to affect the distribution and composition of the alpine flora both directly and indirectly (Pickering, 1998). The rarest and most specialized plant communities, namely short alpine herbfield, fens, valley bogs, raised bogs and sod tussock grasslands are likely to shrink in area. The more generalized communities, namely tall alpine herbfield and heaths, are likely to increase in the short term, but decrease in the longer term, and the diversity and abundance of weeds are likely to increase even more. These processes are likely to cause extinction of some or many of the rare and endemic Australian alpine plant species. Changes in snow cover will also threaten endemic alpine and subalpine animal species, such as the mountain pigmy possum and specialist alpine grasshopper species (Walter and Broome, 1998).

Interaction Between Climate Change and Tourism

The impacts from tourism in the Australian alpine are likely to increase and diversify as the total number of tourists increases, summer tourism increases both in and away from resorts, and climate change affects the alpine ecosystem. These three factors are interlinked. For example, visitor activities are likely to change as the ski season shrinks and resorts focus more on summer activities and on conferences, educational and health tourism, and adventure sports (Keage, 1990; Konig, 1998). These changes in tourism activities, timing and intensity, associated with climate change, will also change the types and intensity of tourism impacts on alpine environments.

In particular, climate change can amplify the impacts of tourism in alpine areas. For example, tourism facilities such as roads, trails and cleared areas provide habitats for weeds, which then disperse into disturbed areas in adjacent natural plant communities (Mallan, 1986; Knutson, 1998). Currently, snow cover and low temperatures limit the diversity and abundance of weeds in the true alpine, with weeds declining with altitude (Mallan, 1986; Knutson, 1998). If these limits are removed, weeds will be able to establish away from trails and roads (Pickering, 1998). In addition, if backcountry summer tourism increases, there will be more trampling disturbance, also increasing the spread of weeds.

Conclusion

Tourism in the Australian alpine region is continuing to grow. Growth in summer and backcountry tourism is more rapid than growth in resort skiing, and this trend is likely to intensify as a result of climate change. The impacts of resorts are far more intense than those of backcountry activities, but both are equally significant for management. Whilst Australia's alpine regions are national parks with conservation as a primary land use goal, tourism is the principal economic activity and one with major implications for land management.

References

Bayfield, N.G. (1994) Burial of vegetation by erosion debris near ski lifts on Cairngorm, Scotland. *Biological Conservation* 6, 246–251.

Brown, J.A.J. and Millner, F.C. (1989) Aspects of the meteorology and hydrology of the Australian Alps. In: Good, R. (ed.) *The Scientific Significance of the Australian Alps.* Australian Alps Liaison Committee, Canberra.

Buckley, R. and Pannell, J. (1990) Environmental impacts of tourism and recreation in national parks and conservation reserves. *Journal of Tourism Studies* 1, 24–32.

Calais, S.S. (1986) Impact of trampling on natural ecosystems in the Cradle Mountain-Lake St Clair National Park. *Australian Geographer* 17, 6–15.

Cole, D.N. (1992) Modelling wilderness campsites: factors that influence amount of impact. *Environment Management* 16, 255–264.

Costin, A.B. (1989) The alps in a global perspective. In: Good, R. (ed.) *The Scientific Significance of the Australian Alps.* Australian Alps Liaison Committee, Canberra.

Costin, A.B., Gray, C.J., Totterdell, C. and Wimbush, D.J. (1979) *Kosciusko Alpine Flora.* Collins, Melbourne.

Cullan, P. and Norris, R. (1989) Significance of lakes and rivers in the Australian mainland Alps. In: Good, R. (ed.) *The Scientific Significance of the Australian Alps.* Australian Alps Liaison Committee, Canberra.

Edwards, I.J. (1977) The ecological impact of pedestrian traffic on alpine vegetation in Kosciusko National Park. *Australian Forestry* 40, 108–120.

Environment Science and Services (1994) *Australian Alps National Parks Visitor Monitoring Strategy.* Australian Alps Liaison Committee, Canberra.

Galloway, R.W. (1988) The potential impact of climate change on Australian ski fields. In: Pearman, G. (ed.) *Greenhouse: Planning for Climate Change.* CSIRO, Melbourne.

Good, R.B. (1992) *Kosciusko Heritage: the Conservation Significance of the Kosciusko National Park.* NSW National Parks and Wildlife Service, Hurstville.

Green, K. and Osborne, W.S. (1994) *Wildlife of the Australian Snow-Country.* Reed, Sydney.

Greller, A.M., Goldstein, M. and Marcus, L. (1974) Snowmobile impact on three alpine tundra plant communities. *Environmental Conservation* 1, 101–110.

Hardie, M. (1993) *Measuring Bushwalking and Camping Impacts: Mount Bogong, Victoria.* Victoria, Department of Conservation and Natural Resources, Melbourne.

Keage, P. (1990) Skiing into the greenhouse. *Trees and Natural Resources* 32, 15–18.

Keane, P.A., Wild, A.E.R. and Rogers, J.H. (1979). Trampling and erosion in alpine country. *Journal of Soil Conservation Service of NSW* 35, 7–12.

Knutson, R. (1998) *Yarrow (Milfoil)* Achillea millefolium L.: *Status, Control and Monitoring in Kosciuszko National Park.* NSW National Parks and Wildlife Service, Sydney.

Konig, U. (1998) Climate change and the Australian ski industry. In Green, K. (ed.) *Snow: a Natural History; An Uncertain Future.* Australian Alps Liaison Committee, Canberra.

Mackay, J. and Allcock, A. (1988) *Recreation in Kosciusko National Park – a Preliminary Estimate of Growth.* Unpubl. Report, NSW National Parks and Wildlife Service, Sydney.

Mackay, J. and Nixon, A. (1995) *Australian Alps National Parks Back-country Recreation Strategy.* Australian Alps Liaison Committee, Canberra.

Mallan, J. (1986) Introduced vascular plants in the high altitude and high latitude areas of Australasia, with particular reference to the Kosciusko alpine area, New South Wales. In: Barlow, B. (ed.) *Flora and Fauna of Alpine Australasia: Ages and Origins.* CSIRO, Melbourne.

Marion, J.L., Cole, D.N. and Bratton, S. (1986) *Exotic Vegetation in Wilderness Areas.* USDA Forest Service Intermountain Research Station General Technical Report INT-212114-120.

Marston, F. and Yapp, G. (1991) *The Impact of Tourism and Recreation on Alpine Water Quality: Issues and their Implications for Integrated Management of the Victorian Alpine Park.* Royal Australian Institute of Parks and Recreation, Canberra.

Meyer, E. (1993) The impact of summer tourism and winter tourism on the fauna of alpine soils in western Austria [in German]. *Revue Suisse de Zoologie* 100, 519–527.

NSW NPWS (1988) *Kosciusko National Park Plan of Management,* 2nd edn. NSW National Parks and Wildlife Service, Sydney.

Pickering, C.M. (1997) Reproductive strategies and constraints of alpine plants as illustrated by five species of Australian alpine *Ranunculus. Opera Botanica* 132, 101–108.

Pickering, C.M. (1998) Climate change and the reproductive ecology of Australian alpine plants. *Australian Institute of Alpine Studies Newsletter* 1.

Preston, F., Whitehead, I. and Byrne, N. (1986) *Impacts of Camping Use on Snow Plains in the Baw Baw National Park.* Victoria, National Parks Services, Melbourne.

Price, M.F. (1985) Impacts of recreational activities on alpine vegetation in western North America. *Mountain Research and Development* 5, 263–277.

Smith, J.M.B. (1986) Origins of the Australasian tropialpine and alpine floras. In: Barlow, B.A. (ed.) *Flora and Fauna of Alpine Australasia: Ages and Origins.* CSIRO, Melbourne.

Timms, B.V. (1980) The benthos of the Kosciusko glacial lakes. *Proceedings of the Limnological Society of NSW* 104, 119–125.

Tsuyuzaki, S. (1990) Species composition and soil erosion on a ski area in Hokkaido, Northern Japan. *Environmental Management* 14, 203–207.

United States Department of Agriculture Forest Service (1994) *Snowmass Ski Area, Final Environmental Impact Statement.* Rocky Mountain Region, Aspen, Colorado.

United States Department of Agriculture Forest Service (1995) *Draft Environmental Impact Statement Steamboat Ski Area Expansion*. USDA Forest Service, Steamboat Springs, Colorado.

United States Department of Agriculture Forest Service (1996) *Final Environmental Impact Statement Telluride Ski Area Expansion*. USDA Forest Service, Delta, Colorado.

United States Department of Agriculture Forest Service (1997a) *Environmental Assessment of Proposed Improvements at Crested Butte Mountain Resort*. USDA Forest Service, Rocky Mountain Region, Aspen, Colorado.

United States Department of Agriculture Forest Service (1997b) *Aspen Highlands Ski Area, Final Environmental Impact Statement*. USDA Forest Service, Pitkin County, Colorado.

Walter, M. and Broome, L. (1998) Snow as a factor in animal hibernation and dormancy. In: Green, K. (ed.) *Snow: a Natural History; an Uncertain Future*. Australian Alps Liaison Committee, Canberra.

Warnken, J. and Buckley, R.C. (1998) Scientific quality of tourism EIA. *Journal of Applied Ecology* 35, 1–8.

Whetton, P. (1998) Climate change impacts on the spatial extent of snow-cover in the Australian Alps. In Green, K. (ed.) *Snow: a Natural History; an Uncertain Future*. Australian Alps Liaison Committee, Canberra.

Willard, B.E. and Marr, J.W. (1970) Effects of human activities on alpine tundra ecosystems in Rocky Mountain National Park, Colorado. *Biological Conservation* 2, 257–265.

Wood, T.F. (1987a) Methods for assessing relative risk of damage to soils and vegetation arising from winter sports development in the Scottish Highlands. *Journal of Environmental Management* 25, 253–270.

Wood, T.F. (1987b) The analysis of environmental impacts resulting from summer recreation in the Cairngorm Ski Area, Scotland. *Journal of Environmental Management* 25, 271–284.

Zimmermann, F.M. (1998) Sustainable tourism in a fragile environment – the Alps. In: Faulkner, B., Tideswell, C. and Weaver, D. (eds) *Progress in Tourism & Hospitality Research*. CAUTHE, Griffith University, Gold Coast, Australia.

Recreation Resource Assessment and Monitoring Techniques for Mountain Regions

Christopher Monz

National Outdoor Leadership School, 288 Main Street, Lander, WY 82520, USA

Introduction

To many, mountains are powerful symbols of an untamed, natural landscape that is becoming rare in our increasingly urbanized world. In cultures on every continent, mountains have evoked fear, reverence and awe. Though mountain regions are important ecologically, economically, spiritually and culturally, they also comprise roughly one-fifth of the earth's surface with one-tenth of the world's population. Ecologically, mountains harbour considerable biodiversity, with rapid changes in altitude yielding multiple climate zones over short distances. Mountain watersheds are the direct source of fresh water for half of the world's population.

Given the significance, importance and attraction of mountain regions, it is not surprising that there has been a recent rise in the popularity of mountain recreation and tourism and consequently, an increase in associated impacts in many areas. Recreation and tourism impacts take two forms: direct, or those occurring directly in protected areas due to recreational activities; and indirect, or impacts on adjacent lands as a consequence of the development of tourist facilities (Wall, 1997). While tourism can contribute to sustaining local and even national economies, it can also have significant consequences on fragile mountain ecosystems. It has been suggested recently that recreation and tourism activities are surpassing the resource extractive economy as the single largest threat to the conservation of mountain ecosystems (Denniston, 1995). Moreover, recreational visits to mountain protected areas in the USA show increases as much as 12-fold since 1945, and analysis suggests that these increases will probably continue for the foreseeable future (Denniston, 1995; Cole, 1996). Similar trends have been reported in many regions worldwide including the European Alps, Indian Himalaya and Nepal (Denniston, 1995).

Direct ecological impacts within protected areas as a consequence of increased recreation are widespread and increasing, and are becoming a worldwide management concern. Land managers are often faced with what seem to be contradictory management goals: to allow for visitor access while simultaneously preserving the naturalness or pristine character of an area. Moreover, recreation impacts in high elevation mountain areas can be particularly problematic, since alpine vegetation is often slow growing and in some cases, can be highly susceptible to impact. Despite the often small spatial scale of recreation impacts, they take on a much greater concern in mountain ecosystems because the areas are often unique and 'high-value' ecosystems containing rare species and are of high aesthetic value. In addition, due to the remote and fragile nature of mountain environments, impacts often progress until significant resource damage has occurred. Subsequent mitigation strategies then become limited to hardening or rehabilitation of trails and sites, which can be logistically difficult and expensive.

The specific desired outcome of management objectives often differ and may be based on varying social, economic and conservation values. For example, the development of visitor facilities in certain areas of a national park may seem appropriate, but in other types of protected areas, or in other zones of the same national park, it may be desirable to provide for a pristine visitor experience. Still, in other areas a bioreserve approach, with little or no visitation, might be more appropriate for conservation purposes. In this chapter, I will discuss the application of existing inventory and monitoring techniques that can help set general thresholds for soil and plant impacts in areas where a pristine, primitive type of visitor experience is desirable. Often, providing for these kinds of experiences is a significant draw for tourism, but to be sustainable, tourism activities must not degrade the natural character of the area (Wall, 1997).

The overall objectives of inventory and monitoring programmes are to identify and quantify site-specific resource impacts. These impacts are often summarized by environmental or use-related factors to detect and evaluate relationships. Of parallel importance (in particular campsite or visitor site monitoring) is to locate all areas of impact, so if the number of sites proliferate in the future, an accurate baseline of site location will have been established (Marion, 1991). Inventory and monitoring measurement indicators and procedures are frequently similar if not identical. The initial inventory provides a baseline assessment of resource conditions using specific impact assessment indicators. The subsequent monitoring utilizes the same indicators and methods for follow-up measurements to assess change over time or as a consequence of management actions.

In the USA, public land management agencies have been in efforts to determine appropriate levels of recreation use by applying objective methodologies. Currently, the best examples of these planning processes in the USA are the US Forest Service's Limits of Acceptable Change (LAC) approach (Stankey *et al.*, 1985) and the Visitor Impact Management programme (VIM) adopted by the National Parks Conservation Association (Graefe *et al.*, 1990). Impact monitoring provides an essential element for these recreational resource planning and management procedures. For example, under the LAC framework, numerical standards are set for individual impact parameters. These standards define critical thresholds between acceptable and unacceptable conditions and act as a measurable reference point to which future conditions can be compared. A monitoring programme provides information for managers to formulate realistic standards and to periodically assess and evaluate resource conditions.

This chapter illustrates how established resource monitoring protocols and field techniques can be utilized to measure resource impacts on soils and vegetation in mountain environments. Monitoring programmes can help guide visitor management strategies, so resource impacts can be minimized. Though the basic principles apply to many ecosystems, examples are drawn from the Phantom Canyon Preserve in Colorado, USA, an environment where a significant increase in visitation is possible, but has not yet occurred. Here, a basic monitoring and assessment project was developed to manage trail networks and visitor sites in light of increasing visitation pressures with the management goal of resource preservation.

Measuring Trail Conditions

Trails provide recreational access to backcountry areas and are a vital component in an overall management strategy. Trails should be carefully located, designed, constructed and maintained to allow for satisfying recreational experiences and to protect resources. Trails in poor condition may result from deficiencies in any of the factors listed above (i.e. location, construction, etc.), or from recreational activities exceeding the physical capacity of the trail segment (Marion, 1994; Hammitt and Cole, 1998).

The most common kinds of impacts observed on trails include excessive widening, multiple treads, muddiness and soil erosion (Leung and Marion, 1996). In order to maintain resource protection priorities, it is often desirable to correct these problems or through proper design and management avoid these problems altogether. Improperly constructed trails often require significant expenditures of funds to maintain and repair. These impacts make recreation travel difficult, unsafe or aesthetically unpleasant.

It is essential to inventory and monitor trails so that problem areas can be identified and the usefulness of management actions evaluated. Trail assessments are often conducted with the following priorities (Marion, 1994):

- Trail inventory – locate and map trails, identify general attributes such as length, hiking difficulty, natural and cultural features, and facilities (bridges, culverts, signs);
- Trail maintenance – locate trail problems and prescribe solutions (reroute tread, reconstruct tread, and construct water drainage bars or dips);
- Trail impact monitoring – assess trail conditions for ongoing deterioration, presence of exotic species, etc.

There are two commonly used approaches for trail assessment: problem-based rapid survey and sampling-based rapid survey (Tables 3.1 and 3.2). A problem-based rapid survey with a measurement approach would have the following procedures: a trail would be hiked while pushing a measuring wheel that records distance walked. The researcher would look for selected trail problems such as excessive width and excessive post-trail construction soil erosion. The measuring wheel distance would be recorded at the beginning and end of each occurrence of a trail problem. This method provides

Table 3.1. Characteristics of two commonly used approaches for trail assessment.[a]

Type of monitoring approach	Measurement options and characteristics
Problem-based rapid survey	1. *Damaged/undamaged* – simple descriptive criteria are applied 2. *Condition class* – trail condition is matched to one of several descriptive trail classes (condition classes which typically are represented by a numerical range, e.g. 1–5). The classes are strictly defined as to the characteristics of such impact parameters as trail width, erosion and excessive slope 3. *Multiple parameter* – individual trail problems (e.g. erosion, muddiness) are rated using descriptive or quantitatively defined classes 4. *Measurement* – individual trail problems (e.g. erosion, muddiness) are measured (length and/or width)
Sampling-based rapid survey	1. *Systematic* – descriptive or quantitative measures are taken at regular intervals (e.g. every 100 m) along the entire trail 2. *Stratified* – descriptive or quantitative measures are taken at regular intervals within selected trail segments stratified by some trail characteristic (e.g. amount or type of use, vegetation type) 3. *Permanent point surveys* – permanent points that allow relocation and re-measurement of specific locations are established

[a]Adapted from Hammitt and Cole (1998) and Marion (1994).

data on the number of occurrences of trail problems, total trail length, percentage of trail affected and number of occurrences per kilometre.

In contrast, in a sampling-based rapid survey with a systematic approach, the trail would be hiked while pushing a measuring wheel, stopping every 50 m to measure the following items:

- trail width – measure the trail width based on obvious disturbance or loss of vegetation cover or organic litter;
- trail erosion – estimate the original trail surface (post trail construction) and measure from this point to the deepest trail tread surface.

This method provides data characterizing the range and mean trail widths and erosion (incision or depth of tread) for a given trail or segments of a trail.

Measuring Visitor Site Conditions

Several types of campsite monitoring systems have been developed and these include photopoint methods, condition class ratings (e.g. 'Frissell ratings'; Frissell, 1978), multiple parameter ratings-based systems and multiple parameter measurement-based systems (Hammitt and Cole, 1998; Marion, 1991). Though these procedures were developed for campsites, they can be applied to virtually any contiguous area of impact, especially areas where visitors congregate for day use.

The different site monitoring systems vary in their precision, reliability, the amount and type of information they provide, and in cost. If two different

Table 3.2.   Advantages and disadvantages of trail assessment approaches.

Type of survey	Advantages	Disadvantages
Problem-based rapid survey	• Permits rapid assessments focused on trail problems of greatest management concern • Characterizes the condition of the entire trail	• Focuses on trail problems • Not able to characterize average conditions for indicators such as trail width or muddiness • Not sensitive to small changes
Sampling-based rapid survey	• Permits rapid assessments of general trail conditions	• May not accurately characterize trail problems unless a large number of sample points are used • Not sensitive to small changes
Permanent point survey	• Provides accurate and precise data on changing trail conditions	• Very time-consuming. Does not characterize overall trail condition

people monitor the same site, substantial differences between measurements often exist, as there are many considerations in the design of a monitoring programme. Different answers may be provided to such questions as: should the assessment provide absolute or just relative measures of change, is an overall index of impact enough or is information of types of impact needed, and are all sites or a subsample of sites to be monitored? In general, research-quality measurements can be expensive, so to keep costs low some sacrifices must be made on the precision, reliability, quantity and type of information monitored.

Photopoint methods, though easy to conduct and low in cost, provide no quantifiable information. Photos are very helpful in relocating sites and in visually conveying impacts and are best used as a supplement to one of the other measurement systems.

Condition class rating systems (Frissell, 1978) involve assigning an overall rating to the campsite, usually a 1–5 numeric scale based on observable characteristics (Table 3.3). Sites are located, mapped, and assigned a rating. This can be done in just a few minutes per site, provided that the general location of the sites is known.

Condition class ratings are an inexpensive and efficient way to determine how many campsites exist and where the campsites are located, which campsites are most highly impacted, if the number of campsites increased or decreased, and if campsite conditions have generally improved or deteriorated.

Multiple parameter systems assess a wide range of impact parameters and can provide specific information on each. Parameters typically measured include:

- vegetation loss
- exposure of mineral soil
- tree damage
- tree root exposure

Table 3.3.   An example of a Frissell condition class rating system.

Class rating	Impact characteristics
Class 1	• Ground vegetation flattened but not permanently injured • Minimal physical change except for possibly a simple rock fireplace
Class 2	• As in class 1 and ground vegetation worn away around fireplace or centre of camping activity
Class 3	• Ground vegetation lost on most of the site, but humus and litter still present in all but a few areas
Class 4	• Bare mineral soil obvious. Tree roots exposed on the surface
Class 5	• Soil erosion obvious. Tree damage extensive

- level of development (facilities)
- level of cleanliness (trash, human waste)
- social trails (i.e. trails developed by visitors and not management action)
- area of the campsite
- area of vegetation loss.

In multiple parameter ratings-based systems (Cole, 1983), these types of impact can be rapidly estimated by just looking around a site. Typically each site is given a rating of 1–3 for each impact parameter. These can be summed to obtain an overall impact rating. In this way one site can be measured in less than 15 min, but precision and reliability can be low. This technique can adequately answer all the questions a condition class rating system can answer. It can also answer which types of impact are most serious and what the area-wide trend is for individual impact parameters.

Multiple parameter measurement-based systems (Marion, 1995; Monz, 1998) provide the only reliable way to obtain accurate data on how individual sites are changing over time. This involves the measurement of individual parameters rather than making categorical estimates. Typically, conducting this kind of assessment can take 30 min or more per campsite, requires significant training of field personnel and, consequently, can be relatively expensive.

Often it is not practical, given the time and funding limitations, to conduct intensive measurements on every campsite (see Table 3.4 for advantages and disadvantages of various assessment approaches). An effective solution is to locate, photograph and assign condition class ratings on all campsites and to conduct the more intensive measurements on a subset of the campsites (e.g. 10–20%). This will provide a set of measurements with the capability of detecting relatively small site characteristic changes, and yield other important information such as the total number of sites, their location and general condition.

Measurement of campsite area: geometric figure and radial transect

An important component of measurement-based assessments is the accurate measurement of the size of the impacted area of recreation sites. This information is vital to the full understanding of the dynamics of resource impacts and to the maintenance of the total area of impact within management objectives. For example, it would be important to know that while the numbers of campsites had remained the same in a given area, their size had increased by twofold.

Two common methodologies have been utilized for measuring campsite areas. The following information is a general overview that describes these methods. A more complete step-by-step description can be found in Marion (1991).

Table 3.4. Advantages and disadvantages of campsite assessment approaches.

Type of survey	Advantages	Disadvantages
Photopoint	• Visually documents extent and location of campsite impacts • Permits rapid assessments • Can be performed with a minimal cost and staff training	• Provides no quantitative information, i.e. average conditions cannot be determined • Not sensitive to small changes
Condition class ratings	• Permits rapid assessments of general campsite conditions • Provides some quantification of the relative degree of impact observed	• Can be somewhat subjective • Not sensitive to small changes • Many types of impact are integrated into one estimate
Multiple parameter ratings-based	• Permits rapid assessments of specific campsite condition parameters with some quantification • Provides information as to which types of impact are the most serious	• Ratings can be somewhat subjective • Not sensitive to small changes
Multiple parameter measurement-based	• Provides accurate and precise data on changing campsite conditions	• Time-consuming and costly • Requires highly trained staff

Geometric figure method

This method involves superimposing one or more imaginary geometric figures (rectangles, circles or triangles) on the site boundaries and measuring appropriate dimensions to calculate its total area (e.g. Fig. 3.1). It is relatively rapid and can be quite accurate if applied correctly, but consistency and good judgement are required as site boundaries rarely match perfectly the shapes of geometric figures.

Radial transect method

The variable radial transect method is recognized as the most accurate method for determining the square area of impacted recreation sites in the field (Fig. 3.2). Currently, most research-level studies utilize this method. It can add a significant amount of time to the assessment procedures, but also provides a substantial increase in accuracy, particularly in re-measurement (Fig. 3.3). The area is measured by determining the azimuth and distance from a designated, permanent centre point to points that adequately define the perimeter of the campsite. The total square area can then be calculated geometrically.

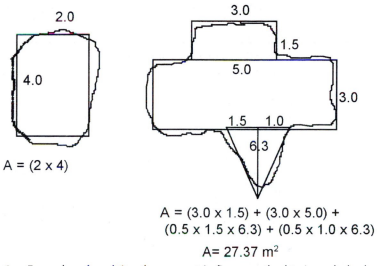

$$A = (3.0 \times 1.5) + (3.0 \times 5.0) +$$
$$(0.5 \times 1.5 \times 6.3) + (0.5 \times 1.0 \times 6.3)$$
$$A = 27.37 \ m^2$$

Fig. 3.1.   Examples of applying the geometric figure method to irregularly shaped impacted areas in the field.

A permanent marker (usually a metal spike with a numbered tag) is buried at the centre point for future reference. Additional compass bearings, location descriptions, site photos, map locations and GPS coordinates can all be useful in relocating sites in the field.

For re-measurement, centre point markers can be found with a metal detector. Original azimuths and distances are determined and decisions are made at each perimeter point as to whether the site boundary should be changed (Fig. 3.3). Transects can be added if needed.

Measuring Trails and Visitor Sites: Examples from the Phantom Canyon Preserve, Colorado, USA

The Phantom Canyon Preserve is located approximately 30 miles northwest of Fort Collins, Colorado, USA and is a core property in the Laramie Foothills Site Conservation Plan Area. The original 650 ha property was purchased in 1987 by The Nature Conservancy (TNC) and protects 10 km of the North Fork of the Cache la Poudre River. The Preserve contains several rare plant populations including one of the largest known populations of Larimer Aletes. Approximately 13 km of hiking trails currently exist in the Preserve and are primarily available for day use during guided events (interpretative field trips and stewardship work days).

Though public access is desirable by TNC and a system of trails exist at the Preserve, the ability of the trail system to sustain current use is not

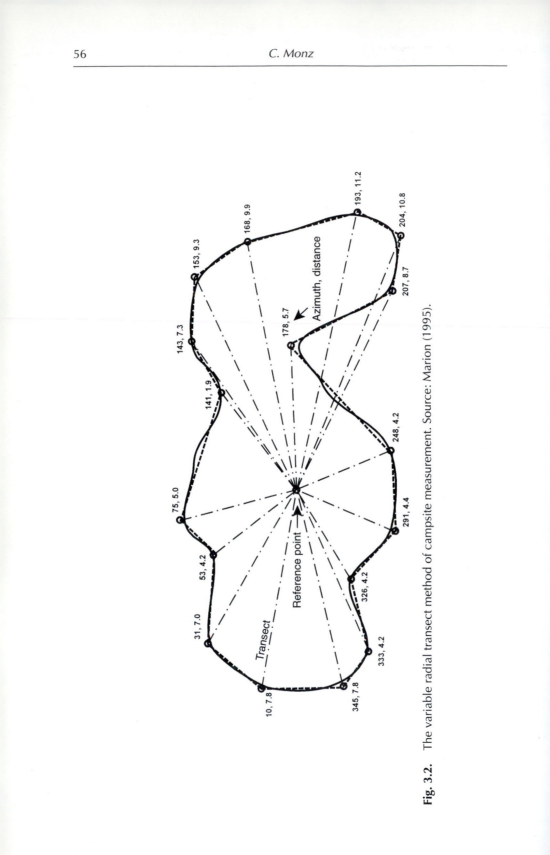

Fig. 3.2. The variable radial transect method of campsite measurement. Source: Marion (1995).

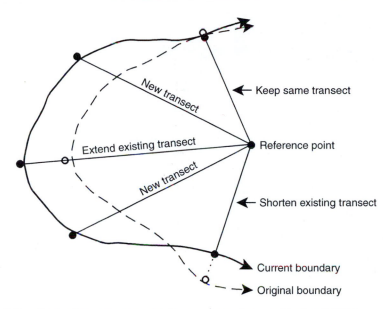

Fig. 3.3. Campsite re-measurement procedures. Source: Marion (1991).

known. Also, while the existing system of trails is acceptable, TNC managers view any proliferation of impact to plant and soil resources as an unacceptable change. Since the protection of biodiversity is the central mission of TNC, finding the appropriate types and levels of visitation, while limiting resource degradation, is of vital importance.

The objective of this study is to provide an initial, basic assessment of the trail and visitation site conditions at TNC's Phantom Canyon Preserve. This assessment will provide the basis for future resource monitoring and will provide valuable information for the development of indicators and standards should a Limits of Acceptable Change (LAC) process be initiated. It should be noted that this study was undertaken mainly for heuristic purposes and cannot stand as a state-of-the art, definitive study of recreation resource conditions at Phantom Canyon. This discussion is provided here simply as a good example of how basic monitoring and assessment can be conducted with limited time and funding and still provide valuable information for management. Several suggestions for further research and analysis are included in the concluding section.

Monitoring trail and visitor site characteristics

The trail assessment describes the current condition of individual trails and trail segments as a function of the linear extent and number of occurrences

Fig. 3.4. Rim Trail Overlook Visitor Site: trail assessment with measuring wheel.

of specified trail parameters. We assessed the overall width and depth of the tread by walking the trail with a measuring wheel (see Fig. 3.4) and measuring the width (see Fig. 3.5) and depth at 30 m intervals. Width boundaries were determined to be the interface where no observable trampling of adjacent vegetation had occurred. Depth was defined as a single measurement of the deepest incision of the tread, using a metre stick spanning the trail as a horizontal reference point.

Trail maintenance features were identified by type and either point measurements (i.e. distance from origin of the trail) or linear extent, or both, where appropriate. For example, the point at which a trail junction occurred was noted as the distance from the origin of the trail or trail segment. Steps constructed in the trail were identified by the distance at the beginning and end of the maintenance feature, thus providing a location and linear extent. Maintenance features that were identified are subdivided into two categories as in Table 3.5.

Permanent plots

Reference points for long-term monitoring were designated at 183 m (600 ft) intervals on the Rim Trail; 244 m (800 ft) intervals along the North Lookout Trail; and 153 m (500 ft) intervals along the River Trail. These varying

Fig. 3.5. North Overlook Trail: measuring trail width using a metre stick.

Table 3.5. Trail maintenance features assessed.

Potential resource problems	Current maintenance features
Multiple tread[L]	Water bar[P]
Side slope[L]	Switch back[P]
Excessive grade[L]	View point/lunch site[P]
	Trail junction[P]
	Steps[P L]

L = Lineal feature parameters, P = Point feature parameters.
After Marion (1994).

intervals were set so adequate replication was included in each trail segment, particularly the River Trail which is naturally divided by river crossings into distinct segments or 'reaches'. These points also serve as photo-monitoring positions. For relocation, two 15 cm steel spikes were driven into the soil approximately 10–20 cm from the trail edge, one on each side, one spike bearing an numbered aluminium tag. One photo with a 35 mm focal length was taken per plot to document the location and provide a visual representation of the trail condition.

Introduction and spread of non-native plant species

At the reference points along each trail and trail segment, a 30×50 cm quadrat frame was placed (see Fig. 3.6) on the vegetation adjacent to the tread. The presence/absence of non-native plant species was determined in these plots.

Fig. 3.6. North Overlook Trail: measuring trail width with a metre stick and presence/absence of non-native plant species with a quadrat.

Assessment of concentration areas

In areas where visitors tend to gather (e.g. vista areas, lunch sites) and soil and plant impacts have become continuous disturbed areas, we employed the variable radial transect method (Marion, 1991) to measure the size of the impacted area. We also estimated the degree of vegetation loss and mineral soil exposure following Marion's (1991) procedures at these sites. Impacted areas were compared to adjacent representative areas (control sites) to determine the degree of vegetation cover loss. Centre points were marked with 15 cm steel spikes with numbered tags and photos and reference bearings were taken to document the site location. The number of trails entering the sites was also noted.

Data analysis

Visitor site areas were determined geometrically from the radial transect data. Relative vegetation cover loss (RC_L) for these sites was calculated by the following formula:

$$RC_L = 1 - \frac{\% \text{ cover in campsite}}{\% \text{ cover in control plots}} \times 100.$$

All data were summarized, and synthetic variables were calculated using Microsoft Excel (Microsoft Corporation, Bellvue, WA, USA) and SPSS statistical software (SPSS Inc., Chicago, IL, USA). Both non-parametric and parametric summary statistics were used where appropriate. For the River Trail width and depth measurements, the Levene's test was used to check the homogeneity of group variance prior to conducting ANOVAs and Tukey's HSD *post hoc* test at alpha = 0.05 was used to determine significant differences in group means.

Results

The current resource status of the trail system at the preserve is described by the results depicted in Table 3.6. Median trail width ranged from 53 cm on the River Trail to 73 cm on the Rim Trail, while depth ranged from 2.5 cm on the River Trail to 5.0 cm on the Cabin Spur. The areas of excessive grade (i.e. steep slopes) and multiple trailing were found almost exclusively on the River Trail, with just one occurrence of excessive grade on the Rim Trail and none elsewhere. Switchbacks were common on the N. Overlook Trail and over 7% of the length of this trail was found to be under current maintenance, most of this length being the construction of steps due to steep grades. Only the River Trail was found to have a significant length in need of maintenance (i.e. the total combined length of the multiple trailing and excessive grade sections) with 1.5% of the trail noted. Further analysis of the River Trail was possible, since it can be divided into discrete segments or 'reaches'. Analysis of variance (ANOVA) results (Table 3.7) examining the

Table 3.6. A summary of some important trail characteristics.

Trail characteristics	River Trail	Rim Trail	N. Overlook	Cabin Spur
Median width (cm)[a]	53.3	73.6	58.4	60.9
	(83.8; 43.2)	(91.4; 53.3)	(91.4; 43.1)	(76.2; 58.4)
Median depth (cm)[a]	2.5	3.0	3.5	5.0
	(5.5; 1)	(5.4; 0.5)	(7; 0.5)	(7.5; 2.0)
Number of steep slopes[b]	20	1	–	–
Number of switch backs[b]	2	–	8	–
Multiple trail sections[b]	3	–	–	–
% length in maintenance[c]	1.18	–	7.00	–
% length needing maintenance[c]	1.58	–	–	–

[a]Summary measurement (median followed by range in parentheses).
[b]Point measurement.
[c]Linear measurement.

Table 3.7. Trail width and depth measurements for the six segments (reaches) of the River Trail.

Reach	N	Width (cm)	Depth (cm)
1	4	58.4 ± 7.1 a	1.5 ± 0.2
2	6	55.9 ± 2.1 a	2.5 ± 0.2
3	5	70.6 ± 4.6 b	3.1 ± 0.5
4	5	47.7 ± 1.7 a	2.8 ± 0.6
5	5	51.8 ± 4.9 a	3.2 ± 0.6
6	8	53.3 ± 1.5 a	3.3 ± 0.4

Values are means ± SE. Means followed by the same letter are not statistically different using Tukeys's HSD at alpha = 0.05. ANOVA did not reveal any significant differences for the depth measurements.

width and depth of the six reaches demonstrate that the third reach had a significantly greater width, while no differences were observed in depth.

Along all of the trails, the majority of the quadrats[1] contained at least one non-native plant species, with the total frequency of occurrence ranging from 71 to 91% dependent on the trail (Table 3.8). *Bromus tectorum* was ubiquitous throughout, occurring at points along all trails and with a range of occurrence of 67–71%. *Lepidium latifolium* was also present along all trails but at a substantially lower frequency than *B. tectorum*. The areas adjacent to the River Trail contained the most weed species, a total of eight, though some species were found in only 3% of the plots (i.e. just one quadrat).

---

[1] A basic sampling unit of vegetation surveys. The size of the quadrat can vary depending on the specific application.

The characteristics of the five visitor sites identified are depicted in Table 3.9. Median RC_L in these sites was 59%, but there was a substantial range observed. For example, the River Overlook Site, on a largely bare rock substrate, showed no observable cover loss, while the Shady site exhibited a 93% RC_L. Exposed mineral soil was high in all of these sites (median 85%) while the proliferation of trails entering these sites was low with a median number of one trail per site. Sites were not excessively large in total impacted area with the largest site being the Sunny Site (see Fig. 3.7) at 41 m² and the median size being 21 m².

Discussion

As with many resource assessment studies, it is impossible at this time with the data represented here to determine use–impact relationships,

Table 3.8. Frequency of occurrence of non-native plant species along surveyed trails.

Non-native species	Frequency of occurrence of non-native plant species			
	River Trail	Rim Trail	N. Overlook	Cabin Spur
Cirsium arvense	24			
Sisymbrium ailtiissiumum	6		3	
Bromus tectorum	67	78	80	71
Lactuca serriola	9			
Lepidium latifolium	3	4	9	14
Verbascum thapsius	15			
Cynoglossum officinale	3			
Allium aparine	3			
Tragapogum dubius		19	9	
Total	91	85	83	71
N	33	27	35	7

Presence/absence of species was assessed in 30 × 50 cm quadrats, placed just adjacent to trails at given intervals (see methods). Total = total number of quadrats that contained at least one non-native plant species; *N* = total number of quadrats assessed along a given trail.

Table 3.9. A summary of important visitor site characteristics. *N* = 5.

Site characteristic	Median (range)
Relative vegetation cover loss (RC_L, %)	59.2 (0–93.4)
Mineral soil exposure (% Area)	85.5 (63–85)
Number of trails	1 (1–3)
Impacted area (m²)	21 (17–41)

Fig. 3.7. View from 'Sunny Site', adjacent to the River Trail.

environmental factors or the acceptable level of visitor impact at the Preserve. The data are, however, an essential step towards meeting the above mentioned goals, and provide an accurate initial description of the current status of visitor resources. Should there be changes in visitor use levels, the temporal or spatial distribution of use, or the types of visitor activities, this analysis will provide an important baseline of knowledge to determine changes in resource condition. Moreover, often the initial steps in the LAC process require a basic knowledge of the current resource conditions in order to begin the development of objectives and standards to be monitored.

Both a limitation and a benefit exist with this current study in that the areas examined have a relatively short history of use, and that use has been restricted to areas largely constructed to tolerate moderate levels of visitation. This limits our ability, even with a more intensive study, to determine much in the way of use–environment relationships. The benefit, of course, is that the majority of these areas have now been documented before substantial resource degradation has occurred and, with continued monitoring and appropriate management action, it is possible that little additional degradation will occur in the future.

Marion's (1994) study is perhaps a landmark effort to relate trail conditions to use and environmental factors. This study measured over 300 miles of historical trails subjected to varying types and intensities of use, and measured a wide range of inventory, resource condition and design and maintenance parameters. This work provides a context for the trail assessment work in this study, and comparisons can be made to these areas of higher use.

The trail width and depth measurements do not currently indicate that significant resource degradation has occurred. Trails for the most part are of the 'single track' variety, in that the current width allows only for hiking in single file. Often, with trail surveys on public lands (i.e. Marion, 1994), the excessive width threshold is usually greater than or equal to 1 m and excessive depth (erosion) is greater than or equal to 30 cm. Trails of this degree may not be appropriate on the Preserve, but for comparison, all trails are currently well below these limits (Table 3.6). Since the Rim Trail, North Overlook and Cabin Spur Trails have all been well constructed via management action and planning, it is likely that with a modest amount of maintenance, these trails can support current use or even increased use without significant degradation.

The River Trail may represent a different management challenge, however. This trail appears to be largely an historical trail for fishing access to the river, and not the result of a management action. A significant number of areas with excessive grade and several areas of multiple tread were identified (Table 3.6). The total lineal distance of these areas was over 1.5% of the total length of the trail. It is not known if the areas of excessive grade will become a particular resource problem (i.e. if they will lead to increased erosion), and at the least they should be monitored. The areas of multiple trailing, however, are of particular concern since they are often the result of a seasonal maintenance problem on the trail, such as poor drainage, that visitors are avoiding. Besides the significant impacts of trail widening and erosion, additional disturbed areas can often provide habitat for opportunistic non-native plant species to proliferate (Liddle, 1997).

An interesting result is the significantly wider trail segment along the third reach of the River Trail (Table 3.7). It is possible that there are some environmental or use-related factors resulting in these effects and this should be investigated further. Elucidation of these causal relationships would be of some assistance in setting visitor use levels in the future for this trail and may actually help preclude significant trail maintenance. Given the nature of the River Trail and its many river crossings, it may be desirable to manage this as more of a 'pristine' area, where little direct resource management is performed. To reach this management goal more research is needed.

Non-native plant species occur frequently in plots adjacent to every trail (Table 3.8). This is possibly a rough index of the overall distribution of the presence of these species across areas of the preserve (assuming trails were located somewhat randomly), or an indicator that there may be a correlation with trail use and the spread of non-natives. This relationship cannot be determined without further study, but these data do raise some interesting questions. Liddle (1997) presents evidence that trail use can lead to the spread of ruderal plant species, particularly since seeds can be carried in mud on visitors' shoes or on clothing, but it is not clear if these mechanisms are at work here. In addition, since TNC is actively involved in a weed management programme on the preserve, it is also unclear how these elimination efforts may have affected non-native plant distributions.

The visitor site characteristics (Table 3.9) are most closely analogous to campsite studies in areas of overnight use (e.g. Monz, 1998). Depending on management objectives, areas such as these are often viewed as 'sacrifice zones' where impacts will be observable, but considerable degradation, enlargement of the impacted area and proliferation of sites will be avoided through management action. Areas of concentrated use frequently exhibit the majority of vegetation cover loss and soil compaction in the initial stages of use and consequently, less overall disturbance often results when use is concentrated in previously impacted areas (Hammitt and Cole, 1998). If the current level of impact is permissible on these sites, these data can serve as a basis for future site monitoring. Should these impacted areas be viewed as unacceptable, a controlled trampling study (e.g. Cole and Bayfield, 1993; Monz *et al.*, 1996) would be valuable in determining the use–impact thresholds needed to minimize site impact.

Suggestions for future research

- The majority of the trail system at the preserve was found to be in better condition than commonly accepted levels of impact for trails on public lands. Several specific resource problems were identified (particularly on the River Trail) that may require maintenance actions.
- Visitor sites, somewhat analogous to backcountry campsites, also demonstrate a moderate, typically acceptable level of impact. These impact levels, for both trails and visitor sites, may or may not be acceptable, and this should be addressed by defining the management objectives for these resources.
- Non-native plant species (especially *B. tectorum*) are prevalent in areas adjacent to trails. Without further investigation, it will remain unclear if there is any correlation with trail use and weed distribution.
- These data can be used as a baseline to determine if visitation is resulting in any additional resource changes on the Preserve. Should there be an interest in determining the use and/or environment–impact relationship factors, additional intensive studies are required.
- A logical next step, from a management standpoint, would be to use these data as a basis for developing objectives and standards for visitor

resource management as is common in the LAC process. Once completed this process may lead to further research, additional site monitoring or both.

Conclusion

Though it is important to provide facilities and services for visitors to mountain protected areas, resources must be allocated for the development of adequate monitoring and assessment systems as part of an overall planning framework. Without monitoring programmes, resource degradation can often proceed to the point where problems become excessive and mitigation difficult and expensive. Monitoring is extremely essential to tourism development, especially in mountain regions, where vulnerable environments can become altered rapidly. Social trail proliferation in alpine environments, for example, if severe enough, can be a significant contributor to the loss of endemic plant species and soil erosion. The Phantom Canyon monitoring system provided here is a model, but the techniques described can be adapted to monitor mountain regions worldwide.

The monitoring of plant and soil impacts in recreation areas is only part of an overall strategy of resource protection. The resource implications of other aspects of tourism and recreation need to be monitored in mountain protected areas, for example:

- the consequences of ski resort development (Buckley *et al.*, this volume);
- fuelwood usage (Gurung and deCoursey, this volume);
- water quality (Hammitt and Cole, 1998);
- wildlife (Knight and Gutzwiller, 1995).

Providing host communities and local land managers with the tools to monitor impacts enables them to better sustain their land, and can generate feelings of control and pride in the resources. Moreover, visitor education programmes are an essential and effective means of allowing visitors to contribute to a sustainable environment. By developing an awareness of the specific concerns of an area and learning effective minimum-impact backcountry travel techniques, many visitor impacts can be avoided before resource problems occur.

References

Cole, D.N. (1983) Monitoring the condition of wilderness campsites. US Department of Agriculture Forest Service, Intermountain Forest and Range Experiment Station. Research Paper INT-302. Ogden, Utah.

Cole, D.N. and Bayfield, N.G. (1993) Recreational trampling of vegetation: standard experimental procedures. *Biological Conservation* 63, 209–215.

Cole, D.N. (1996) Wilderness recreation use trends, 1965 through 1994. US Depart-
    ment of Agriculture Forest Service, Intermountain Forest and Range Experiment
    Station. Research Paper INT-RP-488. Ogden, Utah.
Denniston, D. (1995) High priorities: conserving ecosystems and cultures. World-
    watch Paper 123. Worldwatch Institute, Washington, DC.
Frissell, S.S. (1978) Judging recreation impacts on wilderness campsites. *Journal of
    Forestry* 76, 481–483.
Graefe, A.R., Kuss, F.R. and Vaske, J.J. (1990) *Visitor Impact Management*, Vol. 2,
    The Planning Framework. National Parks and Conservation Association,
    Washington, DC.
Hammitt, W.E. and Cole, D.N. (1998) *Wildland Recreation: Ecology and Manage-
    ment*, 2nd edn. John Wiley & Sons, New York.
Knight, R.L. and Gutzwiller, K.J. (eds) (1995) *Wildlife and Recreationists.* Island
    Press, Washington, DC.
Leung, Y. and Marion, J.L. (1996) Trail degradation as influenced by environmental
    factors: a state of the knowledge review. *Journal of Soil and Water Conservation*
    51, 130–136.
Liddle, M. (1997) *Recreation Ecology.* Chapman and Hall, London.
Marion, J.L. (1991) Developing a natural resource inventory and monitoring program
    for visitor impacts on recreational sites: A procedural manual. Natural resources
    report NPS/NRVT/NRR-91/06. US Department of Interior, National Park
    Service.
Marion, J.L. (1994) An assessment of trail conditions in Great Smoky Mountains
    National Park. USDI National Park Service research/resources management
    report.
Marion, J.L. (1995) Capabilities and management utility of recreation impact
    monitoring programmes. *Environmental Management* 19, 763–771.
Monz, C.A., Meier, G.A., Buckley, R.C., Cole, D.N., Welker, J.M. and Loya, W.M.
    (1996) Responses of moist and dry arctic tundra to trampling and warmer
    temperatures. *Bulletin of the Ecological Society of America* 77, 311.
Monz, C.A. (1998) Monitoring recreation resource impacts in two coastal areas of
    western North America: an initial assessment. In: Watson, Alan E., Alphet, Greg
    and Hendee, John C. (comps) *Personal, Societal and Ecological Values of
    Wilderness: Sixth World Wilderness Congress Proceedings on Research,
    Management, and Allocation*, Vol. I, Proceedings. RMRS-P-4. U.S. Department
    of Agriculture, Forest Service, Rocky Mountain Research Station, Ogden, Utah.
Stankey, G.H., Cole, D.N., Lucas, R.C., Peterson, M.E. and Frissel, S.S. (1985) The
    Limits of Acceptable Change (LAC) system for wilderness planning. USDA
    Forest Service, Intermountain Forest Experiment Station General Technical
    Report INT-176. Ogden, Utah.
Wall, G. (1997) Is ecotourism sustainable? *Environmental Management* 21,
    497–510.

Conservation and Development in Greek Mountain Areas

Georgia Valaoras

Asklepiou 14, GR-10680 Athens, Greece

Introduction

Much of the territorial extent of modern Greece consists of mountainous terrain. Sparsely populated today, the mountains of Greece have had a long history of human use and habitation. Since Neolithic times, nomadic tribes have shifted their herds seasonally on mountain slopes, while villages and fortifications were built at high altitudes (see Fig. 4.1) to protect populations from piracy, occupying forces or disease. The most dramatic demographic changes in modern times occurred in the post-civil war period after 1950, when rapid growth and development occurred along coastal areas and in major cities, virtually emptying the countryside, especially the mountain areas, of its people. Nomadic tribes such as the Vlachs and Sarakatsani were forced to settle, and animal husbandry declined. Employment shifted to urban centres or to large-scale intensive cultivation, replacing the mixed, subsistence economy of rural areas.

Today mountain areas face a number of threats, including the following:

1. Deterioration of rich cultural heritage (Byzantine churches, monasteries, stone bridges and vernacular village architecture) caused by abandonment of human settlements;
2. Erosion of formerly cultivated step terraces or aggressive colonization by maquis species and other species of wild plants, caused by abandonment;
3. Fragmentation of habitat and erosion of slopes caused by excessive road-building;
4. Deforestation and erosion caused by fires, quarrying, dam construction and road construction;

Fig. 4.1.   Typical mountain village, Perista Nafpaktias, photographed by Vasilios G. Valaoras in the 1950s.

5.   Congestion of mass tourism at ski resorts;
6.   Uncontrolled access to rare mountain flora and fauna by collectors and poachers;
7.   Uncontrolled grazing of sheep and goats.

This chapter describes some features of Greek mountain areas, which include a number of important national parks and protected areas. It identifies current problems regarding their conservation and development and illustrates the potential for ecotourism as a model for sustainable development.

Characteristics of Greek Mountains

The core area of Greece is characterized by a large and complex mountain range, an extension of the Dinaric Alps extending from north-northwest to south-southeast. This range forms the backbone of central Greece and extends south to the Peloponnesus. Another range extends west to east, starting with Mount Belles and then forming the Rhodope mountain range at the border of Greece and Bulgaria. Greek mountains are characterized by a typical Mediterranean climate in the lowlands and reach alpine conditions above 2000 m. More than 60 peaks of Greece's mountains rise above 2000 m, with seven of these above 2500 m (Sfikas, 1997).

Vegetation below 1000 m is primarily maquis and garrigue, representing not only climax vegetation but also degraded forest caused by fire and grazing. Maquis is a tall thick scrub, including juniper, holm and kermes oak growing as high as a person or taller. Garrigue (known as *phrygana* in Greece) is low scrub, and includes aromatic herbs such as lavender, sage, rosemary and thyme, which flourish on limestone-based hillsides all over Greece. Between 800 and 2000 m forests consist of mountain pine, fir and beech at lower altitudes, with fir, oak, beech or cedar further up (McNeill, 1992). Since the Second World War, the settlement of nomadic tribes reduced grazing and allowed regeneration of thick forests in many Greek mountain ranges.

The rich mountain flora in Greece is an important contribution to the world's biodiversity. The number of Greek floral species has been estimated at 5700, with a high rate of endemism (730 species, or 1130 subspecies, G. Sfikas, Athens, 1998, personal communication). One of the reasons contributing to the richness of this species has to do with the fragmented island habitats such as mountain tops, cliffs and islands (Phitos *et al.*, 1995). Other reasons relate to the geographic location of Greece at the juncture of three major continental land masses, and the fact that the eastern Mediterranean is considered to be the main glacial refuge for Mediterranean flora (Roberts, 1994). During the last two ice ages, glacial ice did not reach southern locations of the Balkan peninsula, allowing some species to survive and then recolonize the slopes (Sfikas, Athens, 1998, personal communication). The isolated character of mountain locations limited seed dispersal and produced a rich genetic diversity. Thus mountains are extremely important habitats for rare and endemic plants, which are found in small populations in isolated plateaux or alpine valleys.

In 1937, the beginning of nature conservation was marked by a law recommending the establishment of national parks for the protection of flora, fauna, forests and natural landscape. Of the ten Greek national parks established after that time, nine of them are in mountain areas. On the other hand, many important mountains, such as Taygetos in the Peloponnesus or the Rhodope virgin forest, do not have national park status despite their rich biodiversity.

The first national park, Mt Olympus, was created in 1938, and has since been declared a biosphere reserve. At 2910 m, it is the highest mountain of Greece and the mythical home of the Greek Olympian gods. It is a popular destination for mountain climbers, and has had a long history of this type of tourism. Other frequently visited sites include Mt Parnassos National Park in central Greece, which has extensive ski facilities and is a popular year-round tourist destination because of the ancient site of Delphi, and Samaria, located in the Lefka Ori (White Mountains) of western Crete. Samaria is also a biosphere reserve, and features one of the longest and most beautiful gorges in Europe. About 300,000 visitors per year walk through the gorge, providing enough receipts to the forestry service to more than compensate for management and maintenance costs. Such receipts provide evidence of the role that site visitation and tourism can play in conserving mountain regions.

Besides the national parks, a unique mountain area occurs in the northern peninsula of Mt Athos in Halkidike. Athos is 'the Holy Mountain', an important Byzantine centre, which until very recently had been inhabited for over 1000 years by monks living frugally, without motor vehicles, electricity or running water. The area had also been free from grazing animals, which allowed the richness and integrity of the forest ecosystem to be a reference point for other sites in the Mediterranean becoming degraded from intense human pressure. Modern times have brought electricity and running water to Athos, but also the opening of roads for heavy logging trucks, which are used to exploit the rare forested areas.

Humans have occupied Greek mountains for thousands of years. The importance of mountain villages throughout Greece's history was highlighted by demographer Vasilios G. Valaoras in 1976, who points out that cities in Greece are a relatively recent phenomenon of only the last four generations. Prior to this time, the country's population was based in villages, the majority being mountainous. The Greek mountain village operated like a city-state and was a refuge from invaders but also from diseases that spread easily in the plains and marshlands. Many villages were centres of learning and culture, ensuring the continuity of the Greek language, folklore, politics and religion throughout a turbulent history of occupation by outside forces. According to Valaoras, an estimated 10,000 individual communities occupied mountain regions in the mid-1970s, with an average population of 150 persons per village. This picture, however, represents a changing situation. At the beginning of the 20th century, only two out of ten people were living in urban areas, while today the number exceeds six out of ten. The demographic decline of mountain villages accelerated after the Second World War and the civil war, which lasted until 1949 (Valaoras, 1976). People emigrated abroad or to the major urban centres of Athens and Thessalonike. In the late 1990s, the associated drop in birth rate dipped below the death rate for the first time since the war years, just as Valaoras had predicted.

Ecologically speaking, Greek mountains are fragile, marginal areas, which have suffered from both over-population and under-population. McNeill (1992) describes the phenomenon of overshoot, when a population has grown beyond the level that is sustainable with its given resources. He argues that the role of the environment in shaping history and culture is much stronger in mountains of the Mediterranean than in the plains. The ideal environment for human settlement lay above the reach of malaria and below the timberline; chronologically it lay between the arrival of maize and the disappearance of forest and soils. In recent history, the mountains provided a variety of resources: olive trees, orange trees and mulberry trees at the lower slopes, forests and pasture lands higher up. Thick forests were habitats for foxes, wolves, bears, wild boar and wildcats as well as game animals such as hares, deer, pheasants and partridges. There was also an abundance of springs with plentiful water, as well as many mines and quarries (McNeill, 1992). Land had been cultivated in valleys or on terraces, combined with animal husbandry to form a mixed economy of terraced wheat and oat crops, vineyards, and orchards. Such an economy could only be maintained by determined people. Stony fields had to be cleared by hand and earth had to be prevented from slipping by dry stone walls, which needed repair every spring. When overpopulation occurred, the tendency was to clear and farm more slopes even though these could not hold soil adequately. This eventually led to an inadequate resource base and to population decline through emigration to urban areas. Labour needed to maintain terraces and irrigation was soon lacking and, as a result, terraces collapsed, soil eroded and water resources dried up. Until recently, the population in the mountains fluctuated in response to food supply, disease, war or work opportunities, and land was cleared or abandoned accordingly. The cycle of overshoot and undershoot occurred throughout history, resulting in a reduction in the productivity of the land, and of its carrying capacity, each cycle rendering the mountain landscape more degraded and barren (McNeill, 1992).

Incomes from the agriculture-based economy were historically supplemented by handicrafts. Women specialized in cloth, and men in wood, metals and leather. In the 17th and 18th centuries, the villagers of the Pindus and Pelopponesus were highly skilled in metal working and wool processing. Silk production was a profitable employment for mountain women and girls, and remains of the thriving silk culture still exist in the Pindus mountains and in the town of Soufli in Thrace. Caravans dispersed the goods throughout the Balkans and central Europe on roads based on a network of steep and winding cobblestone paths known in Greece as *kalderimiat*. Craftsmanship decayed after the 1930s when competition from the British undercut the Balkan cloth manufacture. As rural crafts came to the brink of extinction in the 20th century, a market value was established among urban people based on their nostalgia value. Today woven and embroidered cloths are popular tourist items sold in the central markets of Athens, providing a small income to village women who can still make traditional handicrafts.

Threats to Greek Mountains

The most serious threat to Greek mountains throughout recent history has been landscape deterioration. Rapid social changes in the 19th and early 20th century intensified grazing and gathering, leading to accelerated deforestation and soil erosion. Terraces crumbled with every rain, and were either turned over to sheep pasture or colonized by shrubs and a few hardy trees. Abandoned houses, churches and bridges collapsed and roads were left in ill repair.

At present as we enter the third millennium, pressures on the land continue. Forests are of particular risk, with damaging forest fires increasing every summer (McNeill, 1992). In the summer of 1998, for example, over 150,000 ha of forested land were burned, including valuable mountain forests on Mt Taygetos and Mt Olympus. Deforestation and soil erosion have impoverished the local economy, contributing to the abandonment of most settlements. Today, mountain villages seem permanently empty, with only ageing populations and annual gatherings during the summer months of relatives and their descendants who travel from faraway places such as the USA and Australia. The only exceptions are the villages that lay close enough to urban centres to provide weekend or vacation housing to prosperous Greeks.

Overgrazing of mountains is also a problem, occurring in concentrated areas near larger human populations and on islands. In contrast with remote areas and higher altitudes where forest regeneration followed the decline of nomadic herding, contemporary grazing of sheep and goats is subsidized by the European Union. This allows an excessive number of animals to feed in the same area, which leads to over-grazing and desertification in areas close to coasts and cities (G. Sfikas, Athens, and K. Pistolas, Dadia, 1998, personal communication).

The mountains of Greece are also being threatened by a renewed interest in tourism, although not yet on a large scale. To date, there are 19 ski resorts in Greece, most of them opened only briefly during the year. This hardly justifies the environmental damage caused by destroying mountain forests for ski-slopes or access roads, which are not maintained outside the season (Weingartner, 1998). In the most popular ski area, Mt Parnassos, the mountain valley near the ski slopes has become a boom town, with indiscriminate building of lodges and restaurants and associated congestion causing pollution, waste disposal problems and destruction of mountain floral habitat (E. Prokopi, Spetses, 1998, personal communication).

The new fad in Greece is adventure tourism: rafting, rock-climbing, off-the-road vehicle racing and other outdoor sports organized by private companies. The invasion into sensitive mountain habitats has been accompanied by little regulation either for the safety of the unsuspecting (and untrained) urban participants, or for the natural landscape and the rare habitats they contain. The absence of a locally based population to direct and control these excursions into nature further exacerbates the problems they cause. To help contain the excesses that might hurt their income, the more serious of these companies have now formed a professional association whose purpose is to promote environmentally and socially responsible special interest tourism, to set criteria for operation, and to identify and isolate the bad actors (I. Sotirakos, Athens, 1998, personal communication).

Last but not least is the destruction caused by the inappropriate use of European Union regional development funding. Massive dam constructions, river diversions and highway systems, financed by the European

Commission, the European Bank for Reconstruction and Development and the European Investment Bank, cause irreversible losses of mountain resources, both natural and cultural. These losses affect downstream communities as well, since freshwater losses and silt retention contributes to the erosion of the coastline and salt-water intrusion in coastal aquifers. This has occurred in the Axios and Nestos river deltas, since large dams and water diversions have been built upstream. Other examples are the Acheloos river diversion project, which consists of a series of five dams and a tunnel designed to shift water resources from western to eastern Greece (see Fig. 4.2), and the Egnatia highway, which is part of the Trans-European Network linking Greece to central Europe and the eastern states. This latter project is fragmenting mountain habitat for brown bears and other species in the Pindus mountains.

Reversing the Trend: Conservation and Development through Ecotourism

The Mediterranean as a whole has long been plagued by unsustainable development associated not only with large-scale development projects but also with conventional tourism. Valuable coastal and marine ecosystems have been destroyed to accommodate marinas, seaside hotels and

Fig. 4.2. Destruction of mountain landscapes caused by dam construction in Mesochora, Pindus mountains, Greece, to divert the Acheloos river from western to eastern Greece. Photo by Kostas Vassilakis, Hellenic Ornithological Society, 1991.

recreational activities at sites that are important natural habitats. An alternative to this model of tourist development has emerged in the form of ecotourism. Sites with important biological diversity have become organized to accommodate nature-seeking tourists, orienting them to the specific interests of the areas. These sites provide a lower level of tourist accommodation and services that is, however, compensated by the outstanding beauty and interest of the areas.

A key to the maintenance and enhancement of parks and protected areas in Europe is the mobilization of public and political support for their conservation. The conservation of nature and sustainable use of natural resources must be shown to be relevant to the daily lives of people, even those who may never visit a protected area. In Greece, as in several other Mediterranean countries, protected areas are usually seen as a problem, an intrusion on the lives of local people and irrelevant to their daily needs. Restrictions on land use or natural resource exploitation are usually ignored, if not actively sabotaged because of the infringement on locally generated income.

One way of developing the support of local people is to encourage the influx of visitors from outside the area, which can bring supplementary income and awareness of the site's importance. Ecotourism has been defined as 'environmentally responsible travel and visitation to relatively undisturbed natural areas, in order to enjoy and appreciate nature . . . that promotes conservation, has low visitor impact, and provides beneficially active socio-economic involvement of local populations' (Ceballos-Lascurain, 1996). A prerequisite for this type of activity is effective communication to the public at large of the values and interests of the park or protected area. Environmental education must be developed in a way that is accessible to ordinary citizens, adaptable to the needs of the old or the young, the city-dweller, the policy-maker or the tourist. Another prerequisite is the consistent presence on site of individuals or groups actively involved in these pursuits. Often this can only be achieved by investment from private sources, in particular, in the case mentioned below, from conservation organizations that have the means and flexibility to ensure continuous support. This support, however minimal, can fill in the gaps between government-funded programmes whose development and implementation are often plagued by bureaucratic delays.

Prespa National Park: a Model for Integrated Rural Development

In Greece, such cases are developing to some extent around protected areas. In the Prespa lakes of northwestern Greece, a national park and Ramsar site has been designated because of the rich biodiversity of the site. Particularly known for the spectacular colonies of Dalmatian pelicans, the area is a rich mosaic of lakes, forests and rural landscape. Conservation bodies followed the initial identification of the scientific importance by investments in public awareness, education and basic conservation activities. In time, these investments attracted visitors, who were able to appreciate the significance of the areas through the information provided by the local conservation projects. Local people have acquired additional income by providing food, accommodation and interpretation services, and additional funds have been provided by government and international agencies.

Lakes Mikri and Megali Prespa are mountain lakes situated at an altitude of 855 m in western Macedonia, on a border area between Greece, Albania and the Former Yugoslav Republic of Macedonia. The lakes as well as their surroundings constitute Prespa National Park, an important centre of biological diversity containing more than 1300 plant species. Also designated as a Ramsar site, they include large freshwater marshes that fluctuate in size, flooding wide expanses of the surrounding land during the spring (Pearce and Crivelli, 1994). Lake Mikri Prespa is an important breeding ground for endangered Dalmatian and white pelicans (Perennou *et al.*, 1996). The lake and flooded meadows also support endemic populations of invertebrates and fish, such as the Prespa barbel, *Barbus prespensis*, one of 11 native species found in the lakes and listed as endangered in the *Red Data Book of Threatened Vertebrates* in Greece (Hellenic Zoological Society, Hellenic Ornithological Society, 1992; Catsadorakis *et al.*, 1996; Crivelli, 1996; Maitland and Crivelli, 1996).

The discovery of the area's biological significance dates from the 1960s when ornithologists visited the area and observed pelican colonies and a rich biodiversity in plants and animals. In 1974, the area was designated a national park, and in 1975, a field biological station was constructed on the banks of Mikri Prespa, funded by the Hellenic Society for the Preservation of the Environment and the Cultural Heritage, or Elliniki Etairia (M. Scoullos, Athens, 1998, personal communication). This station was subsequently used to host students and visiting researchers. Investments in scientific research continued with the monitoring of endangered species as well as the fish fauna of the lakes, forest birds, mountain flora, reptiles and amphibians, soil, aquatic vegetation and water quality (Crivelli and Catsadorakis, 1997). Funding for this research came from many international and national organizations, such as the Royal Society for the Protection of Birds (RSPB), the World Wide Fund for Nature (WWF), the MAVA and A.V. Jenson Foundations, the Danish Ornithological Society, and other non-governmental organizations (NGOs).

In 1990, four international conservation organizations and six Greek NGOs formed the Society for the Protection of Prespa (SPP). This locally based society served to coordinate conservation actions and provided a base for public awareness and education. In 1992, an information/visitor's centre was established, the first ever existing in a Greek national park, and guided tours were developed as well as an environmental education programme for schools. Annually at least 6000 visitors pass through the centre to view the exhibits, and 5000 schoolchildren from all over Greece participate in the programmes (Crivelli and Catsadorakis, 1997).

Since Prespa is located in a remote area, the Greek part is permanently inhabited by only 1200 people in 12 settlements. A traditional subsistence economy combined crop farming with livestock, fishing and collecting from nature following the end of the 1940s. In 1962, a surface irrigation network converted rain-fed crops to irrigated ones. Policy-makers expected to retain the population at this border area and reduce or halt emigration. Assisted by government subsidies, the increasing intensification of agriculture gradually displaced the subsistence economy. By 1985, the monoculture cultivation of beans replaced mixed farming methods and in 1993, livestock dropped by more than 56% compared to the mid-1960s (Catsadorakis *et al.*, 1996).

The issue of organic versus conventional farming has been relevant to conservation efforts of Prespa. Today about 80% of the local people are cultivating beans with conventional methods. These methods threaten the wet meadow habitats for breeding birds as well as water quality of the lakes from runoff of agricultural chemicals. The promotion of organic bean culti-vation in the surrounding hillsides was assisted by the SPP by providing technical and marketing assistance as well as by seeking organic certifica-tion. Organic bean production has higher than average yields and premium prices. During a recent crisis in the bean market, conventionally grown Prespa beans were sold at very low prices or not sold at all, while organic beans remained unaffected, and were in high demand. Interest in organic cultivation has increased, with at least ten farmers practising organic meth-ods in 1996. Such interest has been largely sparked by the organic farming promotional efforts of Conservation and Development in Sparsely Populated Areas (CADISPA), an EU programme jointly funded by the WWF and the European Commission.

Aside from the support of organic farming, CADISPA aids the marketing of local products, such as woollen socks, herbs, dried beans and preserves, through the information centre. CADISPA also has funded studies on the preservation of local architecture and of a local breed of dwarf cattle. In par-allel, conservation activities have been conducted in the form of wardening pelican colonies and providing information about the region. Volunteers now come regularly to Prespa to designate hiking trails, collect refuse or renovate buildings.

As a result of the many efforts and programmes geared toward conserva-tion, local people gradually have begun to take interest in the development of the area. Rooms for accommodation and taverns have started operating, and the village of Psarades has requested assistance to establish a second information centre, this time focusing on the traditional fishing practices and the rich variety of endemic fish found in the lakes. The guesthouse at Aghios Germanos, built in the traditional style with wood-burning stoves, now offers comfortable, though simple, accommodation to visitors. Through the

Table 4.1. Increase of visitors to Prespa's visitor centre.

	1993	1994	1995	1996
Students	2,300	4,000	5,500	8,400
Tourists	3,027	7,328	7,649	12,123
Totals	5,327	11,328	13,149	20,523

Source: Society for the Protection of Prespa, Prespa, 1998, personal communication.

provision of services such as food, accommodation, boat trips and guided tours, local income has increased, supplementing the traditional occupations with income from visitors. It has been estimated that at least 50–60 people are now employed in ecotourism related activities, usually on a part-time basis to supplement other occupations. Infrastructure is still limited and insufficient to meet demand in peak seasons, but the visitors are increasing (Table 4.1) and visits tend to be distributed throughout the year, with the exception of the cold winter months (Crivelli and Catsadorakis, 1997). The two visitor centres, one in Psarades and the other in Aghios Germanos, are run by trained ecoguides: young persons from the local community trained in environmental management, interpretation and ecotourism, through EU-funded programmes. Although local residents were initially hostile to the establishment of the national park, fearing restrictions from legally mandated management measures, ecotourism has succeeded in raising awareness and instilling pride in the ecological value of the area. Private citizens have an incentive to provide services such as food and accommodation, thus enhancing the potential of further development in the area (Tables 4.2 and 4.3).

This, in turn, has renewed the interest of state development funding. Initially the Greek government was not able to stimulate economic and social development. Past investments were poorly planned and of inappropriate scale, often diminishing the ecological values of the area (Cuff and Rayment, 1997). Recently, the Development Company of Western Macedonia in Kozani completed a development study funded by the Prefecture of Florina. The European Community Support Framework Environment Funds were committed up to a level of 350 million drachmas (see Table 4.2). Another EU funding mechanism, the LEADER II programme, allocated 356 million drachmas to local entrepreneurs through the funding cycle, culminating in 1999. This is administered by the Development Company of Florina, which also handles other EU budget lines consistent with the trend towards ecotourism (ANFLO, Florina, 1998, personal communication). It is ironic that an application to the first LEADER programme in 1991 was rejected by the EU because Prespa was considered a poor investment, having a small resident population and inadequate development structures to absorb and implement development aid.

Table 4.2. Investments in conservation in Prespa.

Category	Amount	Years
EU Cadispa programme	44,000,000	1993–1997
EU Cadispa programme	6,000,000	1997–1998
Elliniki Etairia (for Biological Station)	10,000,000	1975–1997
EU Cadispa	43,500,000	1994–1997
EU Petra programme	2,900,000	1994
Community Support Funds	350,000,000	1995–1999
MAVA Foundation (for restoration of education centre)	35,000,000	1996
Leader I	not successful	1991
Leader II	356,000,000	1995–1999
Totals	897,400,000	

All amounts quoted are in Greek drachmas for the years specified. Sources: Myrsini Malakou, Director of the Society for the Protection of Prespa, Christina Golna, Development Agency of Florina, Michael Scoullos and Elliniki Etairia.

Table 4.3. Benefits and income to the local community[a].

Category	Prespa	Years
Jobs (numbers)	4 full-time, 16 part-time	1990–1997
Visitors (numbers)	49,000	1994–1996
of which students:	18,000	
Guided tours (income)	1,200,000 per year	1995–1997
Shops and information centre including publications (income)	10,276,000	1996
Sales of organic beans (income)	1,620,000	1996–1997

Source: Myrsini Malakou, Director of the Society for the Protection of Prespa
All income and sales numbers are in Greek drachmas for the years specified.
[a]Table includes only cases directly cooperating with the SPP; many more income benefits have accrued to enterprises in the area, including the guest rooms managed by the women's cooperatives, for which figures are not available at this time.

Conclusions and Recommendations

If one were to identify the most important threats to Greek mountain areas in order of priority, then regional development funding would probably be the highest. To counter the destructive impacts of large-scale development projects one needs an informed and active civil society, with strong non-governmental organizations and an independent and well-documented media. Unfortunately these conditions are only in their nascent stages in Greece, and are hardly sufficient to act as a buffer to the excesses of the construction industry and the state's development mentality, which provides sources for funding.

Another solution is emerging, however: a renewed interest in rural mountain areas, by investments in conservation, and by establishing the basis for sustainable ecotourism. The restoration of guesthouses in traditional architectural style, the preparation of local recipes and the revitalization of handicrafts can generate local income. In time, combined with associated actions for nature conservation, these activities may be successful enough to maintain or attract people to settle in more remote homelands. Ecotourism can give back value to the wealth of nature and village life, which was so recently lost.

Despite its unique characteristics, the example of Prespa can serve as a model for other natural areas in the Balkans and the eastern Mediterranean. It demonstrates a number of principles that could be transferred:

1. The successful combination of tourism and conservation relies on the involvement of the local community. The level of tourist services in Prespa has evolved gradually and is in the hands of the local people. They have developed tourism at an appropriate scale and do not infringe on the ecological integrity of the areas.

2. The attraction of visitors outside the area has provided additional income which otherwise would not be generated. This is particularly relevant to the supplementary income of women in the cooperatives, most of whom have families and therefore would not have the opportunity to seek regular employment elsewhere.

3. The basic infrastructure that is in place has given incentives to private entrepreneurs to provide food, accommodation and other services. This in turn has had a multiplier effect by attracting public investments, which are now oriented towards ecotourism. Government and EU funding provide a basis to continue appropriate development in the future, thus strengthening the local economy and enhancing present activities.

Perhaps the most important aspect that is relevant to other valuable habitats in the region is that ecotourism has provided the means to conserve these sites effectively. Neither international treaties nor protected area legislation had been implemented during the two decades or more since the sites were first identified as important for biodiversity. Local people could not understand nor support the land-use restrictions and limitations on activities that were seen as fundamental to their livelihoods.

Ecotourism has introduced alternative income and has created new jobs centred on the protection and promotion of the natural values of these habitats, thus creating a new awareness and interest in their conservation. The increase in social activities associated with ecotourism has kept young people in the area and reversed the trend towards emigrating to larger cities.

In such cases, the most important factor that has led to the transformation from isolation to well-publicized centres of ecotourism has been the

continuous financial support given to the individuals who lived and operated on site. Also, the crucial involvement of one or two local persons who
were engaged from the very beginning played a key role. These people
were important agents to facilitate the work and to 'interpret' the message of
conservation to the rest of the local inhabitants, their own relatives and
neighbours who needed to be convinced that protecting the area would
eventually bring benefits to their families. It is a well-demonstrated fact that
unless means are found actively to involve the local people and render them
beneficiaries of conservation activities, then parks and protected areas have
little chance of being protected in the long run (Valaoras, 1997).

Are the successes of Prespa sustainable? Can they continue to bring
benefits to local people and at the same time preserve the rich biodiversity
that constitute the main attraction of visitors and scientists? Such questions
remain to be answered. Certainly dependence on only one form of income
renders these societies even more vulnerable than before; ecotourism is
subject to the same fluctuations that conventional tourism experiences.
Social and political conditions can change radically in less-developed areas,
and disturbances can completely cut off tourist influxes for many years.
These efforts must always be developed in combination with other economic activities, especially those that are self-sustainable and somewhat
independent of outside inputs (Y. Moussouris, Athens, 1998, personal
communication).

Much depends on the determination and resilience of the local people,
to continue their present involvement and to resist the 'easy' paths of mass
tourist exploitation, which has destroyed so much of Greece's natural
wealth. Much also depends on wise investments of the state and prefecture
bodies who can bring European Union funding to the areas for further development on an appropriate scale. Finally, the role of national and international conservation NGOs is critical in funding the continued monitoring
of the sites, the exchange of know-how, and the active involvement in
conservation management. Based on such a network of partners, the model
of integrated rural development including both nature conservation and a
revival of some aspects of traditional village culture can perhaps become
one of the viable alternatives to the abandonment and deterioration of Greek
and other Mediterranean mountain areas.

References

Catsadorakis, G., Malakou, M. and Crivelli, A.J. (1996) *The Prespa barbel*, Barbus
    prespensis, *Karaman 1924, in the Prespa lakes basin, north-western Greece.*
    Tour du Valat, Arles.
Ceballos-Lascurain, H. (1996) *Tourism, Ecotourism and Protected Areas.* IUCN,
    Gland.
Crivelli, A.J. (1996) *The Freshwater Fish Endemic to the Northern Mediterranean
    region.* Tour du Valat, Arles.

Crivelli, A.J. and Catsadorakis, G. (1997) *Lake Prespa, Northwestern Greece: Unique Balkan Wetland. Developments in Hydrobiology 122.* Kluwer Academic Publishers, Dordrecht, Netherlands.

Cuff, J. and Rayment, M. (eds) (1997) *Working with Nature: Economies, Employment and Conservation in Europe.* Royal Society for the Protection of Birds Policy Research Department on behalf of Birdlife International, RSPB, Bedfordshire, UK.

Hellenic Zoological Society, Hellenic Ornithological Society (1992) *The Red Data Book of Threatened Vertebrates of Greece.* World Wide Fund for Nature, Athens.

Maitland, P.S. and Crivelli, A.J. (1996) *Conservation of Freshwater Fish.* Tour du Valat, Arles.

McNeill, J.R. (1992) *The Mountains of the Mediterranean World: an Environmental History.* Cambridge University Press, Cambridge, UK, New York, USA and Australia.

Pearce, F. and Crivelli, A.J. (1994) *Characteristics of Mediterranean Wetlands.* Tour du Valat, Arles.

Perennou, C., Sadoul, N., Pineau, O., Johnson, A. and Hafner, H. (1996) *Management of Nest Sites for Colonial Waterbirds.* Tour du Valat, Arles.

Phitos, D., Strid, A., Snogerup, S. and Greuter, W. (1995) *The Red Data Book of Rare and Threatened Plants of Greece.* World Wide Fund for Nature, Athens.

Roberts, N. (1994) *The Holocene: an Environmental History.* Blackwell, Oxford, UK and Cambridge, USA.

Sfikas, G. (1997) *The Mountains of Greece.* Efstathiadis Group, Athens.

Valaoras, V.G. (1976) The Greek village: its history, contribution and decline. *Nea Estia* 100, 1177, 925–929.

Valaoras, G. (1997) A paradise only for birds: travels to an Indian biotope. *Nea Oikologia* 149, 38–39.

Weingartner, H. (1998) An outline of environmental problems caused by the construction of skiing tracks in Pilion and Pindus Mountains. In: Katsifarakis, K.L., Korfiatis, G.P., Mylopoulos, Y.A. and Demetracopoulos, A.C. (eds) *Proceedings of an International Conference, Protection and Restoration of the Environment IV.* Halkidiki, Macedonia, Greece, pp. 780–786.

Tourism in Bioregional Context: Approaching Ecosystemic Practice in the Šumava, Czech Republic

5

Laurence A.G. Moss,[1] Jan Těšitel,[2] František Zemek,[2] Michael Bartoš,[2] Drahomíra Kušová[2] and Michael Heřman[2]

[1]*Laurence Moss & Associates, PMB 422, Santa Fe, NM 87505, USA;* [2]*Institute of Landscape Ecology, Academy of Sciences of the Czech Republic, Na Sádkách 7, České Budějovice, Czech Republic*

Introduction

Tourists continue to be a significant force for change, having profound impact on the places that attract them, and throughout the global political–economic, financial and social web forming the support system for these places and tourism itself. As we transform into post-industrial ways of life, considering tourism as an integral part of its ecosystemic context is a strategic way significantly to reduce its negative impact on local culture and symbiotic natural environment. If not done, in all probability the continuing degradation will bring about a marked reduction of tourism *per se*, if not its demise where it relies primarily on local cultural and environmental attributes. It will occur principally through destroying these attributes or the limiting of access to them. Moreover, the negative aspects of tourism appear more pronounced and critical in the comparatively vulnerable ecosystems of mountains (Harrison and Price, 1996).

Such an outcome is undesirable for alpine visitors, and both undesirable and dire for inhabitants as well as the many lowlanders dependent on the maintenance of alpine ecosystems (Bandyopadhyay *et al.*, 1997; Hamilton *et al.*, 1997). It is an outcome that may be avoided; however, not without changes in awareness, attitude and behaviour, if not a fundamental shift from the dominating Cartesian scientific and social paradigm (see especially Capra, 1983). These changes are reflected in the bioregional ecosystemic

(BRES) approach to tourism described here: the integrated use of a set of dynamic, organic systems, analytical and action concepts and methods. This essay draws on work in progress, but far enough along to indicate the likely positive outcome of practising the BRES approach that is described below. Over the past several years we have been engaged as an interdisciplinary team in understanding and formulating this strategic approach to sustaining the beauty and ecosystemic integrity of the Šumava bioregion, while improving the well-being of its inhabitants (see Acknowledgement).

Increasing global attention to leisure, learning and physical and spiritual well-being, and the commoditizing of these concerns and the cultural and environmental heritage they use, is being manifest in the rapidly growing attraction of tourists, amenity migrants and others who follow to make a living, to previously remote and marginal regions. Commonly these are mountainous areas. Around the world, these groups are increasingly finding the means to sojourn or reside in these comparatively environmentally pristine and/or culturally distinct places (see Moss, 1994, 1999; Price *et al.*, 1997). The Šumava bioregion is one such place. Here our focus is on tourism in its ecosystemic context. However, a more recently emerging, and quite significant part of this global condition is amenity migration, which is addressed by Glorioso and Tonderayi in this volume.

A Profile of the Šumava Bioregion

The bioregional concept and Šumava application

Bioregions are geographical areas whose delineation primarily follows natural parameters rather than human administrative jurisdictions. A bioregion is distinguished by characteristics of flora, fauna, water, climate, geology and often their co-existing human settlements. Subsequently defined by watershed for biodiversity protection, they also enable large-scale ecosystemic approaches in planning and management. Bioregions have typically been delineated within countries on differing spatial hierarchical levels. Quite often artificially isolated by national borders, European integration, for example, is now offering opportunities to consider ecosystems that cross political boundaries. 'Bioregion' is also used in a more subjective sense, whereby an individual or group feels a strong spiritual association or affinity with a bio-geographical place, usually where they reside. This perception appears basic to the 'deep ecology' movement (Devall, 1988). While a bioregion so defined is often coterminous with the previous definition, it is not necessarily so, and here we use the term mainly in its earlier meaning.

The Šumava Mountain range in the Czech Republic makes up one of the most naturally valuable bioregions in the Central Europe. The massif it dominates emerged by elevation and the consequent breaking of a levelled plane some 60 million years ago. Geologically it belongs to the Central

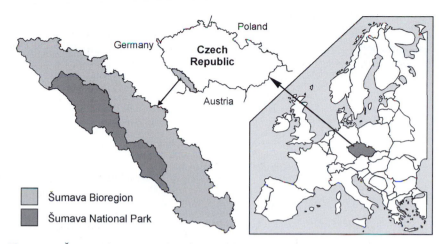

Fig. 5.1. Šumava bioregion, Czech Republic, Europe. Source: Institute of Landscape Ecology, České Budějovice, 1999.

Moldanubian Pluton Formation. The central part of the mountains form extensive flats in an average height of 1150 m, over which the highest peak rises to 1457 m. The upper plateau slopes down steeply in the Bavarian Forest, crossing the German border (south-southwest exposition), and gently in the Šumava Mountains (north-northeast exposition). These geomorphological differences are followed by a different gradient of land-use intensity in the two parts. What we refer to as the Šumava bioregion is the Czech Šumava Mountains and their piedmont; a total area of some 2600 km², inhabited today by about 63,000 people (see Figs 5.1 and 5.2). Importantly, this bounding crosses administrative jurisdictions, focusing on the unity of the natural condition in the included territory.

Historical sketch

The Šumava Mountains retained their predominantly natural character almost to the mid-1900s, with human settlement and natural resources use existing for centuries in a tradition of harmony. However, since then the bioregion has undergone several significant land use changes, most notably an increase in forest cover (Table 5.1), then from about the beginning of the 1990s a reversal of this condition. More disaggregated data than that available for Table 5.1 indicates that in the 1987–1995 period, meadow and pasture land increased from 17 to 24%, and clear cut areas from 2.6 to 5.3% (Zemek and Heřman, 1998). Before 1938 Šumava was inhabited by a relatively stable population and managed predominantly by small and scattered, low impact farms. However, the period following World War II is characterized by considerable ethnic change (Mejstřík *et al.*, 1995; Bartoš

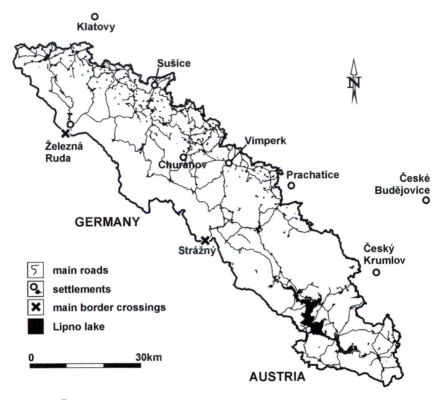

Fig. 5.2. Šumava bioregion: human settlements and arterial roads. Source: Institute of Landscape Ecology, České Budějovice, 1999.

Table 5.1. Forest area change: 1830–1995.

Territory	Area (km²)	Forest (km²)		Grassland (km²)		Change (%)
		1830	1995	1830	1995	
Šumava bioregion	2515	1132	1559	1383	956	17
Biosphere reserve	1674	887	1172	787	502	17
Šumava N. Park	684	479	554	205	130	11

Source: digitized military maps 1830 and 1995, ILE, České Budějovice.

and Těšitel, 1996; Johnson, 1996), resulting both in decreasing population density (Table 5.2) and cultural heterogeneity in the mountainous part of the bioregion. Following from the Yalta treaty there was a transfer of the centuries old ethnic German population, or *Sudetendeutsche*, to

Table 5.2.   History of population density in Šumava (inhabitants km^2).

Territory	1869	1900	1930	1950	1961	1970	1980	1991	1997
Šumava Bioregion	53.3	57.9	56.5	25.7	25.2	24.6	25.2	24.5	25.0
Klatovy District	73.3	77.0	73.9	51.7	51.2	48.6	47.7	46.4	47.6
Prachatice District	63.2	66.2	62.8	34.8	35.1	34.9	36.5	37.0	37.4
Č. Krumlov District	54.9	58.4	58.2	29.0	30.1	30.9	34.3	35.5	36.6

Source: Czech Statistical Survey 1997, České Budějovice.

Germany and subsequently a relocation to Šumava of Slovak and Rom peoples from Romania and Volyne Czechs from the Ukraine. The establishing of military zones adjacent to the international border and large-scale, poorly managed state farms were other specific characteristics Šumava became known for.

Location on the border separating East and West European political alliances, at a distance from political and cultural centres and a predominantly rural economy were the main factors maintaining Šumava as marginal. However, changes after the 1989 Czech 'Velvet Revolution' resulted in a new milieu exhibiting the following main trends:

1.   Nature protection regulations beginning to play a more important role in the type, location and magnitude of land use activities;
2.   Growth of amenity/ leisure activities and development of related facilities and services;
3.   Rapidly declining intensive agriculture with local farming transforming into a 'service' playing primarily a landscape-forming, rather than a traditional productive, role;
4.   Local industry developing very slowly within built-up areas of existing human settlements; and
5.   Freer access to and by western European and more global political–economic and socio-cultural forces.

Due mainly to its historical marginality, the natural beauty and ecosystem of the bioregion have been sustained, resulting in much of the mountainous area being proclaimed a Protected Landscape Area in 1963, and subsequently in 1991, a national park. Because of its uniqueness it was also made a world Biosphere Reserve by UNESCO in 1990 (see Table 5.1). Along with the strictly protected wilderness core of the Šumava National Park, it is important to realize that the cultural landscape of much of the bioregion is also protected. The need for appropriate human activities to sustain this cultural character is also viewed as an imperative (see especially the Ministry of Environment, Nature and Landscape Protection, 1992).

A Bioregional Ecosystemic Approach (BRES)

The construct

Our ecosystemic approach to understanding and management assumes a bioregional perspective, in which the ecosystem is treated as a whole – a symbiotic web of relationships among species and their activities within their spatial territory. It further assumes that we need to plan and act with careful consideration of this interdependent system. It also espouses a holistic intent, even though our present understanding, skills and technology may not allow us to function as holistically as we wish. This construct is applied to the understanding and sustaining of a bioregion, and in this context, to the management of tourism, especially as it influences the natural environment and human culture. Moreover, for tourism to survive, it must function in a manner that sustains these primary attributes on which it is dependent. This ecosystemic approach, however, is still rather experimental and problematic, including technical issues and a limited awareness and acceptance by key stakeholders and their institutional processes.

The regional perspective

The strategic advantages particular to a regional view are as follows:

1. Especially with a primary concern for effects on natural ecological systems, we obtain the needed large scope for forest ecology, whole watershed or systems of watersheds;
2. Similarly there is the regional scale of human built and operated systems, such as networks of roads, water and waste water facilities, hydro-electric power, health care, etc. There are also economies of scale associated with regional delivery of these facilities and services; and
3. The regional scale also offers socio-cultural and political–economic benefits of complementarity among communities. For example, municipalities in Šumava have come together to form mutual interest groups, the Association of the Šumava Municipalities and its Šumava Regional Development Agency, thereby creating a presence in and outside the bioregion that each alone could not have. It may also appeal to and harness regional cultural communal sentiments.

A good example of use of a BRES approach is the recent analysis of the ecological status of Sierra Nevada in California, a mountainous bioregion of some 83,625 km^2. This major project brought together extant information about this bioregion's ecosystem and natural resources, including human settlements, assessed their condition and recommended protective management strategies. It also strongly recommended a BRES approach as the most appropriate framework for sustaining and rehabilitating this bioregion, but recognized that considerable change in management and administrative cultures would be necessary to implement its recommendations (Centers for Water and Wildland Resources, 1996).

Strategic enhancement of BRES

We have identified and are experimenting in an integrated manner with three additional analytical and planning constructs and techniques that appear considerably to enhance the bioregional ecosystemic approach outlined above (see Fig. 5.3). In addition, they have brought considerable insight to our understanding of the present and potential role of tourism in Šumava. The first is a complementary set comprising strategic analysis and planning, key stakeholder analysis and local sustainable development indicators.

Strategic analysis and planning
'Strategic planning' is used by many with little knowledge of what it actually is or how to apply it, especially in public sector institutions. As a result much of its potential is lost. Yet, strategic planning when used with knowledge and skill is capable of providing a framework for analysing and managing complex and highly uncertain conditions, ones more successfully treated in a holistic manner, principally through the identification and understanding of behavioural patterns of open systems. Recently a research tool, 'strategic analysis', has been derived from strategic planning and seems quite effective, especially in the policy arena. Due to the poor understanding of these methodologies and their exceptionally fine fit with our subject, we offer the following detailed description.

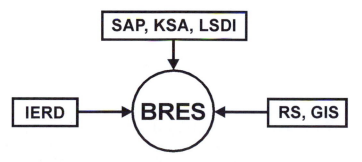

Fig. 5.3. Scheme of the enhanced BRES approach. BRES – Bioregional Ecosystemic Approach; SAP – strategic analysis and planning; KSA – key stakeholder analysis; LSDI – local sustainable development indicators; IERD – integrated endogenous regional development; RS, GIS – remote sensing and geographic information systems.

Strategic planning and analysis is long term and relativistic, focusing on understanding and manipulating key factors, and in this sense is not comprehensive. It relies on multi-skilled and oriented group participation involving all key stakeholders. It takes advantage of the 'whole brain' capability of marrying logic and intuition to analyse, plan for and manage a concern or task. A key principle distinguishing strategic planning from other planning methods is its focus on the importance of factors that are external to the system under consideration and on their likely impacts. This focus must be integrated into the analytical process early in the formulation of a plan or strategy. The external or 'strategic' environment is studied for opportunities and threats to task achievement, in parallel with the more traditional analysis of strengths and weaknesses of the subject being considered. In 'rational' or 'comprehensive' planning practices, these exogenous factors are usually considered after plan formulation, and typically reactively through a feedback loop after attempts at plan implementation. While there may be some consideration of external factors earlier in these processes, they are typically *ad hoc.*

We suggest that this strategic approach is particularly appropriate where long-term guided change is desired of complex open systems, ones that are likely to be considerably affected by the uncertainty of external factors. This is the case with bioregions generally and for the Šumava bioregion specifically. How is such an external environment considered in the strategic approach, especially as this methodology distinguishes itself by recognizing and accepting that while some external key factors are quantifiable, and to limited degrees predictable (e.g. some demographics), more typically they are imprecise, qualitative and unpredictable? Typically, and especially recommended for a BRES approach to understanding and managing regions, it is done with 'multiple scenario analysis'. This method for forecasting and identifying conditions likely to cause significant change, assumes that understanding of conditions and informing important decisions are based on a complex set of relationships among socio-cultural, economic, political, technological and physical key factors. Significant numbers of these are external to the decision-making system under consideration, such as a bioregion, or more specifically here, tourism in Šumava. Yet these relationships must be identified and reasonably understood to provide essential knowledge and make successful decisions.

Note that multiple scenario formulation uses key factors, and in this sense does not attempt to be comprehensive, but strategic. Also, a set of alternative future scenarios are formulated, for given the high uncertainty in the strategic environment in our turbulent and swiftly changing times, uncertainty can at best be reduced, not eliminated. Therefore, a single view of the future strategic environment is inherently inaccurate. Of the three general styles of multiple scenario analysis the 'intuitive logic' approach is recommended, as it seems most appropriate for large, complex open systems analysis and management (see especially Mandel, 1983; Ringland, 1998).

While to date there appear to be few applications of strategic analysis and planning to regions, the following examples demonstrate an understanding of the methodology and skill in its use. Probably the most successful, but poorly documented, experience to date is that of the province of Alberta, Canada. A strategic planning unit, The Futures Compendium, functioned in the Department of Economic Development and Trade, as an intelligence and advisory body to the Department and government cabinet committees between 1985 and 1990. Subsequently the unit was privatized. More recently several American states have begun to use strategic planning at the state-wide scale (see especially Goldschmidt, 1989; Utah Tomorrow Strategic Planning Committee, 1993). Also, the Northeast Regional Water Management Plan for Bangladesh used strategic planning to assist in guiding the development of a region of 24,200 km^2, emphasizing water management (Canadian International Development Agency, 1994).

The following three examples treat tourism in particular within a regional context: an analysis and policy recommendations for amenity migration and tourism in the Baguio bioregion of the Philippines (Dimaculangan, 1993); a study of the Doi Ithanon National Park, Thailand, with a proposed development strategy focused on the role of resident hill tribes (Bhatta *et al.*, 1993); and the Šumava Bioregion studies being drawn upon for this analysis (Moss, 1994; Těšitel *et al.*, 1997; Glorioso, this publication). In the Šumava case methodologies have only been partially applied to date – what we consider an experimental phase of a larger task.

Key stakeholder analysis (KSA)

Key stakeholder analysis is commonly considered a component of strategic planning, but this appears to be more the case with private sector strategic planning than in governmental and volunteer sectors to date. It originated as a discrete methodology in the field of business policy and strategic management, and continues to also be used independently of strategic management or planning.

In a planning or research task, KSA provides one means for stakeholders' input as well as a research tool for the analyst. Some users consider the improved openness to knowledge and influence that it offers as being helpful in deflecting criticism and paving the way for smoother implementation. It also offers opportunities for negotiations and bargaining among stakeholders, and so has been described as 'a means of increasing the chances of successful strategy implementation by explicitly addressing the politics of implementation during the formulation process itself' (MacMillan and Jones, 1986: 1). However, care should be taken that this tool becomes neither the main arena for interest bargaining nor a substitute for other forms of democratic participation. A greater diversity is needed, such as self-organized collaborative community groups, in order to learn about each other's concerns, invent new opportunities and solutions, and shape, reshape and implement strategies and plans.

As a mechanism for identifying and understanding stakeholders, as one means to democratizing decision-making and management, and as a method integrated into strategic planning, we suggest KSA is an important complementary tool to the bioregional ecosystemic approach. So far in our Šumava work it was used in the sustainable biodiversity strategy and the Český Krumlov sustainable development strategy projects (see Acknowledgements). It was also part of the methodology for the Doi Ithanon and Baguio studies mentioned above. In all of these, tourism was important. For key stakeholder methodology see Glorioso and Moss (1995), MacMillan and Jones (1986) and Nutt and Backoff (1992).

Local sustainable development indicators (LSDI)
Of the three methodologies in this cluster, the design and use of sustainable development indicators is still in the earliest formulation phase. The need for such indicators probably first drew significant attention in 1987 with the Brundtland Commission Report's call for developing new ways to measure and access progress toward sustainable development. One of the best descriptions of the sustainable development paradigm, the need for it, and the generation and use of associated indicators comes from Henderson on the future role of the Bretton Woods institutions in more equitable, sustainable and participatory development (Henderson, 1996). However, a caveat is necessary. As a technique originating in economic theory, and thought of by many as a means to predominately economic ends, care must be taken in its use not to overemphasize economic development through manipulating sustainability.

Despite the short history of LSDI use, experience from their application to date strongly suggests a strategic role in sustaining bioregional integrity. They can assist in analysis, strategy or plan formulation, and monitoring and evaluation during and after implementation. Most of the experience with these new indicators has been in urban centres and at a national level; however, three experiences have come to our attention which may be considered bioregional in intent: British Columbia, Canada; the Feldbach Region, Austria; and the Puget Sound Region, USA (Sustainable Seattle, 1993; Hardi and Zdan, 1997). In the Šumava context, the authors have proposed the use of LSDIs in the recommendations of three projects, but the use of LSDIs has been taken furthest in the Český Krumlov strategic planning project. In late 1996, a project proposal for the design and institutionalization of LSDI was developed at the request of the town's mayor and submitted to several foreign aid agencies for joint funding. Unfortunately, with the exception of initial seeding from the Canadian Ambassador to the Czech Republic, it has not yet attracted financial support.

Integrated endogenous regional development (IERD)
Integrated endogenous regional development also enhances the BRES approach, and in particular strengthens the internal analysis of strategic

planning. It is an effort to go beyond a single sectoral view when using land-scape resources, and it stresses the bioregional aspect of land use practices. Jehle (1998) identifies the key attributes of this method as: viewing the area as a whole, not from one sector perspective only; participation of local social group in the decision making; and developing a region based pre-dominantly on its endogenous potential. In recent regional development, the issue of endogenous versus exogenous emphasis is an important theme (see particularly Storper, 1997).

In Europe for example, the concept began to be discussed in the early 1970s, by politicians seeking new strategies for assistance to less developed countries, and it is now taken into account by the European Union for devel-oping European 'disadvantaged' rural areas, such as in LEADER programmes ('Links between actions for the development of the rural economy') of the European Commission. For example, the Finnish Saimaa Lakes Region pro-ject, which aimed at better management of natural resources and tourism, and the education of local communities about environmental quality (Leader, 1998).

Remote sensing and geographical information systems (RS & GIS)

One of the difficulties that landscape management had suffered until quite recently was the lack of tools for gathering information on a regional scale. However, much of this difficulty is beginning to be overcome with the intro-duction of computer-based systems for handling geographical or spatial data, geographical information systems and digital image analysis systems for handling remotely sensed data about landscape phenomena. The use of these technologies in landscape analyses is well documented both independently (for example Richards, 1986; Chrisman, 1997; Burrough and McDonnell, 1998) and together (Ehlers *et al.*, 1989; David, 1991). A review of GIS and RS use in landscape ecology is given in Haines-Young *et al.* (1993) and Turner and Gardner (1990). Even though many other GIS undertakings dealt with evaluation of landscape, from the perspective of a passive viewer to informed decision-makers, only recently was the consider-able potential of GIS recognized as a process modelling tool, with potential in simulation modelling, particularly regarding the spatial character of socio-economic issues and their relationship to nature (Eastman *et al.*, 1995).

We used GIS and RS facilities in two ways in our Šumava bioregion work. Firstly, in reconstructing the historical development of population, land cover and land use, in a retrospective analysis for understanding recent 'natural potential' on the basis of its development in time, and for estimating future trends in the bioregion. The results of our GIS layering of the informa-tion we generated included the spatial location of all types of tourist accom-modation and related services, such as restaurants and pubs (see Fig. 5.4).

Secondly, socio-economic data were integrated into a GIS framework representing the perceived socio-economic development potential of

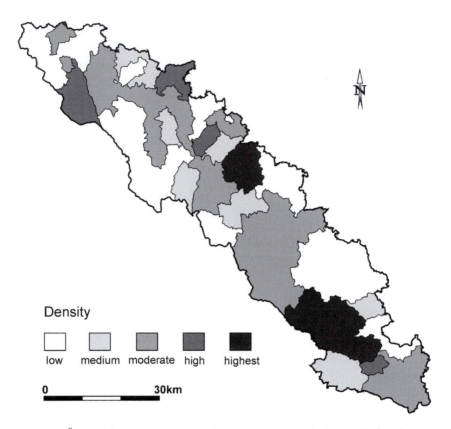

Fig. 5.4. Šumava bioregion: density of tourist accommodation and related services. Source: Institute of Landscape Ecology, České Budějovice, 1999.

Šumava (see Fig. 5.5). This calculation used the modified spatial multi-criteria evaluation (MCE) model of Eastman (1995), human settlement cadastre data from the *Czech Statistical Yearbook* (1997), key informant interviewing of local key stakeholders and external experts, and a bioregion-wide sample survey of 500 interviews. Sixty-four parameters were used, grouped into six data categories (demographic characteristics, transportation facilities, technical facilities, public services, private and state organizations, tourism facilities, and cultural facilities), and each category was assigned a weight based on opinions of local inhabitants and experts (Zemek and Heřman, 1998). Such key social and economic factors must be taken into account both for the general objective of supporting social and economic stability while sustaining the natural values of the bioregion, and for managing tourism's particular role.

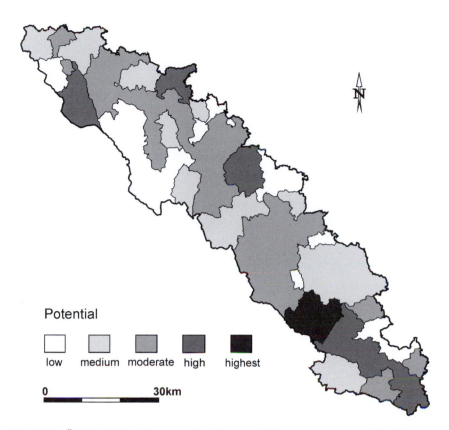

Fig. 5.5. Šumava bioregion: perceived potential for socio-economic development. Source: Institute of Landscape Ecology, České Budějovice, 1999.

Šumava Application of Enhanced BRES to Date

The enhanced BRES approach has been used as the principal conceptual framework and methodology for three Šumava projects to date (see Acknowledgement). It was used to identify key issues in sustaining the bioregion's integrity in development, namely the identification and analysis of key stakeholders, the more important internal strengths and weaknesses and external threats and opportunities, and subsequently it was used to formulate preliminary strategic thrusts, or strategic objectives. These are briefly outlined below along with tourism aspects of the strategic thrusts identified to date.

Key stakeholders

Four internal key stakeholders in the Šumava bioregion were identified, along with their predominant behavioural patterns, authority, human and financial resources, and agendas. They are:

1. The National Park Administration, representing and implementing national policy for nature conservation and its Šumava implications;

2. Municipalities, a group having common general interests and agenda and to this end having established two stakeholder organizations, the Regional Association of Šumava Municipalities and the Šumava Regional Development Authority;

3. Entrepreneurs in agriculture, a heterogeneous group defending their individual interests but not having a local or regional association to represent their common ones; and

4. Entrepreneurs in the amenity/leisure sector, a heterogeneous group, typically perceiving themselves as catering to tourists, each representing her/his own individual interests. To date several attempts to establish a group association have been unsuccessful.

In addition the following four external key stakeholders have been identified, but not sufficiently analysed to date:

5. The new Ministry of Regional Development, established in 1996, and given responsibility for the following activities significant to our subject: tourism, coordinating regional policy with other governmental bodies, facilitating and implementing regional programmes, supporting regional development agencies, providing regional training and information on local and regional subjects, and revitalizing the countryside (Blažek, 1999);

6. The three central government regional administrative 'district' administrations, Český Krumlov, Prachatice and Klatovy, having jurisdictional authority in the bioregion (which for some issues may also be considered internal stakeholders);

7. The Bavarian Forest administration in the adjoining German part of the larger mountain massif; and

8. Tourists and amenity migrants, along with their support and promotion systems.

Internal key strengths and weaknesses

Strengths

1. The dominant strength of the bioregion is its beautiful and relatively well sustained natural landscape, unpolluted air and its characteristic harmonious human settlement pattern; and

2. While living ethnic cultural heritage is no longer highly differentiated, the historical built environment is exceptional and high cultural events, such as serious music offerings and spectacles, are significant when the adjoining district capitals are included, especially Český Krumlov.

Weaknesses

1. Lack of skilled human resources and investment capital;

2. Ambiguity of land ownership and use regulations and anticipated and actual changes occurring to the same, due to the previous communist system and *Sudetendeutsche* restitution claims;

3. Lack of communication and participatory means among key stakeholders, especially with the Šumava National Park administration, and limited living traditions as a base for developing these;

4. Demographic and social structure of local people (see discussion below); and

5. No representative regional level body having responsibility and authority for developing the bioregion as an entity, paralleled by unfamiliarity of decision-makers and other key stakeholders with ecosystemic management and the bioregional perspective.

External key opportunities and threats

From our analysis to date, the opportunities and threats in the bioregion's strategic environment do not appear to fall well into positive and negative categories. This seems mainly due to growing international awareness of Šumava, especially through the Czech Republic's integration into western Europe. But it is also because of the considerable uncertainty in the surrounding political-economy of both the Czech Republic and the more global situation, particularly as manifest in amenity/leisure activities, and the need for much better understanding of this subject. However, there appears to be three clusters of opportunities and threats of primary significance during the next decade or so.

1. A new situation was introduced into Central and Eastern Europe after 1989, which is resulting in changing roles of individual regions. The Šumava bioregion is progressively being perceived as less socio-economically marginal with political–economic change drawing it into pan-European context (Těšitel *et al.*, 1999). Adjacent to a comparatively densely populated and highly developed Europe, the 'underdeveloped and empty state' of Šumava is beginning to attract the attention of tourism and recreation developers from outside the bioregion – Czech and foreign. Real development pressure, however, is expected to start with the Czech Republic entering the European Union, when the flow of labour and capital is expected to be unrestrained;

2. Unclear national policy on the future of Šumava, along with quite limited awareness of the emerging global amenity/ leisure economy and BRES among policy-makers and implementors. Yet, regional representative government is expected to be established soon, which through a greater regional perspective may improve this situation;

3. The bioregion's location bordering Germany and Austria also presents ambivalence. This delineation between unequal economies with a significant welfare gap generates socio-economic dynamics within the bioregion. One manifestation was local Czechs working abroad as cheap labour just after the opening of the border, and subsequently Austrian and German entrepreneurs operating in Šumava and offering some employment to local people. When and to what extent this welfare gap will disappear is uncertain. Also, penetration of foreign capital systems without sensitivity to local conditions can lead to the bioregion losing its 'genius loci', and so compromise its above-mentioned strengths.

Šumava Tourism

Early tourism in the Šumava Mountains

Tourism is a Šumava tradition dating back to the 18th century when its alpine Black (see Fig. 5.6) and Devil Lakes became significant attractions. At the time it was difficult to approach the many interesting places in these

Fig. 5.6. Restaurant and tourists by Black Lake; today the lake lies within the Šumava National Park's most protected zone (postcard, circa 1910, collection of M. Pouch).

Fig. 5.7. Postcard illustrating the attractions of Železná Ruda or Eisenstein, western Šumava (1898, collection of M. Pouch).

mountains because of dense forest and sporadic byways. Later, as the consumption of wood increased with the growing glass industry, the woodcutter's trails made possible excursions to previously inaccessible places. These early sojourners may be characterized as the wealthy, naturalists, artists and adventurers. During the next century or so the Šumava Mountains and the rustic folkways of their inhabitants became more publicized, notably through the romantic writings of Adalbert Stifter (1805–1886) and Karel Klostermann (1848–1923). The region took part in the period's growing vogue for alpine touring – there to be awed by the landscape, commune with nature, delve into natural history, linger in a Baroque square and dine in a medieval inn. This image of Šumava, or der Boehmerwald, and its strong sense of place still motivates the tourist gaze today.

The first tourist facilities were hostels, and the earliest of what was to become typical late 19th through early 20th century tourist centres in these mountains developed in the small town of Eisenstein, or Železná Ruda (see Fig. 5.7 and in Glorioso, this publication). In 1877 this settlement was connected by railroad to the central European urban centres of Plzeň and Prague, and 3 years later had 1500 inhabitants and four tourist hotels built to take advantage of its lovely alpine setting. Šumava also developed a few spa health resorts, but this activity has been far less than in central and northern Bohemia. Table 5.3 indicates tourism related activity at the end of the 19th century and a contemporary comparison.

In the 1880s German- and Czech-speaking alpine clubs were established and they promoted tourist activity in Šumava through building tourist

Table 5.3.   Historic alpine tourism centres in Šumava.

Settlement	Population		No. hostels and hotels	
	1900	1997	1900	1997
Čuina	396	0	2	0
Kvilda	1412	147	4	4
Strážný	725	281	4	2
Modrava	56	58	1	3
Železná Ruda	2756	1777	6	41

Sources: Basta, 1913; Czech Statistical Survey, 1997.

accommodations and publishing tourist guides. The Czech Tourist Club (Klub Českých Turistů), established in 1888, was particularly important, giving the public popular view towers (see Fig. 5.8), building many tourist hostels and less expensive student accommodations. This organization also created the network of world acclaimed Šumava hiking trails. During World War II the Czech alpine clubs were closed, and although begun again when hostilities ceased, they were once more shut down at the beginning of the communist period. Since the 'Velvet Revolution' in 1989 an attempt has been made to revive them, but with limited success.

A post World War II tourism profile

During the communist era foreign tourism was carefully controlled and discouraged in alpine Šumava. On the other hand, the piedmont was open, with most visitors coming from Czech urban centres and other Soviet bloc countries. Hiking, swimming, boating and fishing were, and still are, the focal activities, particularly in the Lipno Lake vicinity during summer months. Among urban Czechs it has been popular to pass weekends and longer vacations in the bioregion, some renting, many taking advantage of accommodation supplied by their public employers and others using their modest second homes (see Glorioso, this publication). Both domestic and foreign tourists were also attracted to the piedmont's cultural heritage resources.

   After 1989, the Czech Republic as a whole saw a marked increase in the number of foreign tourists; between 1985 and 1997 the numbers increased approximately ten times (Czech Statistical Survey, 1998). The Šumava bioregion reflected this national condition, especially with Austrian, German and Dutch visitors. For foreigners, the little known cultural heritage, charming landscapes and the comparative low cost of vacationing in the Czech lands have been the main attractions. In addition, the novelty of a society changing from a communist system was important. Also associated with the early phase of economic integration into a wider Europe, but now lessening,

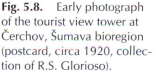

Fig. 5.8. Early photograph of the tourist view tower at Čerchov, Šumava bioregion (postcard, circa 1920, collection of R.S. Glorioso).

were day-trippers bargain hunting in the Czech Republic for cheaper food, liquor and tobacco; farm and sports equipment; garden tools and ornaments; and sex. However, with a waning of the novelty, rising costs and down-turns in neighbours' economies, foreign tourism now appears to be decreasing – nationally some 10.7% from 1996 to 1997 (Ministry for Regional Development, 1998). German visitors are now estimated to be only one-quarter that of the mid-1990s.

Many Czechs have taken advantage of their new freedom to travel beyond their nation's borders. Again, however, the wearing off of this novelty along with rising cost of foreign travel and a worsening domestic economy are causing the number of domestic tourists to increase recently. In parallel, Šumava appears to be reflecting this national pattern.

In a country well endowed with attractive historical settlements, typically located in bucolic landscapes, Šumava foothill towns stand out. Český Krumlov leads in attracting the tourist, second only to the national

capital of Prague. The most important cultural monuments (historical buildings, townscapes, landscapes and other structures) throughout the country
were reasonably well maintained and promoted as tourism attractions
during the communist period, and this governmental activity continues. But
in the context of tighter budgets for all public expenditures, the government
struggles to do justice to the very large number of worthy Czech attractions.
In addition, financial responsibility for much of this heritage has been given
to municipalities, who have very limited revenue-raising authority and so
even slimmer budgets. Therefore, while there is considerable awareness of
the need for maintenance and restoration, especially in view of potential
foreign tourism revenue, taking care of this heritage is a major issue, and one
also evident in Šumava.

Český Krumlov: Mark I or model?

In this context, the town of Český Krumlov has done well. It has a most
attractive morphology, including fine Gothic and Baroque townscape and
almost a surfeit of handsome individual buildings, enhanced further by
dramatic siting around an ox-bow of the beautiful Vltava River. In recognition it was designated a UNESCO World Heritage Site in 1992. The town
has also been fortunate to have a number of elected officials and other leaders who in this critical period comparatively swiftly became aware of both
the opportunities and threats of tourism. In 1995 they initiated a strategic
planning process for sustaining the town's cultural and environmental
heritage. (See Glorioso in this publication for additional information on
Český Krumlov's strategic planning.)

From 1990, a new mayor initiated a concerted effort to promote tourism
as a primary means for improving the economy of a town quite neglected for
some 50 years. Most of the initial tourists in this border town were country
people from neighbouring parts of Austria and Germany. Considerable effort
went into courting more prosperous and sophisticated foreign visitors, and
although having very limited professional tourism expertise and funds, the
mayor and his staff mounted a successful campaign. Against the backdrop
of the town's superlative heritage resources, key components of this
programme have been: development of a Summer cultural calendar highlighted by serious music; revival of the traditional Rose Festival; location
of scarce resources for restoration of the town-owned historic buildings;
promotional visits of European royalty and senior diplomats; development
of a competent town and regional tourism information centre; and 'Czech
Inspiration', an innovative cooperative programme of six Czech towns that
promotes their collegiate as an alternative to the nation's capital city.

Today this town of some 15,000 inhabitants caters to a spectrum of
visitors with an emphasis on cultural tourism. As it may be a harbinger for
Šumava's historic settlements more generally, in the absence of comparative

data, we continue with a description of the impacts of tourism on Český Krumlov.

The period from 1989 to 1998 saw an enormous increase in tourists, estimated as growing from several thousand to 1–1.5 million visitors annually (Schel, 1998). The considerable spread in these current figures probably reflects the large shadow economy and unreliability of related local and state tax statistics. With this influx, the town is changing from a place for the living of local lives to that of a contemporary museum, offering for learning and diversion, artefacts, spectacles and eating. In common with many towns that have taken this path before, its land use is becoming more characterized by the wants and needs of the visitor than of locals: hotels, pensions and hostels; craft boutiques, art and antique galleries; souvenir, book and liquor stores; restaurants, bars, and banks abound.

The town's administration receives modest additional revenues, and a few inhabitants make significant profit from this conversion. Some obtain employment, but few attest to being satisfied with the new situation, and many in this minority are recent arrivals occupied in tourist promotion and support services. So far the local municipal services are coping with increasing demand, although related greater public expenditures are recognized as essential. Most locals appear to be adjusting to the stress of increasing cost of basic needs, with the exception of housing. As residential buildings shift into commercial use related to tourism, earlier tenants must move out of the historical town.

Although many of the town's citizens and their local elected representatives are concerned about this changing character and state a desire to control negative impacts, change continues. The pace of change is swift, while community response is slow, especially in a society still rediscovering democratic processes. Yet, some battles appear to have been won. Progress is made with solving the parking problem, augmenting local employment alternatives to tourism, strengthening some town ordinances and regulations being manipulated by the unscrupulous, and using the recommendations of the town's strategic planning exercise as guidelines for a revised physical development plan. Perhaps most importantly to date, there has been growth in awareness of the issues that the town faces from successful tourism promotion and their systemic interdependence.

While other towns and villages in the bioregion seem eager to risk Český Krumlov's problems to also experience its successes, others hesitate (Fig. 5.9). The surrounding natural environment that is fundamental to the appeal and sustenance of this bioregion seems to date to have suffered little from tourist activities. The heavy recreational use of the major waterways, especially the Vltava River and Lipno Lake, needs greater and improved regulation, and the lands adjacent to arterial roads have higher deposits of trash. As tourism can very likely continue to be significant in the bioregion, we have outlined below some strategic considerations generated from our enhanced BRES analysis to date.

Fig. 5.9. New pension and restaurant at Stožec, central Šumava (photograph: L.A.G. Moss, September 1996).

Strategic thrusts for future tourism

Local perceptions

Development of 'tourism and recreation' was generally perceived by the local inhabitants in a 1996 surey as the most promising shorter-run focus of an economic strategy, while development of spa and sanatorium facilities was identified as the longer-term 'desired future'. For the shorter term, 27% of the respondents identified tourism and recreation, and 8% each for agriculture and forestry (Těšitel *et al.*, 1997). Aside from the health–leisure facilities proposed for the more distant future, other knowledge-intensive and amenity/leisure activities that are now occurring in similarly endowed bioregions globally were not mentioned by the Šumava respondents (see Moss, 1994, 1999).

Taking into account the decline in traditional agriculture and forestry practices and the relatively large and well-sustained protected areas, 'nature' is becoming, at least potentially, the predominant income generator for the bioregion. This seems well perceived by local inhabitants, along with some insight into the relevance of their present abilities. They are also reasonably aware of the potential negative impacts of tourism on their surroundings and ways of life. This is reflected in their wish for a shift to the health sector longer term, particularly spa resorts and sanatoriums now that

Šumava's environmental quality, especially clean air, is superior to that of its earlier central and northern Bohemian competitors.

Strategic thrusts

Regional development in mountain regions that is principally dependent on one economic sector is very vulnerable and not strategic. Tourism has the same risk, although probably further increased by its primary reliance on discretionary income, fashion and image or perception; and even less reliable within the strategic or external environment of the Šumava bioregion. For example, immediately after 1989 a wave of foreign visitors flooded the Šumava Mountains – it was fashionable, and cheap, to visit 'our wild and left behind' neighbours. But it was also short-lived.

Based on our analyses to date, we suggest tourism should be considered as only one component of a sustained Šumava bioregion. Firstly, there is need for more sophisticated understanding that tourism is only one part of an amenity/leisure economic sector that appears to be globally and rapidly growing. Another key component is amenity migration (Moss, 1994, 1999; Price *et al.*, 1997; Glorioso and Tonderayi, this volume). However, despite the difficulty, an even more diverse economy based principally on local attributes needs to be pursued. This is a precondition for the needed flexibility that can strengthen the bioregion's adaptability in the unpredictable longer term, and seems essential for maintaining the integrity of its ecosystem and cultural heritage.

In several similar bioregions, for example Baguio, Philippines and Sierra Nevada, USA, we are seeing a shift from tourism *per se* toward other amenity and associated knowledge-intensive activities (Dimaculangan, 1993; Centers for Water and Wildland Resources, 1996; Moss, 1999; Glorioso, this publication). While the spa and sanatorium use suggested by Šumava inhabitants appears to fit, its timing should be moved forward. This diversification, however, needs to be combined with much greater attention to policy and action that will encourage the type of Šumava visitors and new residents that will respect and participate in sustaining the bioregion's attributes. This in turn takes us back to the Introduction of this chapter, where we pointed out the need for shifts in awareness, attitude and behaviour, which is also identified as a common major issue for future mountain tourism strategy (see Chapter 16, this volume).

Šumava's environmental and cultural attributes appeal to both domestic and foreign tourists. Also, from the viewpoint of western visitors in particular, the 'unused and undeveloped' image of the bioregion appears to considerably enhance its attractiveness. However, sustaining this 'genius loci' will be a considerable challenge. One way is by keeping Šumava comparatively 'undeveloped'. Tourist services and facilities are presently concentrated mainly in two centres – Železná Ruda and Lipno Lake area. Excluding some neighbouring towns, especially Český Krumlov, the rest of

Šumava from this perspective is undeveloped (see Fig. 5.4), a pattern that should be maintained.

Another strategic thrust suggested from our findings is integrating development of the alpine and piedmont zones. Foreign visitors in particular appreciate the bioregion's attractions being typically quite spatially proximate and concentrated, yet offering opportunity for diverse experiences. For example, Český Krumlov's cultural attractions are less than 1 h by car from the Šumava National Park's wilderness, and the variety of aquatic activities of Lake Lipno are even closer. The same attractions should not be developed everywhere, but rather the existing complementary specialities of particular places should be reinforced. The bioregion as a whole however, while continuing to offer a range of attractions, should focus on components that least compromise its ecosystem and cultural heritage, yet contribute to economic welfare.

Existing mountain recreation facilities, such as ski lifts and accommodation, are generally considered of lesser quality than those in western European and North American locations, which to many suggests that considerable investment will be needed in order to compete. More generally, a higher standard of public facilities and services, such as telecommunications, water and sewerage, and public transportation seems called for and needing considerable public and private investment. Should Šumava copy its competitors? Its late-comer position should be viewed as an opportunity for avoiding earlier errors, particularly through innovative design, engineering and management systems that are resource conserving and having low environmental impact. For example, the environmental and socio-economic trade-offs between alpine and Nordic skiing and the use of integrated multiple use, cross-seasonal facilities need careful analysis.

Careful consideration should be given to the demographic and social characteristics of the local population from the perspective of their participation, today and in the future. Qualified human resources in the amenity/leisure sector, including tourism, are still very limited both locally and nationally, and those available are soaked up in Prague and across the border in Bavaria in higher-paying jobs. The dearth of local entrepreneurs and capital is crucial. Risk aversion is evidently a main cause, along with the lack of capital and collateral for loans, and of course, knowledge. These are deep structural problems that again require innovative solutions. The key will be a combination of guided community self-help and public and private assistance.

This takes us full circle to another overarching strategic thrust – the need for a vehicle for bioregion-wide guidance and support for socio-economic development and ecosystems maintenance. While the establishment of a regional representative level of governance noted above could assist, any successful entity representing or undertaking bioregional visioning and strategy formulating, guiding, monitoring and assessing roles needs to be established and maintained through the core involvement of local stakeholders. A command-and-control system with delegation of responsibility and action from the top down is not likely to sustain the bioregion. It needs the committed and sustained involvement of local people. Therefore, support to local formal and informal institutions in the broadest sense should be a main objective of sound governmental policy and undertakings.

Next Steps

The above strategic tourism thrusts can and should be pursued within a bioregional ecosystemic context to sustain Šumava's integrity and improve its inhabitants' welfare. This suggests proceeding immediately on two fronts:

1. Increasing the familiarity with and support for the enhanced BRES approach from its political and cultural environment, and
2. Undertaking projects at the Šumava bioregional level that further use and develop the enhanced BRES approach. Such projects, if skillfully formulated and executed, should *inter alia* also contribute to the first front's objective. Two such projects are outlined here.

Amenity migration and tourism strategy for a sustained Šumava bioregion

Conditions in the Šumava offer an opportunity to tackle the issues of amenity migration and tourism (AM & T) with reasonable odds for obtaining development that maintains local culture and natural environment while supporting AM & T. The project's mission is to formulate and put into effect a strategy for future AM & T in the Šumava within an ecosystemic managerial context, with the objectives of sustaining biodiversity and improving the welfare of the inhabitants. Being strategic, the project will also include formulating a set of local sustainable development indicators, and priority will be placed on involving local people and their use of the project's methodologies.

Tactical improvement of Šumava stakeholders' skills

While key stakeholders in the Šumava wish to carry out sustainable development, some major obstacles stand in the way. Poor communication among disparate interested parties is one immediate constraint, while another is the lag between acquisition of knowledge and its transfer to the bioregion. Therefore, this project aims to:

1. Enhance communications among key stakeholders through workshops for facilitating consensus building; and

2.   Improve the understanding of GIS and its potential role in the decision-making process, including the testing in multiple scenarios context of alternative policies and decisions.

The comparatively early phase of tourism's reappearance generally in the Šumava bioregion, and the possibilities of the enhanced BRES approach for appropriate planning and management of Šumava's attributes, should be viewed as an opportunity to harness the potential of this potent societal phenomenon. But in doing so there must be constant and sensitive vigilance for the particular welfare of Šumava and its people.

Acknowledgement

The three Šumava bioregional projects referred to here and undertaken between 1995 and 1997 are:

- 'Sustainable Development Strategy for Český Krumlov and its Bioregion', funded by the Foundation for a Civil Society, New York, and the town of Český Krumlov;
- 'Sustainable Development Strategy for the Šumava Biosphere Reserve', funded by the International Bank for Reconstruction and Development, Washington, DC; and
- 'Land Use and the Future of the Šumava Mountains', funded by the Grants Agency of the Czech Republic (No. 512/95/0725). We also wish to thank Josef Hejzlar, of the Hydrobiological Institute of CAS for sharing the Landsat 5 TM 1995 data used in this project.

We also wish to thank Miroslav Pouch, for the use of his Czech historic postcard collection.

References

Bandyopadhyay, J., Rodda, J.C., Kattelmann, R., Kundzewicz, Z.W. and Kraemer, D. (1997) Highland waters – a resource of global significance. In: Messerli, B. and Ives, J.D. (eds) *Mountains of the World: a Global Priority.* The Parthenon Publishing Group, London and New York, pp. 131–155.

Bartoš, M. and Těšitel, J. (1996) Large scale land abandonment: problems of reinhabitation, Czech Republic examples. In: Steinberger, Y. (ed.) *Preservation of Our World in the Wake of Change, Vol. VI A/B, Proceedings of the Sixth International Conference of the Israeli Society for Ecology & Environmental Quality Sciences, Jerusalem, Israel, June 30 – July 4, 1996.* ISEEQS, Jerusalem, pp. 871–874.

Bašta, A. (1913) *Průvodce šumavou (Guide to Šumava Mountains)* Narodní Jednota Pošumavská, E. Beaufort, Prague.

Bhatta, B.R., Clarete, C., Figueroa, S.D. and Ratnayake, K. (1993) *A strategy for resource conservation with income generation from cash crops by hill tribes in*

Doi Inthanon National Park, Chiang Mai, Thailand. Unpublished practicum study, INRDM Programme, Asian Institute of Technology, Bangkok, Thailand.

Blažek, J. (1999) Regional development and regional policy in Central and East European in the perspective of the European Union eastern enlargement. In: Hampl, M. (ed.) *Geography of Societal Transformation in the Czech Republic.* Charles University, Faculty of Science, Prague, pp. 181–207.

Burrough, P. and McDonnell, R.A. (1998) *Principles of Geographical Information Systems.* Oxford University Press, Oxford.

Capra, F. (1983) *The Turning Point: Science, Society and the Rising Culture.* Simon and Schuster, New York.

Canadian International Development Agency (1994, May) *Bangladesh: Northeast Regional Water Management Plan: Final Report.* Canadian International Development Agency – Northeast Regional Project, Bangladesh.

Centers for Water and Wildland Resources (1996) *Status of the Sierra Nevada: Sierra Nevada Ecosystem Project, Final Report to Congress,* Vols I, II, III. University of California, Davis, California.

Czech Statistical Survey (1997, 1998) Data base of Czech Statistical Office, (Český statistický úřad), České Budějovice (unpublished data).

Czech Statistical Yearbook (1997) Czech Statistical Office, Prague, p. 422 (in Czech).

David, F.D. (1991) Environmental analysis using integrated GIS and remotely sensed data: some research needs and priorities. *Photogrammetric Engineering and Remote Sensing* 57, 689–697.

Devall, W. (1988) *Simple in Means, Rich in Ends: Practicing Deep Ecology,* 1st edn. Peregrine Smith Books, Salt Lake City, Utah.

Dimaculangan [Glorioso], R.S. (1993) Key policy implications for strategic use of amenity resources: A study of longer-term amenity migration, Baguio Bioregion, the Philippines. Unpublished M.Sc. thesis, INRDM Programme, Asian Institute of Technology, Bangkok, Thailand.

Eastman, J.R., Jin, W., Kyem, P.A.K. and Toledano, J. (1995) Raster procedures for multi-criteria/multi-objective decisions. *Photogrammetric Engineering and Remote Sensing* 61, 539–547.

Ehlers, M., Edwards, G. and Bedard, Y. (1989) Integration of remote sensing with geographical information systems: a necessary evolution. *Photogrammetric Engineering and Remote Sensing* 55, 1619–1627.

Glorioso, R.S. and Moss, L.A.G. (1995) *Notes on Key Stakeholder Analysis.* International Cultural Resources Institute, Santa Fe, New Mexico.

Goldschmidt, N. (1989) *Oregon Shines: an Economic Strategy for the Pacific Century.* Office of the Economic Development Department, Salem, Oregon.

Haines-Young, R., Green, D.R. and Cousins, H.S. (1993) *Landscape Ecology and GIS.* Taylor & Francis, London.

Hamilton, L.S., Gilmour, D.A. and Cassells, D.S. (1997) Montane forests and forestry. In: Messerli, B. and Ives, J.D. (eds) *Mountains of the World: a Global Priority.* The Parthenon Publishing Group, London and New York, pp. 281–311.

Hardi, P. and Zdan, T. (eds) (1997) *Assessing Sustainable Development: Principles in Practice.* International Institute for Sustainable Development, Winnipeg, pp. 37–52; 67–76.

Harrison, D. and Price, M.F. (1996) Fragile environments, fragile communities? An introduction. In: Price, M.F. (ed.) *People and Tourism in Fragile Environments.* John Wiley & Sons, Chichester, pp. 1–18.

Henderson, H. (1996) Changing paradigms and indicators: implementing equitable, sustainable and participatory development. In: Griesgraber, J.M. and Bernhard, G.G. (eds) *Rethinking Bretton Woods:* Vol. II. *Development: New Paradigms and Principles for the Twenty-first Century.* Pluto Press, East Haven, Connecticut, pp. 103–136.

Jehle, R. (1998) The concept of endogenous rural development in the framework of its introduction in the regional policy in the Czech Republic. *Economy of Agriculture* 44, 9–12 (in Czech).

Johnson, L.R. (1996) *Central Europe: Enemies, Neighbors, Friends.* Oxford University Press, Oxford, New York.

Leader (1998) A thousand opportunities around a thousand lakes, *Leader* Autumn 1998, 13–17.

MacMillan, I.C. and Jones, P.E. (1986) *Strategy Formulation, Power and Politics,* 2nd edn. West Publishing Company, St Paul, Minnesota.

Mandel, T.F. (1983) Future scenarios and their uses in corporate strategy. In: Albert, K.J. (ed.) *The Strategic Management Handbook.* McGraw-Hill, New York, pp. 10-1–10-21.

Mejstřík, V., Bartoš, M., Těšitel, J. and Hanousková, I. (1995) Abandoned landscapes in Czech Republic. In: Schoute, J.F.Th., Finke, P.A., Veeneklaas, F.R. and Wolfert, H.P. (eds) *Selected and Edited Proceedings of the Symposium Scenario Studies for the Rural Environment, Wageningen, The Netherlands, 12–15 September 1994.* Kluwer Academic Publishers, Dordrecht, pp. 717–723.

Ministry of Environment (1992) Czech National Council Act. No. 114/1992, On nature and landscape protection, Czech National Council, Prague, pp. 666–693.

Ministry of Regional Development (1998) *Věstník Ministerstva pro místní rozvoj,* 1/98. http://www.obce.cz/mmr/vestniky/vestnik98-01 (in Czech).

Moss, L.A.G. (1994) Beyond tourism: the amenity migrants. In: Mannermaa, M., Inayatullah, S. and Slaughter, R. (eds) *Coherence and Chaos in Our Uncommon Futures: Visions, Means, Actions.* Finland Futures Research Centre, Turku School of Economics and Business Administration, Turku, Finland, pp. 121–127.

Moss, L.A.G. (1999) *Policy Issues Brief: Sustaining the Sierra Nevada Bioregion's Integrity under Growing Human Population Pressure.* Public Policy Institute of California, San Francisco, California.

Nutt, P.C. and Backoff, R.W. (1992) *Strategic Management of Public and Third Sector Organizations: A Handbook for Leaders.* Jossey-Bass Publishers, San Francisco, California.

Price, M.F., Moss, L.A.G. and Williams, P.W. (1997) Tourism and amenity migration. In: Messerli, B. and Ives, J.D. (eds) *Mountains of the World: a Global Priority.* The Parthenon Publishing Group, London and New York, pp. 249–280.

Richards, J.A. (1986) *Remote Sensing Digital Image Analysis.* Springer-Verlag, Berlin.

Ringland, G. (1998) *Scenario Planning: Managing for the Future.* John Wiley & Sons, Chichester.

Schel, A. (29 August 1998) The 15,000 population Krumlov is packed with the same number of tourists. *Českokrumlovske listy,* p. 11 (in Czech).

Storper, M. (1997) *The Regional World: Territorial Development in a Global Economy,* 1st edn. Guilford Press, New York and London.

Sustainable Seattle (1993) *The Sustainable Seattle 1993: Indicators of Sustainable Community: A Report to Citizens on Long-Term Trends in Our Community.* Sustainable Seattle, Seattle, Washington.

Těšitel, J., Bartoš, M., Cudlínová, E., Heřman, M., Kušová, D. and Zemek, F. (1997) *Sustainable development strategy for the Šumava Biosphere Reserve: Final report.* Institute of Landscape Ecology, Czech Academy of Sciences, České Budějovice.

Těšitel, J., Kušová, D. and Bartoš, M. (1999) Non-marginal parameters of marginal areas. *Ecology (Bratislava)*, 18, 39–46.

Turner, M.G. and Gardner, R.H. (1990) *Quantitative Methods in Landscape Ecology: The Analysis and Interpretation of Landscape Heterogeneity.* Springer-Verlag, Berlin.

Utah Tomorrow Strategic Planning Committee (1993) *Utah tomorrow: Annual report.* Office of the Legislative Research and General Counsel, Salt Lake City, Utah.

Zemek, F. and Heřman, M. (1998) Natural and socio-economic potential of landscape integrated in GIS frame. *Ecology (Bratislava)*, 17, 232–240.

Mountain Culture as a Tourism Resource: Aboriginal Views on the Privileges of Storytelling

6

Robert E. Pfister

Resource Recreation and Tourism, University of Northern British Columbia, 3333 University Way, Prince George, British Columbia, V2N 4Z9, Canada

Introduction

In tourism, culture counts! It is readily understood that tourists will travel to distant and remote locations because of a desire to learn about culture. In some cases, the desire may be to discover one's own cultural roots, but for the majority of travellers, it is to explore a different way of life. Culture can be defined as the shared products of a given society: its values, knowledge, norms and material goods. Thus, culture includes the non-material aspects (knowledge, norms, values and ideals) and the material aspects (arts, crafts, clothing, dwelling, tools, etc.) of society. Every individual who is an active member of society shares in its own culture, although the level of involvement may vary along lines of power, gender, ethnicity or equality. Based upon the interests, perceptions and aspirations of travellers, culture is an important place-specific resource that is incorporated into tourism. For some, it may be the tangible components of culture (arts and crafts) and for other tourists it may be the intangible components of culture (values, beliefs, legends, etc.) that attract them to the homeland of an indigenous community.[1]

---

[1] 'Aboriginal' herein is used interchangeably with the term 'indigenous'. It denotes indigenous people, that is, existing in the land at the dawn of history or before the arrival of the colonists. This reference would include such terms as First Nations (Canada), Aborigine (Australia), Native American (USA), Indigena (South America), and many other such terms.

Indigenous Culture and Mountains

Without doubt, the mystery and spiritual value of travel to inaccessible, less known and remote locations in mountainous regions has long been part of travel and tourism. Just what it is that most appeals to the urban dweller may be uncertain, but it likely includes a desire to experience nature on its own terms and get back to the basics of observing what it is to live close to the land. Indigenous culture in mountainous regions brings together two positive elements, which readily serve as an attraction to travellers: the mountains and indigenous culture. As noted in the introductory chapter, mountains have been described as spiritual centres and places of worship. Again, it is culture that can give unique meaning and value to these special and sacred places. It is often the belief and practices of a people living in that region that give rise to the images and legends that pervade the intercultural encounters which travellers cherish. In other words, it is the beliefs, or non-material elements, of culture that give significance and meaning to mountains as sacred places. As stated by Bernbaum (1997: xxi):

> Just as traditional cultures frequently separate the sacred from the profane, so they cordon off certain mountains with rules and rituals. Only those of spiritual power and purity may venture up these mountains without fear of provoking the anger of the gods or the spite of the demons. In North America, for example, many Native Americans believe that only people with the proper ritual preparation can climb to the summits of sacred peaks without being struck by spirits.

The desire to explore remote and less accessible locations of the world seems to be a universal motivation for travellers attracted to the mountainous regions. When those areas are settled by an indigenous people, the opportunity presents itself for an intercultural experience. It offers images of mystery, wonderment and serene lifestyles, as they become elements of the exploration. Around the world, it has been observed how stark mountainous environments have been revered for some idealized settlement and set apart from the more common populated areas in which the travellers live. Again, Bernbaum (1997: 55) illustrates this point when he writes about the ranges of Central Asia:

> Cultures of both East and West have turned to these little-known ranges in quest of earthly paradises impossible to reach or attain by ordinary means – the hidden kingdom of Shambhala, the cosmic axis of Mount Meru, the palace of Hsi wang-mu, the monastery of Shangri-La. The mountains that conceal such sanctuaries . . . represent the extreme limits of the physical world, the borders between the possible and the impossible, the known and the unknown, the imaginable and the unimaginable. Their remoteness and inaccessibility are a measure of their power to evoke the ultimate mystery of the sacred.

The aim of this chapter is to:

- distinguish between the material and non-material components of culture;
- introduce several general observations applicable to non-material culture;
- illustrate the importance of the spoken word to indigenous communities, the roles of storytelling and intercultural issues arising in tourism when aboriginal people share non-material cultural experiences with their guests; and
- identify some strategies that may support and enhance the capability of indigenous communities to maintain control over non-material culture, particularly storytelling, and ensure the strategies help to sustain the culture.

The case study selected to illustrate the culture–general issues is a coast mountain territory occupied by the Nisga'a people of British Columbia, and the secondary source material, to elaborate on the strategies, is drawn from case studies that relate to New Zealand, Australia, the United States, and other indigenous communities of Canada. Given the cultural diversity of the aboriginal groups in the diverse geographical locations, it is inevitable that some information may be overlooked or perhaps not highlighted in context. Every effort is made to avoid an ethnocentric perspective and to recognize the ever-changing situation of all cultures.

Tourism as a Resource: Shared Views and Expectations

How does culture become a resource? By definition, 'a resource is an abstraction that presupposes a person and it represents an expression of human appraisal . . . Resources have meaning, utility and consequences since they serve as a means to an end' (Pfister and Ewert, 1996: 3). The 'end' for travellers may be described as learning, discovery, satisfying curiosity or an inquiry about alternative lifestyles. Moreover, what is sought may vary from one tourist to the next. Indigenous culture 'becomes a tourism resource' because, collectively the appraisal of one or more elements of culture are recognized by a group of travellers as an attraction or something of value. Whether it is based on an idealized mental image or 'reality' is less important than the fact that the perception has created a motivation to discover and learn.

The fact that indigenous culture attracts people to remote locations poses a variety of questions about the very culture itself.

- If it is a valued resource, then who owns it?
- How do the members of indigenous communities see cultural tourism?
- What is the role and responsibilities of elders, hereditary chiefs and others?

- Does marketing cultural products affect the set of values, beliefs or traditions from which the products originate?
- How do we begin to understand an indigenous worldview of their culture before attempting to package it as a tourism experience?
- What distinctions in terms of a code of conduct for tour operators should be made between material and non-material culture?
- Are issues of cultural authenticity critical to the market value of the experience?
- Is it appropriate to promote a culture of which you are not a part?

An appraisal by a tourist is based on a 'constellation of the individual's background, training and personal belief systems. Related to these personal belief systems is the issue of worldview' (Pfister and Ewert, 1996). With the growth in indigenous tourism, a discussion of the premise of a 'worldview' by groups involved with tourism is in order. A worldview can be the way a particular group of stakeholders see the phenomenon of tourism. It is a point of view which often reveals a set of values inherent in their general orientation or worldview. Four stakeholder groups can be considered to illustrate this point: the tourist, the tour operator, the cultural scientist and the resident of an indigenous village. Each group observes the dynamics of tourism in terms of their own worldviews.

Consider each of the following four views:

1. The responsible traveller. Of interest to us are their perceptions of culture, its diversity and the unique elements of culture that can create a sense of place. In questioning his instinct to explore, McLaughlin (1999: 1) states:

> The landscape belongs to another culture and as I move through it, I slowly realize I cannot understand or even see the people of this foreign civilization from my perspective as a western scientist and museum curator.

2. The tour operator. Their product and practices in packaging the cultural experience as part of their tour can sway the balance between the consequences of tourism (Klieger, 1990; Higgins, 1996; Norman et al., 1997). Research has looked at both outbound nature tour operators and inbound nature tour operators as part of an effort to describe the structure of an industry, which includes ecotourists, tour operators and local businesses. As part of the Green Evaluation Programme (Norman et al., 1997: 18), the researchers took a close examination of the information and education provided by tour operators to their clients during the trip. That study reported:

> Nearly nine out of ten (87.2%) of the respondents reported that they were briefed prior to each stop of their tour, with 82.9% reporting that briefings on proper behavior while on trails, in campsites, around wildlife of fragile plants, took place. The two areas of mild concern are the advisement against purchasing specific crafts that are produced from threatened natural resources (69.4%) and the discouragement of having unrealistic expectations of observing rare wildlife or plants (60.7%). Overall, there is not as strong support for the

provision of information to minimize cultural impacts as was provided by the tour operators in an effort to minimize environmental impacts.

3. The cultural scientist or the business academician. This group is concerned about culture and also links together a shared set of values held by indigenous people in general and their relationship to place (Booth and Jacobs, 1988; Sweet, 1990; Wood, 1991; Walle, 1993; Jostad, 1994; McDonald and McAvoy, 1997). As will be discussed in the next section, there are common values that seem to create bridges across the indigenous boundaries and provide a basis for contrasting indigenous culture with western culture. Anthropologist Jill Sweet (1990: 8) states:

> As more and more tourists search for contact with 'real natives', and as the tourist industry continues to nourish these wishes, native people will have to be forthright about the nature of these encounters. If they do not meet this challenge, they will be reduced to nothing more than passive tourist attractions.
>
> [The task is] . . . finding the balance between maintaining their cultural autonomy and benefiting from tourism economically and socially. The fact that people travel long distances to see them presents problems of intrusion but also provides them with a market for their arts and sends a positive message to Indian people about the strength and beauty of their cultural ways.

The business professionals recognize as well the dangers of homogenization of culture and have addressed the consequences of tourism upon traditional people. Walle (1993: 15), a market professor in the business school, writes:

> . . . folk cultures (as well as individual traditional people) tend to be intimately niched within their society and environment and changes wrought by marketing and tourism can trigger a host of side effects which affect the entire culture. Marketing, even if well intended, can disrupt social relationships and thrust people into a whole new web of life: the mainstream culture. On a positive note, marketing might also validate a culture and lead to a tangible recognition of traditional people and their accomplishments. The respect many tourists show for a people's traditions is an example of that potential . . . .
>
> Marketing is seen to be profoundly interrelated with the entire culture; the health and well-being of that culture and the people comprising it may be linked to marketing decisions. Cultural conservationists have to become concerned with marketing and its impacts . . .

4. The indigenous resident. Often the resident of an indigenous community is concerned with self-destiny and cultural issues that relate to the right, privileges, duties and practices of their community. Such traditions maintain or restore a living culture. Kevin Brown, a Haida from the Queen Charlotte Islands, cites McDonald (1994: 5) who comments:

> Wealth consisted of the right of access to both natural and supernatural resources. Rights and privileges belonged to the lineage and were exercised by the lineage chief. Prerogatives assigned to a particular lineage might include the rights of hunting land and fishing streams, rocky islets where sea

mammals could be clubbed, berry picking areas, stands of fine timber, or stretches of beach where whales might be stranded. Each lineage had a founding ancestor and an accumulated history, which was the basis for claiming these rights and privileges. Linking the lineage with the ancestral and supernatural sources of power were the songs, dances, crests used in the carvings and names belong to lineage.

The above commentaries illustrate the diversity of views on indigenous tourism that exist among the stakeholders. Among the four perspectives present, the indigenous resident will be given depth and breadth.

Tourism resources, as with all its cultural components, increase in value, as they become scarce. For those cultures that are endangered (Davidson, 1993), it is apparent that the recognition they now receive from the tourism industry may be in part related to the dilemma they face as a sustainable culture. As such, travellers from around the world tend to value those experiences that enrich our own values and experience, stimulate our intellect and give purpose to our existences. Cultural encounters, where travellers experience a way of life quite different from their own, and then return home to support or to advocate its existence, may be at the very essence of what it is to be human and to be part of responsible tourism.

Understanding Aboriginal Worldviews

Recognition and understanding of aboriginal worldviews can help begin to bridge the gap between aboriginal and non-aboriginal peoples. In examining aboriginal worldviews, it is critical to keep in mind that aboriginal peoples living in mountainous regions are not a homogeneous group who, once placed in such a category, can be treated one way. Rather, they are composed of a multitude of peoples with distinct languages, cultures and beliefs. This variation may be seen in the other contributions to this book. Within western Canada, there are exceptional opportunities for visiting mountainous parks, natural and wilderness areas, and engaging in educational tours focusing on nature or indigenous culture. For example, Murtha (1996: 40) points out the mountainous Province of British Columbia alone has 590 provincial parks and ecological reserves, six national parks and an immense diversity of aboriginal cultures. He goes on to state that:

British Columbia is the most geographically and biologically diverse region in Canada, with 27 mountain ranges, intermontaine plateaus, and incised canyons. Elevations range from sea level to over 4,500 meters, creating a mosaic of ecological conditions – the northern tip of the Sonaoran Desert, grasslands, temperate rainforests, boreal forests, taiga, muskeg, alpine tundra, glaciers, and icefields. The deeply indented fiord coastline and fringing island archipelagos create a Pacific coastline of 2,700 kilometers . . . (Moreover) British Columbia has the greatest diversity of aboriginal cultures in Canada. There are 120,000 'Status Indians' (people of aboriginal ancestry who are legally recognized under Canada's Indian Act). They belong to 25 ethnographic groups and speak 27 native languages from seven linguistic families (out of a Canadian total of 37 languages in 11 families).

A review of the cross-cultural literature on indigenous worldviews does reveal some striking similarities. Thus while we acknowledge that we cannot hope to elucidate the full complexity of indigenous worldviews in the current context, it is possible to identify some of the common elements which contribute to the indigenous way of seeing, feeling and knowing. The theory of culture suggests that any synthesis of an indigenous worldview reflects the point of view of a cross-cultural scientist or the 'etics' of culture. As stated by Bhawuk and Triandis (1996: 23):

> The 'etic approach' is mainly followed by cross-cultural scientist (both anthropologists and psychologists), who believe that cultures have both specific and universal dimensions and are interested in observing these universals. It is now generally accepted that similarities between cultures must be established before their differences can be studied, because if a framework of universal constructs is not observed, it is impossible to distinguish cultural differences . . ..
>
> Etics are theoretical concepts that allow generalizations about relationships among variables across cultures. For example, even animals other than humans have pecking orders, and thus social hierarchy is an etic.

McDonald and McAvoy (1997) in their pursuit of an *etic* approach, identify five elements of a generalized indigenous worldview based upon their work with several communities of Native Americans.

The first element they identify is the pervasive belief in the sacredness of all life. This concept can even be expanded to include the sacredness of all creation, whether animate or inanimate. Couture (1991: 57) summarizes this perception in his remark that 'traditional Indian knowing is an experience in matter and spirit as inseparable realities . . .'. Similarly, Meyer and Ramirez (1996: 100) explain that in the Dakota/Lakota worldview, 'the physical appearance of "hard things" is simply a manifestation of the spiritual reality which underlies everything.' The Maori in New Zealand share this concept with the indigenous people of North America. *Wahi Tapu*, or sacred space, extends 'all aspects of the environment or *papatuanuku*, from which Maori base their descent' (Keelan, 1993: 98).

Directly linked to this, Native Americans possess a clear sense of a reciprocal and interdependent relationship with all creation (Couture, 1991; Jack *et al.*, 1993; McDonald and McAvoy, 1997). This element is also part of the worldview of New Zealand aboriginal people whose creation myths express 'the indivisible nature of the Maori people with their environment . . . [thus] the wretched nature of the environment is analogous to that of the people' (Keelan, 1993: 97, 99). Similarly, the Australian Aborigine communities perceive places of significance 'as part of a complex system of relationships with the land and the Dreaming' (Boyd and Ward, 1993: 113).

A third element identified as part of the Native American is an un-wavering belief in the importance of harmonizing their relationship with other humans and with the land (Hart, 1996; McDonald and McAvoy, 1997). The critical nature of harmonization is also implicit in the typical consensus-based decision-making process of Native people (Hart, 1996).

A fourth dimension of an indigenous worldview is the pervasive belief in the cyclical pattern of life. This conceptualization is manifested in many concrete ways such as the sun dance ceremonies common to the Plains tribes. It also underpins the 'First Salmon' ceremonies that are common to Native peoples who reside on the coast and salmon rivers in British Columbia:

> If bones of animals and fish are not treated with . . . respect . . . they will not
> return to give themselves up to humans. In this way, a person's actions not
> only interact with those of the animals and the spirits, but also have repercus-
> sions for future generations, deprived of the food that will ensure their survival
> (Wa, 1992: 23).

A fifth aspect of the indigenous worldview is an emphasis on the importance of the spoken word. This pertains to trust, which is freely given on the basis of spoken agreement as well as the transmission of culture through oral methods. Rupert Ross (1992: xiii) explains that 'for a community to regard a person as one worth listening to was the highest distinction they could confer.' The spoken word is also important among the Maori who view ceremonial speech-making as a highly valued art form (Keelan, 1993: 101). It is this fifth aspect of an indigenous worldview that will be examined next in terms of tourism and non-material culture.

The Spoken Word and Storytelling: Issues of Non-material Culture

The indigenous worldview pertaining to the importance of the spoken word is supported and illustrated by the phenomenon of storytelling. Indeed, the two are intertwined in a symbiotic relationship. Thus, it may appear that the potential incorporation of storytelling into cultural tourism encounters with indigenous communities may be a very effective way to deepen visitors' understanding and appreciation of aboriginal non-material culture. The Australian National Museum's recent exhibit, 'The True Story' illustrates how this can be achieved:

> From sitting in a rock cave listening to an elder recount stories from the
> Dreaming to standing in a wooden bush chapel hearing a Torres Strait Islander
> choir sing hymns in language, the new Indigenous Australians exhibition at
> Sydney's Australian Museum, offers a vivid perspective of life through indige-
> nous eyes (ATSIC, 1997).

The role that storytelling plays may vary between aboriginal cultures, but nevertheless they are critical to sustaining the integrity of most aboriginal cultures. For many aboriginal cultures such as the Gitksan and Wet'suwet'en of northern British Columbia, storytelling is a highly ritualized process that confers spirit power:

> The formal telling of the oral histories in the Feast, together with the display of crests and the performance of the songs, witnessed and confirmed by the Chiefs of other Houses, constitute not only the official history of the House, but also the evidence of its title to its territory and the legitimacy of its authority over it. The oral history, the crests, and the songs of a House are evidence, however, of something more than even its history, title, and authority. They represent also its spirit power, its daxgyet (Wa, 1992: 26).

Another example can be drawn from the Shuswap for whom 'the greatest value of the legends and stories . . . are in the values and attitudes towards all relationships in the world' (Jack *et al.*, 1993). Because of this powerful and pervasive relationship between oral tradition and cultural sustainability, the use of aboriginal oral histories in an interpretative context must be approached with caution and sensitivity. The commodification of culture has been frequently treated in the literature as a topic of widespread concern of social scientists. It is worthwhile to identify and understand some of the key issues pertaining to the process of sharing aboriginal oral histories with tourists. Briefly, some of these issues are (i) trivialization and simplification, (ii) respect for privacy and sacredness, (iii) accuracy or 'authenticity', (iv) protocol, and (v) permission and authority.

Trivialization and simplification

When aboriginal stories are told within the context of a casual tourism experience, guides may inadvertently simplify or trivialize the content and meaning of the stories because of time constraints or lack of knowledge. Non-aboriginal tour guides, as cross-cultural facilitators, and aboriginal elders, as stewards of the oral tradition, should consider the impact of their actions upon the way tourists perceive aboriginal cultures.

The danger of trivializing meaning is addressed in the *Shuswap Community Handbook*, which cautions teachers not to present traditional non-material culture in isolation. Decontextualizing intangible culture (as well as tangible culture) cuts the threads of the complex web of factors and conditions that contribute to its importance. 'The presentation of legends for example in isolation of the purpose, may trivialize the importance of the beliefs and values that were inherent in the stories' (Jack *et al.*, 1993: 4). Meaning can also be trivialized and simplified when people sharing stories attempt to explain their meaning by comparing aboriginal stories with those of other cultures. For example, non-aboriginals often draw parallels between oral stories and European fables, by pointing out that both are used to teach a moral lesson. Ross (1992: xviii–xix) reflects on the stories told to him by Charlie Fisher, an elder from northwestern Ontario:

> In time I learned how to listen to those stories, how to see beyond their casual appearance. To say that they contained lessons would be wrong; instead, they crystallized various scenarios within which some choices would clearly be wise and others inappropriate. The ultimate choice, however, would always be mine.

Another reason why non-aboriginal tourism operators or guides may inadvertently simplify the nature of aboriginal cultures is due to the tendency to homogenize, rather than to recognize and discuss diversity. Tourists may be unaware of the extent of diversity in the traditions, languages, opinions and beliefs of aboriginal peoples. Interpreters who share aboriginal stories with tourists can help develop awareness of this diversity by telling different versions of stories that are common to more than one aboriginal group. In doing so, the differences and similarities between aboriginal peoples will become apparent to tourists and they will learn how each story may be equally valid and useful:

> There were many versions of similar stories. Each storyteller added his or her own adaptations according to their style, their purpose and their audience. The message may have been very clear in some cases and in other, very symbolic and subtle (Jack *et al.*, 1993: 11).

Comprehension of diversity is also important because diversity between aboriginal groups is not just reflected in stories. As pointed out in the ATSIC submission to the Joint Parliamentary Committee (1998), different perspectives which aboriginal groups hold on current issues often arise out of their respective oral traditions.

Respect for privacy and sacredness

The pervasive belief in sacredness among aboriginal people is often reposited in, and transmitted through, oral histories. These stories simultaneously rest upon and support worldviews relating to the sacred elements of culture. Because of this, it is imperative that their integrity be strictly protected. While many steps can be taken to ensure that storytelling to tourists does not depreciate the value of some stories; aboriginal people may feel that others are too precious and private to share. ATSIC clearly articulates this concern in its Cultural Industry Strategy:

> There are strong traditions of storytelling amongst both Aboriginal and Torres Strait Islander cultures. Some stories have spiritual significance and can only be told to certain people. Others can be presented more widely (Commonwealth of Australia, 1997).

It is clear that aboriginal people who are involved in tourism in Australia act as cultural facilitators and cultural protectors. For example, a recent travel review describes how guides with Umorrduk Safaris in Australia impart their people's deep sense of connection with Arnhem Land by sharing stories about the ancestral beings who created their land. It is also emphasized in the review, however, that 'Some of the stories and aspects of local culture remain secret' (Taylor, 1997). This principle is also practised by a Wardaman guide in Australia who informs tourists that he will share 'some of the non-secret stories associated with the paintings' (Northern Territory Tourist Commission, 1994 in Zeppel, 1998a: 5).

Accuracy and authenticity

The question of accuracy and authenticity can be a very contentious issue. It raises many questions to which aboriginal peoples respond in a variety of different ways. Some of the questions raised at the Australian Eco-tourism workshop are: 'When is an indigenous guide 'traditional'? [and] Where did they learn or obtain their information from?' (Bissett *et al.*, 1999: 2). Laurie Perry, an Aboriginal (*Wonnaruha*) from Singleton, New South Wales and the operator of Gringai Aboriginal Cultural Tours, believes that Aboriginal cultural knowledge contained in books is not accurate. In her opinion, the only truth is that which is obtained from Aboriginal elders (Bissett *et al.*, 1999: 2). Indeed members of her community feel so strongly about this issue that they are setting up an 'Elders Court' in order to verify which stories are correct.

Many other questions relating to the issue of accuracy in storytelling can also be raised. One of these, 'Is there only one correct version of a story?' can be answered with an unequivocal *no* – at least according to Rita Jack and Marie and Robert Matthews who write about the culture of the Shuswap or *Secwepemc* in the Interior of British Columbia:

> There were many versions of similar stories. Each storyteller added his or her own adaptations according to their style, their purpose and their audience. The message may have been very clear in some cases and in others, very symbolic and subtle (Jack *et al.*, 1993).

Even the *Anishinaubaeg* of Ontario, Canada where speakers are complimented with '*w'daeb-wae*', a word which loosely translated means 'truth', recognize that a person's desire to convey the truth is limited by their abilities. The compliment acknowledges that:

> One casts one's knowledge as far as one has perceived it and as accurately as one can describe it, given one's command of language. In other words, the best one can do is to tell what one knows with the highest degree of accuracy. Beyond this one cannot go. According to this understanding there is or can be no such thing as absolute truth (Johnston, 1992: xii).

Another question that could be posed is whether stories that incorporate elements of contemporary culture could be considered authentic. One of the principles espoused in the *Shuswap Community Handbook* affirms this. They identify and validate 'adapted and borrowed non-material culture' and state that these cultural elements 'are the most difficult to interpret but are so necessary in the understanding of contemporary Shuswap communities' (Jack *et al.*, 1993: 4). This concept has been illustrated in Table 6.1.

It should be noted that the author has attempted to illustrate Jack's conceptual matrix with examples from the Secwepemc culture. The 'traditional culture' category illustrated by Jack has also been expanded in order to illustrate how change is a constant part of Secwepemc culture. Further, for simplicity, the author has presented 'traditional' and 'adapted' cultural attributes and activities as if they did not overlap in practice. It should be noted that many activities, such as salmon drying and learning by doing, continue to be practised today.

Reflecting on the fourth aspect of aboriginal worldviews, belief in the cyclical nature of life, may provide further insight regarding how other aboriginal people might answer the question posed above. In the aboriginal worldview, all life exists on a continuum and includes animate as well as inanimate life, including time (Ross, 1992; Wa, 1992). The past, present and future are not arbitrarily defined and separated along a linear path. Rather,

Table 6.1.   Traditional, adapted and borrowed elements of Shuswap Culture.

	'Traditional' Shuswap culture	Adapted and borrowed Shuswap culture
Material		
Food	Dried salmon	Canned salmon
Clothing	Hide clothing	Native print T-shirts
Shelter	Pit houses	Mobile and wood frame homes
Transportation	Feet	Pickup trucks
Tools	Large, stemmed points	Hunting rifles
Non-material		
Values	Learning by doing (education by family)	Learning by reading (education by teachers)
Beliefs	Belief in a protective guardian spirit	Catholic and traditional beliefs syncretized
Stories	Only orally told and in the Shuswap language	Now written in books and told in English
		Grass Dancing (borrowed from Plains)

Adapted from Rita Jack *et al.* (1993).

they are intimately connected. So too are the past, present and future generations. It could be argued that in this view, the knowledge and experiences of ancestors, the people of today and descendants cannot and should not be separated. Thus, the contributions each generation makes to aboriginal oral histories could be interpreted as overlapping, integrating and together, developing the cultural value and strength of the stories. Though not discussed with direct relation to oral stories, this interpretation can be supported by Wa's (1992: 43) comment that, for the Gitksan and Wet'suwet'en, '. . . developments have been incorporated into an existing framework and structure of their society in ways which are a part of a chain of continuity with the past.' It can be inferred that Aboriginal people in Australia would concur with this belief because the ATSIC submission to the Joint Parliamentary Committee on Native Title (1998) states that 'traditions may change . . . Culture is dynamic and adapts to changes in the social and physical environment.'

Protocol

Adherence to appropriate protocol is another critical factor in maintaining the integrity of aboriginal oral traditions, and in turn aboriginal cultures. Protocol permits a relationship of mutual responsibility and respect between a storyteller and his/her audience to be established and maintained. Some protocols, such as asking permission to write down or repeat stories, or to tape record and/or photograph the storyteller, may seem fairly obvious. However, differences between the worldviews held by tourists and aboriginals may make it difficult for visitors to identify and practise the attitudes and behaviours that aboriginal people believe constitute respectful treatment. This situation is complicated by the likelihood that tourists' will not be provided with a clearly articulated list of 'dos' and 'don'ts' prior to being invited to listen to an aboriginal story. Nor is it likely that guides who receive permission to share aboriginal stories with tourists will be instructed on their responsibilities as a storyteller. Contemplation about the worldviews elaborated earlier as well as careful reading of accounts written by other individuals about interactions with aboriginal peoples may provide some tentative guidelines.

Ross (1992) recounts how an aboriginal speaker discussed past treatment of aboriginal people by whites, and how the audience felt uncomfortable and defensive, even though they did not disagree with what was being said. Ross was surprised at the man's approach, because he 'was used to Elders who were able to make these kinds of points while at the same time keeping everyone present at ease and receptive'. Later the man's older brother both acknowledged and apologized for this breach of protocol in a very subtle but effective way:

> Finally he said, 'He is a young man yet.' In those six words he had, I am
> certain, offered an apology for the discomfort his brother had caused me. He
> had also asked me to be patient with him. It was his way of saying that the
> younger man had not yet leaned how to speak with care and respect, but
> that I shouldn't write him off (Ross, 1992).

Unsure of what protocol he should follow, Ross responded by replying with
a simple nod, smile and a quiet 'um-hmm', because he had enough experience interacting with aboriginal people to know that a flood of words is
unnecessary. 'As every Native [can] tell you (but won't), white men spend
too much time talking' (Ross, 1992: 27).

It is possible to infer from Ross's last comment that it would be appropriate for tourists who listen to aboriginal stories to refrain from asking questions to show interest. Instead, they could convey their enthusiasm and quest
for understanding by actively, but quietly listening. Operators can assist their
clients in adhering to this protocol through careful logistical planning of the
tour itself. The nature of aboriginal storytelling frequently involves lengthy
accounts of situations and a great deal of repetition. One of the reasons for
this is because 'there is hope that in multiplying the glimpses and using the
multiplicity of accumulated glimpses, we may obtain more reliable and
composite representations . . .' (Bahr, 1994: 57). Because of this, the summa-
rizing of stories will deeply affect the message, and so it should only be done
with caution and permission. Tourists will not be able to give their full
attention and respect to the oral histories, thereby forming more accurate
perceptions of native culture if the operator has scheduled the group's
activities too tightly.

The Maori have developed very formalized and elaborate rituals
designed to establish and maintain an appropriate relationship between
hosts and guests. The actions and activities of tourists who experience
Maori culture through 'homestays' are regulated by this well-defined code of
social conduct (Keelan, 1993). Whether similarly detailed protocols govern
the words and behaviour during storyteller and audience interactions is
not clear. However, given the parallels between the worldviews of the
Maori and American/Canadian aboriginal, it is likely that adherence to
protocol is an important element of the storytelling process in Maori culture
as well.

Permission and authority

Museums, galleries, governments and even private businesses now generally accept and respect the position of aboriginal peoples regarding past
appropriation of material culture. In the past, artifacts, artworks, cultural
symbols and other elements of material culture were collected, reproduced
and used without the informed consent of their aboriginal owners. This
breach of trust is beginning to be rectified through repatriation processes,

new aboriginal heritage protection, as well as copyright laws, which are being enacted in many countries around the world. Legally encoded regulations pertaining to publishing, repeating and using non-material elements of aboriginal cultures have yet to be developed. However, it is clear that because of the sacred nature and deep value of aboriginal stories, operators and guides should not share stories with tourists without obtaining permission from the appropriate groups and/or individuals. Carol Bissett, an Aboriginal (Worimi) woman from Nelson Bay, New South Wales, has emphasized that questions pertaining to permission are critical. 'Interpreting Aboriginal culture is about asking for permission and showing respect for Aboriginal culture and traditional owners' (Bissett *et al.*, 1999).

While most aboriginal peoples and (hopefully) tour guides and operators agree that it is imperative to obtain permission to share aboriginal stories, it is not as easy to reach consensus regarding who has the authority to give permission. Although they refer primarily to places and objects, ATSIC makes a very strong and clear statement about authority in its submission to the Joint Parliamentary Committee on Native Title. They state that 'the authority for the significance of areas and objects must rest with indigenous people as only they can make statements about their heritage values' (ATSIC, 1998). Like most policy statements, this one is very broad and does not delve into specific details on the matter of authority. It can be argued that this respect for the authority of indigenous peoples can and should be extended to include intangible elements of culture such as stories.

Participants in a workshop recently held to develop key principles for integrity in Aboriginal ecotourism in Australia do explore and make decisions regarding a wide range of issues associated with authorization. Participants were careful to distinguish between two types of authorities: (i) 'official permission' by national or provincial parks offices, individual landowners and elected Aboriginal councils, and (ii) 'cultural approval' by traditional Aboriginal 'owners', who may be individuals, communities or groups. Understanding who has the authority to give permission to operators and interpreters who wish to share specific stories with visitors is an important factor in ensuring that the cultural integrity contained within oral histories is maintained.

In many cases indigenous people agree that elders are the only individuals who have the authority to give permission to share stories with tourists. Even when it has been agreed that only elders can provide 'cultural authority', the issue becomes even more complex because of the difficulty in establishing who is, and who is not, an elder. For some it is worthwhile to differentiate between an 'elder' and 'a non-traditional owner living in an area, aged around 50 years . . . [and] a 'traditional elder' [who is] one born in that country, a 'knowledge holder', who does not have to be 50 years old' (Bisset *et al.*, 1999). Not all communities will be able to clearly articulate what and who an elder is.

A Nisga'a First Nation Story

Guides to the Nisga'a Memorial Lava Bed Provincial Park in the Nass Valley of Northern British Columbia tell a story about the cause of the volcanic eruption that occurred in the area. The story belongs to the Raven Clan and is as follows:

> From time immemorial, the Nisga'a have always valued the salmon. They believed it to be a sacred gift from the Chief of Heaven. Our ancestors therefore set down taboos regarding the salmon, the first and foremost being: you must not ridicule or abuse the salmon! The year of the eruption a group of boys were catching humpback salmon and putting a slit in the back in which they placed a piece of slate. The youth had been instructed regarding the sacredness of all life and knew that they were going against the teaching of their elders. The boys found it quite amusing to see the salmon swimming with the slate showing above the water. Not long after these boys started to make fun of the salmon, the eruption occurred.
>
> At first it was only big smoke, as if a house were burning up. The fire then began to slide down the mountainside coming very slowly. When the people started to smell it they began to suffocate, their bodies grew stiff. The Gitwinksihlkws on the far side of the river began to dig holes in the ground and bury themselves. The Gitlaxt'aamiks did likewise. A few people were asphyxiated especially at Gitwinksihlkw because this village was lower.[2]

As the Nisga'a story illustrates, storytelling, as an interpretative technique, can be a very engaging and effective way to communicate vital information about values, beliefs and a tragedy that nearly destroyed a culture. Such rich stories create tremendous opportunities to develop and enhance cross-cultural understanding and respect. Yet the issues raised previously must be addressed as well.

The BC Parks/Nisga'a Strategy

The area included in Nisga'a Memorial Lava Bed Park is a special place not only in terms of geology and human history but it is also ' the first park in the BC Parks system which is jointly managed by a First Nation organization and BC Parks. The park is administered by the Skeena District under the direction of the Nisga'a/BC Parks Joint Management Committee' (Copeland, 1995). As is the case in most parks, there are comprehensive policies governing all activities, services and development within its boundaries (see Figs 6.1–6.3).

The volcanic areas sacred to the Nisga'a people have been zoned for restricted access and, to enter into the sensitive areas, tourists must be

---

[2] This account is a product of many versions of the story with the most detailed provided by Eli Gosnell (Ayuukhl Nisga'a Dept, 1992).

Fig. 6.1. Non-material elements of cultural and languages. The language of the Nisga'a gives cultural meaning to special and sacred places in the coastal mountains. Their language is descriptive of their deeply rooted identity with the land. The park interpretive signs carry educational messages about the values, beliefs and legends of the Nisga'a culture.

Fig. 6.2. Entrance sign to the park. The tourist is welcomed in the Nisga'a language at the entrance to further enhance the cultural significance of the protected area they are about to enter.

Fig. 6.3. Nisga'a sacred mountains. From this vantage point, travellers can learn about the legend of Txeemsim (a story of creation) and view Mt Hinkley (Sganism Laxswa), one of the four sacred mountains in the Nisga'a territory. By park policy, guided interpretive walks to the lava cone are restricted and the Nisga'a stories of the eruption are told to the visitors by the descendents of the Raven Clan to whom the stories belong.

accompanied by an official park guide. These guides are contracted to provide visitor services and their services are secured in accordance with the guidelines set out by the joint committee. Today, the official guides are Nisga'a, and as members of the Raven Clan, they have the right to tell the above-referenced story. From personal experience, the author is certain the key issues addressed in the previous sections have been successfully addressed in this approach. While there is no certainty that permission will be sought by unofficial tour guides within the area, the fact that access to the sacred area is restricted encourages others to comply with policies and practices set out for the park. This is part of the policies developed for the area to achieve provincial goals. As Copeland (1995: 9) writes:

> The Park features the rich culture of the Nisga'a people who have lived in their territory . . . since time immemorial. The Park serves as a memorial to over 2,000 Nisga'a, who were killed by the eruption. It is intended that an interpretative center will be constructed within the Park to provide historical, natural, and cultural interpretation and as a place where the Nisga'a people can share their culture with the outside world. A key role of the Nisga'a Memorial Lava Bed Park in British Columbia's system of parks will be to study, investigate, and implement traditional Nisga'a sustainable management approaches and techniques.

Government officials and indigenous people have seldom succeeded in working as closely together, as has been the case with the Nisga'a. However, when traditional societies draw strength from their holistic relationship to the environment and to the spirits present in the landscape, then the government policy-makers perform a critical role. The Nisga'a Memorial Lava Bed Park serves to illustrate what can be achieved when a collaborative process is initiated to ensure that special heritage and cultural meanings are protected. In referencing the role of researchers and policy-makers, Bernbaum (1997) sets out the steps that assist in mitigating the impact that modernization can have on traditional beliefs and practices.

> We need first to identify the groups and individuals for which the mountain or sacred site under consideration is sacred . . . The second step is . . . an examination of pertinent myths, stories, rituals, and other practices . . . The third step is to ascertain the meaning and relevance of the themes at a specific site . . . Consultation with local people entrusted with traditional knowledge about a particular site is essential.

The Province of British Columbia and the Nisga'a have also continued to negotiate on establishing rights to traditional land beyond what is contained in the co-managed park. Nonetheless, the steps outlined previously produced a strategy that would ensure protection for the culturally important areas and the stories that establish the Nisga'a relationship to the spirits of the area.

Conclusion

The five issues associated with storytelling serve as a reminder about the need to protect non-material cultural in dealing with aboriginal tourism and it presents an illustration of the dilemmas and the complexity facing isolated mountain communities. There are diverse stakeholders involved in a tourism phenomenon that is culturally oriented. This chapter presents a specific illustration of storytelling and oral history as basis for strengthening the forum involving a critical dialogue on the concerns raised when non-material culture becomes a tourism resource. The questions are numerous and this chapter barely scratches the surface when it comes to the survival of indigenous communities versus the potential benefits that tourism may bring. The dialogue is an important one and as stated by Davidson (1993, p. vi):

> All around the world, enlightened people anxiously follow the fate of sea turtles, condors, spotted owls, black rhinos, and hundreds of other endangered species. But they forget or never realize that whole peoples can be endangered, too. Before our eyes, human diversity is vanishing, but few seem to notice . . . In almost every country, indigenous peoples, the first people native to their lands, are fighting for their lives, their identities, and a future for their children.

Oral traditions, such as storytelling, are a vital part of aboriginal culture and the messages they convey contribute to the cultural identity of the people to whom the stories belong. The strategies that will permit the tradition of story-telling to reinforce the values and beliefs, in which the tradition is anchored, will vary from place to place. In the case of the Nisga'a, there has been many years of shared decision-making on the co-management of a protected area during the time treaty negotiations have been underway. It would have been commonplace, from a western perspective, to interpret the landscape as a geological feature and as one of the youngest and most accessible volcanic features in British Columbia. However, to do so would ignore the cultural landscape, and the 'wealth of stories related to Nisga'a cosmology . . . would never have been told . . .' (Murtha, 1996: 43).

The consequences of initiatives to co-manage protected areas seem to vary from one jurisdiction to another, but it would appear that if trust and mutual respect are the foundation for the partnership, then co-management should succeed. There are often a variety of factors that yield success in the dialogue and exchanges that must occur across cultural boundaries but a fundamental element is perhaps attitude. As put forth by one partner to the Nisga'a co-management experience:

> Despite sometimes profoundly different cultural environments, there can be common interests in respect for the natural world . . . in sustainability, in sharing knowledge with visitors, in celebrating diversity . . . in employing time-proven resource management techniques.

> . . . Translating the ideals and the enthusiasm into a successful reality
> requires creativity, sensitivity, patience, innovation, and perhaps even imagi-
> native interpretation of rules. A fundamental requirement is a recognition that
> it is not primarily a technical issue but an attitudinal one – how to accommo-
> date two worldviews (Murtha, 1996: 45).

Thus, worldviews can be a beginning point for discussion. One solution to
ensure that tourism is a positive influence in mountain environments, and
with aboriginal culture, certainly involves the attitudes of the guest. Tour
operators can help in creating favourable perceptions of aboriginal tourism
and making travellers more knowledgeable of cultural issues. To paraphrase
Aldo Leopold (1966: 295), responsible tourism is a job of not transporting
visitors 'into lovely country, but of building receptivity into the still unlovely
human mind.' Building receptivity is a personnel responsibility both for the
traveller and for those organizing such tours.

If the cultural encounters that are marketed for tourism are to be beneficial for the indigenous communities that generate the travel, then it is necessary to place the contact between aboriginal and non-aboriginal people in
the context of a cross-cultural experience. It may be logical to require the
tour operators to adopt the ethical standards set for cross-cultural training
and to recognize the special experiences they offer are an 'inherently
transformative form of education which demands of its practitioners the
highest form of professionalism . . . a deep concern for the welfare of their
clients, and ethical behaviour in all aspects of their work' (Paige and Martin,
1996). While many tour leaders may embrace a set of standards prepared to
mitigate the environmental, economic and cultural impacts of tourism
(Ecotourism Society, 1993), the success of translating the core principles and
guidelines into successful practices lies in the future. It may be time to revisit
the guidelines and incorporate ethical standards that are part of the
intercultural training literature.

> What sets worlds in motion is the interplay of differences, their attractions and
> repulsion's. Life is plurality, death is uniformity. By suppressing differences and
> peculiarities, by eliminating different civilizations and cultures, progress weak-
> ens life and favors death, impoverishes and mutilates us. Every culture that
> disappears, diminishes a possibility of life (Octavio Paz).

References

Aboriginal and Torres Strait Islander Commission (ATSIC) (1998) ATSIC Submission
    to the Joint Parliamentary Committee on Native Title and the Aboriginal and
    Torres Strait Islander Land Fund on the Aboriginal and Torres Strait Islander
    Heritage Protection Bill. ATSIC web site: http://www.atsic.gov.au.
Ayuukhl Nisga'a Department (1992) Interviews containing stories related to lava
    beds. Unpublished Monograph. Prince George BC: BC Parks Library.
ATSIC (1997) The true story: The Australian Museum's latest exhibit. In *ATSIC News*
    6(4). ATSIC Web Site: http://www.atsic.gov.au/news/winter97/pate16.htm

Bahr, H.M. (1994) Multiplying glimpses, gleaning genres: a multidisciplinary approach to the study of change among Navajo peoples. *Human Organization* 53 (spring), 53–73.

Bernbaum, E. (1997) *Sacred Mountains of the World.* University of California Press, Berkeley.

Bhawuk, D.P.S. and Triandis, H.C. (1996) The role of culture theory in the study of culture and intercultural training. In: *Handbook of Intercultural Training*, 2nd edn. Sage Publications, New York, pp. 17–34.

Bissett, C., Perry, L. and Zeppel, H. (1999) Land and spirit: Aboriginal eco-tourism in New South Wales. In: *Ecotourism through to the year 2000: Proceedings of the 1997 National Ecotourism Conference.* Ecotourism Association of Australia, Brisbane (in press).

Booth, A.L. and Jacobs, H. (1988) *Environmental Consciousness: Native American Worldviews and Sustainable Natural Resource Management: An Annotated Bibliography.* CPL Bibliography. Council of Planning Libraries, Chicago, p. 214.

Boyd, W.E. and Ward, G.K. (1993) Aboriginal Heritage and Visitor Management. In Michael Hall and Simon McArthur (eds) *Heritage Management in New Zealand and Australia: Visitor Management, Interpretation, and Marketing.* Oxford University Press, Oxford, pp. 103–118.

Commonwealth of Australia (1997) National Aboriginal and Torres Strait Islander Cultural Industry Strategy. ATSIC Web Site: http://www.atsic.gov.au

Copeland, G. (1995) *Anhluut'kwsim Laxmihl Angwinga'asanskwhl Nisga'a (Nisga'a Memorial Lava Bed Park).* Grant Copeland & Associates and BC Parks, Prince George, BC.

Couture, J.E. (1991) Explorations in native knowing. In John W. Friesen (ed.) *The Cultural Maze: Complex Questions on Native Destiny in Western Canada.* Detselig Enterprizes, Calgary, pp. 53–67.

Davidson, A. (1993) *Endangered Peoples.* Sierra Club Books, San Francisco.

Hart, M.A. (1996) Sharing circles: utilizing traditional practise methods for teaching, helping, and supporting. In: O'Meara, S. and West, D.A. (eds) *From Our Eyes: Learning from Indigenous Peoples.* Garamond Press, Toronto, pp. 59–72.

Higgins, B.R. (1996) The global structure of the nature tourism industry: ecotourists, tour operators, and local business. *Journal of Travel Research* xxxv, 2.

Jack, R., Matthew, M. and Matthew, R. (1993) *Shuswap Community Handbook.* Secwepemc Cultural Education Society, Kamloops, BC.

Johnston, B.H. (1992) Foreword. In: Rupert Ross (ed.) *Dancing with a Ghost: Exploring Indian Reality.* Reed Books, Markham, ON, pp. vii–xvi.

Jostad, P. (1994) Cultural perspectives: an alternative view of land management. *Trends* 33, 31–34.

Keelan, N. (1993) Maori heritage: visitor management and interpretation. In: Hall, M. and McArthur, S. (eds) *Heritage Management in New Zealand and Australia: Visitor Management, Interpretation, and Marketing.* Oxford University Press, Oxford, pp. 95–102.

Kleiger, P.C. (1990) Close encounters: 'intimate' tourism in Tibet. *Cultural Survival Quarterly* 14, 38–42.

Leopold, A. (1966) *A Sand County Almanac. With Other Essays on Conservation from Round River.* Oxford University Press, New York.

McDonald, D. and McAvoy, L. (1997) Native Americans and leisure: state of the research and future directions. *Journal of Leisure Research* 29, 145–166.

McLaughlin, H. (1999) *The Ends of our Exploring-Ethical and Scientific Journeys to Remote Places.* Malcolm Lester Books, Toronto.

McDonald, G.F. (1994) *Haida Monumental Art.* UBC Press, Vancouver, p. 215.

Meyer, L.N. and Ramirez, T. (1996) 'Wakinyan Hotan': The inscrutability of Lakota/ Dakota Metaphysics. In: O'Meara, S. and West, D.A. (eds) *From Our Eyes: Learning from Indigenous Peoples.* Garamond Press, Toronto, pp. 89–106.

Murtha, M. (1996) *British Columbia Parks' Partnerships with Aboriginal People. Trends* 33, 40–45.

Norman, W.C., Bauman, E., Toepper, L. and Sirakaya, E. (1997) *Green Evaluation Programme and Compliance of Nature Tour Operators.* http://www.ecotourism. org/res.html.

Northern Territory Tourist Commission (1994) Come share our culture: a guide to Australia's Northern Territory Aboriginal tourist, arts, and crafts. Darwin: Northern Territory Tourist Commission. In: Heather Zeppel (1998a) 'Come Share our Culture': marketing Aboriginal tourism in Australia. *Pacific Tourism Review* 2 (1).

O'Meara, S. and West, D.A. (eds) (1996) *From Our Eyes: Learning from Indigenous Peoples.* Garamond Press, Toronto.

Paige, R.M. and Martin, J.N. (1996) Ethics in intercultural training. In: *Handbook of Intercultural Training,* 2nd edn. SAGE, New York, pp. 35–60.

Pfister, R.E. and Ewert, A.W. (1996) Alternative worldviews and natural resource management: introduction and overview. *Trends* 33, 2–8.

Ross, R. (1992) *Dancing with a Ghost: Exploring Indian Reality.* Reed Books, Markham, ON.

Sweet, J. (1990) The portals of tradition: tourism in the American Southwest. *Cultural Journal Quarterly* 14, 6–8.

Tayor, J.B. (1997) Umorrduk exposes glimpse of aboriginal culture. In *ATSIC News* 6 (3). ATSIC Web Site: http://www.atsic.gov.au.

The Ecotourism Society (1993) *Ecotourism Guidelines for Nature Tour Operators.* Ecotourism Society, North Bennington, Vermont.

Wa, G. (1992) *The Spirit in the Land: The Opening Statement of the Gitksan and Wet'suwet'en Hereditary Chiefs in the Supreme Court of British Columbia.* Reflections, Gabriola, BC.

Walle, A.H. (1993) Tourism and traditional people: forging equitable strategies. *Journal of Travel Research (Winter),* 14–19.

Wood, D. (1991) Earth values of the native American people: a comparison of cultures. Unpublished Ph.D. Dissertation. California School of Professional Psychology, Fresno.

Zeppel, H. (1998a) 'Come Share our Culture': marketing Aboriginal tourism in Australia. *Pacific Tourism Review* 2(1).

The Economic Impacts of Different Types of Tourism in Upland and Mountain Areas of Europe

7

Patrick Snowdon, Bill Slee and Helen Farr

Department of Agriculture, University of Aberdeen, 581 King Street, Aberdeen AB24 5UA, UK

Introduction

The geography of Europe is characterized by a wide variety of upland and mountain areas, ranging from plateaux to highly dissected mountain ranges of varying geological age. These include Mediterranean ranges in southern countries such as Spain and Greece, maritime ranges in the Alps and Pyrenees, continental ranges in the Carpathians of central Europe, to sub-arctic and western temperate ranges in northwestern countries such as Scotland and Norway.

The variable topography of Europe's uplands and mountains has partially sheltered a rich diversity of cultural and environmental qualities from economic and political forces, which have wrought greater changes in many lowland areas. These qualities represent a rich resource base for the tourism industry. However, these mountain areas are also highly susceptible to inappropriate forms of tourism development, which may undermine rather than sustain the traditions and well-being of their populations and threaten the quality of the natural environment.

This chapter provides an analysis of the economic impacts of different types of tourism development in upland rural areas of Europe. Its empirical content is based on recent research carried out in Portugal, France and the UK, and funded by the European Commission (EC), which compared the economic impacts of 'hard' tourism (large-scale, capital-intensive developments) with 'soft' tourism (small-scale, land-based enterprises). It discusses the role of tourism activity in the context of rural development policy, and considers the significance for tourism development of both locally specific factors, and wider economic and political changes that are reshaping the socio-economic fabric of rural areas of Europe.

Tourism and Development in Mountain Areas of Europe

Most mountain areas of Europe are predominantly rural, and many have
been subject to significant changes in their social and economic structures
in recent decades. Declining agricultural employment and a growth in
demand for services associated with the countryside (e.g. recreation and
tourism activities) have encouraged rural–urban and urban–rural migrations
and a growing emphasis by policy-makers on employment provision in the
tertiary sector. Tourism has acquired a central position in thinking about the
future of rural, upland and mountain economies across Europe, at a time
when there has been both increasing recognition of these service functions
and growing concern (and demand) for the natural environment. Many
upland and mountain areas are remote and disadvantaged but can, nonetheless, provide specific tourism opportunities due to the high quality of their
natural environments. Such opportunities have been promoted as important
means of arresting further decline in the social fabric (e.g. structure of local
populations) of rural areas.

Within the European Union, which covers much of northern, western
and southern Europe, tourism now supports over seven million jobs, approximately 6% of employment, and in some countries generates up to 18% of
the GDP (Leal, 1996). Although these figures include urban as well as rural
tourism, the proportion of economic activity attributable to rural tourism has
grown substantially as demand has increased for independent holidays in
country areas and for specific market niches, such as heritage and green
tourism.

Rising demand for rural tourism trips and increases in the supply of rural
tourist accommodation have been widespread in Europe. However, the
nature of tourism provision in upland areas of Europe has been very
heterogeneous. Differences in the historical background and evolution of
tourism in France, Portugal and the UK have resulted in major variations in
the conceptualization of tourism and in tourism policy and practice. This
produces significant variations in the socio-economic, cultural and political
contexts in which rural tourism operates in the different countries.

Tourism has been widely advocated as a means of economic restructuring at regional, national and supranational levels (HMSO, 1985; Grolleau,
1988). Recent changes in agricultural and rural policy – including the 1988
reform of the European Union (EU) Structural Funds[1], the 1992 reform of
the Common Agricultural policy (CAP) and the 1994 Uruguay Round
Agreement on Agriculture – have stimulated a more multi-sectoral approach
to rural policies. The EU has actively supported rural tourism since the late
1980s through the reformed Structural Funds and through schemes such as
the LEADER and LIFE Initiatives. Increasing prominence of tourism as a

---

[1] The European Regional Development Fund, the European Social Fund and the European
Agricultural Guidance and Guarantee Fund.

policy objective at an EU level has been illustrated through an EC Green Paper on tourism in 1995, and discussions have been held on inserting a chapter on tourism in the Treaty establishing the European Communities. However, the tourism-related effects of the EC's Agenda 2000[2] remain unclear, and concerns exist that it may limit Structural Fund spending on employment measures in the non-agricultural sector and on rural infrastructure provision, particularly in the more prosperous Member States (Agra-Europe, 5 June 1998).

Tourism policy in Europe, at both a national and supra-national level, has tended to be fragmented in nature. The EU does not have a common tourism policy, as it does for agriculture and fisheries, although, in any case, it may be argued that an integrated rural policy would be preferable to one focusing on tourism. In the three countries involved in this study (France, Portugal and the UK), national governments, public and private organizations have given increased support to tourism as a development tool in rural areas. However, in all three countries, there are numerous and diverse institutions involved in rural tourism. Institutional support has tended to be fragmented, resulting in considerable overlapping and confusion of responsibilities between agencies. The respective governments and many other institutions continue to regard rural tourism as a relatively unimportant sector of the tourism industry. Rural tourism has often been weakly represented in tourism strategies and policies, with inadequate coordination between the visions of central government and the needs of rural areas.

Since the late 1980s, interest has grown in styles of tourism, which are seen as more environmentally, socially and culturally sensitive than mass tourism. A variety of terms were used to describe these alternative types of tourism including 'soft', 'green', 'responsible' and 'sustainable', although these terms, while promoting a broadly common ethos, should not be regarded as synonymous. In some cases, these alternative models focused on ecological sensitivity (Hunter and Green, 1995), while in others priority was given to socio-cultural impacts on local communities (Lane, 1994). However, despite the importance of these alternative types of tourism in a rural, mountain development context, such models have not been subject to economic analyses.

Wider development policies, which have undergone major changes in recent decades, are also important in an understanding of the development of mountain tourism, as many upland areas have been classified as economically disadvantaged and have therefore been the object of a range of policy assistance. Development policies in Europe in the 1960s and 1970s were characterized by a largely top-down approach through which development was often promoted through growth nodes (an exogenous approach). However, since the early 1980s, development thinking has shifted towards a

---

[2] Agenda 2000, introduced in July 1997, sets out the EC's proposals for agricultural and rural policy beyond the year 2000.

more endogenous approach founded on locally based, bottom-up forms of development. This was evident in a number of action research studies in the early 1980s, which promoted the theme of integrated rural development, including the Peak District Project in England (see Parker, 1984), and three EU-supported pilot Integrated Development Programmes in the Western Isles of Scotland, Luxembourg and France.

The locally based approach to development has perhaps been best exemplified by the EC's LEADER[3] Initiative, which has supported tourism-related projects in many mountainous areas across Europe. LEADER is administered through Local Action Groups (LAGs) and partly funds innovative approaches to development in disadvantaged rural areas. The initiative has sought to foster local entrepreneurship and is based on an ethos that development actions should respect and enhance the socio-economic, cultural and environmental distinctiveness of rural areas. Its focus has been to stimulate appropriate *processes* of development, rather than simply consider the *product* of interventions.

The European Commission (EC) has been a major force in formulating and implementing policies affecting mountain areas of Europe. Enlargements to the European Community, and more recently the European Union,[4] and the introduction of a Single European Market in 1987, underlined the need for policy assistance to reduce regional socio-economic disparities and to promote economic and political cohesion. Since the mid 1980s, the EC has injected large amounts of aid through its three Structural Funds into regional economies in Europe on a range of development priorities, including infrastructure, business development, the environment, primary industries, tourism, community development and training.

In addition to EC-related development actions, there has been increasing evidence of more integrated approaches to development affecting mountain areas in individual countries in Europe. In the three countries studied in this chapter, this is illustrated in the emergence of partnership arrangements between institutions. Partnerships have been formed at local, regional and national levels within the public, private and voluntary sectors in order to coordinate the resources and actions of different agencies and actors in policy design and implementation. In some instances, they have also enabled the participation of local communities in the development process.

---

[3] LEADER is a French acronym: 'Liaisons entre actions de developement de l'économie rurale'.

[4] The European Union was created by the 1991 Maastricht Treaty, although the commitment to such a union was first made by Member States governments approximately 20 years earlier. The term 'European Community', is a separate entity within the European Union, and denotes the European Coal and Steel Community (Treaty of Paris 1951), the European Economic Community (the EEC of 'Common Market'; Treaty of Rome 1957), and the European Atomic Energy Community (Treaty of Rome, known as the Euratom or EAEC Treaty, 1957).

Moves towards more integrated and locally based approaches to development in rural areas have encountered some resistance. For example, a set of principles agreed at an EC-sponsored conference at Cork (in Ireland) in 1995, were dismissed at a subsequent EU summit of Member States. Nevertheless, there is widespread recognition across Europe of the need to reform agricultural and rural policy in order to reduce budgets, enhance the rural environment, and encourage economic diversity and resilience in rural areas.

The Economic Analysis of Tourism Impacts

The analysis of the economic impacts of tourism presents considerable challenges to economists. The amorphous nature of the tourism industry creates major difficulties in defining what constitutes tourist activity and what types of enterprise should be considered as tourism businesses (Smith, 1989).

On the demand side, tourists are considered in this analysis to comprise holiday-makers and people on business trips staying overnight away from their normal place of residence. On the supply side, the tourism industry consists of a core of businesses that are wholly dependent on tourists for their income and a very wide range of businesses for which tourism provides part of their income. The structure of the latter group varies geographically. Some businesses (e.g. garages) may be totally dependent on the resident population in some areas and largely dependent on tourists in other regions. Thus, it is not possible to define the boundaries of tourist activity by the type of industry, as would be the case in some other types of economic activity.

Many mountain areas are characterized by fragile economies. This fragility derives from various factors including over-dependence on a single industry, weakly competitive firms, and remoteness from suppliers and markets. An important area of investigation concerning the role of tourism in the development of such areas – particularly from a policy perspective – is the identification of types of tourism development that are most beneficial to local economies, particularly in generating sustainable incomes and employment.

A widely used technique for identifying the economic impacts of tourist spending on income and employment is input–output (I-O) analysis, which enables the estimation of income and employment multiplier effects of economic activity in different sectors. Multiplier effects of tourist spending can be sub-divided into direct, indirect and induced impacts:

1. The *direct* impact is the effect of tourist spending on incomes and employment at businesses where tourists spend money. Direct income effects comprise wages, salaries and profits of employer(s)/employees resident in the local area and any rent payments to local residents. Direct employment effects relate to the ratio between turnover and employment.

2. The *indirect* impact results from successive rounds of local business transactions that are triggered by tourist spending. It calculates the income and employment generated as a result of purchases by tourism businesses from suppliers, and the subsequent purchases by suppliers from other suppliers.

3. The *induced* impact represents the impact on incomes and employment of the spending of income by local residents earned as a result of spending by tourists (i.e. the respending of income earned in tourism businesses and their suppliers).

The direct and indirect impacts are calculated using data on the expenditures and employment of local tourism businesses. Local household expenditure data are used to calculate the induced impacts. All income effects refer to income after the deduction of income and corporation tax and social security payments.

When analysing the economic impacts of tourism at a local level, it is necessary to produce local I-O tables that depict inter-industry transactions in the local economy. This can be achieved by 'localizing' national I-O tables using techniques such as GRIT (Generated Regional Input–Output Tables). Such techniques cannot substitute – in terms of accuracy – for bespoke I-O tables of a local economy created through business surveys of inter-industry transactions at a local level. However, the cost of the latter option is normally prohibitive. A compromise – in terms of accuracy and cost – is to create a partial I-O table of the local economy covering the sectors relevant to tourism. This allows the estimation of direct and indirect effects, after which a traditional Keynsian method is used to calculate the induced effects. This is the approach adopted in this study.

For this approach, three main sets of data are required:

1. Estimation of the amount and distribution of tourist spending between different types of business (e.g. accommodation, food and drink, travel, etc.);
2. Estimation of the allocation of business turnover between different expenditures, signifying linkages within the local economy (e.g. local purchases, income to local owners and employees) and leakages to the external economy (e.g. taxation, imports);
3. Estimation of household expenditure in the local economy, including the destination of that expenditure on different goods and services.

Multipliers are conventionally expressed as ratios of the direct effect : direct and indirect effects in the case of a Type 1 multiplier and of the direct : direct, indirect and induced effects in the case of a Type 2 multiplier. When the object of interest is income and employment creation, it has been argued (e.g. Vaughan, 1994) that the proportional multiplier is a more meaningful way to express multipliers. This is defined as the direct and indirect effects per unit of tourist spending in the case of the Type 1 multiplier and the direct, indirect and induced effects per unit of tourist spending in the case of the Type 2 multiplier. This form of expression was used in this study and is particularly useful for policy-makers and tourism institutions as it illustrates the amount of tourism expenditure required to achieve a given impact on income or employment. Proportional multiplier analysis has been used in a number of studies of tourism since the early 1970s, including Archer (1973), Henderson and Cousins (1975), Vaughan (1988, 1994), and Walker and Vaughan (1992).

The interpretation of multipliers requires particular care in two ways. First, they do not indicate the actual value of tourism to the local economy. This requires data on the multiplicand – i.e. the total value of tourist spending in the area – which determines the absolute impact of tourism activity on the local economy. Thus, multipliers in one sub-sector of tourism accommodation (e.g. bed and breakfast) may be significantly greater than in another (e.g. holiday villages), but a much larger multiplicand in the latter sub-sector (perhaps due to higher numbers of tourists or higher daily expenditure) may result in a greater absolute impact on income and employment in the local area. Second, multiplier results reflect the specific characteristics of a particular local economy. Therefore, results should not be extrapolated from one geographical area to another.

The Research Study

The research described in this chapter used the hard-soft dichotomy to conceptualize different styles of tourism development upon which the subsequent economic analysis was based. The concept of soft tourism emerged in the European Alps in the 1980s, and was strongly advocated by Krippendorf (1987). In the UK, Lane (1994), a prominent proponent of soft tourism, describes it as tourism activity that:

- is embedded within a diverse local economy
- makes use of local products as inputs (crafts, food, etc.)
- employs local people and yields them satisfaction and enhanced self esteem
- does not place unacceptable burdens on the environment
- respects local traditions and ways of life.

Soft tourism typically comprises businesses that are small-scale and locally owned, and based on resources that are distinctive to the local area, such as the natural environment and local products, and that are embedded in the local economy. Examples include farm-based accommodation and local craft and food enterprises. The counterpoint to soft tourism is hard tourism, which is characterized by externally owned large-scale developments, with limited local linkages in an economic, socio-cultural or environmental sense. Such developments may create single industry 'enclave' resorts, highly dependent on tourism for their well-being. Examples in Europe include many large-scale developments in coastal areas and alpine ski resorts, which have undermined local cultures and created negative impacts on the natural environment. The Aviemore Centre in Badenoch and Strathspey is an example of hard tourism in Scotland.

The distinction between 'soft' and 'hard' described here depicts two extreme types of tourism development. In practice, 'soft' and 'hard' should be seen as opposing ends of a continuum along which most tourism businesses display, in varying degrees, both hard and soft characteristics. Table 7.1 depicts this continuum, albeit in a generalized fashion. Clearly, different establishments of the same type (e.g. small hotels) will vary in the extent to which they are hard or soft. The visual impacts of hard and soft tourism enterprises are illustrated in Figs 7.1 and 7.2, which contrast the Aviemore Centre development with a farm accommodation site in the neighbouring area.

The methods used in this study are based on those used in a number of tourism-related partial I-O studies carried out in the UK in the last two decades. They rely on sample-based, labour-intensive interviews with both tourists and tourist-related businesses in order to elicit tourist and firm spending behaviour. These data are then used as inputs into the model to estimate direct, indirect and induced impacts of tourism activity on the local economy.

This study compared the economic impacts arising from tourist spending in the accommodation types that lie at opposite ends of the

Table 7.1. The hard–soft tourism continuum in the accommodation sector.

SOFT TOURISM ⇐ = = = = = = = = = = = = ⇒ HARD TOURISM

Attributes				
Socio-cultural affinities	Strong	Significant	Limited	Weak
Local business linkages	Strong	Significant	Limited	Weak
Ownership and labour	Local	Mainly local	Mainly external	External
Negative environmental effects	Limited	Variable but limited	Variable	Significant
Scale	Small	Small/medium	Medium/large	Large
Product	Locally-specific			Standardized
Example	Farm accommodation	Small hotel/ guesthouse	National hotel chain with regionally specific product	National/ International hotel chain

Fig. 7.1. Hard tourism – the Aviemore Centre.

hard–soft continuum, in particular, whether tourist spending in soft tourism accommodation generates higher levels of local and regional income and employment than tourist spending in hard tourism accommodation. The types of hard and soft accommodation examined in the study are shown in Table 7.2.

Earlier studies (e.g. Coppock *et al.*, 1981) have shown that multipliers may be low at a local level but increase substantially at the sub-regional level. Therefore, two levels of geographical analysis were used in this study: a core area (i.e. the selected study area) and an extended area, which covers the area within 25 km of the core area boundary, therefore including important regional service centres.

The research involved extensive fieldwork in six economically disadvantaged regions in France, Portugal and the UK.[5] These are shown in

[5] The project on which this work was based was AIR3-CT-92-0477 and was a collaborative project between the University of Aberdeen, the Institut d'Etude Politique in Grenoble and the University of Trás-os-Montes e Alto Douro in Vila Real.

Fig. 7.3. The areas for study were selected to reflect the diversity of rural tourism provision in Europe, particularly with respect to both the level and style of tourist activity, and were all located in upland or mountain areas.

Fig. 7.2.   Soft tourism: farm accommodation in the Highlands of Scotland.

Table 7.2.   Types of hard and soft tourism accommodation in France, Portugal and the UK.

	Hard accommodation	Soft accommodation
France	All hotels	Gites ruraux, chambre d'hote, fermes auberges, farm camp-sites
Portugal	Hotels and guesthouses (pensões)	All TER[a] accommodation – Turismo de Habitação, Turismo rural, Agroturismo
UK	Hotels with over ten rooms, holiday villages and timeshare developments	Agricultural holdings providing bed and breakfast, self-catering or camping and caravan pitches

[a]TER = Turismo en Espaço Rural, or Tourism in the Countryside.

Two study areas were selected in each country, and were chosen to contrast different levels of provision of hard and soft tourism, and are shown in Table 7.3. Administrative boundaries were used to delimit the study areas,

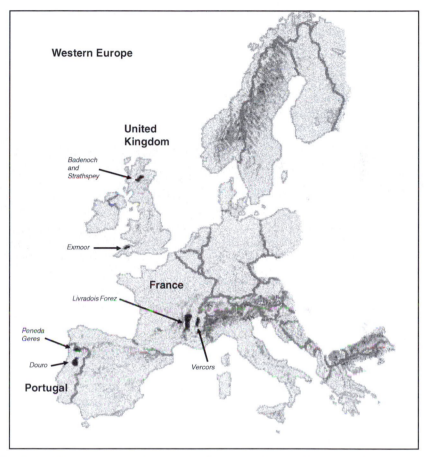

Fig. 7.3. Western Europe showing the locations of the study areas in France, Portugal and the UK.

Table 7.3. Study areas in France, Portugal and the UK.

	France	Portugal	UK
Lightly developed soft tourism	Livradois-Forez	Douro	Badenoch and Strathspey
Well developed soft tourism	Vercors (agrotourism)	Not applicable	Exmoor
Hard tourism	Vercors (ski-resorts)	Peneda-Gerês (Minho)	Badenoch and Strathspey

although it is recognized that these may not define functional economic areas.

The study areas display significant similarities in terms of their physical characteristics and their socio-economic profiles. All lie in upland areas and are designated by the EU as Less Favoured Areas. Their economies, dominated until the recent past by the traditional primary sector, have experienced multiple symptoms of decline, and in recent decades have been peripheral to national development processes. Livestock rearing and milk production are the principal agricultural activities in most areas, although vines and cereals are of particular importance in the Douro and Peneda Gerês respectively. In all areas, pluriactivity is an integral facet of farm household activities. All of the study areas are of high landscape quality and most are designated as national or regional parks.

As shown in Table 7.4, there are also significant differences in the physical size and populations of the study areas. Population densities are more consistent, with the exception of Badenoch and Strathspey, and are substantially below national averages in all areas. The Portuguese areas are continuing to experience depopulation, while in the French and UK areas the principal demographic change in recent years has been in-migration.

Table 7.5 shows the structure of employment in the study areas. Despite significant declines in recent decades, employment in agriculture remains comparatively high in all areas, particularly in Portugal. The incidence of pluriactivity has increased in all areas in the past 20 years. Manufacturing activity comprises mainly small and medium-sized enterprises and is limited in all areas, except Livradois-Forez where indigenous industries and crafts remain important activities. The tertiary sector is the most dynamic in all areas in terms of local employment and provides a wide range of jobs in tourism, commerce and public services.

In all of the study areas, there is great potential for tourism activities to supplement local incomes and provide employment. Opportunities exist for

Table 7.4.   Socio-economic structure of the study areas.

Study area	Population 1991	1981–1991 Population change (%)	Area (km^2)	Population density (per km^2) 1991
Livradois-Forez[a]	133,768	+0.7	3053	44
Vercors[a]	29,875	+6.4	1300	23
Peneda Gerês	37,800	−16.9	700	54
Douro	145,000	−8.4	2000	58
Badenoch & Strathspey	11,008	+13.5	2291	5
Exmoor	10,494	+4.0	265	40

Source: University of Aberdeen *et al.* (1994).
[a]1990 figures, and 1982–1990 for Population change.

Table 7.5. Structure of employment in the study areas (%) 1991 (unless stated).

Study area	Primary	Secondary	Tertiary
Livradois-Forez	22	64	14
Vercors	19	32	48
Peneda Gerês (1981)	68	16	14
Douro (1981)	50	20	30
Badenoch & Strathspey	8	10	80
Exmoor	24	11	65

Source: University of Aberdeen *et al.* (1994).

tourist development linked to enjoyment of the natural environment, local crafts and gastronomy, and historic and architectural assets.

Fieldwork for the study took place in the latter half of 1994 and early 1995. Data were collected both through 'face-to-face' interviews and self-completion questionnaires conducted by the research teams employed on the project in the three countries.

Data on the amount and destination of tourist spending were gathered through surveys of tourists staying in hard and soft accommodation. Data on business expenditures were collected through surveys of tourism businesses in the study areas and their suppliers in both the study areas and the extended study areas.

Tourist surveys

Tourist surveys were held in at least 50% of the total population of hard and soft tourism accommodation establishments in the study areas. The precise types of tourist accommodation defined as hard and soft varied between countries, reflecting the different types of accommodation provision available in France, Portugal and the UK (see Table 7.1). Interviews were conducted on every day of the week to eliminate bias from daily variations in tourist spending.

Quota sampling was used to ensure that adequate sample sizes were obtained (for each tourist sub-group) to give statistically significant results. A comparable number of questionnaires was gathered from tourists staying at soft and hard tourism accommodation, except in Badenoch and Strathspey where low numbers of tourists at farm bed and breakfast and self-catering establishments reduced the sample size of tourists in these accommodation types.

Following completion of the survey, a weighting procedure was applied to the data to ensure that the number of bednights covered by questionnaires in each accommodation type was representative of the number of bednights sold in each accommodation type during the period of the survey. This removed bias, which might result from the gathering of a disproportionate number of bednights from any particular accommodation provider.

Business surveys

In each country, the following stratification of businesses was adopted for the business survey.

- hard tourist accommodation
- soft tourist accommodation
- other businesses benefiting directly from tourist spending
- suppliers to these businesses.

The accommodation categories were further stratified into different types of accommodation (e.g. bed and breakfast and self-catering) and different sizes of accommodation (e.g. large, medium and small hotels). At least 50% of the accommodation businesses in the hard and soft sectors were interviewed.

Businesses in the third category included a diverse range of businesses that receive tourist spending; for example, restaurants, cafes, shops, art and craft centres, visitor attractions and public sector facilities. The population base of businesses was obtained from local databases and business directories provided by local authorities, and a random selection of ten businesses was made from each business group.

The fourth category of businesses included wholesalers, building contractors, business support services and office suppliers; five businesses were randomly selected from each sub-group. The population base of suppliers was obtained during interviews with the accommodation providers and the other businesses benefiting directly from tourism, and included businesses within the 'extended area' to allow the exploration of business linkages within the regional economy.

In some cases, there were small numbers of enterprises in certain groups. In such situations, the aim was to interview two-thirds of all firms in that group. The size of the business survey samples is shown in Table 7.6.

The response rate to the detailed business questionnaire varied considerably from 30 to 100% between business types and study areas. The overall response rate for a country was highest in the UK at 89%, where business owners and managers appeared less reluctant to provide sensitive financial information. This contrasts favourably with the 38% response rate of a recent Scottish tourism study (Surrey Research Group, 1993).

A model of the tourist sector of the local and regional economies based on partial I-O analysis was constructed, which yielded a wide range of results relating to the overall economic impacts of spending of soft and hard tourists, as defined by accommodation sectors used. The results of the research are presented in Tables 7.7–7.9. The soft tourist sector generated higher local income multipliers than the hard tourism sector in four out of six areas (see Table 7.7). This was most pronounced in Livradois-Forez and Badenoch and Strathspey, respectively, where soft tourism generated 77 and 36% more local income per unit of tourist spending than hard tourism. In relation to employment, soft tourism generated higher employment multipliers than hard tourism in five out of six areas (see Table 7.8), particularly in Livradois-Forez and the two Portuguese study areas.

The finding that soft tourism does not outperform hard tourism in all areas may be due to the types/styles of soft and hard tourism found in some local economies. For example, in Douro, many soft businesses retained social links with Oporto and consequently obtained supplies from outside the area, thereby reducing the multiplier effects. The hard tourism sector also produced higher multipliers than soft tourism in Exmoor. This is most likely due to the lack of typical hard tourist accommodation in the area. Most of Exmoor's hotels are small to medium sized and are in many ways characteristic of soft tourism in terms of their ownership and expenditure patterns.

Between 70% and 99% of income and employment effects in all the core study areas, in both hard and soft tourism, accrued as direct effects (see

Table 7.6.   Business survey samples in the six study areas.

Business category	France		Portugal		UK	
	Vercors	L.Forez	Douro	P.Geres	Exmoor	B&S'pey
Hard accommodation	13	15	10	11	16	15
Soft accommodation	12	12	23	14	30	25
Other tourism businesses	16	14	22	18	68	56
Suppliers (core+extended)	11	8	9	13	28	23
Total	52	49	64	56	142	119

Source: authors' survey.

Table 7.7.   Proportional multipliers for hard and soft tourism in the core areas and the core + extended areas.

Region	Core area		Core + extended area	
	Hard tourism	Soft tourism	Hard tourism	Soft tourism
Livradois-Forez	0.31	0.55	0.43	0.60
Vercors	0.30	0.37	0.35	0.40
Douro	0.46	0.40	0.52	0.47
Peneda Gerês	0.45	0.46	0.57	0.59
Badenoch and Strathspey	0.22	0.30	0.30	0.42
Exmoor	0.23	0.21	0.34	0.34

Source: authors' survey.

Table 7.8. Standardized employment (another term for full-time equivalent employment) created in core areas per 100,000 ECU of tourist spending in soft and hard tourism.

	Direct standardized jobs		Total standardized jobs	
Region	Soft tourism	Hard tourism	Soft tourism	Hard tourism
Livradois-Forez	5.6	1.5	6.3	1.9
Vercors	2.8	1.7	3.1	2.0
Douro	9.2	3.7	10.3	4.8
Peneda Gerês	10.2	4.7	12.4	6.7
Badenoch and Strathspey	4.0	2.2	4.8	2.8
Exmoor	2.3	2.1	2.7	2.6

Source: authors' survey.

Table 7.9. Daily expenditure per person in different types of local business by tourists staying in hard and soft tourism accommodation (ECU).

Accommodation type	Daily expenditure	
France	Livradois-Forez	Vercors
Hard	54.58	48.68
Soft	23.78	17.20
Portugal	Douro	Peneda Gerês
Hard	61.06	89.96
Soft	70.55	53.67
UK	Exmoor	Badenoch and S'spey
Hard	54.38	45.34
Soft	20.11	20.35

Source: authors' survey.

Table 7.8 for employment effects). Indirect effects varied significantly between core study areas and were less significant in regions such as the Vercors and Exmoor, which had major commercial centres in their extended areas and where less use was made of local suppliers. Induced effects were low in most study areas, suggesting that there was limited recycling of income within the local economy. Therefore, a large increase in tourist spending would be necessary to have any significant effect on induced income and employment in the area.

At an extended area level, the income generated per unit of expenditure increased by between 10 and 50% (see Table 7.7). This was most evident in Exmoor where the local economy contains few settlements of any size but is strongly linked into the wider regional economy.

Table 7.9 shows that daily tourist spending in hard tourism accommodation is significantly higher than in soft accommodation, except in Douro.[6] Further disaggregation of the results in the UK reveal that small hotels generate the highest levels of daily expenditure of any type of accommodation, and that farm bed and breakfast produces the highest levels of expenditure in the soft sector. These expenditure levels have important effects on the economic impacts of tourist spending. For example, when considering the total (as opposed to proportional) economic impacts of tourist spending, the effect of lower multipliers associated with hard tourism may be offset by higher levels of spending (and, incidentally, higher numbers of tourists).

Discussion and Conclusions

There can be no doubt that different styles of tourism are characterized by different types of economic relationships. These differences are of more than intrinsic interest. They are relevant in policy development because they represent key concerns in the development of alternative policy options, which can be seen to have significantly different economic and wider consequences. They are significant in determining whether tourism is more or less embedded in local economies, which has implications on the economic, social and cultural impacts of tourism.

The choices in determining options for tourism development are by no means simple. Differences of spending between hard tourists and soft tourists, with soft tourists spending substantially less per day in five out of the six case study areas studied in this chapter, means that it is necessary to have larger numbers of soft tourists to deliver a given level of spending in the local economy. Normally, but not universally, the higher level of circulation of spending in local economies (and resulting multiplier effects) compensates for the low level of spending by soft tourists. However, in different parts of Europe, the different characteristics of tourism in local economies result in substantial differences in the 'capture' of economic benefits. In the three EU countries studied, soft tourism normally created higher levels of benefit retention and higher levels of direct, indirect and induced employment per unit tourist spend.

The advocacy of soft tourism on social or environmental grounds can thus be supplemented by its advocacy on economic grounds. However, the processes by which higher levels of soft tourism benefits are realized cannot always be readily replicated. There must be a demand for tourism in the region. Whereas it is possible for hard tourism to develop in rural locations with modest endowments of intrinsic attractions by supplying a full range of

---

[6] The low level of expenditure reflects the fact that on cruise boats on the River Douro the principal component of holiday costs are paid in advance.

facilities, for example, within a holiday village, this is not possible with soft tourism. Further, it is essential that there is a range of suppliers of regional products to meet the demands of tourism providers for inputs, and that there is a pool of local labour willing to work in the tourist sector. In the absence of these suppliers and of a willing labour force, it can be anticipated that the soft businesses will take on many of the economic characteristics of hard tourist businesses.

The compatibility of soft tourism with the development strategies of empowerment and the development of place-specific niche products, supported by a range of local value-added activities, which have been promulgated within the EU over the last decade, is self evident. However, the vision of embedding tourism in local economies is still frustrated by institutional structures which, if not inimical, are often less than supportive of effective integration of local economic development strategies. The replacement of sectoral planning in rural economies with effective integrated spatial planning is far from complete and this has implications on the policy interventions of key agencies.

From a development perspective in upland and mountain areas, it may be legitimate to ask just how far the process of embedded tourism development can be pursued. Although the rapid expansion of supply has been complemented to date by a rapid expansion of demand, there is no guarantee that this will continue. Competition between tourist places is inevitable and with increasing global competition, areas which cannot innovate sufficiently fast, or which have only modest place-specific assets, are likely to experience tourist sector decline. It is necessary for those promoting tourism, whether soft or hard, to be confident of future demand for the range of products and services on offer. There is a danger that an overenthusiastic espousal of tourism could lead to unfilled bedspaces and few of the economic benefits that at least some types of tourism can confer on their recipient communities.

The question of the potential of tourism in different upland areas can be better answered if good economic data are on hand to answer key questions about profitability, demand and local linkages. The research which forms the heart of this chapter begins to explore some of these issues and throws light, for the first time, on the economic characteristics of the different types of tourism in upland and mountain areas of Europe.

Acknowledgement

The authors gratefully acknowledge the assistance of Dr R. Vaughan.

References

Agra-Europe (1998) Will the Structural Fund plans dilute farm reform? *Agra-Europe*, 5 June 1998, Agra-Europe (London) Ltd.

Archer, B.H. (1973) *The Impact of Domestic Tourism*. University of Wales Press, Cardiff.

Coppock, J., Duffield, B. and Vaughan, D.R. (1981) *The Economy of Rural Communities in the National Parks of England and Wales*. Tourism and Recreation Research Unit, University of Edinburgh, Edinburgh, 47, pp. 1–399.

Grolleau, E. (1988) *Rural Heritage and Tourism in the EEC*. CEC, Brussels.

Henderson, D. and Cousins, L. (1975) *The Economic Impact of Tourism. A Case Study in Greater Tayside*. Tourism Recreation Research Unit, University of Edinburgh, Edinburgh.

HMSO (1985) *Pleasure, Leisure and Jobs, the Business of Tourism*. London, HMSO.

Krippendorf, J. (1987) *The Holidaymakers: Understanding the Impact of Leisure and Travel*. Butterworth Heinemann, London.

Hunter, C. and Green, H. (1995) *Tourism and the Environment: a Sustainable Relationship?* Routledge, London.

Lane, B. (1994) What is Rural Tourism? *Journal of Sustainable Tourism* 2, 7–21.

Leal, A.C. (1996) *Policy on Rural Tourism in the European Union*. European Parliament Working Document, Division for Agriculture, Fisheries, Forestry and Rural Development, European Parliament, Luxembourg.

Parker, K. (1984) *A Tale of Two Villages: the Story of Integrated Rural Development in the Peak District*. Peak Park Planning Board, Bakewell.

Smith, S.L.J. (1989) *Tourism Analysis: a Handbook*. Longman, Harlow.

Surrey Research Group (1993) *Scottish Tourism Multiplier Study*. Vol. 1, *Main Report*. Scottish Office, Edinburgh.

University of Aberdeen *et al.* (1994) *Agrotourism and Synergistic Pluriactivity – First Progress Report*, report to the European Commission, unpublished.

Vaughan, D.R. (1988) *Tourism in Eastbourne: Visitor Characteristics, the Economic Impact of Visitor Spending and the Businessman's Experience*. Eastbourne Borough Council, Eastbourne.

Vaughan, D.R. (1994) The impact of visitor spending: a review of methodology. In: University of Aberdeen, Institut D'Etudes Politiques de Grenoble, and Universidade de Trás-os-Montes e Alto Douro (eds) *Agrotourism and Synergistic Pluriactivity. First Progress Report*. University of Aberdeen, report to the European Commission, unpublished, pp. 31–90.

Walker, S. and Vaughan, D.R. (1992) *Pennine Way Survey 1990. Use and Economic Impact*. Countryside Commission, Manchester.

The Economic Impacts of Ecotourism: Conflicts and Solutions in Highland Mexico

David Barkin

Department of Economics, Universidad Autónoma Metropolitana, Apartado 23-181, 16000 Xochimilco, Mexico City, Mexico

Introduction

Ecotourism projects must go beyond prevailing notions of 'the overlap between nature tourism and sustainable tourism'[1] to encompass the social dimensions of productive organization and environmental conservation. Ecotourism must do more than simply create a series of activities to attract visitors. Not only must it offer an opportunity to interact with nature in such a way as to make it possible to preserve or enhance the special qualities of the site and its flora and fauna, it must also allow local inhabitants and future visitors to continue to enjoy these qualities. If ecotourism is to be part of a successful strategy for promoting sustainability, it must incorporate other complementary activities that produce basic needs for the local population, as well as tourism goods and services. There is a need, in other words, to create a diversified economy and to support an effective social and political organization so that all of the local inhabitants might enjoy a sustainable standard of living. This is a particular concern in fragile mountain environments where already marginalized groups of people often become even more marginalized when ecological missions taken up by lowland policy-makers and corporations come into play.

A close study of ecotourism in mountain regions offers many opportunities to reflect on the importance of sustainability in these environments, and

---

[1] A definition offered by a leading scholarly participant in the discussions of the theme, Kreg Lindberg, of Charles Sturt University in Australia, in the Internet discussion group 'Green-travel' (@igc.apc.org) on 14 March 1996. He adds: 'because 'true' ecotourism (i.e. verifiably sustainable nature tourism) is comparatively rare, perhaps we are left with ecotourism as a goal.'

the possibilities of implementing approaches that move us in a new direction. But it also suggests that there are significant obstacles preventing a potential cornucopia from benefiting mountain people. Overcoming these obstacles requires more than well-intentioned policies; it requires a new correlation of social forces, a move towards broad-based democratic participation in all aspects of life, within each country and in the concert of nations. Strategies to face these challenges must respond to the dual challenges of insulating these communities from further encroachment and assuring their viability.

Unfortunately, these obstacles are an inseparable part of the world system, a system of increasing duality, polarized between the rich and poor – nations, regions, communities and individuals. A small number of nations dominate the global power structure, guiding production and determining welfare levels. The remaining nations compete among themselves to offer lucrative conditions that will entice the corporate and financial powers to locate their enterprises and monies within their boundaries. Similarly, regions and communities within nations engage in self-destructive forms of bargaining (compromising the welfare of their workers and the building of their own infrastructure) in an attempt to outbid each other for the fruits of global growth. The regions unable to attract investment suffer the ignoble fate of losers in a permanent economic Olympic, condemned to oblivion on the world stage, their populations doomed to marginality and permanent poverty. Ecotourism planners often find themselves caught up in this vicious circle, feeling compelled to concede on key issues of environmental conservation and social welfare when negotiating with outside contractors who are attempting to obtain the most profitable conditions for their corporate directors.

Sustainability is not possible as long as the expansion of capital increases the ranks of the poor and impedes their access to the resources needed for mere survival and for their participation in environmental maintenance. Capitalism no longer needs growing armies of unemployed to ensure low wages, nor does it need to control vast areas to secure regular access to the raw materials and primary products for its productive machine. Today the world market and the institutions of global finance do the job of imperial armies much more thoroughly. The increase in indebtedness of poor countries obliges them to implement structural adjustment programmes that systematically force wages down for their workers and indiscriminately open national frontiers to international trade and investment. In their desperate search for exports to service their debt, countries throughout the Third World find their local industries being destroyed by competition from well-financed international consortia, dismembering national economies, denationalizing their most productive enterprises, and mining their own natural resources. As a result, people are uprooted from their traditional homes and the ecosystems they once cared for with great pride are devastated. This productive and human destruction is accompanied by environmental disasters, caused by the excesses of unbridled production and consumption that leave treasure troves of resources unprotected and urban centres functioning under clouds of poisonous gases while discharging torrents of contaminated water into neighbouring watersheds. Profound changes are required to facilitate a strategy of sustainable development, a strategy that encourages people to rebuild their rural societies, produce goods and services in a sustainable fashion and expand the environmental stewardship services they have always provided.[2]

Research shows that when given the chance and access to resources, the poor are more likely than other groups to engage in direct action to protect and improve the environment (Toledo, forthcoming). From this perspective, an alternative development model requires new ways to encourage the direct participation of peasant and indigenous communities. Such a model would offer a programme for creating jobs in rural areas in order to increase incomes and improve living standards. By proposing policies that encourage and safeguard rural producers in their efforts to become once again a vibrant and viable social and productive force, this chapter attempts to add another dimension to our understanding of the complex process of promoting sustainability.

Although ecotourism is an ideal economic activity for promoting both sustainability and development, it cannot be successful in isolation. Such an activity must be actively integrated into a broader institutional nexus in which diversified production and social organization are reinforced. There are too many examples of cases in which the region and the people who husband the resources have been damaged, sometimes irreparably, by people purporting to be promoting ecotourism. This chapter examines the relationship between these goals and finish by proposing specific approaches to ensure that ecotourism will contribute to improving general well-being.

The Monarch Butterfly: Changing Fortunes in its Winter Home

The 5000 mile trek of the Monarch butterfly between Canada and Mexico has come to symbolize the bridge forging the three nations of North America into a single trading bloc. The phenomenon of the overwintering of the Monarch butterfly was 'discovered' some 25 years ago (1974–1976) when researchers from the University of Florida finally traced its flight path from Canada. Of course, their presence was well known to local residents and to a broader segment of the population in the Sierra Madre of west-central Mexico from time immemorial. At least one curious Mexican peasant

---

[2] For a fuller analysis of this approach to sustainability, see Barkin (1998a,b).

followed them from Canada, as part of his own return journey from his job as war-time guest-worker in the early 1950s. But with the publication of the details of the journey in *National Geographic* (Urquhart, 1976), its social and economic significance altered conditions in the region (Chapela and Barkin, 1995).

Fig. 8.1. Monarch butterfly in the Reserve, Michoacan, Mexico (photo © Jürgen Hoth).

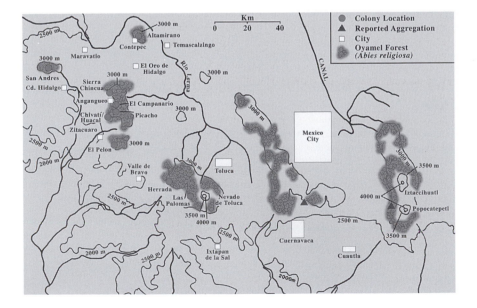

Once announced to the world, the spectacle of the wintering lepidoptera attracted visitors in droves. A special biosphere reserve was created in 1986 to offer this winged caller some degree of protection from the ravages of encroachment by human activities. The World Wildlife Fund supported the Reserve through a grant to a nascent Mexican environmental non-governmental organization (NGO), which was founded by a group of concerned but poorly informed businessmen. The NGO did not undertake any prior consultation with local communities but obtained the concession to manage the Reserve, producing a deficient programme based on a paternalistic attitude towards the people and a miserly strategy of corporate environmentalism. No compensation was offered for the reclassification of the lands nor was any consideration directed toward creating alternative productive opportunities that might have contributed to their earning a livelihood elsewhere in ways that would not degrade or deforest the region. Quality facilities were not constructed and the day-to-day activities were sub-contracted to just one of the dozens of communities in the area, offering

Fig. 8.2. Milkweed, ambrosia of the Monarchs, grows plentifully in the Reserve (photo © Jürgen Hoth).

Fig. 8.3.   Children sell Monarch theme items and are becoming active protectors in the Reserve (photo © Jürgen Hoth).

jobs to but 80 of the thousands of people who needed jobs. The NGO barely tolerated the initiative of community members to operate make-shift stands offering souvenirs and light meals.

In spite of efforts to impose a 'low-profile' on the phenomenon of the nesting butterflies, tourism grew rapidly. The visitors stream exploded during the following years, from about 25,000 people a season to some 250,000 in the 1998–1999 season. These visitors came from other parts of Mexico to observe the Monarchs during their 4-month visit, creating a human tidal wave that now virtually swamps the region at the same time every year. Foreign tourists still make up an insignificant proportion, certainly less than 5% of the total visitor population, and yet international concern for the welfare of the Monarchs has mounted, along with tensions between various interest groups. Outside groups and interests irrupted in the area, staking a privileged claim on fast solutions to local problems. In 1997, ecologists went so far as to propose buying the local peasants' lands and moving them out, as the only viable way to protect the butterfly's habitat (Aridjis and Brower, 1996). They did not, however, give any consideration to what thousands of families might do instead or the impact these families might have on other regions if forced to migrate.

With the establishment of the Monarch Reserve came dramatic changes to the lives of the people living in and around the Reserve, people who trace their origins back hundreds of years. After the conquest, the indigenous population intermingled with settlers early in the Colonial period, transforming the region into a typical peasant society, organized into more than 50 communities dispersed throughout the highland plateau. At the turn of the century, they actively participated in the revolutionary struggles and were rewarded with communal titles to the dense forests, previously controlled by descendants of the colonial aristocracy. The villages evolved into prosperous rural economies, with a diversified production system that combined the cutting of timber with low-intensity farming. This combination assured the supplies that met their needs: the basic crops for their diet (maize and beans) as well as artisanal pottery and furniture to complement sales of logs.

Despite the hardships that the Reserve brought to the local communities, the region's problems and those of the communities cannot be attributed solely to the Reserve. Many are simply local manifestations of the larger crises of Mexican society, making it difficult for poor rural producers to survive by continuing their traditional activities. Orthodox models of local development have proven inoperative, because the region is ill equipped to compete with nearby areas to generate productive modern employment opportunities. Official policies that discourage peasant agriculture and local systems of control by economic élites and political bosses have long been an important part of the local scene, predating the newfound fame of the winged visitors. Industrial demand for new sources of pulp has created a thriving illegal, but tacitly acknowledged, market for wood that many impoverished families have supplied. This, in turn, has generated pressures on the forests and has caused social conflict, pitting neighbours against each other. In spite of a heightened consciousness of the benefits that butterfly tourism can potentially bring and an explicit commitment by communal authorities to support conservation and protection measures, many peasants are violating the logging ban in order to earn a little extra money. Just as troublesome, however, is the present institutional impasse, which denies local communities of both the resources and the autonomy for the management of their lands, and thereby prevents them from implementing the resource conservation practices that everyone recognizes as being essential for the health of the ecosystem and its people. Thus, the unbridled expansion of 'ecotourism' and the appropriation of the spoils by a very small group of outsiders have further compounded the problems of social polarization and environmental decay.

At the beginning of the 21st century, then, the communities find themselves at a complex crossroads. Shorn of their traditional sources of income, by the prohibition or severe restriction on traditional forestry activities with the creation of the Monarch Reserve, and with no recourse to agriculture and artisan production that have become unprofitable, traditional leaders and institutions are also being ignored or frankly undermined. Outside interests (paper companies, tourist agencies and regional power brokers) are exploiting the void created by the erosion of local community pillars. As a result, many people must leave to support their families, who remain in their communities to maintain the elements of the traditional society that are still

Fig. 8.4.   Forests within the Reserve suggest opportunities for agroforestry as a supplementary income-earner to tourism (photo © Jürgen Hoth).

so important. Migrating in search of jobs elsewhere, these people suffer the ignominy of poor pay as well as unhealthy work conditions in the nearby towns or in Mexico City. They often earn barely enough to allow their families to continue living in their communities. Some venture further, assuming the risks of crossing the border with the USA, with hopes for better pay.

The Plight of Ecotourism and the Search for Alternatives

With the expansion of the North American Free Trade Agreement (NAFTA), the region has become the centre of a political maelstrom. The Monarch (*Dannaus plexippus*) was adopted as the symbol of the process of integration and environmental concern by the environment ministries in all three countries, along with pious declarations of concern for the well-being of all involved. The international Model Forests Project selected the region for special attention and the North American Commission on Environment Cooperation convened an international symposium to confront the challenge (NACEC, 1999). Aside from a number of small community-run projects that siphon off small numbers of tourists from the principal sites during the winter months, no credible alternative has emerged for this region because of the shortsightedness of the planning and implementation process. Many of the local managers of the state and federal agencies responsible for operating the reserve are cognizant of the contradictions, but are without the authority, skills or resources to propose realistic alternatives. As a result, they have become the target of acerbic attacks from within the regions and have been charged with incompetence or corruption from without.

With so much international attention, years of experience with conflict, and hoards of 'experts' offering their frequently contradictory and almost invariably unrealistic solutions, it is little wonder that the communities are incredulous. The peasant communities do not have the resources to construct their own alternative. Nor can they afford to take the risks and make the sacrifices required to initiate a long-term process of building new enterprises and reconstructing the diversified resource-based productive structure that would be required successfully to incorporate this short-term avalanche of tourists into the region. No group is seriously considering the possibility of diversification, so that people from Mexico City and Guadalajara might enjoy the region's natural beauty and cultural variety during their traditional vacation periods. Although complementary, non-tourist related projects are essential for any tourist programme to become a successful link in a regional development programme, none of the outside agencies have shown any interest in a more ambitious programme.

Bureaucratic imposition, outside control, poor planning and lack of organization have fuelled a debilitating competitive struggle among the communities. Yet, the principal problem facing the region at this moment is the lack of understanding by the outside agencies charged with managing the Reserve of the need for initiating a broad variety of complementary productive activities to create employment that will allow the 65,000 people in the region to improve their quality of life while also exploiting the forest in a more sustainable way. As long as the corrective measures are focused exclusively on the minuscule areas defined as sanctuaries, they will only deepen the social chasm and environmental decline generated by limited opportunities and self-interested tourist developers from outside.

A new strategy requires re-examining the resource base so that agroforestry and other forms of cultivation and gathering of wild products might provide a basis for forging a new vision for the regional economy. At the heart of the problem is the limited conception of the region as a passive receiving area for the butterflies and their visitors during the winter months. Any alternative would redefine the region to include a larger area where new small-scale agro-industries would induce a demand for agricultural and agroforestry products and where communities could offer services to 30 million Mexicans who are anxiously searching for attractive, healthy, affordable recreation and vacation spots (Barkin, 1999a).

Tourism services themselves must be diversified, in both time and space, to accommodate a broader base of visitors for longer stays that also extend the region's attractiveness beyond the 4-month period of the Monarchs' visit (Chapela and Barkin, 1995). To implement more comprehensive production strategies, including a range of new activities, additional information about opportunities and markets must be disseminated, as well as mechanisms to channel available resources more effectively. Local organizations must create structures to institutionalize cooperation, constructed on the basis of broad-based effective participation. This is the route to creating a strategy of autonomous local development in which ecotourism, based on the wonderful spectacle of the Monarch butterfly, would contribute to an overall strategy of sustainability.

Although all agree that any alternative will have to consider the needs of people in more than 50 communities, few are cognizant of its cost, given the years of neglect and destruction that the communities have suffered. This is largely due to lack of infrastructure coupled with the communities' desire to maintain traditional forms of social organization and production. There are groups attempting to promote an alternative, more balanced programme of year-round tourism. Among them, a local confederation of communities (*Alianza de Ejidos*) has begun to play an important role in creating new opportunities to replace the unravelling economic system. To be successful, however, such a programme requires a diversified regional resource management scheme, including recreational facilities, agro-industrial production and a broad-based programme of local investment in small-scale enterprises. Unfortunately, these grassroots initiatives, and the model of small-scale, community-controlled activities they propose, face considerable political opposition from local power hierarchies who understand that it might erode their political control of the region's natural and human resource base.

Solutions for Regional Resource Planning

A new approach to regional development is required if the vicious circle of impoverishment and degradation is to be broken. While there is a general recognition that ecotourism can offer more opportunities to the people, it is also clear that without other complementary productive activities that create jobs and income, the people in the region will continue with environmentally destructive activities that also threaten the viability of the fir forests in which the Monarch nests.

The implementation of an ecotourism programme as part of a strategy for autonomous sustainable development requires a series of important advances on a number of different fronts:

1.   There is a need to recognize the local communities as the rightful claimants to speak for and benefit from any programme that protects and exploits the Monarch butterfly. During the years of debate and conflict, it has become apparent that local communities are not only committed to but are also essential in protecting the butterfly habitat. Their involvement in productive projects depends on their access to training, technical assistance, and resources. Yet few people are willing to confront the market's inability to supply the local communities with capital to invest in agro-industrial installations, tourist facilities, hotels and even basic infrastructure. Nor do the analysts consider that these same projects must include mechanisms for strengthening traditional systems of food production and production of other needs. These systems are essential if local structures of community organization and authority are to remain intact and effective. The traditional food and forest products and the community social and political organizations that support them are a fundamental part of any sustainable development and conservation scheme. The social structure and political organization facilitates the application of inherited knowledge to the management of the region's natural resources for the conservation of the habitat that the Monarch butterflies require. Without this support, not only will the habitat suffer, but the communities themselves will continue to be torn from within by conflicts among their members as they desperately seek to survive. This crucial support is needed because at present they are no longer capable of producing even a minimum living for themselves without resorting to predatory practices or receiving remittances from family members who work outside the region.

2. The diversification of productive activities that allows local communities to generate income in a dynamic global market place is essential. The pent-up demand of the Mexican people to know more about their own country creates a rich opportunity for a programme of sustainable tourism, involving the management of natural, social, and cultural resources. By creating a tourist complex and supporting services for environmental management of the region's resources, a wide range of opportunities could be created for significant numbers of people in the region. This would include the identification of non-timber forest activities (agrosilvicultural production) that could complement proposed forest management programmes needed to restore the region's environment. In addition, the region is rich in geothermal energy, some of which is harnessed for electricity generation and for poorly maintained local spas. This energy could be more intensively used for agroindustrial, recreational and medicinal purposes that would generate income and employment, thereby reducing pressures for the direct exploitation of the forest. Unfortunately, the Federal Electricity Commission, which controls the wells, is not sufficiently organized to support these non-traditional energy uses, and the state government has blocked this type of development for its own selfish reasons.

3. There must be a reorganization of tourist services to overcome seasonality and the concentration of control by a few outside operators who bring their clients in without contributing to the maintenance and welfare of the region. Since most Mexicans vacation at periods when the butterflies are not present, it is important to develop mechanisms to attract part of this demand, thereby encouraging year-round tourism as well as greater stability for host groups. The cultural, ethnic and biological diversity as well as the geographical variety offer great opportunities to increase and diversify the range of tourist services, as suggested above, thus allowing for year-round tourism. Such opportunities, if properly implemented, could generate additional sources of financing to pay for the environmental services that are required if the overall programme is to be successful.

4. Finally, some serious consideration should be given to the environmental services generated by this approach. Like the carbon-sequestration bonds being used in the joint implementation schemes in Costa Rica and Bolivia, and more recently in Mexico,[3] the management scheme offered here would improve the health of the ecosystem and the flow of water into the major watershed supplying Mexico City and Guadalajara.[4] Similarly, by reversing the process of deforestation, the programme would also be contributing to reducing greenhouse gases. The collateral benefits should be recognized and be remunerated as part of the programme to protect the region that hosts the Monarch.

It is unlikely that the Mexican government will recognize the potential and significance of the type of tourism proposed here as a mechanism to promote sustainability and rural development. The model of locally controlled, resource-based tourism that caters to a middle-class domestic clientele, is not part of the image of the 'smokestack-free export industry' that tourism authorities cherish so dearly. The government is unprepared to consider this alternative a priority in its own right, much less as an instrument for environmental management and social well-being. There is no place on its neo-liberal agenda for the provision of services to meet the needs for recreation and relaxation of the large majority of urban denizens who cannot aspire to visiting the large scale upper-income tourist developments on which the government is focusing. Such neglect of a valuable, productive and low cost instrument is likely as long as public policy is driven by the service providers organized to respond to the demands of the tour operators who focus their efforts on the most profitable segments of the globalized market (Barkin, 1999b).

---

[3] The growing concern for the problem of global warming, and the commitments made in the Kyoto Protocol to deal with the problem, has promoted a number of countries to oblige local companies to reduce their emissions of 'greenhouse' gases. As an alternative to installing expensive equipment to eliminate these emissions in the first place, or reduce their release into the environment, many comply with the local regulations by purchasing 'carbon-sequestration offsets' from countries in the South that can guarantee certain parts of their forests will not be cut. This apparent 'win–win' solution has been roundly criticized by many concerned with the long-term implications of poor countries 'mortgaging the rights of present and future generations' (Agarwal and Narain, 1998).

[4] Ghimire (1997) examines the potential for mass tourism to promote a sustainable pattern of growth in developing countries. His comprehensive review of recent experience in the Third World presents a sobering evaluation of the obstacles confronting planners seeking to reorient public policy in this direction. Barkin (1999a) offers an evaluation of community-based tourist initiatives in Mexico.

This existing model of tourist service provision is environmentally destructive and contributes to further social polarization. Ironically, it does not even generate the volume of employment and the net earnings of foreign exchange that its promoters claim. There are too many leakages from the system, and the technology generally used is too advanced to deliver significant benefits for local development. We are not suggesting that the government abandon this pattern of tourist development for its international clientele, but rather that there is a need for a critical reconsideration of the present policy of generously subsidizing this strategy with credit and infrastructure so that it can promote a less damaging model of tourist development, in Mexico and elsewhere.

The alternative model proposed here offers an important counter-weight with considerable benefits for rural communities and the Mexican working class. It would contribute substantially to breaking down some of the obstacles to building a more balanced national society. A pro-gramme of socially oriented tourism would open a new model for decentralized development that would respond to the urgent needs of present-day society. If well organized, it could be financed much more readily than the international model and would offer more employment and an inexpensive way to improve the quality of life for both consumers and providers.

It is clear that an initiative for developing this local capacity would be an imaginative and inexpensive way to promote rural sustainable develop-ment in some selected areas of Mexico. The knowledge, skills and capacity exist to implement such a programme. Given the current character of government policies, it would be unreasonable to expect a public sector programme to champion this approach, but with the capacities already in the hands of many communities and intermediate level organizations, such a programme might be promoted by the social sector (e.g. NGOs and community) itself. At present, official policy actually discourages these initiatives.

The analysis confirms a crucial lesson learned in Mexico and elsewhere: these small-scale rural sustainable initiatives must not be stand-alone projects, but rather they must be fully integrated into a broader programme of regional development. Thus, if mass tourism is to emerge in Mexico as part of a strategy for local development and environmental management, it will have to come from the organizations representing the 'popular' sectors of the population and the receiving communities themselves. Therefore, if there were to be any public sector action in this area, the most productive policy would be one to facilitate initiatives by NGOs and intermediate level community organizations already in place.

Conclusion

The people living in the mountains around the Monarch Butterfly Reserve are like their brethren in other mountainous areas. Most are attempting to find a way to create a dignified way of life in a changing world that disdains and impoverishes them, even though global economic forces have no real need for them or their regions. In the face of a multitude of crises, however, increasing numbers of outsiders are beginning to appreciate the qualities that these ecosystems offer to their residents and almost as generously to visitors.

The montagne communities suffer an ignoble fate in today's world economy, and yet they struggle to preserve a way of life, joined by others who offer to help improve conditions. This effort is not simply an altruistic outpouring of goodwill or charity. There is an increasing recognition that these regions make important contributions to improving environmental conditions in the lower reaches. One particularly eloquent publication proclaims them to be the 'water towers for the XXI century' (Liniger *et al.*, 1998). It goes on to elaborate: 'More than half of humanity relies on the fresh water that accumulates in mountains – for drinking, domestic use, irrigation, hydropower, industry and transportation' (Liniger *et al.*, 1998).[5] It would be tragic simply to reduce these communities and their ecosystems to their resource contributions to the globalized sectors of the world economy; this would miss an important facet of their significance to the world today. In the face of cumulating crises of production and social organization, the mountain regions and their people continue to offer alternatives for humanity. But well-meaning pundits may exacerbate the growing pressures threatening these regions, accelerating their integration into a model of production that will destroy their communities and impoverish rather than enrich their people. Fortunately, many rural communities are wiser than these erudite globalized do-gooders; they are strengthening their capacity to resist or modify these outside projects so that they might better serve the needs of their people and their regions. We would do well to begin to hone our own toolboxes and learn from these societies rather than simply to assume that we must transform them.

---

[5] The Monarch Butterfly Reserve is in the principal watershed supplying water to two of the country's largest cities, Mexico City and Guadalajara, as well as to its largest natural lake, Chapala. With the unravelling of the peasant economies, as a result of policies to promote 'rural modernization', impoverished communities throughout the watershed are no longer able to implement the conservation programmes they traditionally undertook. Consequently, the volume of rainwater captured for urban and industrial use is actually declining. An effective resource management plan for the region would also compensate the communities to enable them to once again carry out these conservation activities (Barkin, 1999b).

References

Agarwal, A. and Narain, S. (1998) Politics in the post-Kyoto world. CSE Briefing Paper, Centre for Science and the Environment, New Delhi (http:///www.cseindia.org/).

Aridjis, H. and Brower, L. (1996) Twilight of the Monarchs. *New York Times.* 26 January, op-ed.

Barkin, D. (1998a) Sustainability: the political economy of autonomous development. *Organization and Environment* 11, 5–32.

Barkin, D. (1998b) *Wealth, Poverty and Sustainable Development.* Editorial Jus and Centro de Ecología y Desarrollo, Mexico.

Barkin, D. (1999a) Strengthening domestic tourism in Mexico: challenges and opportunities. In: Ghimire, K. (ed.) *Emerging Mass Tourism in the South.* United Nations Research Institute for Social Development, Geneva.

Barkin, D. (1999b) The production of water in Mexico. In: Whiteford, S. (ed.) *Managing a Sacred Gift: Changing Water Management Strategies in Mexico.* Center for US-Mexico Studies, University of California at San Diego, La Jolla, California.

Chapela, G. and Barkin, D. (1995) *Monarcas y campesinos: una Estrategia de Desarrollo Sustentable para Oriente de Michoacán.* Centro de Ecología y Desarrollo, Mexico.

Ghimire, K. (1997) Emerging mass tourism in the south: reflections on the social opportunities and costs of national and regional tourism in developing countries. Working paper DP 85, United Nations Research Institute for Social Development, Geneva.

Liniger, H., Weingartner, R. and Grosjean, M. (1998) Mountains of the world: water towers for the 21st century. A Contribution to Global Freshwater Management, Mountain Agenda. Institute of Geography, University of Berne, Switzerland.

North American Commission on Environmental Cooperation (1999) *Proceedings of the North American Conference on the Monarch Butterfly.* NACEC, Montreal.

Toledo, V.M. (1999) *Zapata Ecológico: le Rebellión Indígena en Chiapas y el Nacimiento de una Nueva Uptopia.*

Urquhart, F.A. (1976) Found at last: the Monarchs winter home. *National Geographic* 150, 160–173.

Mountain Tourism and Public Policy in Nepal

L. Rory MacLellan, Peter U.C. Dieke and Bhim Kumari Thapa

The Scottish Hotel School, University of Strathclyde, Curran Building, 94 Cathedral Street, Glasgow G4 0LG, UK

Introduction

In the Himalayan areas of Central Asia, mountains are important for a number of reasons. They exemplify what has been called 'the natural infrastructure' of a country (Jenkins, 1997: 53) and, in development terms, they have 'zero opportunity cost' because of their 'marginal cost' relative to the development of other tourist assets. As a significant tourist attraction, mountains could, with proper management, engender economic benefits to the receiving country and society, primarily in the areas of government revenue and employment creation. These benefits stem from 'the fees paid to guides and porters, for government permits to visit the area . . . tourists paying substantial amounts to engage in these activities . . . (or even) mountain villagers' supplies to the tourists' (Inskeep, 1991: 168–169; 248–249).

While there is no doubt that mountains enhance the economic potential of countries, their capacity to confer such benefits might be questioned from a planning perspective. Given the popularity of trekking and mountaineering, a particular planning concern is the sustainability of this type of tourism, particularly with regard to whether mountain tourism is environmentally and socially suitable, and whether it is marketable. There is also concern about the availability of supplies and services – equipment, medical and even observance of safety measures especially in an emergency. All these factors may prompt the following questions: (i) what has been done to minimize these 'areas of concern'? and; (ii) what else needs to be done?

The aim of this chapter is twofold: first to review the comparative advantage of using mountains relative to other tourist assets as instruments of development, and second to consider the problems of implementation that arise in the context of Nepal. The second objective is to highlight strategic policy implications of mountain tourism and the development of mountain regions for tourism. In considering these issues, it seems reasonable to review the current situation in the Nepalese tourism industry and, in particular, to examine the role of mountains as an important component of the country's tourist product.

Tourism in Nepal – The Current Situation

The country, its people, short history and politics

Nepal is a tiny Himalayan Hindu Kingdom, landlocked between India and Tibetan China in South Asia. The latest World Bank's demographic data (population, life expectancy and infant mortality) shows that this country's population in 1996 was estimated at 22,037,000, an average annual population growth between 1990 and 1996 of 2.7% (World Bank, 1998). It is further estimated that for 1996, life expectancy was 57 years with an infant mortality rate of 85%. David Reed (1998) reports that the country's terrain is mixed, from subtropical jungle to the icy Himalayas, and contains eight of the world's ten highest mountains. The cultural landscape is similarly somewhat diverse, containing about 12 major ethnic groups who speak well over 50 indigenous languages and dialects. Its religious landscape is a mixture of Hinduism and Buddhism.

Despite a new democratic constitution established after the 1990 people's movement (*jana andolan*), most Nepalese believe that nothing has basically changed for the average struggling family. As in other developing countries, Nepal suffers from many development travails (see World Bank, 1998). The economy is undiversified with over 80% of the population living off the land. In 1996, agriculture accounted for about 42% of the gross domestic product (GDP). As will be discussed below, the tourism sector is particularly significant to the Nepalese economy.

Typical of most developing countries, Nepal relies on international aid to support development efforts. For instance in 1996, foreign aid brought in around US$250 million in direct grants and concessionary loans. In general, foreign direct projects are of three categories: projects in which most of the infrastructure is financed by bilateral (and multilateral) agencies; small projects carried out by non-governmental organizations (NGOs; e.g. Oxfam); and big projects with commercial potential (e.g. irrigation) made possible by loans brokered by lending bodies (e.g. The World Bank). The over-reliance on these foreign sources undermines Nepal's ability to do things for itself, thereby engendering aid dependency, which now permeates almost every level of the society. In 1991, against this difficult background, Nepal embarked on a mission of economic liberalization to pull the country out of the economic malaise. One objective was to encourage tourism development.

Developing tourism in Nepal

Facts and figures
Tourism in Nepal was initiated by adventure tourists between 1950 and 1960, but was soon overwhelmed by conventional tourists who came for pleasure and sightseeing. Since then, tourist arrivals have been increasing gradually (see Table 9.1).

In 1998, it was estimated that 418,000 international tourists visited Nepal, and as a consequence between 12,000 and 15,000 direct and indirect jobs were created, generating US$1.64 million in 1997 (see WTO, 1998: 43). The main motivations for visitor arrivals were recreation (75%), trekking/mountaineering (16%) and business purposes (5%). Further estimates also showed that over 31% of all visitors came from four countries – India, Sri Lanka, Bangladesh and Pakistan. Tourists from India comprised about 20% of the total arrivals (over 120,000) with the majority of other international tourists coming from Japan, the UK, Germany and the USA. The average length of stay was 11 days (see Table 9.2).

On the basis of these statistics, a number of caveats can be made. First, there is a heavy reliance on tourists from South Asia region and a small but significant core of trekking/mountain tourists, with recreational tourists forming the bulk of the arrivals from Europe. Second, it is clear that tourism is still important to the Nepalese economy and has great development potential. Part of this significance stems from recent government initiatives in collaboration with the private sector to focus on new tourism objectives relating to product development and promotional issues, as reflected in the theme 'Visit Nepal Year 1998'. These initiatives are 'intended to highlight the need to make tourism work for Nepal and to ensure that it develops environmentally sound products, improves service standards and distributes the benefits of tourism to all local communities' (Cockerell, 1997: 42).

Policies and institutional framework
In 1995, the Government of Nepal published a policy document for the tourism sector (see MTCA, 1995: 1–7). In the main, the document

Table 9.1. International tourist arrivals and receipts in Nepal, 1990–1997 (thousand of arrivals, receipts in millions of US$ and percentages).

	1990	1991	1992	1993	1994	1995	1996	1997
Arrivals (thousands)	255	293	334	294	327	363	394	418
% annual change	6.25	14.90	13.99	−11.98	11.22	11.01	8.54	6.09
Receipts (US$ mn)	109	126	110	157	172	177	161	164
% annual change	1.87	15.60	−12.70	42.73	9.55	2.91	−9.04	1.85

Source: WTO (1998), p. 43.

Table 9.2. Tourist arrivals in Nepal by selected main markets of origin, 1994–1996 (number of arrivals and percentage).

Origin	Number of arrivals			% change	
Markets	1994	1995	1996	1995/94	1996/95
India	102,540	120,268	123,390	17.3	4.5
Japan	19,569	26,934	28,531	37.6	12.3
UK	22,504	27,793	25,488	23.5	7.4
Germany	44,530	27,118	24,537	−39.1	−24.5
USA	21,646	25,491	24,080	17.8	0.3
France	18,638	18,670	19,525	0.2	1.9
Italy	9,715	10,415	9,978	7.2	−2.3
Australia	7,947	10,631	9,885	33.8	5.2
Spain	6,228	8,143	8,649	30.7	21.7
Netherlands	8,669	8,000	8,393	−7.7	−1.1
Switzerland	4,921	6,198	7,270	26.0	16.4

Sources: WTO (1998), p. 44; Cockerell (1997), p. 45.

recognized the strategic importance of tourism, among other sectors (e.g. with water resources, human resources, etc.) to the national economy. The overall aim was to increase productivity, national income and foreign currency earnings; to create employment opportunities, improving seasonal imbalances; and projecting the image of Nepal in the international arena through the development and diversification of the travel and tourism industries. Features of the policies include attention to:

- the preservation and conservation of historical places and monuments
- bio-diversity of wildlife tourism
- new trekking routes and peaks
- rural tourism development
- national environmental guidelines for tourism
- land policy for tourism development
- classification of the tourism industry
- concessions to travel and tourism industries
- provision for human resource development
- institutional strengthening

But at the heart of the policies was an understanding that some functions of government were best handled by a partnership between government and the private sector.

To support the above policies, new institutional arrangements for the tourism sector were put in place. Thus the Ministry of Tourism and Civil Aviation (MTCA) was strengthened and given the sole responsibility for tourism matters, by taking over the existing department of tourism. Also, a new body, the Nepal Tourism Board was created. Each body was given a specific remit. For instance the MTCA was responsible for policy, planning and regulatory controls. These were in the areas of the monitoring of standards and trekking agencies, as these measures reflected the consensus need for a regulatory mechanism to ensure that the established policy objectives were achieved.

The Tourism Board was to operate under guidelines from a Tourism Council, which was an advisory body with representatives from both the key public and private sector organizations. The representations might directly or indirectly linked to tourism. The significance of this advisory body was in coordinating relations with all interested parties, be they government or the trades, for example, hotels, travel agents, airlines or indeed surface transport.

Mountain Tourism in Nepal

Growth of mountain tourism

As noted earlier, Nepal has experienced unprecedented tourism growth in the past 25 years, and is now among the more popular of the international tourism destinations. International tourism receipts increased steadily up to 1997, with only two dips in 1992 and 1996 (WTO, 1998: 73). Much of Nepal's fame lies in trekking and mountaineering, and it was here in the 1960s that the world's first commercial treks took place. Trekking and mountaineering visits to the Himalayas region of Nepal accounted for a 15.5% share of all arrivals in 1997, up from 13.6% in 1975 (Cockerell, 1997).

To maintain the growth of high mountain visitation, the Ministry of Tourism and Civil Aviation developed an infrastructure in existing mountain parks, and opened up new trekking areas (such as Mustang and Dolpo, previously restricted areas opened in 1992), where they have diverted some of the growing number of agency organized groups of adventure travellers. However, the tourism authorities in Nepal face a number of difficulties in managing growth of tourism in the mountain areas, not least of which is the lack of accurate tourism data. The following review of demand and supply of mountain based tourism in Nepal should be viewed in this context.

Demand

The Master Plan 1972 suggested organized sightseeing tourism, independent 'Nepal-style' tourism, trekking and pilgrimage tourism as the favourable tourism forms for Nepal. Mountain tourism in Nepal is composed mainly of recreational tourism (mountaineering, fishing, trekking, rafting, etc.), cultural tourism (archaeology, historical sites) and ecotourism (bird and wildlife watching, photography, scenery, scientific tourism, etc.). Within the framework of adventure and ecotourism, the most commonly measured categories in Nepal are trekking tourism and mountaineering tourism. Trekkers are often, in turn, subdivided into free independent travellers (FITs) and group trekkers (Lama and Sherpa, 1994; ICIMOD, 1995; Pobocik and Butalla, 1998).

Trekking

The growth rates for total trekking tourism indicate that this activity is healthy in Nepal. According to Ministry of Tourism and Civil Aviation figures, trekking now accounts for around a quarter of Nepal's tourism (MTCA, 1995). FITs travel exclusively in the Solukhumbu, Annapurna and Langtang regions where lodges and food are easily available. In 1997, the total number of individual trekkers visiting different trekking routes (shown in Table 9.3) was 39,988. Group trekking activities tend to be organized by overseas adventure travel companies and handled by agencies based in Kathmandu. Group trekkers are self-sufficient and can travel into wilderness areas and away from villages as long as there is water and a place to pitch tents (Lama and Sherpa, 1994). Table 9.4 indicates that the total number of group travellers in 1997 was 51,537. From this total of 91,525 trekkers, 59.1% visited the Annapurna area while those visiting the Everest and Langtang regions accounted for 19.9% and 9%, respectively (Department of Tourism, 1997).

Mountaineering

Mountaineering tourists are classified into two categories: those who climb peaks above 6000 m and those who climb peaks below 6000 m. As a means of controlling numbers, and therefore damage, permits are required to climb mountain peaks of any altitude. For peaks above 6600 m, permits have to be obtained from the Ministry of Tourism, and for peaks below 6600 m, permits are issued by the Nepal Mountaineering Association. A total of 120 expedition teams were granted permits to scale peaks during 1997 which involved 861 mountaineers employing 7003 persons in support (Department of Tourism, 1997).

Supply

Most tourist destinations comprise a core of the following components: attraction, accessibility, accommodation and activity (Cooper *et al.*, 1998). Accessibility and activity assume critical importance in the context of supply of mountain tourism in Nepal. Attraction in the form of natural or cultural heritage is outstanding and unique in the country, but access to these places and activities is problematic.

A key issue for Nepal's tourism industry is the lack of inbound and internal airline seats. Although the liberal sky policy has relieved the seat

Table 9.3. Total number of individual trekkers, 1997.

Trekking routes	Jan	Feb	Mar	Apr	May	Jun	Jul	Aug	Sep	Oct	Nov	Dec	Total
Everest trek	228	423	955	830	336	98	151	216	812	1,765	998	377	7,189
Helambu, Langtang valley trek	195	321	695	688	291	91	140	171	423	1,144	803	439	5,401
Annapurna, Manang, Jomsom trek	1,056	1,981	3,918	2,939	1,216	430	524	798	2,617	5,342	3,182	1,743	25,646
Jumla and Dolpa trek	nil	–	1	4	3	1	1	1	–	–	3	–	14
Others	80	113	216	134	95	73	88	47	175	401	166	150	1,738
Total	1,559	2,838	5,785	4,495	1,941	693	904	1,233	4,027	8,652	5,152	2,708	39,988

Source: Ministry of Finance (1997).

Table 9.4. Total number of trekkers (agency handled), 1997.

Trekking routes	Jan	Feb	Mar	Apr	May	Jun	Jul	Aug	Sep	Oct	Nov	Dec	Total
Everest trek	388	351	1,522	1,299	247	56	90	74	677	3,563	1,831	892	10,990
Helambu, Langtang, Valley trek	77	76	457	384	88	61	96	7	256	603	485	200	2,800
Annapurna, Manang, Jomsom trek	1,234	2,054	4,108	2,974	806	235	479	465	2,299	6,372	4,732	2,674	28,432
Dolpa trek	nil	2	24	29	15	9	96	83	137	–	10	9	414
Kangchanjunga trek	–	2	75	99	17	nil	3	nil	42	329	51	13	631
Others	123	265	694	590	193	77	77	339	964	1,944	680	477	6,423
Restricted area													
Mustang trek	nil	2	14	82	69	21	104	118	130	195	18	nil	753
Dolpa trek	nil	nil	4	8	9	nil	45	16	81	32	4	nil	199
Jumla trek	nil	nil	nil	20	131	37	34	157	nil	25	nil	nil	404
Manaslu trek	nil	3	27	60	2	3	2	25	nil	295	64	10	491
Total	1,822	2,755	6,935	5,545	1,577	199	1,026	1,284	4,586	13,358	7,875	4,275	51,537

Source: Ministry of Finance (1997)
The figures do not include trekkers around Kathmandu and Pokhara valley. Figures for Annapurna, Manang, and Jomsom treks also include permits issued from Pokhara.

capacity constraints of air travel to remote mountain areas since 1992, problems related to landing sites and equipment continue. This is compounded by poor land-based access and inadequate tourism infrastructure throughout the country.

Table 9.5 shows that the Annapurna region is by far the most popular region for trekking, with Sagarmatha National Park (SNP) and Langtang National Park (LNP) following as second and third respectively. The newly opened regions account for less than 3% of trekkers. The Sagarmatha region contains the world's highest mountain and, is therefore a special draw for tourists. The Annapurna and Langtang regions are easily accessible from Pokhara and Kathmandu. Other tourist areas in the mountains are not protected areas, but the number of tourists is restricted by higher trekking fees and an annual quota system (Department of Tourism, 1994).

In terms of mountaineering, there are 142 peaks in various mountain ranges from east to west open, with various levels of restriction. Eight additional peaks in the far-western region were opened in the spring mountaineering season of 1993, with a view to decongesting such activities in the eastern region and to distributing them evenly throughout the country (ICIMOD, 1995).

Tourism industry ownership patterns

The tourism industry in Nepal does not necessarily reflect those development models, which suggests that tourism in developing countries will be effectively dominated by the major industrialized countries, and that peripheral areas will be dominated by the country's capital city. While Kathmandu is clearly the dominating city in the country, receiving all the international flights, the current ownership patterns and the slow pace of tourism development illustrate that Nepal does not readily conform to Dependency Theory (Pagdin, 1995). The exception may be organized tour groups and packaged

Table 9.5. Mountain tourism by destination (1994–1997).

Year	SNP	LNP	ACAP	Dolpa	Kanchan-junga	Jumla/Dolpa	Others	Total
1994	13,461	8,167	44,733	434	575	28	7,842	75,240
1995	14,997	8,427	50,012	500	667	10	8,281	82,894
1996	16,921	7,687	52,399	553	608	33	8,655	86,856
1997	18,179	8,201	54,078	414	631	14	8,161	89,678
	(7.4)	(6.7)	(3.2)	–(25.1)	(3.8)	–(57.6)	–(5.7)	

Source: Department of Tourism (1997), p.51.
SNP – Sagarmatha National Park; LNP – Langtang National Park; ACAP – Annapurna Conservation Area Project.

travel, which are a relatively recent phenomenon, evolving in the 1970s from extensions to India tours. Some dependence on Indian tour operators is still evident, and a significant share of the initial tour operators in Kathmandu, now the market leaders, were originally Indian. This does not indicate major foreign domination of the tourism sector, as the government has exercised considerable control over tourist arrivals and movement around the country, even using tourist fares to subsidize air travel for the local population. According to the Ministry of Tourism and Civil Aviation, no tourist facilities were completely owned by foreign companies, although many were in joint foreign–Nepalese ownership (MTCA, 1995).

Impacts

Economic

Tourism has brought economic opportunities to remote mountain areas of Nepal where agriculture and animal husbandry were traditionally the main occupations of most households. In areas such as SNP, as well as Tatopani and Bagarchap villages in the Annapurna Conservation Area (ACA), agriculture has gradually become secondary to tourism-related activities (CEDA, 1988; Stevens _et al._, 1993; Nepal, 1997).

In parts of SNP, many households have abandoned their traditional cropping practice of buckwheat and barley to cultivate more potatoes, which find a ready cash market (Nepal, 1997). Households along the trekking routes have began cultivating fruit and other high-value crops. Changes in the cropping pattern are positive as long as they earn a relatively higher income than traditional cultivating practices and do not harm the environment (ICIMOD, 1995).

Tourism has changed employment patterns in mountain areas with increased demand for tour support staff: such as jobs for porters, cooks, kitchen boys and guides. However, not all of these employment benefits accrue to the local population: quite often, people outside the area exploit this opportunity. Different employment patterns seem to be generated by group and individual trekkers. Studies in the past found that an average group size (group tourists) ranges from six to ten trekkers, and the average number of support staff hired ranges from about two to four per trekker as opposed to between 0.5 to 1.5 persons per trekker for free independent travellers (Upadhyay, 1984; Banskota and Upadhyay, 1991). Clearly, in terms of direct employment generation, group trekkers have a greater impact on employment than FITs. On the other hand, independent trekkers outnumber group trekkers three to one in popular areas such as the ACAP (Pobocik and Butalla, 1998).

In addition, individual trekkers generate other forms of employment. Since a large number of them depend on local lodges and hotels for food and accommodation, they generate employment in these facilities. In SNP, LNP and the ACA, a large number of such lodges, hotels and tea stalls would go out of business if individual trekkers did not visit or were not permitted to visit such areas.

Direct employment generated by mountaineering expeditions shows a declining trend, especially during the period 1990–1992. Direct employment generated by mountaineering teams declined from 9154 persons in 1990 to 8251 persons in 1992 because of reduced numbers of mountaineering teams and members per team. Figures for 1997 show this declining trend has continued with total direct employment from mountaineering expeditions falling to 7003 (Department of Tourism, 1997).

A 1995 study by ICIMOD produced figures for the generation of income from mountain tourism, and these indicate significant differences between group tours, independent trekkers and mountaineering teams (see Tables 9.6, 9.7 and 9.8). Unfortunately this one-off study has not been repeated to give an indication of changes to the present day. Group tourists have a greater impact on income as they generally hire larger numbers of support staff. The effect of mountain tourism on income, however, does not end here. Individual tourists pay for local accommodation and food while both group and individual tourists spend money on drinks, fruit, handicrafts and other items (Sharma, 1989). However, the generation of income through employment is the most substantial effect that trekkers have. Income generated by mountaineering tourism is also substantial and competes fairly closely with that generated by trekking tourism. Income generated by mountaineering teams in Nepal generally shows a steeply increasing trend. Between the period from 1980 to 1992, the average annual growth rate in income was 17% (ICIMOD, 1995).

Socio-cultural

The impact of tourism on culture, traditions and values is more difficult to assess. In addition to exposure to tourists, local people increasingly travel for education, trade or other purposes, which brings in new ideas and behaviours that affect cultural practices. Changes in the local economies and employment patterns also must be considered in social and cultural contexts. For example, the trend of adult members leaving home for prolonged periods for tourism employment is believed to affect Sherpa society and to cause family break-ups in some cases. Further, it is said that the Sherpas have become overly westernized, and that their religious faith has diminished. It is argued that most families prefer their children to undergo the new system of education rather than to join the monastery as monks (ICIMOD, 1995).

Although clearly not all impacts on Sherpa culture have been positive, it could be argued that tourism generally has had more positive than negative

Table 9.6. Income generated by mountain tourism.

Year	Wages (NRs)	Food (NRs)	Mountaineering Expenditure and Royalties (NRs)	Trek and park (NRs)	Peak fees (NRs)	Total mountain revenue (NRs)	Expenditure per trekker per day (NRs)
1985	31,483	64,272	21,168	3,928	3,646	124,497	272
1986	52,485	117,298	32,917	5,949	5,602	214,251	309
1987	55,596	115,481	38,350	5,673	7,770	222,870	337
1988	81,310	159,630	47,661	7,353	8,523	304,477	355
1989	89,938	184,416	71,198	7,303	1,389	354,244	416
1990	103,952	197,112	75,634	7,451	1,605	385,754	444
1991	120,225	309,618	165,292	7,892	13,053	616,080	669
1992	146,663	332,836	131,706	8,573	20,883	640,661	641

Source: ICIMOD (1995), p. 57.
NRs = Nepalese Rupees.

Table 9.7. Income and employment generated by group and individual tourists: 1988.

Types of tourist	Employment (man days)	Income (Rs)
Group tourists		
High	914,920	61,299,640
Low	457,460	30,649,820
Individual tourists		
High	238,425	15,974,475
Low	79,475	5,324,825
All tourists		
High	1,153,345	77,274,115
Low	536,935	35,974,645

Source: ICIMOD (1995), p. 87.
Notes: The high and low income estimates provided in the above table are multiplied by the average weighted wage rate of Rs 67 per day.

Table 9.8. Income generated by mountaineering teams.

Year	No. teams mountaineers	No. of mountaineers	Income (Rs 000)	Royalty
1985	91	824	17,871	3,298
1986	94	807	28,854	4,063
1987	98	796	34,020	4,330
1988	92	936	42,583	5,079
1989	125	1,053	63,976	7,222
1990	120	966	68,368	7,266
1991	130	1,038	156,363	8,929
1992	113	929	101,355	30,351

Source: Ministry of Finance (1993).

effects. The changes that have occurred, far from being devastating, seem to be closer to the normal process of societal change, and this change has been welcomed by the Sherpa themselves (Haimendorf, 1984; Upadhyay, 1984; Chetri *et al.*, 1992; Robinson, 1992; Stevens *et al.*, 1993; Lama and Sherpa, 1994; Sharma, 1995).

Physical environment

Construction
Some of the most obvious, and frequently cited, impacts of tourism on the mountain areas of Nepal have been on the physical environment. The construction of new buildings is a visible sign of land-use impact in many of

the protected areas frequented by tourists (Byers, 1987). Aside from park headquarters and other buildings, construction of lodges and tea stalls has occurred extensively in SNP, the ACA and LNP, both inside and outside the park area. In SNP and LNP, smaller temporary lodges have also been built at higher altitudes to cater for tourism. In the newly opened Makalu-Barun National Park and Conservation Area (MBNPCA), the land-use changes have occurred along the Makalu Base Camp trail in the conservation area as well as outside the area.

Litter
The increasing amount of littering taking place at high altitudes in the mountains is a major negative environmental impact that has received a great deal of attention in Nepal. Litter includes non-biodegradable rubbish such as plastics, glass bottles, tins, foil and batteries, improperly deposited or discarded along trails, at campsites, outside trekking lodges and at base camps by tourists, trekking staff, porters, trekking lodge staff and local residents. Inadequately covered toilet pits and scattered toilet paper around campsites and trails are another serious problem (Lama and Sherpa, 1994). The dimensions of this problem are worth emphasizing. In one study, it was estimated that an average trekking group of 15 people generates about 15 kg of non-biodegradable, non-flammable garbage in 10 trekking days (Lama and Sherpa, 1994). Tables 9.9 and 9.10 provide an idea of the amount of litter deposited in and garbage cleared from protected areas. Since then several projects have been initiated to address this issue. For example, the Sagarmatha Pollution Control Committee (SPCC) collected 145 tonnes of burnable and 45 tonnes of non-burnable garbage between July 1995 and 1996. In 1995, SPCC collected nearly 2 tonnes of disposable and 1.5 tonnes of non-disposable garbage from mountaineering expeditions alone in the Everest region (Nepal, 1997). As such, the Nepalese Himalayas have been regarded as 'the highest junkyard on earth' (Cockerell, 1997: 42).

Pollution
The pollution of water resources from setting toilets too close to streams and drinking water sources, use of chemical soaps for bathing, and the washing of dishes and clothes in streams are of increasing concern. Water pollution is exacerbated by disposing of human waste directly into rivers and streams, customarily done by lodge owners and also a common practice of local people (Gurung, 1990; Lama and Sherpa, 1994).

Deforestation
One of the most widely discussed topics on mountain environments is forest degradation and deforestation. The demand for firewood by tourism and associated tourism activities in the mountain areas has the most significant

Table 9.9. Litter deposits in the mountain environment, 1988 (in kg).

Area	Number of trekkers	Average deposited	Total deposited
Annapurna	37,902	15	56,853
Khumbu	11,366	15	17,049
Langtang	8,423	15	12,635
Other	3,582	15	5,373
Cumulative total	1976 to 1993	640 mt	

Source: Lama and Sherpa (1994), taken from ICIMOD (1995), p. 81.

Table 9.10. Mountaineering (1979–1988), garbage cleared from Everest base camp – Spring 1993.

	Disposable garbage	Non-disposable garbage	Oxygen/gas cylinders	Total
14 expeditions	7,030	2,350	3,444	12,824
Average teams	502	168	246	916
Range	90–1,350	60–360	356–540	390–1,820
Total (1979–1988) total for 840 teams	421,680	141,120	206,640	769.44 Mt

Source: Lama and Sherpa (1994), taken from ICIMOD (1995), p. 81.

effect on forest, vegetation and wildlife. The demand for firewood seems to differ for FITs and group tourists. This difference in consumption arises because group tourists are self-supported in food, shelter and fuel for cooking, as demanded by His Majesty's Government law while travelling in protected areas. This rule is also applied for mountaineering teams. However, the enforcement has not been effective enough to make this policy an overwhelming success (Banskota and Upadhyay, 1991; Lama and Sherpa, 1994; Pobocik and Butalla, 1998). Individual trekkers depend on local lodges or hotels, tea houses, and locals for food and accommodation. A study in SNP indicated 30% of visitors were individual trekkers, out of which 73% ate in lodges or tea houses (ICIMOD, 1995).

However the pattern of firewood consumption for tourist types is far from clear and may have changed in recent years due to the ban on firewood consumption by trekkers. Other detailed studies on the ACAP have cast doubt on the assumption that independent trekking necessarily places a greater burden on natural resources than group treks. Low-technology methods of conserving energy have been introduced and kerosene is viewed as a short-term fuel alternative but with associated economic costs. Hydro-electricity is viewed as the long-term solution although forest protection must be improved until this is available (Pobocik and Butalla, 1998).

The Organization and Regulation of Mountain Tourism

Most of the tourism policies and institutional arrangements for Nepal are general to all tourism: specific mountain tourism arrangements are confined to mountain tourism rules and protected areas policies. This is not to diminish the importance of national tourism policy, as certain inherent weaknesses have a profound influence on effective management of mountain tourism growth.

Government intervention and policy weaknesses

The failure of the market to allocate value to environmental resources and the externalities that have occurred in the context of mountain tourism can be identified as the main problems demanding government intervention. In the context of Nepal, there are inadequate and inappropriate policies, which lead to conflict between tourism development and conservation of the protected areas. This lack of cohesive policy joining tourism development with environmental protection is linked to central government departmental divisions and exacerbated by a lack of continuity of tourism civil servants and personnel in government with tourism expertise. There also tends to be a lack of communication between government and the private sector in tourism and little or no funding support from the tourism authorities for private sector initiatives (Cockerell, 1997). This has led to demand-led growth with crisis management at pressure points and *ad hoc* implementation of policies.

   For example, in protected areas, policies have failed to eradicate the continued use of firewood and poaching. Lack of coordination between the Department of Wildlife and National Parks and the Ministry of Tourism and Civil Aviation has led to *ad hoc* changes in visa fees and an absence of an appropriate pricing mechanism in the case of park entrance fees, trekking fees and mountaineering fees. The opening of new areas by the Ministry of Tourism and Civil Aviation, without prior assessment of their potential value and logistical support is another example of lack of strategic thinking (MTCA, 1999). At the local level, these problems are manifested in the lack of awareness of linkages between economic benefits and environmental protection at community level (ICIMOD, 1998).

   The national policy of diversification of tourism and dispersal to all potential tourist sites, in a phased manner, is another example of policy failure. There seems to be no commitment to priority setting in a time frame, and no tourism development area has been declared as yet in the mountain region or even in Kathmandu Valley. When the basic infrastructure reaches a potential area, tourists start visiting and the private sector provides services and facilities on demand. Although tourism policies have emphasized the promotion of trekking and mountaineering activities to remote areas of the country, the mountain areas closest to Kathmandu and Pokhara have seen the most impressive growth.

Recent changes in the organization of tourism in Nepal led to the establishment of the Nepal Tourism Board, which replaced the Department of Tourism on 2 December 1998. A key objective is to establish a more effective partnership between government and the private sector to strengthen the overall development of tourism in Nepal. The Nepal Tourism Board has been assigned the prime responsibility for marketing and promotional activities whilst responsibility for regulatory and policy making functions have been retained by the Ministry of Tourism and Civil Aviation (Thapa, 1999, private communication with His Majesty's Government Ministry of Tourism, Kathmandu). These changes may address some of the administrative issues and lead to more effective mechanisms for policy implementation.

Rules and regulations

Tourism policies more specific to mountain areas tend to be confined to control measures. This again tends to alienate the private sector. Rather than developing a harmonious relationship and public–private cooperation in mountain tourism, this sometimes heavy-handed approach can be viewed as stifling development and leading to non-compliance by the tourism sector and locals.

An example of over-bureaucratic regulation and control of the tourism sector and tourist activities, particularly mountaineering, is the Tourism Act of 2035 B.S. under which several regulations pertaining to various sub-sectors are implemented. This Act consists of six chapters, of which the first is devoted to a description of terminology used in the act. The second chapter, concerned with travel and trekking agencies, including hotels, lodges, restaurants and bars, clearly stipulates that a licence is necessary to open a travel or trekking agency. Unlicensed activities are liable to punishment, which includes the closure of operations and a fine. The Department of Tourism is given the authority to execute this Act; however, enforcement is in reality more problematic.

Mountaineering and trekking activities also have specific environmental rules and regulations. Garbage management and fuel usage are very sensitive issues. The Sagarmatha Pollution Control Project in Khumbu and the Annapurna Conservation Area Project (ACAP) in the Annapurna area are making significant headway with this, although there is still a need to create a more effective organization for garbage management in other areas. The ACAP's minimum impact code for tourists advises staying in lodges that use appropriate waste control and fuel management. Interestingly, a study in the ACA showed that 80% of all trekkers surveyed stated they would be willing to pay more for their trek to protect the environment (Pobocik and Butalla, 1998).

Extensive rules also exist for mountaineering where climbing permits are mandatory for all mountaineering teams attempting to climb the mountain peaks of Nepal. Rules are laid down for reporting the progress of the expedition and for the hiring of mountaineering support staff through a government liaison officer. There is provision for personal health checks and insurance against accidents for the safety and well-being of the Nepalese staff attached to a mountaineering expedition. Similarly, there is provision for emergency rescue arrangements through a representative agency in Kathmandu. The duties and responsibilities of the team leader, liaison officer and *sardar* are specified and there are strict environmental regulations for the course of the expedition. The news of the expedition's progress should be reported first to the Ministry of Tourism. The Ministry of Tourism can authorize the Nepal Mountaineering Association to issue climbing permits for a fixed number of peaks. No expedition team can change the climbing route without written approval from the Ministry of Tourism. Similarly, climbing attempts without a permit and any action or behaviour in defiance of the regulations are punishable. Most of these regulations are valid and necessary, however, the means of implementation and enforcement through tourism authorities are far from ideal.

Protected areas and mountain tourism

Most of the mountain areas in Nepal have some level of protection. Protected area management in Nepal began in the 1970s and is thus relatively new. Currently, there are 14 protected areas of different status in Nepal (Table 9.11), covering roughly 12% of the country's surface area. Of these, nine are in the hill and mountain areas. The creation of protected areas has brought changes to the traditional life of the people living in these areas. These local people have derived benefits from the protection of their environment, although conflicts have also arisen between park authorities and tourism (Shrestha *et al.*, 1990; Stevens and Sherpa, 1993; Yonzon, 1993). The management of protected areas is carried out by the Department of National Parks and Wildlife Conservation. The most frequently visited protected areas and national parks in Nepal are SNP, ACA and LNP.

Public Policy Issues

Lack of accurate data on tourism

The lack of periodic surveys on tourism, with consistent definition and coverage, makes it difficult to determine the demand and supply of tourism in the country. On the demand side, proper knowledge of characteristics of tourist types and expenditure patterns is important to understand the tastes

Table 9.11. Protected areas in Nepal.

Name	Area (km²)	Location	Gazetted
Hill and mountain			
Rara National Park	106	High mountains	1976
Shey Phoksumdo NP	3555	High mountains	1984
ACAP	7000	High mountains	1988
Langtang National Park	1710	High mountains	1976
Sagarmatha NP	1148	High mountains	1976
Makalu-Barun NP and CA	2330	High mountains	1992
Shivpuri Watershed Protected Area	144	Mid mountains	
Dhorpatan Hunting Reserve	1325	High mountains	1987
Kaptad National Park	225	High mountains	1985
Terai or inner terai			
Royal Sukla Fata Wildlife	305	Terai	1976
Royal Bardia NP	968	Terai	1988
Royal Chitwan NP	932	Terai	1873
Parsa Wildlife	499	Terai	1984
Kosi Tappu Wildlife	175	Terai	1876

Source: Master Plan for Forestry Sector Project (1988), Main Report.

and preferences of the tourists with regard to different domestic products. This is evident in some of the conflicting findings on group and independent trekkers.

The lack of periodic data on companies providing tourist services (hotels, airlines, travel agencies, trekking agencies, handicraft shops, carpets and garment industries, etc.) makes it difficult to assess the supply components of the industry. The information on the tourism industry has been viewed as so inadequate and limited that it is surprising how any policies have ever been formulated (ICIMOD, 1995). Estimates indicate that 37% of the total tourist expenditure in Nepal is exchanged in the black market. The only comprehensive study that has attempted to link the tourism industry with the entire economy has been conducted by the Nepal Rastra Bank (NRB; Khadka, 1993). One major conclusion emerging from this study is that a great portion of the revenue generated by tourism in Nepal actually flows out due to the capacity constraint in the domestic economy. Such studies should be conducted on a periodic basis to formulate new policies and fine-tune the old ones.

Absence of institutional coordination

The absence of accurate market data is compounded by a lack of a systematic approach to information sharing and feedback between the ministries related to tourism. The lack of coordination in the formulation and implementation of sectoral plans and programmes is another problem on the institutional front. Thus, for mountain tourism in Nepal, like any other developing country, scholars agree there is an urgent need for government to actively intervene (Jenkins and Henry, 1982) for the systematic development of tourism. Without political stability and political determination, the national objectives for the betterment of mountain tourism and mountain environment cannot be achieved.

No clearly defined role for tourism in mountain area development

There has been no concerted effort by the government to view the mountain areas as potentially rich in a variety of unique natural resources. The value of these resources needs to be identified and their potential role in mountain development needs to be assessed. Furthermore, the role of tourism in mountain development needs to be clearly identified. This lack of perspective appears to have led to a demand-induced tourism growth pattern that has not formed a sustainable basis for mountain tourism (ICIMOD, 1995). Opening new areas and building some rudimentary infrastructure has been the main basis for tourism and mountain development. Government policies to encourage the private mountain tourism sector have been lacking, the preference being towards tourism investment in urban areas. As a result, only small pockets have benefited.

It is necessary to diversify tourism to new areas to ensure environmental conservation. This strategy should generate more income, employment and a better distribution of income. The development of new areas depends primarily on the strength of the forces that operate on the supply side, although the demand side will also be important. Unique characteristics of the area have to be identified and innovative strategies need to be promoted. With old areas already overcrowded, there is a growing need to disperse tourists to newer areas.

Lack of linkages of tourism with local and regional production systems

Tourism is a multidisciplinary sector that needs a lot of coordination and cooperation between different disciplines in society to achieve sustainable development. The main problem encountered by most developing countries is the lack of linkage of tourism with other sectors of the economy. In the context of Nepal's mountain tourism, it is felt that there is a weak linkage between mountain development and tourism and that the development benefits of tourism have not spread equitably. The manner in which the development of the mountain environment and mountain tourism has taken place is partly responsible for this problem. The weak linkage of local areas with mountain tourism also results from the absence of clear policy directives.

Lack of retention of benefits in particular for local communities

One of the major problems in Nepal is minimal retention of foreign exchange earnings from tourism. Approximately 90% of total foreign exchange earnings goes back to tourism-generating countries in the form of imports of goods and services for the tourist. There is no long tradition of tourism in Nepal, so many of the inputs of tourism development are imported from the developed countries. Moreover, where tourism has reached a mature level of development, there are difficulties for the local suppliers to enter the market because they are not capable of supplying the scale and quality of product or services required by the industry. A study of the Hindu Kush-Himalayas (HKH) emphasized how this problem is not unique to Nepal:

> In almost all of the mountain areas of the HKH the earnings from tourism mostly, and naturally in the scheme of things, flow to large urban-based tour and travel agents and entrepreneurs in the hospitality industry (ICIMOD, 1998).

The involvement of local people in areas where tourism occurs has, in the past, been minimal. In the ACAP area, and in the Makula-Barun National Park and Conservation Area (MBNPCA), this has changed. But the lack of evaluation of the new approach in the ACAP area makes it difficult to conclude how well the new process is contributing to mountain and tourism development. In the MBNPCA, the process has only begun, so it is too early to judge.

Managing the growth of tourism

Mountain and trekking tourism has played a significant role in transforming rural communities in certain areas. However, these areas are often composed of sensitive micro-ecosystems with meagre tolerance to stress and limited carrying capacity. Aggressive tourism activities in such areas, without proper mountain resource management, have created serious environmental threats. Clearly promoting mountain and trekking tourism without consideration of an area's specific carrying capacity under the given state of technology, infrastructure and policy environment is unlikely to make tourism sustainable (see Gurung and DeCoursey, this publication).

Remedial actions and code of conducts have been formulated, but the fact that negative impacts or excess stress on the environment continue to occur indicates that policies have failed or that their enforcement has been ineffective.

Recent evidence reveals that the return from tourism in the mountain areas has been very low due to the undervaluing of the environmental resources that the mountains harbour (ICIMOD, 1998). Moreover, mountain environmental resources are directly consumed by the local people as well as by tourists. Tourists purchase goods and services and consume them jointly with non-priced natural amenities such as natural beauty, scenery, climate, and so on. Local people use environmental resources to produce goods and services for their sustenance or for tourist consumption. Many other potential values of the flora, fauna and nature functions remain unknown. Mountains are thus a store of unique environmental resources that have value and have no close substitutes.

Forest degradation and the increased use of firewood are key problems that have received much attention. Alternative sources of fuel and regulating consumption can alleviate critical situations but these should form part of a comprehensive management strategy, recognizing wider capacity measures and environmental values.

Conclusions

Mountain tourism in Nepal has grown rapidly in recent years, but not in a planned, systematic manner. Indeed, the accurate data which exist indicates dispersal of economic benefits to more remote mountain areas has been restricted, whilst more accessible mountain locations have suffered environmental damage.

The existing policies are based on weak information, and institutional structures seem inadequate for linking mountain tourism and other mountain economic activities. Scarce resources are exploited by a few for small gain. Yet there is no institution specifically to look at mountain tourism in Nepal.

It is essential to have a clear long-term policy on what is desired from tourism in the context of mountain tourism development. The national objective of tourism is to increase revenue growth, but there are several ways to achieve this growth. For example, growth can be achieved by encouraging: (i) more tourists to visit the country, (ii) tourists to spend more nights, (iii) more spending, and (iv) the development of import substitution industries. For a small country like Nepal, tourism development must be defined in terms of the national goal and an appropriate growth path must be prioritized. This growth must complement environmental conservation if tourism growth is to be sustainable, especially in the fragile environment of the mountain areas. Tourism development cannot be viewed in isolation from conservation, natural resource management and mountain development. Thus, in the first instance, a clear objective for mountain development and the role of tourism needs to be assessed for all mountain areas that already have tourism and in other areas that have tourism development potential.

The unique mountain environment of Nepal is increasingly being degraded, thereby reducing tourist amenities and the visual appeal of the area. The scattered evidence on protected mountain areas in Nepal clearly points to this. Since the nature of studies conducted vary considerably over time, it is difficult to form a clear picture of the various impacts and determine their trends, severely limiting policy analysis as well as formulation. Clearly, there is a need for generating systematic information on the various dimensions of mountain areas and mountain tourism for guiding, planning and managing mountain and tourism development.

Policies specifically designed for mountain tourism tend to be restricted to rules and regulations for visitors. Nepal's mountaineering tourism is now suffering from self-glorifying *ad hoc* policy changes. The application procedures for mountaineering are cumbersome. The requirement of a cash deposit to ensure garbage disposal, despite a hike in royalties and attachment of a government liaison officer, is negatively perceived as unnecessarily troublesome by mountaineers and trekkers (ICIMOD, 1995). Despite periodic increases in royalties, no additional facilities have been erected at important tourist areas in the mountains.

There is an urgent need to improve the information base of the tourism sector in terms of the quality and quantity of information. A well-planned research agenda should be conducted to assess the environmental resource base, its value, socio-cultural and economic characteristics, together with the feasibility of an investment package, before opening up new areas for tourism.

Key Recommendations

- Review institutional arrangements for tourism
- Include specific mountain tourism policies in national tourism plan
- Combine tourism development policies with protected area conservation policies
- Encourage greater public–private sector collaboration
- Improve provision and dissemination of tourism data on supply and demand: visitor segment characteristics, economic values, local community views, environmental impacts.

References

Banskota, K. and Upadhyay, M. (1991) Impact of rural tourism on the environment, income, and employment in the Makalu-Barun area. *Report 17. The*

Makalu-Barun Conservation project. Department of National Park and Wildlife Conservation, HMG and Woodlands Mountain Institute.

Byers, A. (1987) An assessment of landscape change in the Khumbu region of Nepal using repeat photography. *Mountain Research and Development* 7, No. 1.

CEDA (Centre for Economic Development and Administration) (1988) *Trekking Tourism in Khumbu and Kanchanjunga Regions of Nepal.* Ministry of Tourism, His Majesty's Government, Nepal.

Chetri, J.K., Neupane, I. and Sharma, B. (1992) Off-farm employment in Nepal: a case Study of Marphs-Jomsom VDCs, Mustang District. *MPE series No. 18.* ICIMOD, Kathmandu.

Cockerell, N. (1997) International Tourism Reports No. 1 – Nepal. *Travel and Tourism Intelligence* 1, 40–57.

Cooper, C., Fletcher, J., Gilbert, D., Wanhill, S. and Shepherd, R. (1998) *Tourism: Principles and Practise.* Longman, Harlow, UK.

Department of Tourism (1994) *Nepal Tourism Statistics 1994.* Department of Tourism, Kathmandu, Nepal.

Department of Tourism (1997) *Nepal Tourism Statistics 1997,* Department of Tourism, Kathmandu, Nepal.

Gurung, H. (1990) Environmental management of mountain tourism in Nepal. Paper presented at ESCAP Symposium on Tourism Promotion in Asian Region, Hangzhou, China.

Haimendorf, C. (1984) *The Sherpa Transformed: Social Change in the Buddhist Society of Nepal.* Sterling Publishers, New Delhi.

ICIMOD (International Centre for Integrated Mountain Development) (1995) *Mountain Tourism in Nepal – An Overview.* International Centre for Integrated Mountain Development, Kathmandu, Nepal.

ICIMOD (International Centre for Integrated Mountain Development) (1998) Environment, culture, economy and tourism: dilemas in the Hindu Kush-Himilayas. In: *Issues in Mountain Development.* International Centre for Integrated Mountain Development, Kathmandu, Nepal.

Inskeep, E. (1991) *Tourism Planning: an Integrated and Sustainable Development Approach.* Van Nostrand Reinhold, New York.

Jenkins, C.L. (1997) Impacts of the development of international tourism in the Asian region. In: Go, F.M. and Jenkins, C.L. (eds) *Tourism and Economic Development in Asia and Australasia.* Cassell, London, pp. 48–64.

Jenkins, C.L. and Henry, B.M. (1982) Government involvement in tourism in developing countries. *Annals of Tourism Research* 9, 499–521.

Khadka, K.R. (1993) Tourism and economic development in Nepal. Ph.D. thesis, Development and Project Planning Centre, University of Bradford.

Lama, W. and Sherpa, A. (1994) Tourism Development Plan for the Makalu Base Camp Trek and Upper Barun Valley. Revised Draft Report. Makalu-Barun Conservation Project, Feb. 1994.

Master Plan for Forestry Sector Project (1988) *Main Report.* His Majesty's Government of Nepal, Kathmandu.

Ministry of Finance (1993) *Economic Survey.* Ministry of Finance, HIs Majesty's Government of Nepal, Kathmandu, Nepal.

Ministry of Finance (1997) *Economic Survey of the Fiscal Year 1996/97.* Ministry of Finance, His Majesty's Government of Nepal, Kathmandu, Nepal, pp. 46–59.

Ministry of Tourism and Civil Aviation (1995) *Tourism Policy Final Draft.* His Majesty's Government, Kathmandu, Nepal.

Ministry of Tourism and Civil Aviation (1999) *New Peaks opened for Climbing with Royalty Exemption.* His Majesty's Government of Nepal Ministry of Tourism and Civil Aviation Mountaineering Section, website 14/5/99 www.south asia.com/dotn/news.htm

Nepal, S.K. (1997) *Tourism Induced Environmental Changes in the Everest Region: Some Recent Evidence.* Centre for Development and Environment. University of Bern.

Pagdin, C. (1995) Assessing tourism impacts in the Third World: a Nepal case study. *Progress in Planning* 44(3), 197–198.

Pobocik, M. and Butalla, C. (1998) Development in Nepal: the Annapurna Conservation Area Project. In: Hall, C.M. and Lew, A.A. (eds) *Sustainable Tourism: a Geographical Perspective.* Addison Wesley Longman, Essex, pp. 159–172.

Reed, D. (1998) *Nepal: The rough guide.* Penguin, London.

Robinson, D.W. (1992) Socio-cultural impacts of mountain tourism in Nepal's Sagarmatha Everest National Park: implications for sustainable tourism. In: Thorsell, J. (ed.) *World Heritage Twenty Years Later: IVth World Congress on National Parks and Protected areas,* IUCN, Gland, Switzerland, pp. 123–131.

Sharma, P. (1989) *Assessment of Critical Issues and Options in Mountain Tourism in Nepal.* International Centre for Integrated Mountain Development, Kathmandu, Nepal.

Sharma, P. (1995) Culture and Tourism: defining roles and relationships. MEI Discussion paper series 95/2. Katmandu, Nepal, ICIMOD.

Shrestha, T.B., Sherpa, L.N., Banskota, K. and Nepali, R. (1990) *The Makalu-Barun National Park and Conservation Area Management Plan.* Department of National Park and Wildlife Conservation, His Majesty's Government and Woodlands Mountain Institute, Kathmandu.

Stevens, S.F. and Sherpa, M.N. (1993) Indigenous people and protected areas: new approach to conservation in highland Nepal. In: Hamilton, L.S., Bauer, D.P. and Takeuchi, H.F. (eds) *Parks, Peaks, and People.* East–West Centre Programme on Environment with Assistance from Woodlands Mountain Institute, U.S. National Parks Service and IUCN – The World Conservation Union.

Stevens, S.F., Sherpa L.N. and Sherpa, M.N. (1993) *Tourism and Local Development in Sagarmatha National Park, Nepal.* Department of Geography and Anthropology, Louisiana State University, Baton Rouge, Louisiana.

Upadhyay, M.P. (1984) *Environmental Impact on Mountain Ecosystem by Trekkers and mountaineers: Mt. Everest Trek Route Survey Report.* NAIS, Kathmandu, Nepal.

World Bank (1998) *World Bank Atlas.* The World Bank, Washington, DC.

Yonzon, P. (1993) Traditional resource use and problems in Langtang National Park, Nepal. In: Hamilton, L.S., Bauer, D.P. and Takeuchi, H.F. (eds) *Parks, Peaks, and People.* East–West Centre Programme on Environment with Assistance from Woodlands Mountain Institute, U.S. National Parks Service and IUCN - The World Conservation Union.

WTO: World Tourism Organization (1998) *Tourism Market Trends, 1998 Edition – South Asia.* WTO, Madrid.

The Role of the Community in Relation to the Tourism Industry: a Case Study from Mount Bromo, East Java, Indonesia

10

Janet Cochrane

Centre for South-East Asian Studies, University of Hull, Hull HU6 7RX, UK

Introduction

In the last few decades, a number of approaches to Third World development have been elaborated. As one method of development apparently fails to achieve its desired results, so another takes its place. By the 1990s, a small-scale participatory model of tourism development was being proposed as the latest answer to global inequalities. As with other development theories, the principles of sustainable and participatory development have been applied in many fields of human activity, including tourism. This has resulted in the establishment of many community-based tourism enterprises intended to attract wealthy tourists and help them to redistribute their wealth to poorer regions. But such enterprises have often been set up by people with little understanding of the nature and complexity of the tourism industry, and the enterprises often fail to achieve the hoped-for results.

   While theories of sustainable and participatory development abound, however, case studies that demonstrate the implications and contradictions of participatory development in practice, are few, especially concerning tourism. It was for this reason that a study of tourism to Bromo Tengger Semeru National Park, in East Java, Indonesia, was undertaken in 1996–1997. This chapter examines the findings of this research and explores ways in which tourism in remote areas can move forward to be of genuine benefit to small communities.

Participatory Development and the Realities of Tourism

Tourism – a huge and complex industry

Tourism is a significant part of the economies of at least 125 nations, and has never experienced a serious decline when measured globally – although individual countries have experienced declines, usually due to political or economic instability, such as with Sri Lanka in the 1980s and Indonesia in the late 1990s.

The central focus of tourism is a range of sensory and intellectual situations that combine to form the holiday experience. In order to provide this experience, a huge network of services and products has evolved. These include the development of a complex regulatory and legislative framework, sophisticated transportation, food and accommodation sectors, and a huge souvenir and handicraft industry. Tangible objects of this kind are only a part of tourist consumption: of equal (or greater) importance are the subjective attributes of beauty, knowledge, companionship, fashionability, spiritual satisfaction or excitement, all of which contribute to fulfilling the aspirations of the purchaser of the holiday product. It is clear that the ways in which people try to satisfy their holiday aspirations are becoming increasingly diverse. For instance, people from the main generating countries are becoming more inclined to travel long distances and to demand better quality transport and accommodation. Some commentators (e.g. Butler, 1995) suggest that tourists are also demanding holidays that are less environmentally and culturally damaging and more 'sustainable'. However, there is little evidence from tourism statistics or from tour operators that their clients pay more than lip service to the ideal of a sustainable holiday, and even the awareness of such an ideal is limited to a very small proportion of the global tourism market.

The notion of what constitutes sustainable tourism is in any case subject to numerous definitions. A review of the relevant literature has revealed several sets of guidelines devised to help assess sustainability in tourism, all of which are basically in agreement that no form of tourism should exceed the capacity of the physical and human environment to withstand it without undergoing serious changes (de Kadt, 1990; Cater, 1992; Eber, 1992; Gunn, 1994; Hunter, 1995). One of the principles of sustainable tourism is that local people should have a decision-making role in any development and be stakeholders in it, in other words that they should participate in shaping any developments which affect them. Of course, as with 'sustainability', the term 'participation' means different things to different people: Pretty (1995) has analysed the different interpretations of participation, ranging from merely imparting information that development is going to occur, to the full involvement of the affected community at all stages, from initial planning through implementation and management. However, in the case of tourism, it is extraordinarily difficult to ensure such a high level of participation because of the extensive needs of government, the mechanisms of the tourism industry itself and the complexity of host communities.

Government requirements and policies

One of the generally accepted tenets of sustainable tourism is that it should be small scale, but as Wheeller (1991) contends, if tourism is to answer the policy aims of governments (increasing foreign exchange, creating employment, promoting regional development) it has to be big, particularly in a country like Indonesia, with a population of over 200 million and where around 2.5 million new people per year were entering the workforce even before the economic crisis of 1997–1998. This means that the small-scale developments proposed by sustainability and participatory development are 'at best . . . a micro solution to what is essentially a macro problem' (Wheeller, 1991: 92). A community of 1500 people constitutes a small village by Indonesian standards, and as the case study of tourism to Bromo will show, it takes a substantial number of visitors to have any meaningful economic impact on this many people. In these circumstances, the micro-projects created by the participatory method of tourism, however noble in aim, are not of major interest to government policy-makers.

The tourism industry and tourists

Tour companies operate in a highly competitive environment, and in the absence of strong controlling regulations, the enterprises showing the best short-term profits will predominate, regardless of environmental or other impact. In the case of Bromo, the absence of strong government support for park protection is a major cause of the inadequacy of conservation of the protected area.

The central element in the tourism industry – the tourist – sometimes seems to be overlooked by proponents of sustainable tourism. And yet the demands of tourists often conflict with the goals of contributing to conservation and minimizing cultural impacts. As many holiday makers choose a different destination every year, they have a short-term interest in seeing the 'best' the destination has to offer rather than a long-term interest in ensuring that cultural and environmental integrity are maintained. Processes that may naturally occur infrequently or over a long period have to be scheduled to fit into fixed itineraries, or in the case of backpackers by the urge to move on and 'do' as much of the world as possible. Providing facilities and services to the standards required by these tourists, many of whom are experienced global travellers, entails expertise that is often lacking in the remote areas of developing countries where much ecotourism takes place. Food, other goods and staff may have to be brought in from abroad or from outside the region, all of which increases the amount of leakages from the tourism economy and reduces the possibility for local people to benefit economically. It is also highly unlikely that under these circumstances the local community could have a decision-making role or be stakeholders, since they lack the experience to make significant decisions and the capital and political resources to acquire more than (at best) a token stake.

The community

Several researchers have remarked on the difficulty of finding an economic mechanism whereby communities coexisting with tourism can be truly involved. A study of tourism in the South Pacific showed local people to be involved in five ways: as observers, entrepreneurs, artisans, attractions and administrators. But it was only as artisans that participation was considered successful in terms of fitting in with contemporary social structures as well as with the demands of the tourism industry (Douglas, 1996). Similarly, consultants trying to ensure that tourism in Lore Lindu National Park, in Indonesia, would benefit as wide a sector of the community as possible found that detailed planning threw up a number of practical problems. For instance, one proposal was to establish community-run guesthouses, but if the building materials were provided by development agencies, would the villagers feel a sense of pride and ownership in the properties, and maintain them? Experience in other areas shows that tourists value tranquillity and privacy more than exposure to the realities of village life, so should the guest houses be sited at some distance from the villages, so they would be quieter, or would this mean that they would not be looked after? Who should run the guesthouses, and on what basis? If it was done on a rota system, could every family in the village participate so that everyone received a share of the economic benefits, or would this be impractical? And how would it be possible to ensure that the management and revenue from the guesthouses were not captured by the most powerful families? (Cochrane *et al.*, 1994).

Taking this point further, exactly what – or who – is meant by 'the community'? Even if they form one administrative unit, any large group of people cannot automatically be considered a homogeneous entity, as it may be composed of individuals subject to ambitions, strengths, family pressures and weaknesses which mean that personal gain may take precedence over the good of the whole. Other development workers too have rejected the myth of a happy peasantry living in harmony with their surroundings and fellows: in the context of Latin America, it has been said that 'the impression of harmony, of cooperation, of community' perceived by outsiders in reality 'masks the real world of conflict, rivalry, and tension' (Carroll, 1992).

As far as decision making is concerned, it is questionable whether the people who host tourism are the best equipped to make decisions about it. They may lack the skills and knowledge necessary to evaluate a particular development, especially its long-term impacts, and they may be unable to take an objective view of the attractiveness of their area in comparison with similar attractions elsewhere, especially when tourists base their discriminations on international experience. Wall (1996) and Cole (1996), both of whom have carried out research into tourism in Indonesia, concluded that it would be preferable for sympathetic outsiders with knowledge of the tourism industry to help guide developments rather than leave it up to the communities most affected.

Finally, the inexperience of many rural communities attempting to operate independently of the mainstream tourism industry, whether catering to group or individual travel, leads to another problem because of the extensive promotion and marketing that tourists rely on. To some extent this can be circumvented by the direct promotional possibilities offered by the Internet, but even this requires a degree of sophistication and resources not available everywhere.

Bromo Tengger Semeru National Park – Case Study

The extent and practice of tourism in and around several villages bordering the national park of Bromo Tengger Semeru was investigated, and conclusions were drawn about the conflicts between the theory and practice of participatory, community-based ecotourism. The study site was chosen because Bromo Tengger Semeru receives the highest number of tourists of any Indonesian national park and because there are numerous villages bordering the park.

Methodology

Five villages with roughly similar underlying characteristics were chosen for detailed research. Two villages, Kandang Sari and Ngadas (in the west of the national park) have virtually no tourism, Wonokitri (northwest) and Ranu Pani (east) have small amounts, and Ngadisari (northeast) is where most tourism takes place.[1] The villages are all situated between 1900 and 2300 m above sea level, and are fairly small by Indonesian standards, with 1000–2600 inhabitants.

A survey of 10% of the households in each village was carried out. Formal and informal leaders such as the village headman, religious and cultural leaders and schoolteachers were interviewed, as well as people servicing the tourism industry and national park staff. Domestic and international tourists at the tourism centres were surveyed with a questionnaire

---

[1] The area of Ngadisari closest to Mount Bromo is called Cemoro Lawang, but as it is part of Ngadisari administratively the latter name will be used throughout.

and semi-structured interviews. The work was carried out by a British researcher fluent in the Indonesian language and with many years' work experience in Indonesia, and by a Javanese field assistant whose knowledge of the Javanese culture and language allowed many insights.

Description and history of Bromo Tengger Semeru

The national park consists of the Bromo-Semeru massif, a block of volcanic highland covering 50,276 ha and with an altitudinal range of 1000–3676 m. The climate is much cooler than in the surrounding lowlands because of the altitude. The principal features are Mount Semeru (see Fig. 10.1), in the southern part of the park, which at 3676 m is Java's highest mountain, and the vast Tengger caldera to the north, in the centre of which is Mount Bromo. Semeru and Bromo are both active volcanoes. Grasslands cover the floor of the Tengger caldera and hill slopes to the south of the Bromo crater, while a desert-like sand sea of lava and ash extends north from Bromo to the caldera wall. The park was established in 1982 for watershed protection, as a buffer zone for volcanic eruptions, and for recreational purposes, rather than for species conservation, although it does contain nine species of plant found nowhere else on Java (FAO, 1977, 1980; Departemen Kehutanan, 1992/93a). Although wildlife is scarce because of hunting in the past, the park does contain much of the typical Javan fauna, including barking deer,

Fig. 10.1. Mount Semeru, highest mountain in Java in Bromo Tengger Semeru National Park.

wild pig, leopard, Javan porcupine, long-tailed macaques, jungle fowl, and Asiatic wild dog.

Administration of the park is the responsibility of the Directorate General of Forest Protection and Nature Conservation (PHPA), which is part of the Ministry of Forestry. The PHPA considers the principal threat to the park's ecology to be wood-cutting, occasioned by the high fuelwood requirement of the surrounding population. The park is also used for fodder for livestock, and there is occasional hunting and bird trapping.

The Tenggerese

There are 167,255 people living in 51 villages abutting the park (Dep. Kehutanan, 1992/93b). The majority of the population is Tenggerese, a remnant group of the Hindu–Buddhist kingdom, which dominated Java until a regime with Muslim affiliations took over in the 15th century. Some of the vanquished peoples fled to Bali, well-known as a stronghold of Hinduism, while others retreated to the mountains of East Java. There, they continued to practise their religion in isolation from other Hindus until links were made with Bali in the 1960s. The best known cultural manifestation of the Tenggerese is the Kasodo festival, which takes place every 9 months. This consists of a huge ceremony centred on the crater of Mount Bromo. For the Kasodo it is estimated that an additional 20,000–25,000 people enter the park, both Hindus from other parts of the Tengger region and domestic non-Hindu tourists.

The Tenggerese have a strong sense of their separate identity from the lowland Javanese who surround them, and while not antagonistic to outsiders, they are self-contained and conservative. One way in which this caution manifests itself is through their traditional laws, which in some areas have been used to great effect to limit the incursion of outsiders into their villages. For instance, in Ngadisari there is a long-standing village law that prevents non-Tenggerese from buying land or from renting it for more than a year, a restriction which apparently pre-dates the advent of large-scale tourism. Similar arrangements have been reached more recently in Ngadas and Ranu Pani.

Livelihood strategies
With the exception of schoolteachers and a tiny number of other civil servants, all residents of the five villages are engaged mainly in agriculture. The majority are land owners, with plots ranging from a fraction of a hectare to 5 ha. The principal cash crops are leeks, garlic, potatoes, cabbages and broad beans. Maize is grown as a food crop. The inputs needed to cultivate potatoes, garlic and cabbages are high in terms of labour, fertilizer and pesticides, and several farmers reported that the need for chemical inputs was increasing every year. The land in Ngadisari was noticeably less

intensively farmed than in the other two villages and more labour from outside the village was employed. The few people in Ngadisari who do not own land are no longer willing to work as day labourers because the wages – Rp2000–2500 (US$0.85–$1.10) per day – are less than earnings from tourism.

About half the families interviewed kept livestock: generally cows, pigs, goats or chickens. Most of the animals live in sheds in the fields rather than being allowed to roam around, necessitating the daily collection of grass as fodder. In Ngadisari over three-quarters of the households keep at least one horse for taking tourists to Mount Bromo.

In four of the villages both men and women do field work, while in Ngadisari the men usually take the horses out for the first shift of tourists from 4 a.m. until 8 a.m., then go to their fields only if it appears no more tourists will materialize that day. Meanwhile the women do much of the farming and wood collection.

Much of the cultivated land is extremely steep and cross-contour cultivation is common, leading to high levels of erosion (see Fig. 10.2). In many places the soil is very deep, which has so far masked the effects of erosion. However, the rates of soil loss are almost certainly not sustainable, as intensive farming has only been practised in Ranu Pani and Ngadas since the early 1970s when roads were built, allowing better access to markets and encouraging greater productivity.

Fig. 10.2.   Steep slopes on the borders of Bromo Tengger Semeru National Park showing erosion.

Culture, education and health

All the villages have groups that perform a type of trance dancing, occasionally for tourists but generally for their own celebrations. Ngadisari also has a dance group, which performs at Hindu festivals, and in Ngadas there are several trained dancing horses (Fig. 10.3), which perform on special occasions. None of these cultural forms are unique to the Tengger people except for the dances performed by the Ngadisari group. Two respondents in Ngadas commented that it was better to grow crops than to dance.

Only elementary school education is available in the villages, and few people go on to high school in most places. In Ngadisari, however, there was a far greater propensity for parents to send their children through junior and senior high school.

It was not possible to carry out a proper statistical survey about births and deaths, but it was clear that many of these are not reported to the correct government office as these are some distance from the villages. Health care is extremely basic and in Ranu Pani, Ngadas and Kandang Sari there was little understanding of basic hygiene procedures. Infant mortality rates were much lower in Ngadisari and Wonokitri than in the other villages.

Utilization of the national park

The major use of the national park by local people is for fuel collection. Over 90% of the households visited in the four villages with little or no

Fig. 10.3. Ceremonial dancing horse in the Tengger village of Ngadas on the border of Bromo Tengger Semeru National Park.

tourism used only wood for cooking. The wood stoves are also the focal point of the home, where people congregate when not working in order to keep warm. Over 70% of respondents in Ranu Pani and Ngadas openly reported collecting wood in the protected area. In Kandang Sari many people produced charcoal from trees within the national park, with the result that tree cover had been substantially reduced within the last three decades (according to older residents). Most of the respondents in Ngadas and Ranu Pani claimed to take firewood from their own land as well as from the forest, but the intensiveness of land cultivation and the relative scarcity of the trees indicated a heavy reliance on the protected area for fuelwood.

The situation in Ngadisari was rather different. There was a higher rate of use of LPG, kerosene and charcoal for cooking and for warmth. There were far more casuarina trees on people's land, which made claims that most fuelwood comes from this source more convincing. The greatest use of the national park here is as a source of fodder for the horses and other livestock. Towards the end of the dry season the grass is burned off to encourage the new season's growth, an illegal practice, but one which the PHPA appear powerless to prevent.

People in all the villages were asked their opinion of the functions of the national park. In Ranu Pani almost a quarter of respondents cited tourism or recreation as a principal function and in Wonokitri a half of respondents said that this was a principal function. (These two villages have low levels of tourism.) In Ngadas and Kandang Sari, where there is no tourism, no positive connection between the park and tourism was made, while in Ngadisari people almost universally thought it was for tourism. Despite this, no correlation was made in Ngadisari between tourism and actual conservation of the park. For instance PHPA's efforts to restrict vehicular access to the crater had been abandoned because of demand from the tourists and jeep drivers, and although the areas of the village on view to tourists were kept fairly clean and arrangements were made to reduce the amount of horse manure on the tourist trails, substantial amounts of rubbish were thrown down the caldera wall out of sight of the tourists.

Involvement with tourism

The villagers in Kandang Sari had seen four tourists in 14 years, three of whom were actually anthropologists or other researchers; the villagers in Ngadas report little contact with tourists, but some tourists do pass through the village on their way into the park, and the hope was expressed by village officials that this passing market could be tapped in some way. In Ranu Pani, the base village for climbing Mount Semeru, half the households reported some contact with tourists, through portering or performing in the trance dancing groups. In Wonokitri around one-third of households had some contact with tourists through driving jeeps or motorcycle taxis, or providing accommodation. There was a general wish in both Ranu Pani and Wonokitri for more tourism because of the economic opportunities offered, and several people believed that it was due to tourism that the government was making infrastructural improvements such as providing a surfaced road and mains electricity.

In Ngadisari three-quarters of the families interviewed were involved in tourism. This mainly took the form of taking visitors to the crater on horses, for which they earn between Rp10,000–20,000 (US$4.35–$8.70) per ride. With between one and three rides per day, their income from this source is therefore considerable (bearing in mind that land labourers earn a daily wage of Rp2500 (US$1.10). Another source of income is from the jeeps. According to another village law, only Tenggerese people are allowed to own horses and jeeps for use with the tourists, which as with the land ownership law is an effective means of keeping control over the basic facilities of tourism.

Many people also rented rooms to tourists, but generally only during the Kasodo and other public holidays. It was noticeable that most of the staff working in the hotels are from outside the region. The reasons given for this were that the local people can make more money by taking horses out with the tourists, and that they lacked sufficient education. However, this situation is likely to change in time, as several of the families interviewed indicated that their children wanted to get qualifications to work in tourism in the future.

In any case, the comments from government officials in the main provincial towns that the Tenggerese made too much money from their agriculture to bother with tourism was clearly a false assumption. Tourism by early 1997 was a significant part of the local economy, with several informants commenting that they now earned as much or more from tourism as from agriculture. Their decision-making inputs and managerial control over tourism, however, are low, as the tour operators who bring groups to the area are all based outside it, and individual tourists base their decisions on where to visit on word-of-mouth or guide-book recommendations.

Tourism to Bromo Tengger Semeru

Tourism activity at Bromo

Mount Bromo is a convenient stop-over point for tourists on overland tours of Java and Bali, and with its dramatic landscape of volcanic craters and the sand sea (Fig. 10.4), combined with the cool mountain air and upland agriculture, the area makes an interesting contrast to the hot climate and rice paddy landscape of the lowlands. It also attracts large numbers of domestic visitors from nearby cities, particularly on Sundays and public holidays. The majority of visitors drive to Ngadisari and ride a horse or walk to the foot of the Bromo crater. From there, it is a steep climb up steps to the rim, traditionally visited at sunrise. There is another viewpoint at

Fig. 10.4. Looking over the sand sea in Bromo Tengger Semeru National Park, with Mount Bromo (smoking crater on left) and Mount Batok.

Mount Penanjakan, which is mainly visited via Wonokitri. The majority of foreign visitors stay only one night, while most domestic tourists drive through the night to arrive in time for the dawn. Both groups depart during the morning, leaving the area almost free of tourists by the afternoon of even the busiest days.

Economic significance

In 1995/96 the 129,148 acknowledged visitors produced Rp246,299,000 in entry fees (US$107,086 at 1996/97 values). This was divided up according to guidelines set out in 1992 legislation covering entry fees to national parks, according to which none of the proceeds return directly to the park. The cost of running the park is Rp1,279,808,000 (US$556,438), about five times as much as the revenue. This funding comes from the central government in one form or another.

Far more significant than the entry fee revenues are the amounts spent by tourists around Bromo and in the province as a whole. According to the East Java government, Bromo is the 'primadona' (*sic*) of its tourism product, being the largest single attraction for foreign visitors. In 1995 tourism to East Java generated foreign exchange of $173.98 million. It is clear, therefore, that the park is an extremely important part of the tourism product at both provincial and national level.

Access and tourism facilities

Access to Ngadisari is by a good quality road built by the provincial government to facilitate tourism. There is also a reasonably good road to Wonokitri, partly thanks to the strong leadership of a former headman of Wonokitri, while there are only poor quality roads to the other three villages. Only Ngadisari is accessible by frequent and regular public transport. Fifty-six households in Ngadisari were reported to provide board and lodging for tourists in 1977 (FAO, 1977), at which time the majority of tourists stayed with villagers, as there was only one hotel. By 1996/97 five more hotels had opened in or near Ngadisari, so that tourists now generally stay with the villagers only when the hotels are full. Only one of the five hotels is owned by a Tenggerese, although three of the others are owned by outsiders in partnership with or married to local people. There are 20–25 cafes, restaurants and mobile food stalls in the touristic part of Ngadisari, around half of which are operated by non-Tenggerese. In Ranu Pani all the Indonesian mountain climbers stay in one of the two climbing huts provided or at a camp site, as do a few of the foreign tourists. Most of the foreigners and a few Indonesians stay at a homestay in Ranu Pani run by a lowland Javanese couple who came to the village as school teachers and are now retired. There are 450 registered horses in Ngadisari, around one-third of which are owned by people in neighbouring villages. There are also around 70 jeeps, which are used for driving tourists into the sand sea or to the viewpoint on Mount Penanjakan. There has been no outside investment by development agencies in tourism in the area, with all accommodation, food and most transport facilities privately owned and developed.

Volume and provenance of visitors

According to national park statistics taken from sales of entry tickets, the park received 129,148 visitors in 1995/96, of whom almost 30% were foreigners (Table 10.1).

Table 10.1. Visitors to Bromo Tengger Semeru National Park.

	Domestic	%	Foreign	%	Total
1976/77	13,113	77.5	3,799	22.5	16,912
1990/91	66,539	72.4	25,352	27.6	91,891
1991/92	84,898	74.7	28,792	25.3	113,690
1992/93	98,728	74.3	34,113	25.7	132,841
1993/94	87,118	73.3	31,713	26.7	118,831
1994/95	88,484	68.5	40,653	31.5	129,137
1995/96	91,459	70.8	37,689	29.2	129,148

Sources: FAO (1977); Dep. Kehutanan (1996a, b).

Table 10.2.   Nationality of visitors to Bromo 1995/96.

Nationality	Numbers	%
Hong Kong	13,208	32.4
Taiwan	6,953	17.1
The Netherlands	5,003	12.3
Other European	6,464	15.9
North America	2,131	5.2
Australia/New Zealand	1,976	4.9
ASEAN	1,383	3.4
Japan/Korea	1,334	3.3
Other	2,192	5.4
Total	40,644	

Source: Dep. Kehutanan (1996a).
ASEAN = Association of South East Asian Nations.

These figures should be treated with some caution, as there is a discrepancy between figures from different sources: for instance data from the provincial tourism office indicates that Bromo received 45,830 foreign tourists in 1995 (Diparda, 1996) rather than the 37,689 indicated by the Forestry Department. There is also an interesting and unlikely decrease in numbers between 1992 and 1993, when formal entry tickets were first issued and better records kept, and the following year, leading one to suspect that by this time methods of 'hiding' visitors – or rather their entry fees – had been perfected. The figures do nevertheless give some indication of numbers, and of the percentage of foreign to domestic tourists.

The country providing the largest number of foreign visitors was Hong Kong, followed by Taiwan and the Netherlands (Table 10.2). The presence of so many Hong Kong and Taiwanese visitors is a relatively recent development, only occurring since the opening of a four-star hotel 20 km from Bromo in 1992, by which considerable marketing effort has been made. As with tourism elsewhere in Indonesia, it is likely that the number of Asian visitors to Bromo has declined since 1997 because of the Asian economic crisis. The large contingent of Dutch visitors is explained by their historical association with Indonesia.

There are no official sources on domestic tourism to Mount Bromo, but according to the visitors' survey carried out for the study, almost all of the domestic tourists came from cities within a 2-h drive of Bromo. Only 12% came from outside East Java. The average group size of foreign visitors was 2.2 people, and of Indonesians 15.5 people. The average length of stay in the Bromo area was 1.65 days for foreign visitors and 0.85 of a day for Indonesian visitors. The majority of tourists were on independently organized tours and aged under 35.

Impacts of Tourism

The amount of tourism activity taking place at Bromo, with 150,000 visitors per year, could be expected to have impacts on the ecology of the park and on the local economy, society and culture.

Economic impacts

The residents of all the villages were universally in favour of tourism for the economic opportunities it offered. In Ngadisari the direct economic impacts were clear, in that the furnishings and material goods in the houses were on average more expensive than in any of the other villages except Wonokitri, and visitors are given shop-bought drinks and snacks rather than home-made ones.

The value of Bromo tourism to the province of East Java in general has already been discussed, and another important finding of the study was that tourism to Bromo is having a direct economic impact in a broader local area than just Ngadisari. Many of the male residents of the village are too busy with the horse rides for tourists to collect the grass for their horses and other livestock, so fodder is brought in by grass collectors from other villages. It was estimated that 30–40 men are engaged in this activity on a daily basis.

An indirect economic impact is that the residents of Ngadisari no longer have time to work their fields themselves, and cannot find labour locally to do so, as earnings are much higher from working directly with the tourists as horsemen. There is therefore a considerable amount of imported labour, mainly from nearby villages.

Socio-cultural impacts

The socio-cultural impacts of tourism generally have been well documented, and include the breakdown of traditional social structures due to an influx of tourists and migrant workers, adoption by younger members of the host community of behavioural traits and morals of the tourists ('the demonstration effect'), and marginalization of the host community. In the case of tourism to Bromo Tengger Semeru, however, these negative impacts have so far failed to materialize. Social and religious structures appear to be intact, and none of the young people showed the signs of cultural breakdown that occur in parts of Bali, such as hanging around the tourist spots and chatting up young foreign women. There is in fact very little social interaction between the visitors and the residents.

There is hardly any out-migration of the Tenggerese, and little in-migration by outsiders. According to the village headman of Ngadisari, outsiders are not allowed to settle in the village unless they marry a local person, and as few outsiders share the religion of the Tenggerese, marriages outside the community are uncommon. The ability of the Tenggerese in Ngadisari to resist outside influences is strengthened by their separate religious and cultural identity and their history of partial alienation from the surrounding lowland community. The structure of land holdings is complex, with people owning land in several different parts of the village due to inheritance patterns. This factor, added to the strong attachment most Tenggerese have to their land, has made it extremely difficult for outsiders to purchase land in the area to build hotels or other tourism facilities. As described above, only one of the hotels in Ngadisari is owned by a non-Tenggerese except where an outsider has married locally, and in Wonokitri villagers have turned down large sums of money offered to buy land for building hotels.

Marginalization of the host community often occurs when tourism becomes lucrative enough to attract outside entrepreneurs. A key factor in the ability of the Tenggerese to resist this trend is that they have succeeded in retaining control of an important part of the provision of tourism services – the horse rides. Horse ownership is restricted to residents of Ngadisari and neighbouring villages, and as the horse ride is an integral part of the holiday experience for many tourists, the vital role of the Tenggerese in the mechanism of tourism in Bromo is guaranteed.

Ecological impacts

Direct effects of tourism
There is trampling of vegetation in the sand sea along the path to Bromo crater, but this is limited in extent as most visitors tend to keep to the path, and the vegetation is anyway rather scarce. More damage is caused by jeeps and motorbikes in the sand sea, but the impact is probably more aesthetic than ecological as, again, the vehicles tend to stay on the same tracks – although a small minority of jeeps and motorbikes zoom around in the sand sea at random.

A more significant problem for the native vegetation is the collection and sale of edelweiss (*Anaphalis javanica*), a protected species. The dried, whitish flowers are considered to be lucky. Edelweiss is collected on mountain slopes within the national park, and is apparently becoming harder to find. It is sold quite openly, with PHPA rangers ignoring the trade and even directing tourists to places where they can buy the flowers.

Indirect effects of tourism
The indirect effects of tourism are probably more significant than the direct ones, in that much of the fodder eaten by the horses used for tourism is collected in the sand sea and on the walls of the caldera. There is also periodic burning of the grass in the sand sea to encourage new growth. The

combined effect of the burning and grass collection is to prevent natural vegetative succession, whereby bushes and eventually trees might be expected to take over from the predominant grassy forms. On the other hand, the grass cutting helps to maintain the sweeping, open landscape so attractive to tourists, and in the park generally volcanic eruptions and deforestation for fuelwood purposes have a more significant impact on natural vegetation cover than tourism.

Another indirect impact is that there is increased litter in Ngadisari as a result of the higher disposable income there. Waste packaging from household goods was observed in litter dumps down the caldera wall at Cemoro Lawang, and there is considerable litter around some of the hotels. This is despite the fact that Ngadisari is the only village out of the ones visited to have an organized rubbish collection.

Induced effects

Ownership of motorcycles and jeeps in Ngadisari and Wonokitri has been encouraged by tourism, and these vehicles are used not only to service tourists but also to facilitate working and ceremonial practices. There are many family ties between the different Tengger villages located around the caldera rim, and there is some vehicular traffic between these villages using the sand sea tracks as a shorter alternative to the longer paved routes around the outside. There is also visitation to the various sacred sites of the Bromo complex, including the large Hindu temple at the foot of Mount Batok, and a holy cave on Mount Widodaren. Journeys to these sites were formerly on foot or on horse-back, and are now often accomplished by motor vehicle.

One of the aims of this study was to find out whether tourism had any beneficial impacts on the environment. As discussed above, the research in villages showed that the most important direct function of the protected area for the villagers is as a source of fuelwood. As described above, in the four villages with little or no tourism, substantial amounts of firewood are collected from inside the national park. However, in Ngadisari it appeared that much less fuelwood was collected. The forest bordering the fields was in good condition, and in many cases the trees actually encroached upon the farmers' land. The casuarina trees on people's land were more numerous, larger and healthier than in the other villages. There was far greater use of other fuels for cooking and heating, such as paraffin, LPG and even electricity. There was also greater use of charcoal, although this merely displaces exploitation of the forest rather than replacing it, as most of the charcoal is bought from another, very poor village which borders the national park.

Given that an estimated 70–80% of the families in Ngadisari are involved in tourism in some way, it is clear that this sector is providing sufficient income to reduce reliance on the fuelwood resources of the national park.

Discussion

The study was designed to find out whether tourism focusing on a protected area can contribute to conservation, and to contribute to the debate on whether participatory, community-based ecotourism as currently proposed is genuinely the best model for achieving economic, social and political improvements. Findings were also made which challenge received wisdom on what constitutes successful ecotourism. From the findings of the study, suggestions have been formulated as to a possible way to move the debate on community-based nature tourism forward.

Tourism's relationship to conservation

As far the first point is concerned, the picture is complicated. On the one hand, it appears that tourism-generated wealth enables people in Ngadisari to buy alternatives to fuelwood, and in Ranu Pani and Wonokitri some people made a clear link between tourism and conservation. On the other hand, tourist vehicles are creating unsightly tracks in the sand sea, and the collection of grass is interfering with the natural ecology of the park. In theory, the outstanding contribution of Bromo Tengger Semeru to East Java's economy should result in increased political will to ensure the park's long-term ecological health, but apart from a few investments in infrastructure no effort is expended on park protection by the local government. The interests of PHPA field staff focus more on making money than on their official duty of protecting the park, and it is a pity that at a more senior level these abuses are not regulated. Such obvious and public negligence is bad for Indonesia's conservation record. It also contributes to the conclusion that the link between tourism and conservation is tenuous, and that ecotourism is unlikely to improve conservation of the target area as a stand-alone policy. Where ecotourism projects are initiated with a conservation aim, official policy support in the form of government incentives and regulations – and enforcement of these regulations – are essential. Another difficulty with claiming that tourism can help park protection is that tourism in national parks generally takes place only in a small area of it, and deterioration of areas outside the touristic zone will have no impact on visitor numbers.

Community-based ecotourism and development

Concerning the second point, the evidence of the Bromo Tengger Semeru study is that, under certain conditions, nature tourism can be directly and indirectly beneficial to people's economic, social and cultural welfare. It was quite clear from people's houses, material possessions and foods that the residents of Ngadisari are wealthier than in Ngadas or Ranu Pani.

Awareness of the need for education is higher, and the number of people reporting infant deaths in the family was lower. These factors are almost certainly not due to greater agricultural productivity, since the land was less intensively farmed while the average farmland per family was no greater. Furthermore, tourism has prompted the local government to make infrastructural improvements such as better road, electricity, telephone and public transport networks, all of which improve the quality of life for residents as well as facilitating tourism.

It is hardly new to say that tourism is responsible for generating economic wealth. What is interesting about the Bromo Tengger Semeru case is that the community with the most tourism, Ngadisari, has remained an important beneficiary of the direct economic impacts by retaining firm control over ownership of tourism services, and this appears to be the key element in ensuring their prosperity. Another key factor arising from the study is that tourism has to occur on a medium to large scale relative to the size of the host community to make a useful contribution to development, such as in Ngadisari, whereas the small scale of tourism in Wonokitri and Ranu Pani provides negligible benefits.

On the subject of community-based and participatory ecotourism, the conclusions of this study do not concur with current development fashion. As described, tourism to Mount Bromo is rooted in the community to the extent that the Tenggerese are benefiting from the industry through their individual involvement in tourism-related enterprises, and they are able by their traditional laws to restrict the incursion of outsiders and the over-development which has resulted in negative impacts in other places. However, their level of participation in decision-making and management is negligible, as they are not involved in promotion and are not in control of whether tourism happens or not. As negative environmental and cultural impacts of tourism currently appear to be low, it therefore appears that a high level of participation in the industry through ownership of facilities and the ability to profit from private enterprise, coupled with a strong local identity and laws, are more important for success and sustainability than involvement in policy and management. Of course, every case study is an isolated example to the extent that local circumstances influence the condition of tourism, and in the case of Bromo the Tenggerese are fortunate in having a strong community identity, a unique, world-class attraction on their doorstep, and sufficient entrepreneurial spirit to exploit the opportunities open to them, while the national park has a relatively robust ecology.

But is it ecotourism?

A more general conclusion concerns the definition of 'ecotourism', to which acres of journal space and hours of conference time have been devoted. Tourism to Bromo is considered by some observers not to be true ecotourism because of its large scale and because most of the tourists are not concerned about their individual impact on the environment and culture of the area. However, this kind of discussion is of more interest to academics than to most practitioners, communities, governments or tourists. What is certain is that the kind of 'mass ecotourism' which occurs at Bromo has to be taken seriously in the context of a developing country in that it is only this level of tourism which can generate sufficient economic benefits to have any impact at all: small scale tourism may be beautiful, but it is also irrelevant to the planner and policy-makers who are trying to make conservation and development compatible, and to the communities who are trying to make a living.

Pragmatism versus purism

If we accept that tourism – even ecotourism – can occur on a large scale, and indeed *must* occur on a large scale if it is to bring recognizable material and social benefits to any given community, then where does this leave the beliefs of many proponents of sustainable tourism? As pointed out in the first section of this paper, communities living near national parks or other attractions generally lack experience of the tourism industry and awareness of what tourists want, and are therefore incapable of planning and managing the development of a successful tourism product – successful, that is, in financial terms, since this is the only type of success which is going to bring in its wake the benefits of an improved standard of living. People who work in the conventional tourism industry have been saying for years that it would be more effective to make conventional, or mass, tourism less environmentally and culturally damaging than pursue the unrealistic aim of replacing mass tourism with an alternative, more aesthetic, 'small is beautiful' type of tourism, which will only ever appeal to a minority market. It is time that community development workers and other advocates of community tourism took this view on board and realized that participation by the host community in tourism does not have to be on the level of making decisions about how tourism will develop.

What is needed is for sympathetic outsiders, whether development workers or commercial investors, to plan a product which uses the labour and resources of as many local people as possible. Government or non-governmental agencies have an important role in trying to ensure that local laws will support the retention of ownership of essential parts of the tourism product in local hands, which in itself will guarantee the long-term future of economic benefits to the area. Governments also have an essential role to play in enforcing a strong regulatory climate so that laws designed to protect environmentally or culturally weak elements of the tourism attraction are upheld.

In general, therefore, to develop a new tourism product a partnership approach is needed, between local people with access to and some control over a tourism resource – preferably one with a unique selling point – and outside individuals or agencies with knowledge of the tourism industry and tourists. Above all, it must not be forgotten that, ultimately, it is the tourist who is central to the tourism industry, and unless his or her needs and aspirations are catered to, there is no chance at all of using tourism as a tool to enhance social and economic welfare.

References

Butler, R. (1995) Introduction. In: Butler, R. and Pearce, D. (eds) *Change in Tourism People, Places, Processes.* Routledge, London, Chapter 1, pp. 1–11.

Carroll, T.F. (1992) *Intermediary NGOs: the Supporting Link in Grassroots Development.* Kumarian Press, Connecticut.

Cater, E. (1992) Profits from Paradise. *Geographical Magazine,* London, March.

Cochrane, J., MacKenzie, K. and Ratcliffe, J. (1994) Feasibility Study for Microenterprise Development in Lore Lindu National Park, Central Sulawesi. Preliminary report for The Nature Conservancy, Jakarta.

Cole, S. (1996) Anthropologists, Local Communities and Sustainable Tourism Development. Paper presented at Sustainable Tourism Conference, Newton Rigg College, Lancashire 17–19 April.

de Kadt, E. (1990) Making the alternative sustainable: lessons from development for tourism. Discussion Paper 272, Institute of Development Studies, University of Sussex.

Departemen Kehutanan, Direktorat Jendral Perlindungan Hutan dan Pelestarian Alam, Taman Nasional Bromo Tengger Semeru (1992/93a) Laporan Pengkajian Zonasi Taman Nasional Bromo Tengger Semeru, Buku I (National park zonation report), Malang, Indonesia.

Departemen Kehutanan, Direktorat Jendral Perlindungan Hutan dan Pelestarian Alam, Taman Nasional Bromo Tengger Semeru (1992/93b) Laporan Identifikasi Daerah Penyangga Taman Nasional Bromo Tengger Semeru (National park buffer zone identification report), Malang, Indonesia.

Departemen Kehutanan, Direktorat Jendral Perlindungan Hutan dan Pelestarian Alam, Taman Nasional Bromo Tengger Semeru (1996a) Laporan Tahunan 1995/ 1996 Taman Nasional Bromo Tengger Semeru (Annual national park report), Malang, Indonesia.

Departemen Kehutanan, Direktorat Jendral Perlindungan Hutan dan Pelestarian Alam, Taman Nasional Bromo Tengger Semeru (1996b), Potensi dan Permasalahan Pemanfaatan Serta Pengembangan Obyek Wisata Alam. Presented at: Rapat Koordinasi Pemanfaatan Obyek Wisata Alam, 5–6 November (Report on Potential for Nature Tourism Development), Malang, Indonesia.

Diparda: Dinas Pariwisata Daerah (1996) *Pariwisata Dalam Angka 1995 (Tourism statistics 1995).* Surabaya, Indonesia.

Douglas, N. (1996) *Tourism in the South Pacific.* Visiting lecture at University of Humberside, UK, 6 June.

Eber, S. (ed.) (1992) *Beyond the Green Horizon.* WWF UK, Godalming, UK.

FAO: Food and Agriculture Organisation (1977) Proposed Bromo Tengger Gunung Semeru Mountain National Park, East Java, Field Report of UNDP/FAO Nature Conservation and Wildlife Management Project INS/73/013, Bogor, Indonesia.

FAO: Food and Agriculture Organisation (1980) Bromo Tengger Gunung Semeru Proposed National Park, Management Plan 1981–85, Field Report of the UNDP/FAO National Park Development Project, INS/73/061, Bogor, Indonesia.

Farrington, J. (n/d) Review of Beyond Farmer First, originally in *Agricultural Research and Extension Newsletter* 31, pp. 15–21, reproduced in *Proceedings of Partici-patory Technology Development Workshop The Limits to Participation*, 23 March 1995, Institute of Education, London (hosted by Intermediate Technology).

Gunn, C.A. (1994) *Tourism Planning.* Taylor & Francis, London.

Hunter, C. (1995) On the need to re-conceptualise sustainable tourism development, *Journal of Sustainable Tourism* 3, 155–165.

Pretty, J. (1995) The many interpretations of participation. *In Focus*, Summer Issue: Tourism Concern, Wimbledon, UK.

Wall, G. (1996) Perspectives on tourism in selected Balinese villages. *Annals of Tourism Research* 23, 123–137.

Wheeller, B. (1991) Tourism's Troubled Times: Responsible Tourism is not the Answer. *Tourism Management* June, 91.

Community-based Tourism for Conservation and Women's Development

11

Wendy Brewer Lama

The Mountain Institute, PO Box 2785, Kathmandu, Nepal

When we first invited the women of Shermathang to the project meetings, they said they could not read nor write, and therefore could not participate. When asked their names, they just giggled. Over the period of two years, through a series of appreciative participatory planning and action workshops and ecotourism training, the situation changed dramatically: a women's group had formed, registered with the District government, and had established its own office; it now holds regular meetings, keeps minutes, and has raised 30,000 rupees (approximately US$500) with which it provides revolving loans to members to start small enterprises. With the interest from the loans, it has set up a small museum to inform tourists about the women's Yolmu culture. Tourists' donations support the women's volunteer efforts to undertake other conservation and community activities, including regular village garbage clean-ups, literacy classes, and performances of traditional cultural dances. (Observations by Langtang Ecotourism Project staff, September 1996 to October 1998)

Introduction

Studies of women in tourism in Nepal show that there are significant gender gaps at the tourism policy, programme design, implementation and decision-making levels that affect women's participation in tourism (Gurung, 1995). There are significant disparities between men and women's status, access to resources, control of assets and decision-making powers that undermine sustainable and equitable development (Gurung, 1995). In mountain villages along Nepal's popular trekking routes, women routinely manage small tourist lodges serving 20–30 foreign trekkers per day and again that many trekking staff, yet they are rarely seen in village meetings or in discussions with government officials about tourism and resource management (Byers and Sainju, 1999). They are usually in the kitchen making tea and caring for the children while the men discuss the issues and set policies.

The lack of gender sensitivity in government tourism development strategies and the socio-economic inhibitions of women perpetuated by society have constrained women from more fully benefiting from opportunities availed by mountain tourism in Nepal. Women often bear the additional burdens of tourism, such as fuelwood and water collection, cooking and cleaning (Stevens, 1993), but the benefits accrue to others (Gurung, 1995).

Women's roles in and benefits from tourism can be enhanced through a participatory appreciative approach to community planning in which the community acknowledges the 'value' of women's contributions to tourism. This assets-based approach builds upon the 'good things' in a community, including natural features, cultural heritage, men and women's skills and institutional capacities, to develop community-based tourism that promotes widespread local benefits and thereby provides financial incentives for conservation of what tourists come to see.

Despite a lack of education and leadership experience, village women of the Langtang-Helambu region have shown remarkable commitment and initiative in carrying out planned tourism and conservation activities on their own. A participatory appreciative approach to village tourism planning is bringing positive changes to women's lives and to the villages where women's initiatives to conserve the cultural heritage and natural environment are promoting community benefits from tourism. The 'observations' (above) reveal the changing roles of women in tourism in one village, Shermathang.

Stories from the Field: Women's Issues in Mountain Tourism of the Himalaya

An analysis of the impacts of tourism on Indian women points out that tourism projects have made no difference to the status of women in the hill states. Declining sex ratio, adult illiteracy, retention of girl children in school, infant mortality rate and infanticide, and life expectancy and birth rates have not 'closed the gender gap' between men and women of mountain regions despite inputs from tourism projects (Rao, 1998).

Tourism is a relatively new phenomenon in the Himalayan communities and has certainly affected the socio-economic structure and cultural environment of mountain communities just as it has the natural environment. Its effects on mountain women's lives and opportunities for betterment vary considerably among mountain ethnic groups as do women's status and their abilities to respond to outside influences. In some mountain communities of Nepal, tourism has ushered in a degree of economic independence for women by extending them opportunities in education, health care, and wage-earning livelihoods. Nowadays, with the new-found wealth and foreign contacts afforded by four decades of trekking and mountaineering tourism in the Everest region, Sherpinis (female Sherpas) of Solu Khumbu travel without husbands or children to the USA where they earn a reasonable living working as domestic childcare givers.

> I stayed in the U.S. for nine months. I loved it. I could do and see so many new things there. I could wear what I wanted, and I was well paid. I'd go back in an instant. (Ms K. Sherpa, married and mother of two children; personal communication)

Such opportunities would have been highly unlikely had not these Sherpinis been accustomed to cooking and cleaning for foreign tourists who stayed in their lodges.

Among the village population of Tarkegyang, Helambu (with approximately 120 households), some 46 men and 40 women are temporarily working in the US as household servants and child sitters. They report that the Lodge Management and Cooking Training certificates they received from an ecotourism project fetches them 66% higher wages than those Nepalis who do not have the certificate.

In the neighbouring northeastern Indian State of Sikkim, several young women of Yuksam village, located at the entry to Kangchendzonga National Park, work as trekking guides. They command a crew of 10–15 male assistant guides and yak drivers, plus a group of foreign trekkers, up to 16,000 ft/4800 m at the base of the third highest peak in the world (Mount Kangchendzonga).

> It was difficult at first to manage the local men. But after a few times, they started listening to me and now I have no problems. I really enjoy the work, meeting foreigners and walking in the forests. I feel that we the local people can give tourists the most authentic experience. (Ms U. Bhutia, age 22; personal communication)

Thus, among these Himalayan communities, tourism has introduced opportunities for women's advancement and empowerment. But while some women enjoy these benefits of tourism, for many, tourism just adds to their daily duties of cooking, child rearing, livestock rearing, farming, fuel and fodder collection, etc. Typically in the less affluent mountain areas where tourists visit, women's normal household responsibilities are compounded when their husbands and sons are away for 6 or more months a year, working as trekking porters and guides. Still, some women manage to do all that, and run a small trekker's lodge to earn a little extra income.

Fig. 11.1. A typical Helambu house kitchen: the Yolmu women.

Social Framework for Women in Community-based Mountain Tourism in the Himalaya

The stories of Sherpinis travelling to the USA without their husbands is not representative of Nepali women's social status. Nepali women cannot get a passport without the written approval of their father or husband. Few women travel within Nepal without a male relative, and those who do are sometimes questioned by airport officials.

There is a pronounced gender imbalance in Nepal, particularly at the village level (Majupuria, 1991). Girl children are often unschooled due to inadequate family funds to pay school costs, which may be the equivalent of only a few dollars per month. Girls are kept home to help with the household and farming chores, and to watch their little brothers and sisters. Although less common today, village girls would traditionally marry by early teenhood and start bearing children shortly thereafter. Women are generally excluded from community leadership and decision-making roles, and in more traditional cultures women are considered pushy for even voicing their opinion. None the less, in recent years, women have begun holding elected local and national government seats, and are increasingly part of the workforce in urban areas but rarely hold management positions.

Women's status is highly variable depending upon their ethnicity. Ethnic peoples of Tibetan origin who live in the middle to higher elevations (e.g. Sherpa, Gurung, Yolmu and the other Bhotia peoples – those whose ancestors originated in Tibet) are generally Buddhist, the social structure of which is considerably less rigid than that of the Hindu castes of the lowlands (those of Indian origin). Mountain women are generally hardy in nature and stature, active in small family businesses and even manage the household finances. Highland men traditionally have travelled away from home for long periods of time, working as livestock herders, traders, labourers and now in tourism, leaving women 'in charge'. Hindus, having a far stricter social structure and a more sedentary lifestyle, generally have more conservative attitudes toward women.

Women's roles in mountain tourism in Nepal are primarily an extension of the home manager and guest caretaker responsibilities. Women operate lodges and teashops along the major trekking routes, sometimes with their husbands or fathers, but often alone. As cooks and primary servers, they have the greatest contact with tourists, trekking guides and porters. The women of Langtang are never idle: whatever time they have to sit down is spent knitting woollen caps, mittens and socks, weaving bags or making handicrafts to sell to tourists. Some mountain women work as porters or pack animal drivers for trekking or mountaineering groups and a handful have broken into the ranks of trekking guide.

The challenges facing village women in mountain tourism are related not only to their lesser socio-economic status, education, literacy levels, inability to speak English, and their low self-confidence, but also to their responsibilities as mothers and homemakers. With the exception of their work in tourism, their contributions to the home and family are largely non-monetary and thus are less valued than the wages earned by males.

> Our women should be more involved in community discussions about tourism and forest management issues, but they are too busy cooking and taking care of the children. (Mr Singhi, village social worker, Shermathang, February 1996, personal communication)

> We would like to learn to speak English so we can communicate better with tourists. Sometimes there is a misunderstanding about the price of the room or food, and we cannot explain the reasons to our guests. Some tourists get angry, and we feel badly and reduce the charges, and then we make no profit. (Ms C. Lama, Shermathang, 1997, personal communication)

Quotations like these suggest some of the obstacles the Yolmu women of Helambu have faced to partake in tourism planning workshops and management training activities: illiterate women's poor self-image; their awkwardness at communicating in their native language (Yolmu) among educated Nepali-speaking men and outsiders; their inability to speak English with tourists; and a lack of understanding or support among male villagers. Despite these hurdles, the women of Shermathang and other Langtang-Helambu communities are gradually gaining the confidence and skills to participate in and benefit more fully from community-based tourism. It is worth looking further at the planning methods and strategies for involving women to see if the approach may have wider application.

Appreciative Participatory Gender-balanced Planning for Community-based Tourism

The Mountain Institute (TMI) is an international non-government organization (NGO) based in the Appalachian Mountains of the eastern USA. It works in partnership with governments, the private sector and non-governmental organizations in Nepal, Sikkim (India) and Tibet (People's Republic of China) to help village communities and national parks plan for and manage community-based tourism that promotes local benefits and conserves the Himalaya's rich biological and cultural diversity. An appreciative participatory gender-balanced approach to planning and management seeks to motivate villagers to conserve their natural and cultural heritage by generating awareness about the environment, and teaching people how to reduce the negative impacts of tourism while improving the tourism service standards that thereby justify greater and more widely available revenues. The approach builds upon the community's assets, strengths and skills in community-based tourism. It formulates a collective vision or 'dream' of how the community will look in 10 or 20 years if tourism is developed and managed properly. Furthermore, it builds the community's confidence and capacity, both institutionally and financially, to achieve the dream under its own initiative and with its own resources.

The premise is that if local people earn an income from tourism, and if tourists are coming to see the natural environment and cultural attractions of

Fig. 11.2. Women of Shermathang find time amidst their household and lodge operation duties to take on community initiatives such as garbage management.

the area, villagers will be financially motivated to value, invest in and practise conservation of their natural and cultural heritage, which in turn will
better serve their own livelihood needs. The sustainability of tourism-linked
livelihoods is thus inextricably linked to conservation. And vice versa. If the
environment and culture are not well cared for, tourists will stop coming and
benefits will cease. A case in point: Nepal's tourist arrivals dipped in the late
1980s as word spread through the media and returning trekkers of the piles
of garbage along trekking routes and at mountaineering base camps. Coordi-
nated efforts by the tourism industry, NGOs and mountain communities,
with backing by the government, have resulted in much cleaner trails,
campsites and villages, and increased awareness among the private tourism
sector that their livelihoods depend on a clean environment. The battle is
not over yet; new tourism operators enter the arena each season, and the
need for generating conservation awareness and incentives for maintaining
tourism standards among a growing industry continues.

For the last 3 years, working with community, government and private
sector partners, TMI has conducted a series of workshops and training
activities on community-based tourism in Sikkim, India, under the Sikkim
Biodiversity and Ecotourism Project (SBE), and in Langtang National Park
and Helambu region of Nepal, as the Langtang Ecotourism Project (LEP)

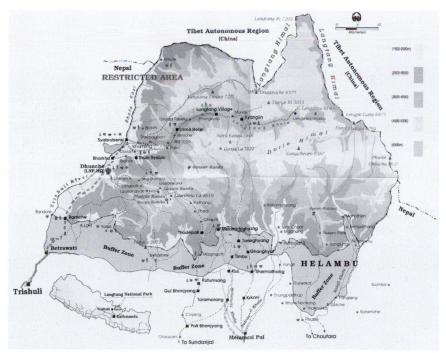

Fig. 11.3. Langtang National Park and Helambu Buffer Zone: the third most popular trekking destination in Nepal.

(Box 11.1). Whereas women's development and empowerment have not been a specific objective of these programmes, an appreciative participatory approach, an emphasis on building self-reliance and institutional capacities, and perhaps the involvement of female project managers, facilitators and trainers have motivated women in these communities to take a lead role in improving tourism management and in conserving the natural and cultural environment.

Strategies for Facilitating Women's Participation in Community-based Tourism

Community recognition of women's contributions to community-based tourism enhances women's overall social status. The development of women's business and service skills prepares them for other income-generating opportunities, and both of these help develop women's self-confidence, self-respect and economic worth. Helping a community to appreciate the 'value' of women and their contributions to sustainable village-based tourism and the community as a whole is the first step toward enhancing women's roles in and due benefits from community-based tourism. Some methods being used are:

Box 11.1.   Major project activities.

These include:
- Training and use of participatory planning and learning tools to develop a village profile and baseline data as the basis for community-based tourism planning and monitoring, and to build interest and ownership among the community;
- Training in lodge operations and management, sanitation and waste management, cooking, hospitality, English language, energy conservation, and promoting indigenous foods and cultural features;
- Exchange study tours demonstrating other conservation and development approaches to community management of natural resources and tourism;
- Village Tourism Planning Workshops, using an Appreciative Participatory Planning and Action methodology to identify current tourism assets, build a collective 'dream' for community-based tourism, develop action plans and strengthen institutional capacities and personal commitments to implement plans;
- Issuance of community matching grants to village tourism management and cultural conservation committees, including women's groups, to undertake activities and enterprises that generate ongoing funds for tourism and conservation.

1. *Valuing women*: holding open discussions with community members, men and women, about what women bring to tourism, their roles and responsibilities, and the unique attributes or skills of women that enhance tourism opportunities and benefits, etc.

2. *Participatory planning and learning exercises*: through such discussions and in participatory planning and learning workshops, facilitating the community acknowledgement of the function and importance of women's groups, their activities and roles. This can be done using participatory learning and action tools, such as:

(a) *Venn diagram*: showing village institutions, including women's groups, their relative importance and roles;

(b) *Trend line*: tracing the historic change in various village conditions in relation to women's group activities and gender issue awareness, e.g. rating cleanliness of village with women's group clean-up activities, support for community infrastructure improvements, such as monastery restoration, education of girl children, increases in cash earned by women entrepreneurs, etc.

(c) *Seasonal calendar for women* (and men, done separately): plotting the multiple tasks performed by women year-round, and focusing on those tasks and skills related to enhancing the tourists' traditional village experiences and income generation through tourism (e.g. teaching tourists to weave, processing food by hand, cooking, making handicrafts). This exercise can also indicate what seasons women (and men) have time to devote to tourism, when tourism attractions are greatest.

3. *Appreciative inquiry*: asking the community in meetings or workshops questions like: 'What is it that you are proud of in your village?'; 'What good things does the women's group do?'; 'How would you (the community) like to see the village/women's group in 20 years?' To the women: 'What are you proud of that you and/or the women's group have done?' These questions help give value to and form a positive basis for a shared vision of community-based tourism for the future. This vision or 'dream' is turned into specific activities that are planned by the community for short, medium and long-term horizons. Action plans emphasize local responsibilities and self-reliance.

4. *Well-planned study tour exchanges*: women naturally network with other women, and often learn best by seeing, hearing and doing. Exchange study tours are an excellent way to open women's eyes to what other women are doing toward tourism, community development, conservation, etc. The study tour is most successful if it is set up as an 'exchange' so that both parties benefit from the cross-fertilization of ideas. The tour should be 'well-planned' so that all participants know exactly what they will share and learn, and plan how they will use it and share with the community upon return home. Following a visit to the Annapurna Conservation Area Project (ACAP) by Langtang-Helambu men and women, one participant told the women of Langtang Village about the ACAPs women's cultural dance programme in Ghandruk, which instantly inspired the women to form their own *aama samuwa* (group). Within a few weeks, the Langtang women started a cultural dance programme for tourists, initiated a revolving loan programme, and began to clean the village every month, with no outside

Fig. 11.4(a) and (b).   Women doing PRA (Participatory Rural Appraisal) exercises as part of the participatory planning process.

assistance from the Project. With the funds raised from demonstrating cultural dances to tourists, the women are planning to restore the monastery.

5. *Women's representation and participation in all project activities and committees*: once the community has discussed the roles and values of women in tourism, it is much more evident that women must be part of all community-based tourism learning, planning and management opportunities (i.e. training and planning workshops, study tours, committees, meetings, etc.). LEP strives for at least 50% women's participation in all activities, and generally achieves 30–60%. Women are represented in almost all village tourism management committees.

6. *'Women-friendly' techniques*: sometimes extra thought must go into facilitating women's participation, to reduce the burden of their other responsibilities as mothers and home-makers, and to conform to social norms. For example:

(a) Workshop organizers might suggest that the community arrange for childcare during day-long, evening, or away-from-home programmes to allow women with children to fully participate.

(b) When women must travel to another village, they should plan to travel and work in twos or more to avoid the social stigma of travelling or working alone or with a man (in some areas, women are 'kidnapped' into marriage while travelling away from home).

(c) Discussions can be held with village men – husbands or fathers of women participants – about the importance and investment value of building women's capacities and confidence so that when appropriate, males step back and give the training opportunity or committee seat to women.

(d) When women are hesitant to speak up in mixed male/female group discussions, consider holding separate break-out sessions for women.

(e) Where women are not fluent in the common language of the workshop, encourage discussions in their local dialect, arrange for simultaneous translation, or use pictures or symbols to illustrate points rather than written words so that uneducated or illiterate women can participate and understand.

7. *Gender-sensitive participation selection criteria*: develop representation and participation selection criteria with the community that include women based on her skills and responsibilities rather than a gender quota, e.g. selected person must be year-round resident of village, or the primary person working in lodge.

8. *Women's quotas*: sometimes, however, it may be necessary to discuss and agree upon mandatory representation by women, though this sometimes relegates the woman as a token, less valued member.

9. *Women's empowerment through improved communication*: village women strive to be literate to reduce their legal and political dependency on men, and are keen to learn English to communicate better with tourists and to learn about the world. Women working in lodges learn a bit of English from trekkers, but are unable to explain why prices have increased to help pay for kerosene, or to 'please order the same food with other trekkers to save fuel.' Communication and self-expression are key to empowerment, and vital to community-based tourism, which depends upon an informed and understanding tourist. The Kathmandu Environmental Education Project (KEEP) an NGO partner in the Langtang Ecotourism Project, raised its own funds to conduct three English language training courses in the Langtang-Helambu area for lodge operators. Local schoolteachers and US Peace Corps volunteers helped in the training and are continuing the language instruction.

10. *Women role models*: engaging women as partners, participants and managers is a priority for TMI's Himalaya Programmes. At present 40% of full-time India (Sikkim Biodiversity and Ecotourism) project staff are women, including the Project Manager. The LEP Manager is also female. A female senior consultant/PRA facilitator who works in the TMI Himalaya Programmes is a Sherpini who heads another of TMI's partner NGOs, Mountain Spirit, to promote mountain peoples as conservation and development professional role models.

Langtang Ecotourism Project

The Langtang-Helambu region of central Nepal is the third most popular trekking area (after the Annapurna and Everest regions). It is visited annually by up to 10,000 foreign trekkers and 10,000–15,000 Nepali and Indian religious pilgrims. The Park was established in 1976 to protect the mountain and glacial landscape, the high altitude fir–rhododendron forests, temperate oak deciduous forests and rare Himalayan larch (*Larix nepalensis*). It was also designed to protect several species of rare, endangered and protected wildlife species including the Himalayan *tahr* and several other mountain goats, red panda, black bear, musk and barking deer, yellow-throated marten and hundreds of species of birds.

The cultural heritage and history of the area is extremely rich with centuries-old Tibetan Buddhist monasteries, meditation sites of early saints and teachers, and high altitude sacred lakes. The carved wooden buildings, hand-woven woollen clothes, and festivals and traditions are unique to the Yolmu and Bhotia peoples of this region, who originated from Tibet. They are primarily herders, farmers and, for the last 30 years, trans-migrant workers who spend long periods away doing manual labour in northern India. There is evidence that the large number of livestock kept to produce milk for the government cheese factories take a heavy toll on high altitude pasturelands, which also support wildlife. Tourism provides an important source of revenue to villagers, reducing their dependency on the land and on taking outside jobs.

The first western 'tourist' to visit Langtang Valley is believed to be explorer H. W. Tilman in 1949. Trekking and mountaineering tourism began in the Langtang-Helambu region some 25–30 years ago. Since the 1980s, trekking lodges have provided food and lodging to some of the 70% of trekkers who travel independently; the other 30% contract for a full-service camping trek with a trekking agency. There are now approximately 140 private lodges and teashops in the Langtang-Helambu area. Most trekkers spend 10–14 days in the area; independent trekkers spend an average of US$10–20 per day eating and sleeping in local lodges, and sometimes hiring a local porter to carry their gear. The mushrooming of lodges in recent years resulted in price wars that drove sleeping charges down to zero, and left little margin for investing in proper environmental management, such as the use of alternative fuels. The national park regulates the number of lodges permitted on government land but not on private land.

In 1996, the LEP was initiated to strengthen the capacities of local communities, Langtang National Park staff and Nepali NGOs to plan and manage community-based tourism, and to develop ways in which tourism can provide benefits to local people and ensure protection of the Park's biodiversity. The project area follows the main trekking routes of Langtang National Park and the Helambu buffer zone. Nine village settlement areas were selected as the places most visited by trekkers, and thus where local people are most experienced, responsive and motivated to conserve what tourists come to see.

The project's main objectives are to build local capacities for planning and managing community-based ecotourism that supports biodiversity conservation. The aim is to help communities improve tourism services, manage the environmental impacts and plan tourism attractions that will help to extend tourists' stays in the Park. If local people can earn an income from tourism, they will be financially motivated to conserve the natural and cultural environment.

Women's Roles in Community-based Tourism and Conservation in Langtang-Helambu

Besides these on-the-ground accomplishments of some 120 women of Langtang-Helambu, the contributions of women in the overall accomplishments of community-based tourism in the region are important to consider in understanding women's roles in community empowerment and participatory management of tourism and natural resources. By nature, women are traditional caretakers, with home, family and farm responsibilities. Their wide-ranging and multiple responsibilities demand that they have a variety of skills and abilities, and be good managers. As collectors and users of the forest products, they are well familiar with the concept of sustainability: if you do not use resources (natural, financial, etc.) wisely, there will not be enough for the future. As skilled caretakers and managers, and in trekking regions with the practical experience of hosting tourists, women are well suited to understanding and managing the impacts of tourism on the natural and cultural environment. They also understand the importance of sharing

---

Box 11.2.   Major project accomplishments.

These include:

1.   *Institutional capacity strengthening*: nine village tourism management committees, six women's groups, and three cultural conservation organizations have been established, or existing organizations strengthened, with a total membership of approximately 300 men and women, who are working toward community-based tourism and conservation in the nine village settlement areas.

2.   *Village ecotourism plans (VEPs)*: all village sectors have developed VEPs laying out detailed activity plans for tourism development and management, and conservation, targeting primarily local funds and resources.

3.   *Community matching grants*: LEP has issued small community matching grants to five village organizations to operate kerosene depots in order to reduce use of fuelwood in trekking lodges and to generate ongoing village organization funds for tourism and conservation activities. In addition, two women's groups have received matching grants to complete a public toilet which one group constructed at the monastery, and to develop a village-wide garbage management system. Matching grants require equal contribution of funds by the village organization.

4.   *Implementation of village ecotourism plans*: activities undertaken by the village tourism and cultural conservation committees with locally generated funds, to implement the VEPs include:

- Monthly trail and village clean-up in all nine village sectors
- Collection of bottles for recycling in four village sectors
- Sale of more than 4000 litres of kerosene
- Use of kerosene stoves in 50% of lodges
- Plantation of 17,500 tree seedlings and employment of forest guard
- Construction and maintenance of 40 km of trekking trails and bridges
- Erection of directional trail signs and removal of large commercial signs
- Increased plantation of vegetables for sale to trekking lodges
- Construction of nine toilets and garbage management at high altitude holy lakes
- Managed cutting and sale of bamboo walking sticks during a religious festival
- Voluntary relocation of four lodges to prevent pollution of the holy lake
- Construction of 55 household toilets supported by US Peace Corps and USAID.
- Initiation of village cultural tours for tourists

benefits of tourism among the community for improved livelihoods and well-being. The experiences from the LEP suggest that women's participation in community-based tourism helps empower women with new skills and confidence and affects their status in the community by 'valuing' their skills as tourism 'assets'. Beyond these gender-based results, women's participation is also *critical to achieving the basic objectives of sustainable community-based tourism*, as summarized below.

Women's involvement helps assure broad-based participation and benefit sharing

Community-based tourism seeks to promote local benefits, which act as financial incentives to conserve the natural environment and cultural heritage that tourists come to see. If only a limited number of people in the community earn income and thereby experience the financial incentives to conserve, there may be an insufficient critical mass to affect a change in resource use patterns and protection of cultural sites and values necessary to support sustainable tourism. Yet, it is often difficult to draw a broad cross-section of the community into community-based tourism planning, particularly community members who are not already involved in tourism. These people may feel they have no experience and nothing to contribute to village tourism planning. Other factors, including socio-economic characteristics, ethnic background, gender and educational level, and village politics are other factors that can sometimes impede widespread participation in community-based tourism. Women's participation in both the planning and operations of community-based tourism and related income generating activities tends to engage a wide socio-economic cross-section of the community in community-based tourism. By involving women as a socio-economic classification or unit of the community, there tends to be a natural cross-section that cuts across other socio-economic and political divisions. In addition, in many village cultures, women are generally not as active in local politics as men are; they are less swayed and biased by political power manoeuvring.

Women are good conservators of tourism resources and managers of its impacts

Women are often the keepers of cultural traditions and knowledge in terms of cooking local foods, wearing traditional ethnic dress, cooperating in support of religious functions, producing handicrafts, knowing about natural medical remedies, performing traditional dancing, and speaking and singing in local dialects. These are the very resources that attract tourists, and through planning and management they can be turned into tourism products. With some training assistance in marketing and financial management, and business planning, village women can manage successful enterprises that rely upon sustainable use of resources. For example, they know what kind of and how much fuel is used on a daily basis. Women who work in lodges are in the position to learn about and use fuel-saving practices. Women who collect fuelwood are aware of decreasing supplies of fuelwood, and the need for and advantages of alternatives. Women also take responsibility for waste management; cooks and kitchen helpers dispose of food wrappings, tins, litter, etc. and thus are responsible for proper treatment of wastes (Box 11.3). Women stay in the villages year-round and thus can follow through on management responsibilities. Women's groups in Langtang-Helambu regularly clean the trails and village area, separating garbage into burnable and non-burnables for burning, burying and/or recycling.

Reinvestment of tourism revenues in conservation

Experiences in undertaking savings and credit programmes in Nepal suggest that women tend to be more careful and responsible about managing money, using it for family needs rather than personal use (e.g. men often use 'extra' income for drinking or gambling). Women tend to work toward the benefit of the family and community over self. For example, women in Langtang-Helambu have formed social service groups to work for cultural conservation and community benefits, performing cultural dances for tourists and cleaning the trails of litter (paid by lodge operators) to raise money to restore the village monastery. Cultural conservation benefits the community with strengthened institutions, identities, moral standards and often with

---

Box 11.3. Activities undertaken by the six village women's groups.

These include:
- Regular village and trail clean-up and disposal, including construction of garbage pits and initiation of household garbage collection and disposal systems
- Establishment of a cultural museum with household and cultural artefacts
- Collection of interest from revolving loans to support activities, including monastery restoration and village clean-up
- Construction of toilets for every trekking lodge
- Construction of a public toilet and water supply at the monastery
- Placement of a painted area map sign for tourists
- Demonstration of cultural dances to generate activity funds
- Planting of flowers around villages, homes and lodges
- Plastering and repair of monastery interior

culturally linked conservation practices (e.g. protection of religious forests or holy lakes).

Conclusion

Although women's empowerment is not the focus of the LEP, enhancing women's roles in community-based mountain tourism is proving to be a key factor in conserving the Himalaya's rich biodiversity and cultural heritage. Three years of community-based tourism planning in nine communities of the Langtang and Helambu region suggest that an appreciative participatory approach that values women for their skills and seeks to enhance their capabilities as tourism and natural resource managers achieves both conservation and women's increased self-reliance. These results are not exclusive to a single national park region in Nepal. Similar results are seen in the West Sikkim where a number of women who participated in an Appreciative Participating Planning and Action (APPA)-based programme have become trekking guides and are actively involved in a grassroots NGO that teaches APPA and community-based tourism elsewhere in India. Women Participatory Rural Appraisal (PRA) facilitators from Nepal are using the APPA approach for community-based tourism and biodiversity conservation planning in Tibet, and now in Sichuan Province of China. In a recent international training in community-based tourism in Nepal, field practitioners from seven countries of South Asia and Africa learned the APPA methodology and are now applying it in their project areas. More evidence will be coming in over the next year or so as to how this approach affects not only biodiversity conservation but also community empowerment and women's upliftment.

Women's empowerment is often hard to measure, but anecdotal evidence such as the stories of Helambu women contained in this chapter shows a significant change in village women's self-image and behaviour that has emerged out of a simple, enjoyable and effective participatory method that builds on what makes a community proud. In the words of one woman from Helambu:

> We never thought about self-initiated village development but this (APPA) workshop has motivated us to look at what (resources) we have, and to think how we ourselves can develop our village for long term benefits. (Shermathang villager, Helambu, May 1996, personal communication)

References

Byers, E. and Sainju, M. (1994) Mountain ecosystems and women: opportunities for sustainable development and conservation. *Mountain Research and Development* 14, 213–228.

Gurung, D. (1995) Tourism and gender: impacts and implications of tourism on Nepalese women. Discussion Paper Series No. MEI 95/3. International Centre for Integrated Mountain Development, Kathmandu, Nepal.

Majupuria, I. (1991) Nepalese women: a vivid account of the status and role of Nepalese women in the total spectrum of life, religious, social, economic, political, and legal : focus on equality, development, and peace. M. Devi, Lashkar, Gwalior.

Rao, N. (1998) India's mountain women kept in the background. In: East, P. Kurt L. and Inmann, K. (eds) *Sustainability in Mountain Tourism*. Book Faith India, New Delhi, and Studienverlag, Innsbruck, Austria.

Stevens, S.F. (1993) *Claiming the High Ground: Sherpas, Subsistence, and Environmental Change in the Highest Himalaya*. University of California Press, Berkeley.

Too Much Too Fast: Lessons from Nepal's Lost Kingdom of Mustang

12

Chandra P. Gurung[1] and Maureen A. DeCoursey[2]

[1]WWF Nepal Program, PO Box 7660, Lal Durbar, Kathmandu, Nepal; [2]PO Box 879, Woodacre, CA 94973, USA

The goose can only lay golden eggs if it is reared properly; otherwise it fouls its own nest. (Gurung and DeCoursey, 1994)

Introduction

Nepal, one of the most scenic and culturally rich countries in the world, has used tourism as a primary source of revenue since the early 1950s when the government first opened its borders to the outside world. Tourism is now the number one industry, generating $117 million a year (DOT, 1996). This is far more hard currency than any other sector. The vast majority of the country's 20 million inhabitants, however, have not benefited from tourism. After almost five decades of tourism development, the fruits of tourism remain concentrated in a few urban areas and popular destinations such as the Annapurna region, Royal Chitwan National Park and Sagarmatha (Mt Everest) National Park. Since there have been few controls, tourism has exacerbated prevailing environmental and social problems, and in several cases, has been the primary cause.

With the restoration of democracy in 1990, demands from the hinterland for more equal distribution of national wealth have prompted successive governments to act in favour of the rural masses. Each successive government has therefore placed greater emphasis on rural needs and aspirations. Given the country's success with tourism, the most obvious strategy has been to use tourism to help alleviate poverty and promote sustainable development in these areas. This strategy is based on successful models of community-based mountain tourism in other areas of Nepal, especially in the Annapurna (Gurung and DeCoursey, 1994) and Sagarmatha regions.

Over the last 6 years, the government has opened four previously restricted areas to trekking tourism for this purpose. These areas, mainly along the Tibetan border, had been closed previously for security reasons. This policy shift can be termed as the beginning of a planned or imposed community-based mountain tourism in Nepal.

This chapter presents a case study of the Upper Mustang Conservation and Development Project (UMCDP). The UMCDP was jointly set up by the King Mahendra Trust for Nature Conservation, a Nepali non-governmental organization (NGO), and the government to oversee conservation and development activities, including community-based mountain tourism in Upper Mustang. Mustang is an extremely isolated, economically impoverished mountain region in mid-west Nepal with strong cultural and historical links to Tibet. Except for a few researchers who were able to undertake studies in the Upper Mustang region (e.g. Peissal, 1968; Jackson, 1976, 1984; Tucci, 1977), Mustang was closed for centuries to all visitors due to its harsh geography and political sensitivity. The Nepalese government opened the borders in 1992 to a limited number of trekkers as well as several bilateral and multilateral aid organizations.

This chapter shows how rapid, poorly planned tourism development in remote mountain areas like Upper Mustang undermines the chances not only for successful community-based mountain tourism, but also for the broader goals of community uplift and biodiversity conservation. This chapter presents background information on Mustang and the UMCDP, followed by an account of the numerous obstacles encountered over the last 6 years as the region has become acquainted with the outside world and UMCDP has tried to implement its programme. While a number of conservation and development goals have been achieved, the community fabric has been ripped apart in the process, and UMCDP continues to face serious set-backs, especially in terms of financial sustainability. Fundamental building blocks of community-based mountain tourism were hastily assembled or omitted altogether, in particular stakeholder identification and coordination, master planning, local capacity-building, infrastructure development, and supportive policy and legal frameworks. UMCDP has learned its lessons the hard way and their experience may be helpful to others embarking on similar undertakings. The more important lessons are summarized in the conclusion.

Welcome to the Lost Kingdom of Mustang

Mustang covers 2563 km² of high-altitude desert in the upper reaches of the Kali Gandaki River near the Tibetan border (Fig. 12.1). Once an independent kingdom, Mustang was consolidated under Nepalese rule but retained a certain degree of internal autonomy, which persists to the present day. Ancient scriptures indicate that the famous Buddhist sage Milarepa

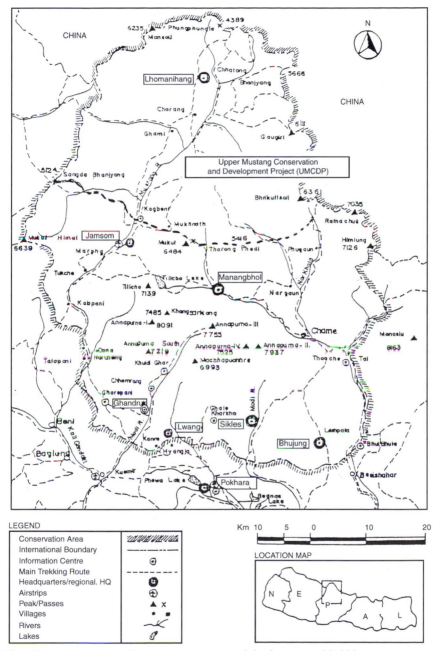

Fig. 12.1. Annapurna Conservation Area and the location of field bases.

visited the area as early as the eighth century, however the kingdom was established much later in the 14th century by the direct ancestor of the present ruler, Rt Honorable Raja of Mustang, Jigme Parbal Bista. To reach Lo-Manthang (3780 m asl), the ancient walled city and the capital of Mustang, it takes 10 days of hard walking from the nearest main road or 4 days from the nearest seasonal airport, Jomsom.

The dramatic landscape is one of windswept plains, craggy rock outcrops, fluted cliffs and snow-covered peaks. The total population is only 6123, separated into 1189 households residing in 32 widely scattered hamlets and isolated settlements (Gurung, 1998). The area has a rich and exotic culture, which is almost purely Tibetan Buddhist. There are several monasteries, cave dwellings, and artefacts, many of superior quality but in desperate need of repair. Biological diversity is equally impressive. Endangered species such as snow leopard, lynx, arghali sheep and wild ass are found throughout the region, as well as several medicinal plants.

Situated in the rain shadow of the Himalaya, the region receives 554 mm rainfall and 782 mm of snow annually. There is very little vegetation and growing seasons are extremely short; most of Mustang remains under snow for 4–5 months a year. Basic necessities such as drinking water, health services, schools and alternative sources of energy are either very primitive or non-existent, and there are no communication links with the outside world. Less than half of the local people can speak Nepali, the national language. The literacy rate among the population aged 10 years and above is about 10% with a marked gender gap (ACAP/UMCDP, 1992). The region is considered one of the most remote and underdeveloped in Nepal.

In contrast to the small human population, Mustang has large herds of cattle, sheep, goats, yaks and horses, totalling over 41,000 (Gurung, 1998). In the past, local people were able to pasture their livestock in Tibet. Since the mid-1970s, however, the Chinese government has restricted this practice, which has led to a severe shortage of forage, serious overgrazing and an overall decline in livestock numbers (Banskota and Sharma, 1998).

Fuelwood is another scarce resource in Mustang. Only a few patches of forest remain, and people are forced to cut or uproot scattered junipers and other types of scrub vegetation for heating and cooking. Yak dung and goat pellets have always been used as a supplemental energy source, but nowadays more people are relying on them almost exclusively. This could eventually lead to a decrease in agricultural productivity due to the shortage of manure (Banskota and Sharma, 1998).

The people adapted to this harsh environment by practising a form of subsistence agropastoralism and seasonal migration. Farming is done wherever irrigation is possible, but only one crop a year can be produced. This barely supports the local population for 6 months a year, and the region is a severe food deficit area (G. Gurung, ACAP Office, Pokhara Nepal, 1998, personal communication). To offset these shortages, almost 70% of the population emigrates to lower altitudes (some as far away as India) during the winter months for employment and trading. The Nepalese Government closes all its offices during this time including schools and police and border security offices. Only old people and young children remain in the villages on a year-round basis.

Trekking for Dollars

Once Mustang was opened for tourism, groups of high-level government delegates assured the local people at various public meetings that 60% of the revenue generated from trekking tourism would be made available to the local community for rural development and heritage conservation. To finance this scheme, a premium fee of US$500 per week (per tourist) was levied with a maximum of 2 weeks allowed in the region. Initially, a limit of 200 international visitors a year was set. Trekkers were required to be part of a group, organized through an authorized trekking agency. Groups had to be self-sufficient in kerosene and all garbage had to be carried out. Each group also had to be accompanied by an Environmental Officer (EO) whose remuneration was paid by the group. The EO's responsibility was to assure that the group followed the prescribed route and environmental protocols, and that they did not purchase or smuggle any valuable artiefacts.

In March 1992, the first batch of tourists arrived in Mustang. Realizing the potential profits to be made, the tourism industry started lobbying the government to increase the 200 tourists per year limit and decrease the premium for the second week. Most treks to Mustang required at least 10 days, and US$1000.00 for an individual permit was seen as too exorbitant. Within a couple of months, the number of visitors authorized to trek was increased to 400 per year and the premium fee was revised to US$700 for 10 days of trekking. Beyond the initial 10-day period, each additional day cost US$70. Six months later, the number of tourists was again increased to 1000 a year. This system continues to the present day. Table 12.1 shows tourist arrival data in Mustang between 1992 and 1997.

Table 12.1. The number of tourists arriving in Mustang (1992–97).

Year	No. of tourists arriving
1992	433
1993	764
1994	773
1995	754
1996	805
1997	783
Total	4312

Source: J.B. Gurung (1998).

The Upper Mustang Conservation and Development Project (UMCDP)

To oversee conservation and development activities in Mustang, the government brought in Nepal's leading environmental NGO, the King Mahendra Trust for Nature Conservation (KMTNC). KMTNC had successfully implemented the Annapurna Conservation Area Project (ACAP) since 1986, and was the logical choice given its expertise as well as its geographical proximity to Mustang. In July 1992, the Nepalese Government officially gazetted the Annapurna Conservation Area and included upper Mustang within its jurisdiction. Thus, full management responsibilities for both areas were handed over to KMTNC. In August, the KMTNC sent a team of experts to Mustang to carry out a feasibility study and identify local needs and priorities. In November, 9 months after Mustang was opened for trekking tourism, the KMTNC initiated the Upper Mustang Conservation and Development Project (UMCDP) to channel tourism revenues into the community in a responsible fashion. A year-round project office in Lo-Manthang was established, and for the first time, local people had a committed group of outsiders working in their villages during the winter season.

The UMCDP staff began its work by gathering basic village information. They spent a great deal of time developing a rapport with the local people and conducting environmental awareness activities. Clean-up campaigns were launched, rubbish pits were dug and waste materials were separated and burnt, buried or hauled out as required. Even the local Buddhist monks were happy to participate. One of the UMCDP staff was a health worker, and again, for the first time, the local communities received medical support in the winter. These activities built up strong feelings of mutual trust and created a positive work environment for future initiatives. One resident from Lo-Manthang remarked, 'This time, the government came to our doorsteps' (ACAP/UMCDP, 1993: 33).

Members of the local community and staff of the UMCDP jointly developed a work plan to guide their activities during the upcoming years. The work plan focused on five key programmes:

1. Sustainable tourism development
2. Natural resources conservation
3. Cultural heritage conservation
4. Community development
5. Institutional development.

These programmes were carried out via numerous training workshops, study tours, demonstrations and awareness campaigns. Representatives of the local community were even brought to ACAP's field sites to learn from communities facing similar issues and see how these communities manage tourism.

Sustainable tourism development

The creation of a sustainable community-based tourism industry was given top priority in order to increase the local share of economic benefits, to ensure a reliable pool of funding from the tourist revenues, and to avoid the trend-based 'boom and bust' tourism experienced in other parts of the country. The three operational objectives have been: (i) to maintain a constant flow of tourists; (ii) to minimize tourists' impacts on the culture and environment; and (iii) to develop local tourism-based enterprises. To date, UMCDP has conducted lodge management training and handicraft development workshops, improved trails and signage, and established a kerosene depot for trekking groups and local villagers alike.

To raise awareness among the visitors, informational brochures and codes of conduct were developed and distributed with trekking permits and through UMCDP's information office at Kagbeni, the gateway village to Mustang. UMCDP staff worked closely with the police at local checkposts to assure that tourists and guides followed the codes of conduct.

Natural resources conservation

As mentioned earlier, pasture and fuelwood shortages are two of the most pressing natural resource problems in Mustang. To help mitigate these problems, UMCDP carried out action-research on fuel needs and potential alternatives, seasonal fodder requirements, and traditional pasture management practices. They also developed an extension programme that included alternative energy, community and private tree plantations, natural forest conservation and agroforestry.

Alternative energy is viewed as an especially important component of natural resource management in light of the critical role it plays in improving local living conditions and reducing pressure on wild flora. Taking advantage of the near-perfect conditions for solar and micro-hydroelectricity, UMCDP has a strong energy programme focused on rehabilitating and expanding micro-hydro facilities and solar lighting, grinding and water heating systems. They have also established a kerosene depot and installed fuel-efficient backboiler stoves.

Cultural heritage conservation

Mustang's centuries of isolation and ancient Buddhist origins (*circa* eighth century) has endowed it with an exceptionally rich yet fragile cultural heritage. There are 25 monasteries, extensive cave dwellings that once housed religious hermits, pilgrims and other practitioners, and a large number of statues, paintings, books and other historical artefacts (Gurung, 1998).

Fig. 12.2. Lo-Manthang, the capital of Mustang (3780 m). Over 800 people reside within this walled city.

Lo-Manthang is also one of the last remaining walled cities in Asia (Fig. 12.2). The local people are strongly Buddhist; rituals and festivals are important events (Fig. 12.3) and the monastery continues to play a key role in village life.

Many of these cultural attributes have never been properly documented and some of the oldest monasteries, paintings and statues had fallen into a serious state of disrepair. To protect these priceless treasures UMCDP and their community counterparts began a programme of heritage conservation which included monastery restoration and renovation, artefact documentation and site preservation. They also developed income generation schemes specifically for the monasteries by printing tickets with a brief description of the *gompas* so that visitors will be willing to pay a donation of NRs 100. UMCDP has also established a school for novice monks. The American Himalayan Foundation has assisted in these efforts by funding the restoration of the Thubchen Gompa, one of the oldest in Lo-Manthang.

Community development

Basic services such as health care, education, alternative food supplies and communications hardly existed in Mustang. To determine the most pressing needs, UMCDP carried out socio-economic surveys in all 32 communities. Health issues topped the list and resulted in the establishment of a

Fig. 12.3. Mustang is rich in cultural heritage. Here the local people are performing a mask dance during the Tenji festival at Lo-Manthang.

permanent health post, a health education programme and regular village clean-up campaigns to improve sanitation and hygiene. UMCDP also helped local villagers to build protective walls around agricultural fields and to improve the facilities at local schools.

Institutional development

In order to carry out and sustain these efforts, local-level conservation and development committees,[1] lodge management committees, and *Ama Samuha* (mothers' groups) were formed. These grass-root committees have been empowered with knowledge, skills, financial support and other resources to co-develop and implement tourism, conservation and community service activities.

Trouble in Paradise

Even though the UMCDP began with a clear set of objectives, several issues plague both the day-to-day operations as well as the sustainability of the

[1] Now referred to as Conservation Area Management Committee as per the Conservation Area Regulations approved by the government in 1996.

Fig. 12.4.   Lo-Manthang Palace where the Raja of Mustang, Jigme Parbal Bista, resides.

project as a whole. Some are the result of the lack of sufficient preparation time which led to design and implementation flaws; others emerged from completely unexpected sources, such as the problems created by disgruntled local and district-level politicians. While some of the issues have been addressed, others continue to spiral out of control. As a result, short-term profit is overriding long-term security, community cohesiveness is breaking down and the environment continues to be degraded. The acrimonious conflict between the Raja of Mustang and some of his closest family members over an upscale resort in the area is apparent.

Research by Baskota and Sharma (1998) and Shakley (1994), along with observations by both authors, suggest several factors at play. These are briefly described below.

Insecure funding and breach of trust

One of the biggest problems for UMCDP has been financial sustainability. For a variety of reasons, the Nepalese Government never provided 60% of the tourism revenue for Mustang's development as promised. On the contrary, as Table 12.2 shows, the amount of funding received by KMTNC has decreased every year, even though the tourism revenue for Mustang has been consistent. KMTNC (mainly through the ACAP budget) has been forced to assume the financial burden, and UMCDP staff and resources have been

Table 12.2. The revenue generation and funding to ACAP/UMCDP by HMGN (1992–97).

Year	Revenue generation (US$)	Funding to UMCDP (NRs)	Funding to UMCDP (US$)[a]	Percentage of the total revenue to Mustang
1992	303,100	6,305,000	126,100	41.60
1993	534,800	6,950,000	139,000	25.99
1994	541,100	6,950,000	139,000	25.68
1995	527,000	4,000,000	80,000	15.18
1996	563,500	4,300,000	78,000	13.84
1997	548,100	1,500,000	25,000	4.56
Total	3,107,600	31,005,000	587,100	19.46

Source: ACAP/UMCDP (1998).
[a]The tourist revenue is always collected in US$. In 1992, the exchange rate for one US$ to Nepali Rupees (NRs) was about 50. Today, the exchange rate for one US$ to NRs is 68. The variation in the UMCDP receipt between NRs and US$ is due to variation in exchange rates at different times.

stretched to the limit. Local people are understandably angry and frustrated at this breach of faith. They can easily estimate how much they should receive and know they are being cheated. UMCDP must operate underneath this cloud of betrayal every day.

Short-sighted policies and poor enforcement

Contrary to all the rhetoric, revenue generation, as opposed to sustainable rural development, was the dominant motivation for opening Mustang. Proper planning and policies were sacrificed to the potentially large profits at stake for the government as well as the private tourism sector. Thus, policies and regulations were weak, changeable and only superficially enforced. Official Conservation Area regulations were not passed until 1996 and until that time UMCDP's limited legal powers left them somewhat crippled in their ability to act decisively on various issues.

Shackley (1994) also notes that government policy towards Mustang was not well-conceived and somewhat duplicitous from the start. This is partially attributed to the lack of experience on the part of government in working with an NGO in this manner. This situation can be readily seen in the confusion and subsequent conflicts over which entity was actually in charge of tourism development in the region: the Ministry of Tourism and Civil Aviation (MOTCA) (whose objective is to promote tourism and increase revenues) and the KMTNC (whose objective is to carry out sustainable rural development using tourism as the main mechanism).

Because UMCDP lacked a strong legal foundation, MOTCA prevailed with a decided bias towards the Kathmandu-based private sector. As described earlier, certain members of the tourism industry were successfully able to lobby the government to raise the number of tourists and reduce the fee, thus undermining the approach of UMCDP. Also, since the policies governing trekking group activities in Mustang were not officially codified, they were only marginally observed and enforced. Porters, cooks, camp helpers and other support staff (an average of four staff to each tourist), for example, were not bound to the kerosene-only and waste management rules. As a result, litter, pollution and resource shortages grew worse (Banskota and Sharma, 1998). Many EOs were known to shrug their duties by staying in the lower valley or turning a blind eye to infractions, yet continued to receive their remuneration from the trekking groups (Gurung, 1998).

Another source of conflict was the lack of clear operational policies and legal jurisdiction associated with the designation 'conservation area' and for regional projects implemented by NGOs, such as ACAP and UMCDP. These approaches were new for Nepal and fairly controversial; as such, the details remained very much in flux. The differences between a conservation area and a national park, for example, were not universally understood nor articulated in the form of policy. In other protected areas of Nepal, the Department of National Parks and Wildlife Conservation is the overriding authority. All activities that take place inside the park boundaries must be approved by the Park Warden and be consistent with the goals of conservation. Both ACAP and UMCDP had virtually the same mandate but were not granted the same kind of legal authority.

Rapid pace of tourism development

The KMTNC lobbied very hard not to open Mustang for 3 years. The experience in Annapurna showed that it would take at least this amount of time to build basic social and physical infrastructures, train local people to manage lodges and camp sites, establish alternative energy sources, develop waste management systems and create functioning local institutions. Government officials did not agree with this approach and the process of opening up Mustang continued unabated.

The rapid development placed an enormous burden on UMCDP. The planning process was almost entirely short-circuited: many projects were implemented on an *ad hoc* basis and lacked clear, demonstrative links to conservation or development. The staff, who were mostly young but had several years previous experience with the ACAP, worked with a high degree of enthusiasm but lacked sufficient expertise and maturity to deal with the bureaucracy and the politicians. Since the funding was coming directly from the government, local politicians felt that they should have a say in the selection of projects. Their demands were often at odds with the participatory approach of UMCDP, and if they did not get what they wanted, they went directly to the highest echelons of the government bureaucracy to get UMCDP to change their course. There was also considerable pressure for quick action and quick results, both from within the region and from the national seat in Kathmandu. All these factors precluded UMCDP from developing a well-articulated, systematic programme. As a result, their efforts focused mostly on containing immediate demands rather than developing long-term strategies and visions (Banskota and Sharma, 1998).

Visitation steadily grew from 433 tourists in 1992 to over 800 in 1996. Because local tourism infrastructure and enterprise were not developed properly, there continues to be a substantial leakage of benefits to outside trekking operators, food suppliers and other entrepreneurs. What little remains tends to be sequestered by local elites.

Poorly defined stakeholder roles and relations

Identifying the stakeholders, working with them to define the roles, responsibilities and rights of each, and maintaining transparency are fundamental aspects of any community-based development programme. In Mustang, numerous organizations and individuals, in addition to UMCDP, initiated projects soon after the borders were opened. These include CARE International, Mustang Development Service Association-Japan, American Himalayan Foundation, National Center for Scientific Research (CRNS)-France, and the United Nations International Labor Organization (ILO). Many well-heeled tourists predictably became enamoured of the land and its people and gave large donations directly to private individuals or even initiated projects on their own. Their charity was naïve and unprofessional, and typically caused more harm than good. Outside assistance descended into '*ad hocism*', which further exacerbated the confusion and opportunism among local communities. Communication and coordination between these entities were minimal, resulting in project duplication, contradictory methods and even competition for community support.

In its zeal to get field projects started, UMCDP overlooked these stakeholder negotiations. Even though they were charged with the overall development of the area, as an NGO they had limited legal authority until formal regulations took hold in 1996. This created tensions with local politicians, government departments and other NGOs, even among the people themselves. In one instance, district political leaders, upset that the tourism revenues were being channelled through UMCDP, purposely derailed UMCDP activities by planting malicious rumours in the local community. Key stakeholders, such as trekking operators (especially field staff) and Environmental Officers, often neglected their responsibilities and in some cases, were completely antagonistic to project goals.

High visibility, high pressure and high expectation

High donor interest, international publicity and rapid tourism development place enormous pressures and high expectation on the people of Mustang as well as UMCDP (P. Sharma, ICIMOD, Kathmandu, 1998, personal communication). Within its first year of opening the area was deluged by foreign dignitaries, filmmakers and photojournalists. At times, helicopters buzzed back and forth from Kathmandu every day, carrying high-level visitors from many parts of the world. The region became a trendy destination for affluent tourists who wanted to be among the first to experience this fabled place. The large donations of many visitors, although well-intended, were given without coordination with responsible organizations. The Raja of Mustang and his son even travelled to America, Europe and Japan as guests of international non-government organizations (INGOs) to raise funds not only for Mustang but for the INGOs. The Mustang Dog and Pony Show had begun.

This hoopla created chaos in the collective psyche of the local community and contributed to UMCDP's difficulties. Prior to 1990, the area had been closed for 500 years. With the exception of traders, most people never left their village and had little contact with the outside world. Few people visited the area, much less set up a major development project. Suddenly a variety of foreigners with different language, dress, customs and mannerisms started coming in droves, handing out money and resources like candy. Opportunistic behaviour and a certain 'begging mentality' began to dominate. (In this context 'begging mentality' refers to local leaders begging for projects with foreign donors as well as common people begging for anything they could get from outsiders.) Prices for horse rental, camp-grounds and other local services sky-rocketed. Valuable art objects and home crafts were sold off to the highest bidder, removed from Mustang forever. Shackley (1994) estimated NRs 8 million worth of artwork and artefacts were removed or smuggled from Mustang in the first 8 months of the introduction of tourism. In some cases, even wild animals were captured to sell to the tourists.

Conclusion: Strategies for Successful Community-based Mountain Tourism

There are many lessons to be learned from the Mustang experience. In order to achieve sustainable community-based mountain tourism, the following strategies are proposed:

Systematic planning

Systematic planning was clearly a major oversight in Mustang. As noted above, it created a sense of '*ad hocism*' in many of UMCDP's activities and allowed the project to get spread too thin. The rapid pace at which the area was opened and with which tourism was introduced left little time for proper planning and preparation, most importantly building the capacity of local people and developing basic tourism infrastructure. As a result, the linkages between tourism, conservation and community development have often been weak and underdeveloped (Banskota and Sharma, 1998).

A slow, iterative planning and management style based on a small pilot project would have been more appropriate to Mustang. The social and eco-logical setting was so fragile that the rapid and widespread development activity, not only from UMCDP but from numerous other projects in the region, led to chaos in the community and increased pressures on the environment.

Clearly defined roles, rights and responsibilities of all stakeholders

The experience in Mustang clearly shows how a lack of structured coopera-tion and communication can undermine a project's viability. Commu-nity-based mountain tourism is a complex undertaking that requires different types of expertise and support on the local, regional and national and inter-national level. As much as possible, all the stakeholders should be identified and engaged from early on so that projects complement, not contradict each other and a consistent message is relayed to the local communities. In Mustang, these would include all NGOs and INGOs, relevant government departments, the local communities, trekking operators and field staff, and visitors. A clear set of general operational principles and well-articulated common goals are key features.

Supportive legal and policy framework

In a place like Mustang, which in many ways was once a wild frontier, community-based mountain tourism would have been greatly aided by a strong legal framework and supportive policy directives. For 4 years, UMCDP implemented its programmes without official legal jurisdiction and had limited powers in times of conflict. This led to turf wars and tussles of various kinds, which clearly inhibited the successful deployment of community-based mountain tourism. In developing countries especially, the legacy of feudalism is still very much alive and personal agendas drive a considerable portion of public policy. Therefore, in order to operate effectively, UMCDP needed the support of clearly written rules and regulations and the authority to enforce them.

Acknowledgements

We gratefully acknowledge the support received from Pitamber Sharma, Sidhartha Bajracharya, Gehendra Gurung, Juddha Gurung and Tshering T. Lama in providing us with valuable comments and necessary information for this chapter.

References

Annapurna Conservation Area Project/UMCDP (1992) Upper Mustang conservation and development project annual progress report for fiscal year 1992/1993 (16 July, 1992 to 15 July, 1993). King Mahendra Trust for Nature Conservation, Kathmandu.

Annapurna Conservation Area Project/UMCDP (1993) Upper Mustang conservation and development project work plan 1992–93. King Mahendra Trust for Nature Conservation, Kathmandu.

Banskota, K. and Sharma, B. (1998) Mountain tourism for local community development in Nepal: a case study of Upper Mustang. Discussion paper series No. MEI 98/1. ICIMOD, Kathmandu.

Department of Tourism (1996) *Nepal Tourism Statistics 1996*. Department of Tourism, Kathmandu.

Gurung, C.P. and DeCoursey, M. (1994) The Annapurna Conservation Area Project: a pioneering example of sustainable tourism? In: Cater, E. and Lowman, G. (eds) *Ecotourism – a Sustainable Option?* John Wiley & Sons, Chichester, pp. 177–194.

Gurung, J.B. (1998) Upper Mustang conservation and development project's field related problems and issues. A Paper presented at the Officers Meeting held at ACAP Headquarters in Pokhara, 2–4 February, 1998, p. 10.

Jackson, D.P. (1976) Early history of Lo and Ngari. *Contributions to Nepalese Studies* 4 (1).

Jackson, D.P. (1984) *The Mollas of Mustang*. Library of Tibetan Works and Archives, Dharamsala.

Peissal, M. (1968) *Mustang, the Forbidden Kingdom*. Collins and Harvill Press, London.

Shackley, M. (1994) The land of Lo, Nepal/Tibet: the first eight months of tourism. *Tourism Management* 15, 17–26.

Tucci, G. (1977) *Journey to Mustang*. Ratna Pustak Bhandar, Kathmandu.

Mongolia's Tourism Development Race: Case Study from the Gobi Gurvansaikhan National Park

13

Alan Saffery

Mangolian National Tourism Center, Chinggis Avenue 11, Ulaanbaatar, Mongolia

Introduction

Contrary to popular belief, the Gobi is not a sandy, uninhabitable wasteland. Only 3% of Mongolia's surface area fits this image. Each year more tourists are discovering this when they travel to the Gobi Gurvansaikhan National Park, one of the most popular destinations within the world's largest land-locked country. For many years, the beauty of the landscape, marked by the Gobi Gurvansaikhan Mountains, was kept hidden from all but the Russians. This changed in 1990 when democratic elections took place and opened the country up to development and tourism.

In 1992 at the Rio Earth Summit, the Mongolian government pledged to designate 30% of its land area as protected zones. There are now 38 protected areas covering 171,000 km^2, 11% of the land surface (Fig 13.1; Shiirevdamba, 1998). There are plans to designate a further 52 protected areas before 2010 to meet the 30% target (JICA, 1998a). The increased efforts to preserve fragile environments in Mongolia has not come too soon, for with the increase in tourism, many of these and other environments within Mongolia are at a heightened risk for receiving tourism impact. This is especially true given the current nature of affairs within the nation's upcoming tourism industry, wherein all participants lend to the heated competition of the tourism race.

Tourism and the Gobi Gurvansaikhan National Park

Changes took place in 1999 to the way in which tourism is developed in Mongolia. Policy-making is now undertaken by the National Tourism Council (NTC), which is made up of heads of ministries, public tourism organizations and representatives of the private sector. Policy implementation, regulation and promotional activities are carried out by the Mongolian National Tourism Center (MNTC), a government agency. Management of tourism within protected areas remains under the jurisdiction of the Protected Areas Bureau (PAB) in the Ministry for Nature and the Environment.

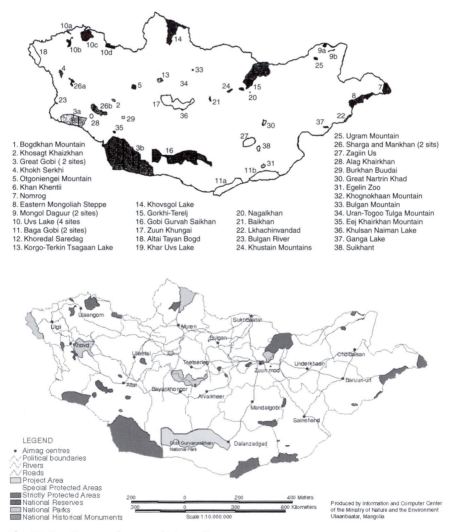

1. Bogdkhan Mountain
2. Khosagt Khaizkhan
3. Great Gobi (2 sites)
4. Khokh Serkhi
5. Otgoniengei Mountain
6. Khan Khentii
7. Nomrog
8. Eastern Mongoliah Steppe
9. Mongol Daguur (2 sites)
10. Uvs Lake (4 sites
11. Baga Gobi (2 sites)
12. Khoredal Saredag
13. Korgo-Terkin Tsagaan Lake

14. Khovsgol Lake
15. Gorkhi-Terelj
16. Gobi Gurvah Saikhan
17. Zuun Khungai
18. Altai Tayan Bogd
19. Khar Uvs Lake

20. Nagalkhan
21. Baikhan
22. Lkhachinvandad
23. Bulgan River
24. Khustain Mountains

25. Ugram Mountain
26. Sharga and Mankhan (2 sits)
27. Zagiin Us
28. Alag Khairkhan
29. Burkhan Buudai
30. Great Nartrin Khad
31. Egelin Zoo
32. Khognokhaan Mountain
33. Bulgan Mountain
34. Uran-Togoo Tulga Mountain
35. Eej Khairkhan Mountain
36. Khulsan Naiman Lake
37. Ganga Lake
38. Suikhant

LEGEND
• Aimag centres
⁄⁄ Political boundaries
⁄⁄ Rivers
⁄⁄ Roads
☐ Project Area
  Special Protected Areas
▓ Strictly Protected Areas
▓ National Reserves
☐ National Parks
▓ National Historical Monuments

200   0   200   400 Meters
300   0   300   600 Kilometers
Scale 1:10,000.000

Produced by Information and Computer Center of the Ministry of Nature and the Environment Ulaanbaatar, Mongolia

Fig. 13.1.   Protected areas of Mongolia.

Aside from these agencies, a number of foreign aid organizations have assisted and are assisting nationally in the development of tourism, including the Japan International Cooperation Agency (JICA), Technical Assistance to the Commonwealth of Independent States and Mongolia (TACIS), Danish International Development Agency (DANIDA), United Nations Development Programme, the International Finance Corporation, and the World Tourism Organization. With these efforts, the tourism industry in Mongolia is thriving. In 1995, Mongolia reportedly earned an estimated US$47 million from tourism which equates to $327 per stay and 4.5% of the GDP.

Mongolia's tourism assets include the natural scenery, history, traditional culture and festivals, lifestyle, wilderness and landscape diversity. Many of these assets are found in the Protected Areas, which serve as the centres for most foreign visitors as they provide the best opportunities for viewing wildlife and experiencing traditional nomadic cultures. The Gobi is one such area, attracting 53% of the total holiday tourists to Mongolia (TACIS, 1998) with the majority of these originating from eastern Asia, Western Europe, North America and Australia. In 1997, over 28,000 tourist nights were spent in the Gobi region (JICA, 1998b), and present tourism numbers are in excess of 5000 annually (TACIS, 1998). At present, Mongolian tour operators supply holidays to the nature and cultural tourism markets and to a lesser extent the adventure tourism market. The independent tourist market (or 'wild tourists') began to grow only last year when restrictions on entry were relaxed. Before this, package tours dominated.

Tourism has existed in and around what is now the Gobi Gurvansaikhan National Park for over 30 years, when the only tourists arriving were usually on tours arranged by the state-owned Juulchin Company. The park stretches 400 km from east to west and an average of 50 km from north to south. Also Mongolia's second largest protected area, it covers 2.17 million hectares. The landscapes of the park include gravel and sandy plains, rocky gorges, saline marshes, springs and oases as well as high mountains reaching a height of 2835 m, with steppe, juniper shrublands and alpine meadows at higher elevations (Wilson, 1997). The mountain gorge, Yolyn Am, covering 69 km^2 had been a protected area since 1965 but has now been incorporated into the larger park, designated in 1993.

Situated at the eastern end of the Gobi Altai mountain range, the Gobi Gurvansaikhan Mountains (Gobi's Three Beauties) form the focal point for the park. Unlike the Northern Altai, which is a single massif, the park is occupied by separate mountain ranges, which increase in altitude from west to east (Fig. 13.2). Wind and drought have heavily eroded all the mountains, resulting in sharp rocky points, steep cliffs and gorges that are teeming with animal life. Within this rich mountain environment, over 290 vascular plant species have been identified, 46 of which have been registered as endangered or rare. There are 52 mammal species including wild ass, snow leopard, argali, ibex and gazelles, with eight species listed in the Mongolian Red Book. Fourteen of Mongolia's 20 species of reptile have been found in

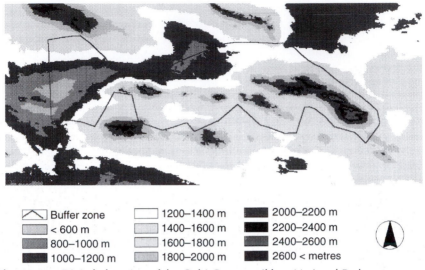

Buffer zone	1200–1400 m	2000–2200 m
< 600 m	1400–1600 m	2200–2400 m
800–1000 m	1600–1800 m	2400–2600 m
1000–1200 m	1800–2000 m	2600 < metres

Fig. 13.2.   Digital elevation of the Gobi Gurvansaikhan National Park.

the park, four of which are listed in the Mongolian Red Book, and over 200 bird species have also been recorded (SGNPAA, 1998a).

Aside from the tremendous diversity of plant and animal species, nearly 1000 nomadic families (approximately 4200 people), most of whom live on subsistence livestock agriculture and depend upon the mountain resources, reside in the park. The majority survive by breeding camels, horses, goats, sheep and occasionally cows and yaks, and their standard of living varies considerably from the suggested figure of 68 extremely poor families with little or no livestock to those with well over 1200 livestock. Those who have livestock sell the meat within the community or commercially in the Sum (small settlement) and Aimag (province) centres, as well as the skins and wool, which are sold throughout Mongolia and often traded with China. The nomads have both summer and winter locations for their *gers* (round tents used as housing) and livestock, with the winter camps located in or around the mountain areas where there is more water, pasture and better shelter. Because of the natural amenities that the mountains of the park hold, the number of park residents is gradually increasing, a situation facing other mountain regions (see Glorioso, this publication; Tonderayi, this publication). For example, between 1995 and 1997, 192 families moved into the park due to better weather conditions, better pasture and accessibility to water, privatization and increasing unemployment in the urban centres.

At present day, there are four tourist *ger* camps of various sizes, all situated in easy reach of the Aimag capital, Dalanzadgad. The main tourist attractions are Yolyn Am, a 10 km gorge, in the Gurvansaikhan Mountain Range with an ice sheet up to 4 m thick for most of the year and Khongoryn

Fig. 13.3.   Also known as the 'Singing Sands', the Khongoryn Els sand dunes stretch up to 180 km in length and their movement creates a sound like the rumbling of a distant fighter aircraft.

Els (Fig. 13.3), a 180 km range of sand dunes that reach up to 180 m in height. In the far west of the park are two dramatic rock formations, Bugiin Tsav and Khermen Tsav (Fig. 13.4), of international palaeontological significance; yet these are difficult to reach for the majority of tourists because of their isolation (few people, little wildlife or water) and the poor quality of the roads.

The management of the park is undertaken by an office staff of seven, representing the South Gobi National Protected Areas' Administration (SGNPAA), which is headed by the PAB. In addition, 11 rangers are employed on a part-time basis. Mostly herders, they fit in their ranger activities around the day-to-day routines of tending their livestock. The GTZ (German Agency for Technical Cooperation) has been assisting in the management of the park since 1995 as part of its 12-year involvement with three of Mongolia's protected areas. They have one permanent member of office staff based at the park office. Support in the project 'Nature Conservation and Bufferzone Development' includes long-term experts on park management, short-term consultants on technical aspects, training, equipment and assistance with establishing park infrastructure. Their overall objectives are ecosystem protection and sustainable use of natural resources, and with regard to tourism, these include:

1.   The management of tourist activities in an environmentally compatible way in accordance with the project's overall conservation goals;

Fig. 13.4.   Resembling an image of a lunar landscape, Khermen Tsav is home to a number of unique fossil discoveries.

2.   The development of mechanisms for the financing of protected areas through tourism; and
3.   The identification of tourism-related income opportunities for local people with the indirect objective to compensate them for conservation-related restrictions and increase their acceptance of the parks (Strasdas and Steinhauer-Burkart, 1998).

The environmental impacts of tourism in the Gobi are not unique, but fortunately at present they are also limited. Examples include the negative effects of concentrations of people in highly visited areas and the lack of sound environmental practice among the tourism industry, principally within the domestic tourism sector. These effects are most notably being felt in the vulnerable ecosystems of the mountain regions of the park, where the majority of the park's endemic flora and fauna reside.

Tourism Development in the Gobi Gurvansaikhan National Park: a Race Towards Change

Many definitions of ecotourism give reference to untouched destinations, and Mongolia can be described as just such a place, particularly the Gobi Gurvansaikhan National Park. The relative remoteness of this region has been realized by the increasing number of people involved in the development of tourism here. A race is the analogy used to describe what is happening at present, as the rapid growth of interest in tourism in Gobi Gurvansaikhan is based on the desire by many people to achieve rapidly the financial benefits that tourism can bring. As with all races towards a common end, the development of tourism in the Gobi Gurvansaikhan National Park is spurred on by organizers, competitors and spectators. While some cooperation exists amongst these groups, the main relationship between those in the tourism industry is one of competition. This sense of competition is heightened given the extreme climate of the Gobi and a tourist season of only 5 months, during which time heavy rains fall, making the development of tourism in the region still more challenging. To add to this, Mongolia's low population and underdevelopment also mean that tourism services and infrastructure will take time and large amounts of finance to develop. For example there are no paved roads at all throughout the south of the country, except for a few concrete paths in the larger settlements.

Organizers

'Race organizers' is perhaps a rather optimistic term to describe those involved in managing tourism since, because of the lack of staff and resources, they are not in a suitable position fully to control the activities of the industry. Yet the MNTC, the PAB and the individual Protected Area Administrations are similar to race organizers in the degree of influence they hold, and they generally decide where, when and how tourism will proceed in the Gobi Gurvansaikhan National Park. Ironically, however, an organizational dilemma is prevalent among these agencies, manifested in an inter-agency communication breakdown. Although representatives from the parties may come together at meetings throughout the year, there has been limited discussion on individual involvement in tourism, resulting in duplication or overlap of activities. The lack of communication appears to be continuing from the communist days, certainly within the park administration. Public consultation for example, with the preparation of the park's management plan, is a relatively new concept that is only starting to be grasped.

Aside from the lack of communication, a number of other challenges face the development of the Gobi Gurvansaikhan National Park. Professional qualification and experience relating to the specific jobs assigned to park staff are missing, and this consequently has led to the very slow introduction of measures designed to develop sustainable tourism. Specific park regulations, adopted zoning, tourism information, defined camping or picnic places and measurements for carrying capacities are largely nonexistent. Also, apart from a small tourist survey carried out in the summer of 1998, research on the views, attitudes or behaviours of tourists is lacking. Yet it has become apparent that research, as well as monitoring on the effects of tourism activities on the environment or culture, is essential, as there has been some discrepancy as to the overall benefits and damages of tourism on the wildlife, wildlife habitats, landscape and culture. It is well known that there have been some illegal excavations of dinosaur fossils and improper disposal of rubbish. Furthermore, it is clear that the size of the park and the difficulty for tourists to access some areas has resulted in tourism being concentrated in the eastern areas of the park, especially in the Gurvansaikhan Mountain Range and Yolyn Am, which house the greatest diversity of plants and wildlife. If tourism develops only in these areas then it is likely that even small numbers of visitors will start to produce negative environmental effects. Yet, without adequate research and monitoring systems on these or other potential problems, it is difficult to ascertain the exact levels of impact.

Control over park finances presents another difficulty. The park is funded by money from the PAB along with park entrance fees. Apart from the fact that there are difficulties in obtaining these monies because of poorly controlled entrance points, there is some doubt to the legality of collection, a situation hampered by the confusion over the legal status of service fees versus entrance fees. Tour operators are refusing to acknowl-edge that their tourists are being given any level of service. A common argument is that tourists do not even know when they are in protected areas because of the lack of visible management, signs or rangers. Entrance fees are and have been paid late, unwillingly or not at all. The low level of income resulting from this situation, coupled with the high costs involved in travelling around the park, result in a lack of control by the park administra-tion on the activities of tour operators and tour companies. Even when there are legal restrictions relating to tourism activities, tour operators often ignore them, running only a slight risk of being caught, or they are unaware of the restrictions placed upon them and, consequently, their infractions of law.

This latter situation results from the lack of communication between the park administration, ministries and tour operators. Unfortunately, the park administration is not well supported by the local government administra-tions or the local people, a situation that stems from the lack of public consultation during the initial development phases of the park and from the current lack of public awareness. As a result, knowledge about public legal codes and equally about ecological (inclusive of the local communities) issues and measures is missing. There is some potential that various restric-tions on the traditional lifestyles of park residents will be imposed in the name of conservation, and as in other mountain regions (see Barkin, this publication; Valaoras, this publication), such restrictions could greatly affect the livelihoods of the landscape and wildlife. As a result, it is possible that conflicts could occur between local people and policy-makers over the development of tourism.

Seemingly at the heart of all these problems lies the lack of promotion and understanding of the established aims and objectives for the park.

Tourists, nomads and the tourism industry need to be aware and understand these aims and objectives in order for their activities to have any chance of being sustainable.

As a pilot to a larger survey in 1999, the SGNPAA carried out a small questionnaire at the *ger* camps among just under 200 tourists. The questions addressed tourists' attitudes toward the park and their suggestions and ideas for improvements. Interestingly enough, the tourists' responses mirrored some of the results in a survey carried out at the same time by TACIS in Ulaanbaatar. The Gobi survey (SGNPAA, 1998b) clearly showed that, while East Asian tourists were not bothered by relatively small numbers of tourists in one place, Western European tourists, especially those travelling independently without a tour, were disappointed to find that the isolated Gobi was not so isolated. In Yolyn Am, for example, 30 tourists might be considered a 'relatively small group'. Although the park covers such a large area, concentrations of people in this mountain region decrease the visual carrying capacities. Put the same 30 people on the open steppe and the feeling of isolation increases. The survey reveals the lack of understanding about the needs of tourists. It is only beginning to be accepted that tourists from Western Europe and East Asia are different in terms of what they want to do, what they want to see and the standards they expect in terms of accommodation, transport and infrastructure. Up until now, all the decisions on the management of the park have been made by the administration with assistance from GTZ and guidance from the PAB. Tour operators, tour companies and local government administrations, who have some awareness of tourist needs, have little chance to voice their opinions.

Competitors

The competitors in this theoretical race include local government administrations and some local people. However, the first and largest group is the tour operators. Before 1990, only the state-owned Juulchin Corporation operated tours, but within 8 years, the number of registered Mongolian tour operators increased to over 200, many still yet to operate tours. The large amount of interest in the industry has resulted in many private companies diversifying their activities and including tourism as a subsidiary. Cooperation between the operators has never been good, although occasionally individual companies have been known to work together, for example by coming together at conferences to give a united front. The central challenge among these competitors is overcoming the limited understanding of an environmentally friendly form of tourism. Tour operators are using the term, 'eco', synonymously with wildlife or nature tourism without regard for true conservation measures or for local community involvement that must be a part of environmentally friendly tourism. Tour itineraries are all very similar, focusing on the nature, wilderness and traditional nomadic culture, but they do very little to conserve these features or to promote local community involvement. Furthermore, the overlap in itineraries leads to strong competition between operators and, as evidenced by some brochures, misleading and exaggerated programmes of activities. Lending to the problem is the unprofessionalism in the form of poorly written literature, little knowledge of the places to visit and a lack of understanding of the requirements of foreign tourists. The operators are unable to distinguish between the need for guides and translators and feel that one person can do both jobs (for the same pay and fewer logistical difficulties) even if they have no knowledge the areas which they are visiting.

Some of the wealthier operators are putting forward enthusiastic plans to develop tourism, for example, building new *ger* camps or even theme parks to highlight Mongolia's pre-history and its dinosaurs. This is worrying many people, since little research appears to be done on demand and supply, local people have not been consulted, and little regard is given to protected area conservation. Three companies are interested in establishing accommodation facilities near the Khongoryn Els sand dunes and have apparently already signed land-use agreements with the local Sum governor. Worse, violations have existed against protected area regulations, such as the illegal construction of toilets and the erection of catering *gers* in Yolyn Am in the Gurvansaikhan Mountains. Despite infractions of law, little has been done to abate the situation. The local government administrations, which have some of their territory within the boundaries of the park, have little understanding and acceptance of the park and its activities, largely because they receive no direct benefits. This is expected to change, however, as agreements have now been made so that the Sum administrations start receiving some of the income from tourism entrance fees.

Spectators

Tourists and the local population appear to be the spectators but for different reasons. Tourists may get the chance to discover how tourism is developing, but it is likely that, because of the little time they spend in the Gobi Gurvansaikhan National Park, their understanding of the relevant issues will remain limited. On the other hand, the local population sees how things are developing over time but feel they can have little influence and empowerment in the industry. In one Sum, in the centre of the park, a small number of nomads were interviewed about tourism. They appeared to have an understanding of why tourists come to Gobi Gurvansaikhan National Park, but only around 50% had any contact with tourists. Fortunately, none of the nomads had any negative experiences, although over 30% of them expected that tourism would have some negative effect on the environment and culture. The lack of involvement at present results from a lack of knowledge on how to become involved and what the tourist industry is all about. Many of the nomads within the park have certainly met tourists at some stage but the language barrier has prevented interaction and understanding of their needs.

Solutions for Sustainable Tourism in the Gobi Gurvansaikhan National Park

Each organizer, competitor and spectator has his or her own individual role to play in tourism development in the Gobi, whether it is big or small, since they are all part of the race. For tourism to develop sustainably within the park, there needs to be cooperation and communication between the government administrations, tourism industry and local people as shown in Fig. 13.5. If roles were more clearly defined and communication was

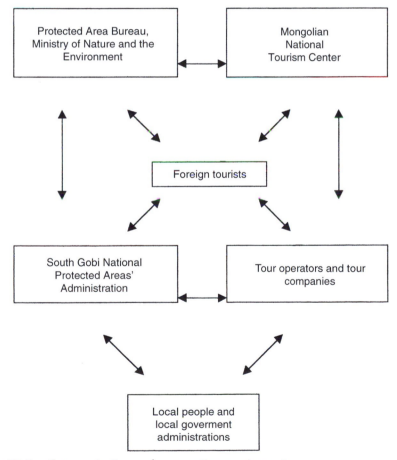

Fig. 13.5. Communication and cooperation requirements.

improved, then the management process might run more smoothly. Equally, there is a need for: participation by local residents; education and training; park tourism management; information exchange; and development of tourism products and services.

Local participation

The park has recently recognized that the principles of ecotourism should involve local people. It also grasps some of the reasons why local communities should be involved in the park's management plan. However, there has been little consultation directly with the people for whom these activities have been designed. In May 1998, the park administration organized a meeting for all those involved in tourism in the Gobi Gurvansaikhan National Park, including tour operators and companies, Sum and Aimag administrations and relevant ministries. Local participation was discussed, but ironically representation by the local population was lacking. Consequently, activities to involve local people were drawn up without consultation, and issues such as the benefits of cultural exchange and international understanding, aside from economic gain, were left unattended. While local people need the freedom to choose whether or not they wish to participate in tourism, it is certain that, because of their unfamiliarity with the industry, they may require support in helping them make such decisions.

Over the past 30 years, local people have been employed through the tour operators or service companies rather than working independently.[1] This may be a sign that support work needs to be directed toward local communities.

At the same time, however, some local families in the eastern area of the park have recently started to take advantage of tourism. The best example of this is at Yolyn Am, where most tourists arrive as part of a larger tour. Each day, during the tourist season, up to 20 horses and their owners can be found offering rides. Artists sit in the car park offering their paintings for sale and, half way down the gorge, there is usually someone selling wooden carvings. The park administration anticipates that the number of these local entrepreneurs will increase unless regulations are put in place and other opportunities are provided for them to sell their products and services. The existence of the local people here, combined with the number of tourists visiting contributes to the tourists' feeling of overcrowding. In order to encourage local people to make an 'honest living', the park administration proposes to centralize the services of these local people at the entrance to the gorge, 10 km away, where the museum is located. Since further tourist infrastructure is planned at this location, including catering, camping and

---

[1] One *ger* camp provides 45 people with 6 months work and pays around $30 a month.

picnic facilities, it is hoped that tourists will spend more time here and less time at the gorge, and that therefore their level of enjoyment and the feeling of isolation at the gorge will increase.

Local entrepreneurs are also working in Dalanzadgad, the Aimag capital. When the planes come in from Ulaanbaatar during the summer, English and non-English speaking untrained guides and drivers await to pounce on the independent traveller. Tourists tend not to be surprised by the lack of experience these local people have in tourism and are aware that if they use them as guides or drivers, they will be receiving only basic services. However, some tourists have complained about the high and often hidden charges that have been imposed upon them.

A number of employment opportunities exist for local people in tourism in the Gobi Gurvansaikhan National Park, and these include:

- general guides for independent tourists and tour groups
- site specific guides with a particular specialist knowledge on nature or palaeontology
- drivers for independent tourists or package tours
- service positions in *ger* camps, at camp sites or in urban centres
- providing tourism activities – horse and camel riding, exhibiting traditional culture and lifestyle
- providing accommodation in private nomads' *gers* and allowing tourists the opportunity to join in the day-to-day routine
- souvenir and handicraft making
- supplying fresh meat and vegetables to the *ger* camps, hotels and restaurants
- infrastructure development.

For most of these, support in terms of training, education and finance will be necessary, and the promotion of domestic and independent tourism will help. Domestic tourism is more likely to benefit local people than foreign tourism, since there is less need to use the services of a tour operator and a greater need to use local goods and services. An encouragement of independent foreign tourists would also have the same effect, as independent tourists too have less need to use tour operators.

Local people obviously know the park better than most guides brought down by tour operators from Ulaanbaatar. As well as knowing the roads, which will help to spread the load of tourists throughout the park, they are more likely to know the wildlife and culture of the park, including some of the nomad groups that can be visited. The Gobi questionnaire (SGNPAA, 1998b) highlighted the finding that guides brought from Ulaanbaatar were unable to cite valuable information about the park, its wildlife or its residents. At highly visited sites, it may be possible to provide guides who are specialized in nature or palaeontology. The *ger* camps already employ some local people, but as infrastructure develops, the number of service positions at new *ger* camps or campsites will increase. If training is provided and pressure is put on the present *ger* camps, catering and entertainment opportunities currently occupied by Ulaanbaatar residents may become available. Like most nomads throughout Mongolia, the residents of the park have a history of making as many items as possible for their *gers* themselves. These include furnishings, cooking equipment, clothing, games and animal husbandry tools. Knowledge and skills have been passed down through the generations so that things are made much the same now as they were decades ago. Many items, because of their ornate decoration, take months to make, and as such are in high demand by tourists. The TACIS question-naire report (TACIS, 1998) showed that the average visitor spent US$129 on handicrafts and textiles. The park administration has now embarked on a project to set up a tourism souvenir cooperative based on other similar projects working successfully elsewhere in the country. This form of income generation is of particular interest to some nomads, as little training is required and the items can be made during the quieter winter months. The major obstacle to overcome, however, is the logistical difficulty with trans-portation and communication, particularly because of the size and shape of the park.

It is clear that in the Gobi, tourism products and activities need diversifi-cation. Some nomads already provide horse and camel riding and this needs to be encouraged along with training on safe riding methods for foreigners. Other possibilities include involving nomads in providing accommodation in their own *gers* and allowing the tourists to participate in the daily routine such as collecting water, cooking, milking the animals and herding. In this way, the tourist gets to feel the real culture of the nomadic people. Activities like these will allow a greater amount of money to go directly into the hands of the nomads and will cause little environmental impact. Since tourism in the Gobi is largely based on the landscape and wildlife, any nomads affected by zoning could be compensated by tourism, preferably by involv-ing them in activities rather than giving handouts generated from tourism income.

Consideration needs to be given to the people of the Aimag and Sum centres outside the park, in the buffer zone. There is little at present to attract tourists to these areas and so the local people have little or no opportunity to become involved. The population centres have an advantage over nomadic people in that it is easier for training groups of people. Sum centres could be developed as service points providing better standard accommodation, small shops and information. One of the big attractions of the Gobi is the nomadic lifestyle, and a number of tourists indicated in the Gobi survey (SGNPAA, 1998b) that they would like more opportunity to join with the local people to experience their lifestyle. A model *hot-ail* or *ger* community could be established near a Sum centre, making use of the available employ-ment. For this, some amount of training on tourist expectations might be necessary. Tourists could then take part in the daily routine of the nomads. In the past, visitors could turn up at a nomad's *ger*, be fed, watered and provided with accommodation without the need to recompense their hosts. Fortunately, the behaviour of foreigners has done little yet to upset this hospitality, but with the growth in tourism expected and the obvious wealth of the visitors, some local people might well see the benefits to the tour operators and want something for themselves. However, if managed properly, some of Mongolia's customs and traditions that were lost during the communist era could be revived through tourism.

Education and training

The organizers would benefit from further training in tourism management, public relations, interpretation and information skills. In particular, the staff and rangers of the park administration need to be trained in general tourism concepts and the importance of developing ecotourism within the park. There is a wealth of experience currently in Mongolia amongst the foreign donor agencies. Instead of these consultants working solely to produce reports for their own counterparts, more emphasis should be placed on sharing information and experience, and training personnel, to enable the park administrations, the MUTC and the PAB to manage tourism themselves.

Many of the larger and more successful tour operators either employ foreign staff with tourism experience or are joint ventures. Foreign involvement has benefited the tour operators in terms of marketing, service standards and the provision of knowledge of some customer bases. Other operators could benefit from either sending staff abroad for training or by cooperating to arrange seminars and conferences in-country with tourism experts or expert organizations. Joint ventures that involve some foreign investment should be encouraged, not just at a national level in Ulaanbaatar, but in the Gobi with planned *ger* camps. Generally, the tour operators and service organizations need to be educated on the importance of protected areas and how they are of benefit to the tourism industry.

The tour operators and protected area tourism officers of the future are today's students attending tourism courses, but it is clear that tourism courses need improvement. Five institutions in Mongolia now provide tourism or tourism-related courses, but the syllabuses are lacking significantly in some areas, for example, in the teaching of tourism management. Students would greatly benefit from outside speakers from the private sector and the MNTC, who are capable of providing knowledge about the foreign tourism industry (Erdembileg, Ulaanbaatar, 1998, personal communication). The JICA report (1998a) makes recommendations in this area: improving the quality of instructors, expanding international education for students, updating training materials, rearranging institutes and courses, and training personnel in the tourism industry. Furthermore, the children in the Aimag and Sum centres need to be given an understanding of tourism, the purpose of National Parks and protected areas, the importance of nature conservation and the uniqueness of their environment. This would ease some of the problems of domestic tourism and give them a greater opportunity to participate in tourism in later years.

Park tourism management

Since tourism in the Gobi is forecasted to grow, the priority is to build foundations on which ecotourism development can take place. Zoning within the park needs to be established along with officially adopting a network of tourism routes, and specific regulations for the park need to be agreed upon and adopted. It is the park administration's responsibility to introduce basic infrastructure, such as roads, toilets, waste disposal points and camping areas; yet with little funds, an understanding of tourists' requirements and the technical knowledge, it is essential for the park, tour operators and tourists to work closely. Cooperation and communication need strengthening, as aforementioned, and on some issues, contracts need to be drawn up to define responsibilities and roles. Regular meetings should be arranged for such discussions. Monitoring methods also need to be established and taught to the rangers so that the effects of several years of tourism can be measured in terms of their effect on the environment and culture. This will also help in defining carrying capacities for the most highly visited sites.

The park administration and its tourism officer have identified and acknowledged some of those problems listed above and have developed activities in the management plan to deal with them. These include: developing tourism impact measuring methods, providing site specific interpretation material, producing training materials, training rangers in tourism management and gathering information on the activities of tour operators. Another tourist survey is planned in cooperation with the tour operators and companies to continue listening to the tourists, seeking and implementing some of their ideas and suggestions. However, the order in which these activities are to be accomplished and the time scales given are often optimistic, given the staff's abilities, knowledge and budget.

The park receives its budget from the PAB and some financial assistance from GTZ but it is conceivable in the future that it will be responsible for raising its own income. This will come through tourism and therefore the need to increase the current numbers of tourists has been identified. This can only effectively be achieved if controlled properly by the administration. The entrance fee for the park is just over US$1 per person per day and nearly $3.50 per vehicle per day. For a long time, the park, the Ministry for Nature and the Environment and tour operators have felt that the fees were too high. The Gobi questionnaire results (SGNPAA, 1998b) conclusively proved the opposite. Almost 50% were in favour of increasing the current amounts, which indicates the value of the landscapes and wildlife within the park. Once issues related to whether tourists should be charged entrance or service fees are resolved, when some improvements have been made to the infrastructure of the park, then consideration should seriously be given to increasing the amounts.

Information exchange

Tourists and tour operators need to be provided with better information by the park administration. A small range of leaflets has been produced, but this needs to be extended to cover aspects such as environmental and cultural issues of the park, regulations, tourist attractions, necessary travel supplies for tourists and travel ethics. The interaction tourists want with the nomads should not cause conflicts or resentments. They need to have knowledge of the customs, culture and traditions in order to respect the local people they visit. They also need to be aware that the standard of tourism in the Gobi is not the same as in industrialized countries; here, roads are often of poor quality, accommodation in the countryside is basic, and many of the local people are not used to tourists. If the information comes directly from the administration, then it is more likely to be accurate.[2] The park should assist in verifying information produced by tour operators and companies and at the same time make suggestions on tour itineraries, content of information, and the layout and presentation. Educational material and information provision is lacking in both the domestic and international markets. A partnership between the park administration and the tour operators could be established to improve this situation by providing a better quality of inter-pretative material in museums, written literature on the wildlife, plants, pre-history and culture of the park, and information boards at highly visited sites. Tour operators need to do more research into the needs of the tourists and get feedback from them. The Gobi questionnaire (SGNPAA, 1998b) found that many tourists accompanied by Mongolian tour operators knew little about their tour itinerary and in some cases did not know the name of the operator.

Development of tourism products and services

As aforementioned, one of the challenges with the present situation of tour-ism in the Gobi is the competition that exists between the tour operators, which is particularly high because of overlap in itineraries and activities. In an effort to reduce repetition, the park should work with the tour operators to develop a greater diversity of tourism products. Suggestions put forward

---

[2] The Gobi questionnaire (SGNPAA, 1998b) highlighted that nearly 20% of tourists did not think or were not sure if the information they received was accurate.

from the Gobi questionnaire (SGNPAA, 1998b) include: hot-air ballooning, wildlife observation, palaeontological tourism, hobby astronomy, cooking Mongolian food and products that include the three Mongolian sports of archery, wrestling and horse racing. The park administration should actively promote the type of tourism they desire in the park and encourage new products in the nature and cultural tourism markets; those that have a lesser environmental impact. The current lack of tourism products could be attributed to the lack of communication between the tour operators, the tourist and the park administration; yet the introduction of these new products needs to be combined with methods to monitor the cultural and environmental impacts. JICA (1998b) suggests targeting the casual nature, adventurous nature, hobby and scientific tourism markets in the short-term (until 2005).

Just as there is a need to create tourism opportunities that are beneficial to ecosystem management, there is a need to limit tourism activities that are not beneficial. Hunting tourism, for example, which still exists as an income generation activity for the government, could hamper the future opportunities to wildlife viewing. Apart from it conflicting with Mongolia's image of a country that cares for its wildlife, 'it should be noted that hunting results in wildlife becoming difficult to approach for watching and photographing' (Munch-Petersen et al., 1993). Furthermore, it is suggested that hunting tourism encourages poaching, which still exists by local people who sell the skins of such species as snow leopards to tourists.

One thing that has surprised the park administration was that in the Gobi questionnaire (SGNPAA, 1998b), 17% of tourists responded to the question of how to make the park more enjoyable by suggesting it be left as it is and not be changed. Previously they thought that much needed to be done to make it an acceptable worldwide ecotourism destination. However, the park administration does need to realize that management is still required to keep it as it is. Since the highest concentration of tourists in the eastern end of the park is already causing some problems (for example, at Yolyn Am), some infrastructure should be improved or developed, so that the numbers of tourists are spread more evenly throughout the park. As well as improving the road system, the development of more accommodation in the park would encourage those tourists who want the relative comfort of a ger camp, compared to a tent, to travel further. JICA (1998b) forecasts that the number of leisure tourist nights could increase from 28,262 in 1997 to over 83,000 in 2005. This will require twice as much accommodation as is currently available, an issue on which the public and private sector will need to engage in discussion. The location, design and size would need careful consideration but as well as the benefit of utilizing more of the park, it would also provide more employment opportunities and income for local people. If the development of new tourism services and activities is planned properly, they can be introduced into currently under-visited locations. Other areas of the park need to be researched for their tourism potential in terms of ability to accept different types of tourism activities, accessibility and aesthetic beauty. Simple solutions could include establishing walking trails or wildlife observation points, the funding for which could come, in part, from fees paid by tour operators. The growth in the tourism industry enables some operators to make considerable incomes. It is not inappropriate, therefore, to encourage operators to reinvest money into nature conservation and tourism infrastructure and to provide incentives for such action.

The need for development also applies to areas outside the park, particularly with regard to the Aimag capital, Dalanzadgad. Dalanzadgad needs to be transformed from an unattractive former socialist town to a centre for tourism accommodation and information. The museum, which has a good array of historical artefacts, could house an information centre for tourists wanting to travel within the park. It could provide a useful base for tourists to meet and share costs into the park, could sell local handicrafts and have a list of suitable and available guides and drivers. If other infrastructure could be developed then tourists might remain in Dalanzadgad a little longer, thus again taking pressure off the highly visited sites within the park. The DANIDA report (Munch-Petersen *et al.*, 1993) even suggested developing Dalanzadgad as a new international point of entry for tourists and constructing an international standard airport.

Conclusion

Forecasts show that in the next 20 years the number of holiday tourists to Mongolia could increase to as many as 172,000 and the number of holiday tourists to the Gobi Gurvansaikhan National Park could rise to as many as 57,000, representing an increase of 1100% (JICA, 1998b). Due to the mystery and image the Gobi holds of being a place where time stands still and to the desires of tourists to keep it as such, ecotourism as a form of tourism is likely to grow rapidly. Yet, at the same time that many tourists wish to keep the Gobi isolated, a certain amount of tourism development needs to take place in order for tourism to provide the economic benefits to this region of low population and low manufacturing output. Importantly, these benefits need to extend to local people, who want to improve their standard of living through participation in the tourism industry. Moreover, a form of tourism development that provides a framework for natural resource conservation needs to take place in order to maintain the pristine environment of the Gobi. Specifically, nature conservation, bearing in mind the country's commitment to protecting large areas of land, needs financing. With an understanding of the concepts of ecotourism and the industry working in partnerships, sustainable tourism development can be implemented successfully and the Gobi Gurvansaikhan National Park can become a popular international ecotourism destination. The keys to this success are cooperation, communication, planning and training.

The race for tourism development in the Gobi Gurvansaikhan National Park will continue as long as tourists continue to come. It is hoped that the organizers will become more organized and start monitoring the competitors, that the competitors will form teams and that there will be opportunities for the spectators to join in. Tourism in Mongolia and in particular, the Gobi, relies on the pristine nature and unique culture. These are the basis for the industry and are therefore fundamental. With the increase in tourism forecasted, improvements in the industry need to be made. The Gobi is not a foreigners' resort; it is the nomads' home. Development should be with their backing, understanding and involvement.

References

JICA (1998a) The master plan on national tourism development in Mongolia – progress report 1. JICA, Ulaanbaatar.

JICA (1998b) The master plan on national tourism development in Mongolia – Interim report. JICA, Ulaanbaatar.

Munch-Petersen, N.F., Sloth, B. and Ramussen, I.L. (1993) *Nature Conservation through Development of Tourism*. DANIDA, Ulaanbaatar.

Shiirevdamba, T.S. (1998) Biological diversity in Mongolia – First national report. Ministry for Nature and the Environment, UNDP and Global Environment Facility, Ulaanbaatar.

South Gobi National Protected Areas' Administration (1998a) *Gobi Gurvansaikhan National Park Management Plan*. SGNPAA.

South Gobi National Protected Areas' Administration (1998b) Report on the 1998 Gobi Gurvansaikhan Tourism Research Questionnaire. SGNPAA.

Strasdas, W. and Steinhauer-Burkart, B. (1998) *The Development of Ecotourism in Protected Areas of Gobi Gurvansaikhan, Gorkhi Terelj and Khan Khentii, Mongolia*. GTZ, Ulaanbaatar.

TACIS (1998) *TACIS Project Development of Tourism for Mongolia – Visitor Survey*. TACIS, Ulaanbaatar.

Wilson, A. (1997) *Mongolia International Country Profile*. WWF, Ulaanbaatar.

Amenity Migration in the Šumava Bioregion, Czech Republic: Implications for Ecological Integrity

Romella S. Glorioso[1]

Laurence Moss & Associates and International Cultural Resources Institute, 2442 Cerrillos Road, PMB 422, Santa Fe, NM 87505, USA

Introduction

Many writing about tourism state it will soon become, or already is the largest global employer and leading income generator (for example de Kadt, 1979; Inskeep, 1991; Eber, 1992; World Travel and Tourism Council, 1995). However, others such as Murphy and Moss suggest a different future. Murphy (1985) proposed tourism will probably decline due to high fuel prices, inflation and recession, and while not disappearing, will change in form and emphasis. Moss identifies these and additional factors for a decreasing tourism, and suggests 'amenity migration' may replace much of tourism (1994, 1999).

This migration for superior amenity potentially offers more opportunities than tourism for places where it is occurring. It: (i) is typically less seasonal; (ii) has less leakage of associated economic benefits; (iii) is characterized by amenity migrants who often bring their knowledge, skills and investment capital with them; (iv) has a greater possibility that amenity migrants, as residents, will develop a sense of belonging to their new place, and responsibility to sustain the attributes that attracted them; (v) enhances potential for participation by amenity migrants in local decision-making and other activities; and (vi) may prove to be a more holistic and equitable vehicle than tourism for linking the local with the global economy (see especially Glorioso, 1998; Henton and Walesh, 1998; Dimaculangan, 1993; Moss,

[1] The author is a PhD student at the Institute of Landscape Ecology, Academy of Sciences of the Czech Republic and a consultant in natural resources and environmental planning and management.

1994, 1999). However, while all these characteristics are evident, the limited studies undertaken of this phenomenon indicate that its impact to date is generally negative. Like much of tourism, amenity migration is resulting in the degradation of natural environment and culture, or amenity attributes,[2] and displacement of local peoples.

Amenity migration is of considerable importance to the Šumava bioregion, as it offers a promising economic alternative to waning agriculture and primary reliance on tourism. In addition, since the phenomenon is at an early phase of development in Šumava, there is an opportunity to capture its positive attributes while ameliorating adverse ones, principally through sensitive management within a bioregional perspective.[3] Here, the primary concern is to maintain the quality of the natural environment and the well-being of the bioregion's inhabitants, and in this context I describe the key characteristics, motivations and behaviour of the amenity migrants and their impacts on the natural environment.

What is Amenity Migration?

Amenity migration refers to the significant contemporary societal phenomenon of large numbers of people moving to places perceived as having superior natural environment and/or distinct culture – amenity attributes (Moss, 1987, 1994). The term was coined by Laurence Moss in 1986, based on his study of the economic success of Santa Fe, New Mexico, which was being propelled principally by such attributes. These migrants may be classified into three types: permanent, seasonal and intermittent. The permanent reside most of their time in the high amenity place; the seasonal for one or several periods each year, such as the summer, the ski season, or the Opera season; and intermittent ones move between their residences more frequently. Amenity migrants may be further generally characterized as resource conservers and resource consumers (Moss, 1994).

The amenity migration construct assumes that the post-industrial information age is in play, and information and knowledge is replacing labour, land and capital (money) as the main producer of wealth (see especially Druker, 1993). In this new economy, six key factors have been identified which coalesce into two societal driving forces (SDF) resulting in amenity migration:

---

[2] Earlier analysis of amenity migration referred to amenity resources. However, to reduce the utilitarian implication of 'resources', I prefer using the word 'attribute'.

[3] Bioregional perspective means that environmental, cultural, social, economic and political policies should be formulated and implemented in an integrated systemic manner within a regional context dictated by natural characteristics, rather than divisions created by state and district jurisdictional boundaries. See also Moss *et al.*, this publication.

SDF 1: increasing motivation for amenity migration
1. Higher valuing of the natural environment,
2. Higher valuing of cultural differentiation, and
3. Higher valuing of leisure, learning and spirituality.

SDF 2: greater facilitation of mobility
4. Increasing discretionary time,
5. Increasing discretionary wealth, and
6. Increasing access through improving and less expensive information and communications (IC) and transportation technology.

(Moss, 1994)

Regarding the factors facilitating mobility (SDF 2), further study of the phenomenon in the past 2 years suggests an important caveat; that discretionary time does not necessarily result from post-industrialization or an IC-based economy. For example, contrary to contemporary folklore, analysis of American work patterns over the past decade indicates that as a result of new IC technologies, such as cellphones, facsimiles, laptops, home computers and beepers, millions of Americans have extended their work at home into the night (Rifkin, 1995; Goozner, 1998). Results of Harris Polls taken periodically over the last 25 years show that the average work week for most Americans has steadily risen from 40.6 h in 1973 to 50.8 h in 1997; and the hours devoted to leisure and hobbies declined from 26.2 h to 19.5 h (Bureau of Labor Statistics, Louis Harris & Assocs, 1998). This condition appears to be manifest in non-telecommuting amenity migrants who choose to work longer hours staying in their high amenity locale for shorter periods and inclined to be intermittent and seasonal types. Moreover, many have more discretionary money to adopt this travel pattern which still has higher transportation costs. Amenity migrants who usually telecommute, along with those who choose more discretionary time in lieu of additional discretionary money, seem to stay longer or reside permanently in their amenity residence.

Although the new economy may not create discretionary time for many, it does make it possible for many more people to live and work in what were previously remote places through its new technology. Or, in the case of intermittent and seasonal amenity migrants who choose to work longer hours and stay in their amenity locale for shorter periods, the new economy gives them more discretionary money to adopt a higher cost travel pattern. This suggests that bioregions such as Šumava can participate in the new economy by creating distinctive habitats for such amenity migrants. Examples of mountainous regions that attracted such amenity migrants and are now a well-connected part of the global economy are the Santa Fe, New Mexico and Sierra Nevada, California bioregions (Moss, 1987, 1994, 1999); the Rocky Mountain Range more generally, which accounted for seven of the ten leading US states in new business incorporation in 1993 (Denniston,

1995) and the eight-state region in the western USA (Arizona, California, Colorado, Idaho, New Mexico, Oregon, Utah, Washington) which harbours more biotechnology companies than any other region of the world (Bolin, 1998).

The Šumava Bioregion and its Amenity Attributes

The Šumava bioregion is centred on the beauty, natural resources and comparative ecological uniqueness of the Šumava Mountains, and extends outward to its principal human settlements: Český Krumlov, Domažlice, Klatovy, Prachatice, Sušice and Vimperk. Although the mountain massif dominated by the Šumava Mountains extends marginally into Bavaria, Germany, and Upper Austria, here I refer only to these mountains and their piedmont. Much of this territory is under three nature protection regimes: a Protected Landscape Area of 1630 km², established in 1963; a UNESCO Biosphere Reserve with an area of 1670 km², proclaimed in 1990; and the Šumava National Park established in 1991, with an area of 685 km². This bioregion[4] of about 3500 km² includes 1670 km² of the best preserved ecosystems in Central Europe, of which about 800 km² has no significant human communication systems and is thus ecologically complete (Price, 1995).

In addition to being comparatively environmentally pristine, the bioregion's built environment is quite picturesque, and especially in its piedmont, historically important. While many European countries lost much of this heritage with industrialization and the devastation of two World Wars, the Šumava bioregion fared considerably better and is now a repository of some 800 years of architecture and townscape. The numerous examples of the Romanesque, Gothic and Baroque periods are generally in good condition and not yet as commercialized as their Western European counterparts. Perhaps, the most remarkable place is the piedmont town of Český Krumlov. It has some 300 fine historical buildings and outstanding townscape. In 1992 this town was declared a UNESCO's World Heritage Site, 'a fact that proves the town's immense historical importance as an intrinsic part of the world's cultural heritage' (Vondrouš, 1995).

Today the bioregion's Czech and German ethnic traditions, while not as pronounced as they were, are still exhibited in behavioural patterns, cuisine, festivals, some folk arts and vernacular architecture. In addition, other ethnic

---

[4] The area of the bioregion in this essay is larger than that used in the Moss *et al.* definition (see Chapter 5) because in addition to identifying a bioregion by physical factors, such as physiography, animal and plant geography, I also used the amenity migrant's and local inhabitants' perception of the extent of their bioregion; their mental map of it. They are the people who will be most affected by the amenity migration phenomenon and who could greatly impact the ecological integrity of the Šumava bioregion. For ways to define a bioregion see especially Berg (1978) and Devall (1988).

Fig. 14.1. A photograph taken some 80 years ago remains a good representation of this western Šumava landscape and the town of Železná Ruda (Eisenstein; postcard, circa 1920, collection of R.S. Glorioso).

Fig. 14.2. The historical centre of Český Krumlov, a principal attraction of amenity migrants and tourists in the Šumava bioregion (photo by L.A.G. Moss, March 1999).

groups have settled in Šumava since World War II (see especially Bartoš and Těšitel, 1996). Romany, or gypsy, living culture should be mentioned in particular. Although not typically considered an attraction by locals I interviewed in the bioregion, the Rom were considered quite interesting by Western European and North American amenity migrants and tourists. They also considered the lifestyle of a people that spent more than four decades living in a communist system an attraction, although this characteristic is rapidly changing.

Amenity Migration and its Key Stakeholders: Past, Present and Future

The historical development of the amenity migration in the Šumava bioregion may be divided into two periods: proto-amenity migration, from the 1850s until approximately the Czech Velvet Revolution in 1989, and amenity migration, from about 1990.

Proto-amenity migration

Proto-amenity migration (PAM) refers to migration principally for greater amenity that occurred before the global IC-based economy and its advent in the Czech lands. The key motivating factors identified for contemporary amenity migrants appear to be the same for Šumava proto-amenity migrants, however, they seem to have been less pronounced, as there was then more pristine natural environment, and cultures were more highly differentiated. Also, regarding the key facilitating factors, PAM was typically more limited to those having discretionary time and/or wealth, mainly because of the underdeveloped communications system, and a parallel condition for transportation until the early 1960s.

The Šumava Mountains were unpopulated until the 13th century when the Bohemian King invited Germans to live in this remote area to strengthen the kingdom's economic power. These first settlers were mainly from 'monasterial demesnes' in the bordering region of Upper Austria (Jelínek, 1995). Settlements were built in the central European alpine vernacular both on the mountain slopes and the foothills, which to varying degrees still exist to attract contemporary amenity migrants.

Human settlement in the Šumava Mountains grew, and from the mid-19th century they became a popular location for socio-economic elites' vacation or country homes. Key informants estimated there were about 200–500 such homes in the bioregion before World War II. Later, such amenity migration was impeded by political upheavals and the resultant deteriorating socio-economic condition. First came the repatriation of the Sudeten Germans, which had made up about 90% of the population. Then the establishment of the communist government in February 1948, resulting in the closure of the bioregion to non-communist proto-amenity migrants, and more generally the demise of the capitalist elite and a reduction in discretionary income (Pokorny, 1994). For more than a decade PAM seems to have stagnated, but in the early 1960s, as the new government stabilized, a new Czech middle class emerged with considerable discretionary time and interest in leisure, especially outdoor recreation.

The Šumava Mountains, having good road and rail access at the time, and ranking as one of the best equipped winter sports centres in the country, were the prime destination for sports enthusiasts. Although personal discretionary income was small, government subsidies, particularly inexpensive petrol and relatively convenient and dependable public transportation, allowed sojourning to the bioregion more often. For these reasons, and the economic difficulties of the 1950s still fresh in people's minds, owning a second home in the Šumava Mountains for leisure was impractical. Although some sports enthusiasts bought houses of the Sudeten Germans inexpensively, which was considered very risky at the time, more common Czech vacation home ownership did not really occur until the 1970s.

From the early 1970s, people's dissatisfactions with the prefabricated high-rise apartments that the government built grew considerably. High density, unattractive designs, small size, noise and limited green space were common complaints from inhabitants. The majority of them did not regard them as their homes, but rather a provisionary solution to a national housing shortage (Plicka, 1994). Missing open and green spaces and the tranquillity of the natural environment, they built second homes in the mountains to spend their leisure time more contentedly. This is reflected in the research on regional and residential preferences of 330 Czech urban high school students in the pre-revolutionary late 1980s by Drhbohlav (1990). They ranked highest mountainous entities and other very little urbanized regions with high quality landscape. 'When it comes to causal specification of the objectives of preferences, there is clear predominance of the factor of "more healthy environment" (in the sense of natural components including "the beauty and picturesqueness of landscape")' (Drhbohlav, 1990: 68).

Although proto-amenity migrants in this period still had little discretionary income to build their second homes,[5] they had learned to manipulate the new political–economic system. Firstly, they took advantage of buying the confiscated Sudeten Germans' real property being sold very cheaply by the Czech government. Secondly, they used their discretionary time in building or renovating their second homes. And thirdly, they traded services and construction materials through personal connections at their place of work or contacts in the large government sector. So unlike the pre-war period, when proto-amenity migrants were characteristically wealthy Germans and Czechs, second home owners were Czechs and represented a broad base of occupations from truck drivers and bricklayers to medical doctors and public officials. The government not only knew what was going

---

[5] Second homeowners did not receive financial assistance from the state. For details regarding housing financial assistance in the communist era see especially Sýkora (1996); and about housing policy in Český Krumlov specifically, Hanšpach and Vajdová (1993).

on, but reportedly supported this use of discretionary time in lieu of political and social activities not supportive of the state.

An estimated 14,000 second homes were built in the Šumava Mountains and foothills between the early 1970s and early 1980s; a marked increase. Different from second homes built before World War II by earlier proto-amenity migrants, these houses were typically much smaller and were used more intermittently rather than seasonally. Also, these proto-amenity migrants relied heavily on the availability and dependability of public transportation.

Amenity migration in a new economic era – a transition period

The end of the communist period in 1989 in the Czech Republic has brought social and political–economic changes that are complex; changes that neither the government nor the people were prepared for. The transition from a centrally planned to a more market-oriented and democratic political-economy, and from an industrial to a more information-based society is resulting in a decrease of discretionary time and wealth generally among the Czech population, and as yet a marked decrease in the general standard of living. While the government considerably reduced its transportation subsidies, such as for gasoline, automobiles and public transportation, the private sector is now investing heavily in communications facilities. Thus, wired and cellular telephones and internet services are not only becoming more

Fig. 14.3.   Southern Lipno Lake and the town of Frymburk (photo by M. Bartoš, March 1998).

available in the capital Prague, but elsewhere, including the Šumava bio-region. Although the quality has not reached western European standards, the cost for these services is still considerably more expensive, especially for the average Czech household and in Šumava.

The amenity migrants' motivating values in this period appear the same as proto-amenity migrants', however, the tangible manifestation of cultural attributes, such as the historical buildings and townscape and alpine vern-acular architecture as motivating factor becomes more apparent. Aside from the post-1989 changes in the Czech Republic mentioned above, other, more external key factors identified as responsible for the increase in amenity migration in the bioregion are: (i) increasing global demand for places with comparatively pristine environment and/or distinct culture; (ii) international-ization of information about the Czech Republic and Šumava; (iii) a shift in perception that investment in this country has become more secure and the likely return more attractive; and (iv) increased availability of employment in the tourism sector.

Key informant interviews undertaken in 1993 indicated the following salient characteristics, which from my later participant observation and the Český Krumlov strategic planning analyses (see below) appeared substan-tially the same in 1995–1996. Approximately 10–20% of the population of the bioregion were amenity migrants, with most residing in the piedmont. Some 10% were foreigners, and about 80% of these were identified as German and Austrian; others being American, Canadian, Italian, Slovak, Romanian, Polish and Ukrainian. Some of these foreign Šumava amenity

Fig. 14.4. Amenity migrants' houses, southern Šumava bioregion (photo by L.A.G. Moss, September 1996).

migrants may have been better categorized as migrants resettling mainly for economic advantage, especially those from central and eastern Europe. Americans and Canadians stated they had considerable choice in migrating and that this bioregion attracted them principally because of its amenity attributes.

While the majority of Czech amenity migrants were from the middle to higher income group engaged in professional activities, such as academics, civil servants, lawyers, environmental designers and scientists, foreign ones seemed to be from the low and middle income groups in their countries of origin. Not many were engaged in the above professions, rather they earned all or part of their income locally as pension, hostel and restaurant owners, and other tourism-based activity. A few were blue collar workers employed in building restoration. Those with professional training were English language teachers, fine artists and environmental activists. There were still very few of the amenity migrants of the types we see in other case studies (Burgess, 1996, 1998a,b; Denniston, 1995; Price et al., 1997; Moss, 1999) – the retiree, the independently wealthy and the teleworker.

Czech amenity migrants usually had two houses in the bioregion, a primary dwelling in town and secondary one in the mountains. It was quite common for Czech amenity migrants to have two sources of income, one from their regular employment and the other from renting their alpine houses. About 80% of these amenity migrants earned their incomes in the bioregion. Foreigners on the other hand typically had only one house, usually located in or close by a town or village due to unavailability of employment and health facilities, and constraints on transportation and telecommunications in the Šumava Mountains. Classification of amenity migrants by key informants was: (i) Czech: 35% permanent; 25% seasonal; and 40% intermittent; and (ii) foreign: 1% permanent; 10–15% seasonal; and 80–85% intermittent.

It is anticipated that amenity migration will increase over the next decade, especially foreign amenity migration, and particularly from Austria and Germany, but the magnitude is uncertain, especially without specific public and private programmes to attract or dissuade them. During the 1989–1992 period, real estate 'for sale' advertisements were common only in the northern part of the country and the capital, Prague. Beginning in 1993, however, they also appeared in local newspapers in the bioregion, seemingly because of an increased demand from Germans and Austrians.

An important hindrance to the development of foreign amenity migration identified was a national law forbidding foreign private land ownership. While some foreigners have legally circumvented this constraint by establishing a Czech corporation (Czech Republic: Facts and Figures, 1994), or by marrying a Czech national, this constraint is expected to disappear in a few years with the Czech Republic joining the European Union. Other foreigners who do not wish to use either of these often costly and time-consuming methods manipulate the law by agreeing with a Czech to buy her or his property, further agreeing that in the event the land ownership law changes, the Czech will sell the property to the real owner for a token amount. This is euphemistically called a 'long-term lease'.

The key informants and the Český Krumlov strategic planning team (see below) also identified other difficulties that appeared to be dissuading foreigners from residing in the bioregion. Principal ones were:

1. Difficulty in dealing with the Czech police in charge of foreign visitors and residents, especially in obtaining and maintaining residence permission;
2. Difficulty in learning the Czech language, as few Czechs in the bioregion speak English. However, this impediment promises to lessen as English is now taught from primary school. Also, although Czechs often speak German, there appears to be some stigma attached to speaking it in this border area;[6]
3. Some animosity toward those thought to be competitors for local perceived scarcities, such as employment – especially foreigners and people of colour;
4. A comparatively lower level of comfort and convenience, e.g. telecommunications facilities were more expensive, less extensive and dependable than Western nationals were accustomed to, public transportation was less convenient, and restaurants with fine international cuisine few;
5. Difficulty in earning income locally. Many amenity migrants moving to Šumava anticipated making at least part of a living there, but were constrained by the difficulties outlined above. Success stories were usually those of a foreigner married to a Czech and being involved in a tourist enterprise;
6. Difficult access to and very expensive health care. In 1996, government hospitals usually charged foreigners seven times the amount paid by Czechs. Semi-private hospital or private clinics charged less, but still higher for foreigners. Health insurance for foreigners not working for the government was also expensive, and English-speaking doctors were few, and fewer still in rural locales; and
7. Foreigners still paid considerably more rent than Czechs, and usually had no access to public housing, still the majority of the housing stock.

While foreign amenity migration appears to have been slowly increasing, Czech seasonal and intermittent amenity migration was decreasing, an estimated 60% between 1989 and 1996. Key informants and documentary sources suggested this may have been due to the following reasons:

1. Considerable decrease in both discretionary time and wealth. In order to survive economically in the transition to a market economy with high inflation, people were working longer and harder. One well-informed interviewee estimated that an average Czech citizen had to earn three times as

---

[6] For interpretations of the historical origin of this Czech–German friction see Johnson (1996) and Pokorny (1994).

much to acquire the same standard of living he/she had during the Communist period;

2. Considerable decrease in public transportation, while both private cars and petrol prices considerably increased compared with disposable income;

3. As Czechs may now freely travel to the West, many preferred to spend their leisure time and money experiencing the rest of the world; and

4. Considerable growth of consumerist and materialist values and behaviour (see especially Greene, 1991)[7]; therefore some potential amenity migrants preferred to refrain from or not take earned vacations and work instead so they could earn more money to buy cars, signature clothing, jewelry, etc.

Due to the above reasons, about 20–25% of second homes, including old hotels and other recreational buildings, were sold between 1989 and 1996. Of this figure about 1% was sold to foreigners. These buyers were usually interested in unusual buildings, such as restored country estates, large farm houses or manor homes, and ones in ready-to-move-in condition, but there were few of these in the bioregion, and for them the owners expected high prices, sometimes almost equivalent to the cost in the foreigner's country. Also, they were too expensive for most Czechs, given their low incomes and that the sweat equity they formerly used was no longer an option.

However, there were Czech amenity migrants overcoming these difficulties (principally the lack of discretionary time and money) and living permanently in the bioregion. One way was owning a restaurant, pension, art gallery or other business catering to tourists. Such amenity migrants had discretionary money but very little discretionary time. While this was a characteristic of both foreign and domestic amenity migrants, the foreign tended to be more permanent while the domestic tended to be more intermittent or seasonal. Also, there were more foreign amenity migrants involved in the tourism industry than Czech.

Another way was through a volunteer simplicity life style – living simpler, less materially demanding lives. Burgess, in his commentary in the *Rocky Mountain News*, 20 January 1998, identified 'simplicity movement', 'lifestyle downscaling' and 'cashing out' as new cultural forces that are motivating amenity migration. Like amenity migrants of this type elsewhere in the world, those in Šumava appeared to be more environmentally aware and educated, have resource conserving ethics and behaviour, and especially motivated by high quality of the natural environment, learning and spirituality. In addition, they tended to have a stronger sense of belonging to their bioregion than seasonal and intermittent amenity migrants. Due to these characteristics they were usually more actively involved in the protection of local environmental and cultural attributes and in local community

---

[7] In addition, the Český Krumlov strategic planning team (CKSPT) identified this reason as a key societal driving force that will influence future amenity migration in their bioregion.

activities; sometimes more involved and committed than the earlier inhabitants. Being typically occupied in the NGO sector, or part time for the government, this type of amenity migrant had discretionary time but little discretionary money, and while growing in number, were still very few in the bioregion as well as globally. An important consideration is, would these two types of amenity migrants have more discretionary money if Šumava had well-developed IC technology? Will there be less foreign amenity migrants involved in the tourism industry if sophisticated IC technology is present?

Key stakeholders – an initial analysis[8]

The key stakeholders identified were: (i) amenity migrants; (ii) tourists; (iii) local inhabitants *per se*, including the out-migrating better educated youth; (iv) the bioregion's political leaders; (v) Šumava National Park's administration; regional offices of the (vi) Ministry of Environment, (vii) Ministry of Regional Development (including the Czech Tourism Authority), (viii) Ministry of Trade and Industry, and (ix) Ministry of Defense (because of the presence of a large military training base in the bioregion); (x) municipalities; (xi) districts; (xii) entrepreneurs; (xiii) the Regional Development Agency of Šumava; (xiv) ŠIPEK (a local environmental NGO); (xv) the repatriated Sudeten Deutsch and their families who may claim property in the bioregion; (xvi) the administration of the adjacent German Bavarian National Park; and (xvii) IC technology private businesses. However, since amenity migration is in an initial phase in the Šumava bioregion, and the Czech political–economic environment is rather fluid, even in the shorter term there may be change in key stakeholders identified above.

As is common elsewhere, there are no public or third sector organizations that promote amenity migration in the Czech Republic. There are, however, a few countries which are more aware of the phenomenon and have special programmes promoting foreign amenity migrants, especially retirees, to locate in their countries. One example is the Philippine government's programme managed by the Philippine Retirement Authority (PRA). This programme encourages foreign retirees or semi-retired younger people to bring themselves, and hard currency, to the country in return for long-term resident visas, which in some cases can be changed into citizenship (Dimaculangan, 1993). According to recent figures from the US Bureau of Consular Affairs, Philippines is in the top six list of Americans' favourite places to live, with 105,000 residing there (Ciabattari, 1998). Yet, similarly to places with more advanced amenity migration, very few planners and decision-makers have an awareness of the global system generating amenity migrants and appropriate planning skills to manage the phenomenon. One

---

[8] This section was written in coordination with Moss *et al.*, this publication.

consequence to date is amenity migration locations have degrading environmental attributes.

However, and quite significant, the Czech Republic has a well-
developed and a long history of nature and landscape protection laws. In the
bioregion, the Boubínský Prales, a primeval mountain mixed forest, was
declared a nature reserve in 1858, the third one in Bohemia, and one of the
best known in Europe today (Price, 1995). More recently, the 1992 Czech
National Council Act No. 114/92, states that, 'the protection of nature and
the landscape is understood to be the hereinafter specified care for wild
animals, wild plants and their communities, minerals, rocks, palaeontological finds and geological wholes, ecological systems and landscape
wholes, as well as for the appearance and accessibility of the landscape,
carried out by the state and by physical and legal persons.'

In Šumava it appears that only the town of Český Krumlov has begun
focusing on amenity migration, and this town is the bioregion's leading
amenity migrants' location. Since about 1993 there has been specific
concern in Český Krumlov over tourism becoming the dominating
economic activity of the town and its surrounding area, as some community
leaders observed the negative impacts of mass tourism on the economy,
culture and environment in surrounding countries. One result was a desire
to develop a more diversified economy, and one better sustaining the town
and its hinterland's environmental and cultural attributes. From September,
1995 to December, 1996, the town's Mayor and Council, assisted by a non-
governmental organization (NGO)-sponsored facilitator, led a volunteer
strategic planning team in formulating a sustainable development strategy
for Český Krumlov. In the course of this activity, amenity migration was
identified as a key factor in the town's future.[9] They began by crafting the
following mission statement:

> Formulate a long range development strategy to facilitate the economic
> well-being of Český Krumlov's citizens, while sustaining the environmental
> and cultural values and resources of the town and its symbiotic hinterland.
> Particular attention will be given to:
> 1. developing the town as a single, harmoniously integrated unit;
> 2. increasing the town's independence, balanced by its own moral and finan-
> cial responsibility for this change;
> 3. sustaining the symbiotic relationship of the town with the natural, social
> and cultural attributes of its region; and
> 4. increasing the capability of the town's administration, including its ability
> to undertake strategic planning and management.
>   (Český Krumlov Strategic Planning Team, 1996b)

---

[9] The 30-person strategic planning team (CKSPT) was composed mainly of local residents,
along with a few professionals drawn from the larger bioregion, and had a wide array of
expertise and experience. The resident advisor and facilitator for the town's 15-month
strategic planning process was Laurence A.G. Moss, a strategic planner and sustainable
regional development specialist, funded by the Foundation for a Civil Society, New York
and Český Krumlov.

The multiple scenario strategic planning process[10] subsequently undertaken identified two societal driving forces critical to mission achievement: there is high global demand for amenity resources, and Český Krumlov bioregion[11] residents' resource-consuming behaviour predominates. Four future scenarios for the 1997–2020 period were derived from these forces, and one, 'Few Surprises', a trends-continue scenario, was chosen as the most likely to unfold at a workshop of the town's strategic planning team, senior administrative officials and members of the Town Council and Mayor. Then, four strategic thrusts for 1997–2001 were formulated to modify the implications of this scenario and achieve the town's mission.[12] They may be summarized as:

1. Be very involved in influencing the future condition of Český Krumlov's bioregion (physical, economic, political, socio-cultural);
2. Skilfully manage amenity migration and tourism to modify the scenario's longer-term negative local development outcomes;
3. Improve local people's level of global strategic awareness and cultural/ environmental appreciation; and
4. Improve the management and hosting skills of Český Krumlov and its people, focusing on appropriate resource-conserving amenity migration and tourism.

As of late 1998, the town had established a standing strategic planning committee for formulating action plans; it had used the strategic thrusts as directives for a new physical development plan and in considering major town investments; and with the town council and ŠIPEK, a local environmental NGO, were attempting to locate funds to formulate and institutionalize a set of local sustainable development indicators[13] for informing strategy implementation and evaluation. Over the strategic planning period there was increasing local interest and involvement in this planning process and outcome, along with expanding local and national media coverage.

---

[10] There is a variety of strategic planning approaches. The one used here relies heavily on the 'intuitive logic' approach to multiple future scenarios. It was developed initially for private sector use by the Harvard Business School in the 1970s, and later in the decade at Stanford Research Institute International. Laurence Moss & Associates further adapted the methodology for the public and non-profit sectors and as an applied research tool. For further details, see especially Ringland (1998) and Laurence Moss & Associates (1999a,b).

[11] For its sustainable development strategic planning exercise, Český Krumlov considered its bioregion the town and surrounding territory extending from České Budějovice in the north to the Austrian border in the south, and between Lake Lipno in the west and Kaplice to the east. In addition, critical to the mission is the condition of the Vltava River, its source to České Budějovice and the southern half of the Šumava Biosphere Reserve (CKSPT, 1996b).

[12] For the four scenario narratives, see CKSPT (1996a, c) for a more detailed discussion.

[13] For detailed discussion, see CKSPT (1996c), and for a description of local sustainable indicators see Moss *et al.*, this publication.

The above condition should be considered in the following context:

1.   Local inhabitants were living in a socio-economic marginal area (Těšitel *et al.*, 1997) and in a rapidly changing political–economic environment. So while it seems difficult for any community to undertake strategic longer-term planning, this was particularly the case in the Šumava bioregion;

2.   A lack of experience with democratic processes, such as open forums with authentic public participation and local community volunteer organizations;

3.   Quite constrained municipal financial resources, and while still reliant on the central government for most funds, its responsibilities considerably increasing after 1989;

4.   A progressive Mayor clearly understood the issues I discuss in this essay, including the global situation and amenity migration, but had inadequate professional and financial support, and significant political opposition; and

5.   More positively, there was growing awareness of what has been discussed and described in this essay among local people and a community-based non-profit environmental organization, ŠIPEK, was established, in which amenity migrants play an active role alongside earlier inhabitants.

Key Impacts

Since amenity migration in the Šumava bioregion is in its nascent phase, there appears as yet little apparent impact of the phenomenon in the bioregion outside Český Krumlov. In the town and its hinterland, as tourism is growing comparatively rapidly, it is even more difficult to assign separate outcomes to the amenity migrants. However, from the information developed it is apparent that even at its initial stage, amenity migration is contributing to the following difficult-to-change pattern, in which there are inherent negatives.

Šumava Mountains

The land use of Šumava's alpine area, virtually constant for more than four decades, now seems to be changing quite rapidly from agriculture, forestry and military to more recreation-related land use (Kušová *et al.*, 1997). This partly results in marked increase in solid and waste-water management difficulties for municipalities, regional districts and the Šumava National Park. Another impact of amenity migration is the introduction of suburban housing and landscaping type and patterning. In addition to more extensive land use, this includes use of spring and well waters and septic systems, manicured lawns and shubbery, non-indigenous trees and plants and increasing hard surfaced areas, especially for roads. These impacts on the bioregion's ecosystems however, have not yet been studied.

Town of Český Krumlov

While there have likely been impacts on other Šumava towns, they are most apparent in Český Krumlov, the premier regional attraction of both amenity migrants and tourists. The town changed considerably since the 1989 Czech Velvet Revolution. From a small subsistence economic base of a local market town, in 1996 the town's small historic core had 17 restaurants and cafes; four hotels, nine pensions, three hostels and other visitors accommodation in private houses; five commercial banks and six additional foreign exchange offices; two cinemas, nine travel agencies, six art galleries, and numerous small souvenir shops selling mostly jewellery, cards and books, glass and crystal, liquor and cigarettes. It also had two theatres and three museums, including the new world-class Egon Schiele International Cultural Centre housed in a skilfully renovated 16th century brewery and exhibiting the works by Schiele and other well-known modern painters (see also Moss *et al.*, this publication). This change brought many newcomers, both Czech and foreigners. While generating some additional income, the historic town core was losing its permanent residents as buildings designed for single family residence were rapidly being turned into restaurants, pensions, souvenir shops, galleries and banks. The Town Ordinance that more than 50% of a residential building must have a permanent occupant to maintain 'life in the town' was proving difficult to enforce.

Most of the above typically thought to result from tourism was also the product of amenity migration. What is not generally realized is that amenity migration is an important promoter of tourism. Many amenity migrants in the Šumava, as in the Baguio, Philippines, Santa Fe, New Mexico, and Sierra Nevada, California bioregions, were not only involved in tourism-related activities but were pioneers in their development. Moreover, in Český Krumlov the leaders of its key institutions, such as the Czech Ceramic Design Agency, the District Museum, the Egon Schiele Centre, the Municipal Theatre and the Český Krumlov Fund, important stakeholders in achieving the town's vision of becoming the cultural centre of the bioregion and South Bohemia, were amenity migrants.

More general bioregional impacts partially attributable to amenity migration were:

1. Increasing cost of basic needs: food, clothing and shelter. For example, housing in the bioregion was becoming expensive, especially in the towns, so that lower and average incomed Czech families found it increasingly difficult to buy a house. At the same time public authorities were attempting to sell or increase rent of public housing to cover the costs of maintenance and renovation of the many houses and historical buildings they own;

2. Some signs of increasing animosity towards foreign amenity migrants as they became more apparent where contact and competition was greater, such as in Český Krumlov; and

3. New ideas and experiences which may be both a value and a threat to the amenity attributes of the bioregion.

The positive aspects of this situation are the amenity migrants' increased motivation for social and environmental activism through learning and spiritualism, usually providing their expertise for little or no monetary return. More generally, amenity migrants also seem to develop a sense of belonging to the place versus a sense of ownership, and therefore are more responsible and involved in the protection of the amenity attributes compared to tourists and earlier migrants (Glorioso, 1998). More difficult to assess is the value of their experience and financial capital. An important question is, to what degree do they have the appropriate attributes sustaining skills, or are they just taking advantage of a comparative opportunity not in their previous locations?

Conclusion

The Šumava bioregion, after more than four decades of virtual stagnation and escape from the negative impacts of industrialization and war, is again at a critical juncture. What was an historical marginal region is now perceived by many as an 'empty place in the heart of Europe waiting to be developed'. In the face of a growing number of increasingly mobile amenity migrants worldwide, searching for comparatively pristine environments like Šumava, bringing with them wealth, entrepreneurial and other skills and new ideas, the bioregion's communities face a difficult task of taking advantage of opportunity while avoiding threat. However, due principally to the national law forbidding individual foreign private land ownership, the bioregion may have a 4–6-year window-of-opportunity before this condition is reversed with the Czech Republic joining the EU. The key issues to be addressed appear to be:

1. The lack of local, regional and national understanding of amenity migration and the appropriate skills to effectively manage it;

2. The need for local people to strategically decide what direction they will take; whether to encourage or dissuade amenity migration. However, informed decision making will rely on resolving issue (1) above, which in turn depends on a significant increase in local participation; then

3. How? This is a difficult question that needs innovative attention. Does strategically manipulating amenity migration to emphasize its opportunities mean making an agreement with the EU for special protection of the bioregion, and selective participation in the IC-based new economy? Encouraging amenity migration may mean displacing local inhabitants from the bioregion due to the mismatch in their skills, the new economy, and the increased cost of living that seems to accompany amenity migrants. Also, amenity attributes degradation due to growing consumer and materialistic attitudes and behaviours locally and globally manifest by many amenity migrants. What is the best way to attract the resource-conserving amenity migrants and those who will actively participate in their local community and help develop an amenity attribute sustaining diversified economy?

In particular, I hope this analysis will help facilitate the people of Šumava in turning complex amenity migration issues into opportunities. Handled with knowledge, sensitivity and commitment, this emerging phenomenon can be a major asset in achieving a healthy bioregional ecology and a decent local quality of life.

References

Bartoš, M. and Těšitel, J. (1996) Large scale land abandonment: problems of reinhabitation. In: Steinberger, Y. (ed.) *Preservation of Our World in the Wake of Change*, Vol. VI A/B. ISEEQS, Jerusalem, pp. 871–874.

Berg, P. (1978) *Reinhabiting a Separate Country: a Bioregional Anthology of Northern California*. Planet Drum Foundation, San Francisco, California.

Bureau of Labor Statistics and Louis Harris & Assocs (19 July 1998) In: *The Sunday Oregonian*, p. G1.

Bolin, F. (1998, June) Biotech century dawns in the western U.S.: an economic geography. *Points West Review* 20.

Burgess, P. (December 1996) *Commentary: Telecomputing Transformation*. http://www.newwest.org/burgess/pb961212.htm.

Burgess, P. (January 1998a) *Commentary: American Outback on the Rebound*. http://www.newwest.org/burgess/pb980120.htm.

Burgess, P. (July 1998b) *Commentary: Recreation Boom Builds New West*. http://www.newwest.org/burgess/pb980707.htm.

Český Krumlov Strategic Planning Team (CKSPT) (1996a) *Český Krumlov Alternative Future Scenarios*. Mayor's Office, Český Krumlov, Czech Republic and The Foundation for a Civil Society, New York.

Český Krumlov Strategic Planning Team (CKSPT) (1996b) *Český Krumlov Strategic Planning Mission*. Mayor's Office, Český Krumlov, Czech Republic and The Foundation for a Civil Society, New York.

Český Krumlov Strategic Planning Team (CKSPT) (1996c) *Strategic Thrusts for Scenario A*. Mayor's Office, Český Krumlov, Czech Republic and The Foundation for a Civil Society, New York.

Ciabattari, J. (12 July 1998) Americans abroad: favorite spots to settle. *Parade Magazine*, p.19.

Czech National Council (19 February 1992) *Czech National Council Act No. 114/92 on the Protection of Nature and the Landscape*. Czech National Council, Prague, pp. 666–693.

Czech Republic: Facts and Figures (1994) Arteria Info Ltd, Prague.

de Kadt, E. (1979) *Tourism: Passport to Development?* Oxford University Press, New York.

Denniston, D. (1995) *Worldwatch Paper 123: High Priorities: Conserving Mountain Ecosystems and Cultures.* Worldwatch Institute, Washington, DC, pp. 36–41.

Devall, B. (1988) *Simple in Means, Rich in Ends, Practicing Deep Ecology.* Peregrine Smith, South Lake City, pp. 57–72.

Dimaculangan [Glorioso], R. S. (1993) Key policy implications for strategic use of amenity resources: a study of longer-term amenity migration, Baguio Bioregion, The Philippines. Unpublished M.Sc. thesis, INRDM Programme, Asian Institute of Technology, Bangkok.

Drbohlav, D. (1990) Regional and residential preferences of the population (example of high school students in three selected cities of the Czech Republic). *Acta Universitatis Caroline, Geographic* 2, 51–72.

Drucker, P.F. (1993) *Post-Capitalist Society.* HarperCollins, New York.

Eber, S. (ed.) (1992) *Beyond the Green Horizon, Principles for Sustainable Tourism.* WWF, UK, pp. vi, 1–2.

Glorioso, R.S. (1998) Amenity migration and tourism in the Baguio Bioregion, Philippines: toward local governance. Contribution to *Community-based Mountain Tourism* e-mail conference, http://ww2.mtnforum.org/mtnforum/archives/document/discuss98/cbmt/cbmt5/051898a.htm.

Goozner, M. (19 July 1998) Burned by the midnight oil. *The Sunday Oregonian Forum*, pp. G1–G2.

Green, P. (1991, June) Bad Czechs. *Connoisseur*, pp. 72–79, 101.

Hanšpach, D. and Vajdová, Z. (1993) *Český Krumlov: Housing Policy, Privatization and Local Development.* Institute of Sociology, Charles University, Prague.

Henton, D. and Walesh, K. (1998) *Linking the New Economy to the Livable Community.* Collaborative Economics, Palo Alto, California.

Inskeep, E. (1991) *Tourism Planning: an Integrated and Sustainable Development Approach.* Van Nostrand Reinhold, New York, pp. 8–15.

Jelínek, P. (1995) The forest wanderer's home. *Český Krumlov, Past and Present.* ORBIS Publishing House, Prague.

Johnson, L.R. (1996) *Central Europe: Enemies, Neighbors, Friends.* Oxford University Press, Oxford and New York.

Kušová, D., Těšitel, J. and Bartoš, M. (1997) *The Role of Tourism in Marginal Areas Development* (Šumava Mts Case). Institute of Landscape Ecology, Academy of Sciences of the Czech Republic.

Laurence Moss & Assocs (1999a) *Multiple Scenarios in Planning.* Laurence Moss & Assocs, Santa Fe, New Mexico and Sunriver, Oregon.

Laurence Moss & Assocs (1999b) *Notes on Strategic Planning Methodology.* Laurence Moss & Assocs, Santa Fe, New Mexico and Sunriver, Oregon.

Moss, L.A.G. (1987) *Santa Fe, New Mexico, Post-Industrial Amenity-based Economy: Myth or Model?* Alberta Ministry of Economic and Trade & International Cultural Resources Institute, Edmonton & Santa Fe, New Mexico.

Moss, L.A.G. (1994) Beyond tourism: the amenity migrants. In: Mannermaa, M., Inayatullah, S. and Slaughter, R. (eds) *Coherence and Chaos in Our Uncommon Futures, Visions, Means, Actions.* Finland Futures Research Centre, Turku School of Economics and Business Administration, Turku, pp. 121–128.

Moss, L.A.G. (1996) *Český Krumlov Sustainable Development Indicators Project Proposal.* Mayors Office, Český Krumlov, Czech Republic and The Foundation For A Civil Society, New York.

Moss, L.A.G. (1999) *Sustaining the Sierra Nevada Bioregion's Integrity under Growing Human Population Pressure: Policy Issues Brief.* The Public Policy Institute of California, San Francisco, California.

Murphy, P.E. (1985) *Tourism: A Community Approach.* Methuen, New York & London.

Plicka, I. (1994) Urban structure of Prague. *Special Issue of the 30th Congress of the International Society of City and Regional Planners Bulletin* 1995/2, 17–32.

Pokorny, J. (1994) *The Czech Lands, 1918–1994.* Martin Vopenka, Prague.

Price, M.F. (1995) The mountains of Central and Eastern Europe. *Environmental Research Series 9*, IUCN European Programme, Gland.

Price, M.F., Moss, L.A.G. and Williams, P.W. (1997) Tourism and amenity migration. In: Messerli, B. and Ives, J.D. (eds) *Mountains of the World: a Global Priority.* Parthenon Publishing, London & New York, pp. 249–280.

Rifkin, J. (1995) *The End of Work: the Decline of the Global Labor Force and the Dawn of the Post-Market Era.* G.P. Putnam's Sons, New York.

Ringland, G. (1998) *Scenario Planning: Managing for the Future.* John Wiley & Sons, Chichester.

Sýkora, L. (1996) Housing policy in the Czech Republic. In: Balchin, P. (ed.) *Housing Policy in Europe*, Routledge, London, pp. 1–17.

Těšitel, J., Kušová, D. and Bartoš, M. (1999) Non-marginal parameters of marginal areas. *Ecology (Bratislava)* 18, 39–46.

Vondrouš, J. (1995) Welcome to Český Krumlov. *Český Krumlov Past and Present.* ORBIS Publishing House, Prague, pp. 4–5.

World Travel and Tourism Council (1995) *Travel and Tourism's Economic Perspective.* World Travel and Tourism Council, Brussels.

Amenity Migration and Tourism in the Eastern Highlands Bioregion of Zimbabwe: Policy Planning and Management Considerations

Desideria Tonderayi

University of Calgary, 2920 5th Avenue N.W., Calgary, Alberta T2N 0V1, Canada

Introduction

In a country badly hit by economic downturn and in which tourism offers a glimmer of hope for economic recovery and growth, it would not be surprising to find tourism development together with amenity migration growing to unprecedented levels in Zimbabwe's Eastern Highlands bioregion (EHBR).[1] If the current situation stands, amenity migration and tourism are not likely to have an adverse impact on the region. However, with potential for growth and left unchecked, they may have significant negative impact on the Eastern Highlands' alpine ecology, perpetuate the legacy of cultural erosion set in motion at the beginning of colonial rule, and result in minimal trickle-down economic benefits to the indigenous local people. Given this potential, it may prove strategically worthwhile to plan for a worst case scenario that may or may never be. This therefore is the thrust of this chapter: a futuristic analysis based on the 'worst case scenario' of plausible multiple scenarios for the uncertain future of the EHBR's strategic environment. In the final analysis, this chapter argues that Zimbabwe's national government, the EHBR's local government and the local communities of the EHBR need to take the lead in strategic policy planning and management for amenity migration and tourism to ensure the best possible near-balance between and within the alpine ecosystem's protection and conservation, including sustained culture, human development and economic growth. Policies that address amenity migration and tourism have to be linked and/or integrated with policies for other sectors, economic and otherwise. This will require

---

[1] 'Bioregion' here used as in Button (1988).

©CAB *International* 2000. *Tourism and Development in Mountain Regions*
(eds P.M. Godde, M.F. Price and F.M. Zimmermann)

collaborative alliances between not only professional planners and policy-makers, but also local organizations, the tourism industry and other multiple and diverse stakeholders involved in mountain communities.

Profile of the Eastern Highlands Bioregion

Main characteristics

The mountains in Zimbabwe's eastern region form part of the border with Mozambique, with parts of this bioregion extending into Mozambique. A 300-km stretch forming the edge of a central plateau, the hills and mountains are collectively known as the Eastern Highlands. The mountain ranges are divided into the Nyanga, the Chimanimani and the Vumba. National parks, botanical gardens and forest reserves are found, including Nyanga National Park, Chimanimani National Park, Vumba Botanical Gardens, Bunga Forest Botanical Reserve, Chimanimani Eland Sanctuary and

Fig. 15.1. Trout fishing in the Chimanimani National Park Eastern Highlands, Zimbabwe.

Chirinda Forest Reserve (Tingay, 1996: 111–131; Swaney, 1999: 271–300). The relatively pristine surroundings are intermittently broken by man-made amenities: roads, small housing estates on tea, coffee and tree (lumber and citrus) plantations, holiday village developments, hotels and archaeological sites. People living in the region travel to the nearest city of Mutare, about 100 km away, to meet much of their needs, but people often must travel 350–400 km to Harare to deal with administrative issues. In the regional town of Nyanga, an administrative service can be provided at a very basic level, and shopping facilities may be adequate.

Tourism is a well-established business in the Eastern Highlands. Tour operators, tourism associations, tourism publicity offices and holiday accommodation (chalets and cottages, with graded hotels also taking a share) are evidence of this. Craft shops everywhere, with artefacts depicting Shona culture, are also earmarked for the tourist. Archaeological sites, some with historical/archaeological interpretive museums are also open to the public. Interestingly, ecotourism and agrotourism do not seem to have taken a firm footing in the EHBR, despite the almost pristine nature of much of the area and the farm-scapes (fruit orchards, tea estates and lumber plantations), particularly in Nyanga. It is also surprising that tourism literature barely mentions the ruins at Nyanga, a historic source of former indigenous ingenuity.

Present-day tourists are drawn to the Eastern Highlands mainly by Chimanimani Park, a roadless park that includes mountains and bush-walking country. There has been no development in the park other than the erection of a simple refuge hut, the aim being to preserve the natural beauty and wilderness aspect of these mountains (Chirawu, unpublished, A Guide to Nyanga Monuments). Bridal Veil Falls, a slender and delicately tiered series of 50 m falls, in a parkland of tall indigenous trees leading to a sylvan pool and into the falls themselves, is a well-known spot in the Chimanimani (Tingay, 1996: 129). Nyanga National Park has some notable attractions: the Mtarazi Falls, which plunge 762 m over the Honde escarpment and the Pungwe Falls and Gorge. Nyanga resort town (Rhodes' former haven) was established as a weekend getaway for Harare residents. Tourists are drawn by highland landscapes, waterfalls, fishing opportunities and by Mt Inyangani, Zimbabwe's highest mountain. This area is said to be the largest and best known of the holiday areas in the EHBR (Tingay, 1996: 111). The Vumba's high and misty forests and botanical gardens provide mystical retreat areas for those seeking quiet or meditative conditions.

As mentioned earlier, archaeological sites, notably the Ziwa National Monument (with an interpretive centre and situated within Nyanga National Park) are a major tourist attraction. The ruins in Ziwa extend over 3337 ha and are perhaps the largest in the sub-continent (Chirawu, unpublished, A Guide to Nyanga Monuments). The sites are cultural landscapes of stone-built agricultural terraces (evidence of land and soil management), stone-lined pits, stone-walled enclosures, defence-related forts and agricultural/

Fig. 15.2.   The Ziwa Ruins at Nyanga, Eastern Highlands, Zimbabwe.

domestic water supply furrows. Household goods, tools and weaponry have been collected for museum display. Also to be seen are the rock paintings in highly stylized figures. These paintings have helped reconstruct early hunter-gatherer settlers' beliefs, economic practices, household goods, subsistence, technological advancement and tools and weaponry. Evidence of a specialized agricultural system has astounded many observers. According to the Department of National Museums and Monuments (1998), total receipts for museums and monuments for 1998 were US$402,150, up from US$273,150 in 1997, suggesting a significant increase in visitation to the park.

The so-called best time to visit, May to September, does not seem to coincide with the period of highest bed nights sold by graded hotels, i.e. October to December (Zimbabwe Tourism Authority, 1998). Rather, this period appears to coincide with the period of harsh weather in the northern hemisphere, from where most non-Zimbabwean visitors originate. May to

September has the most sunshine and least rain, ideal weather for hiking, climbing and horse riding, but the November to March rainy season is also pleasant.

Visitation to the parks is on a fee basis, with foreigners paying several times the resident rates. This strategy is ethical, as high fees may shut out poorer residents. Unfortunately (or fortunately for those opposed to too much commercialization of tourism), the parks administration has been undergoing chronic budgetary problems (Swaney, 1999: 131). This filters through to negatively affect public facilities and services such as water supply, facilities and the reservations system. How much this affects visitor numbers has to be the subject of research.

Park activities include horse riding, scout-led walking and hunting. Park accommodation falls into three categories: chalets, cottages and lodges. Campsites are also available. For tourism statistics purposes, the EHBR is divided into Nyanga and Mutare-Vumba (Zimbabwe Tourism Authority, 1998). Figure 15.3 shows graded hotel bed numbers sold, and from this data it becomes clear that in a regional comparison, the bioregion gets as large a share of bed nights as other areas, with the exception of Harare. It may be noted, however, that according to 1996 figures, operations may be below expectation. There may be periodic effects on visitor numbers, such as the food riots of January 1998 and the civil service strike of August 1997 (figures for these years not available), but even so, a month to month analysis shows an average of beds sold to be around 48% of the beds available. Whether hotels' operating at below capacity is due to low visitation or competition from chalet, cottage, lodge, backpacker dormitory, wilderness cabin, farm homestead and private homeowners' accommodation, or both, has yet to be

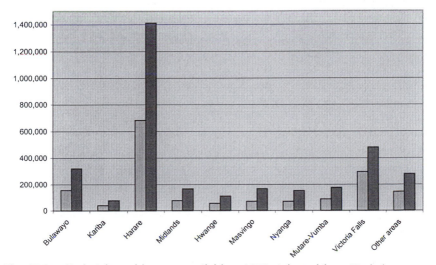

Fig. 15.3.   Bed nights sold versus available – 1996. Adapted from Zimbabwe Tourism Authority Research Development Division (1998).

established. It may also be noted that Harare is showing somewhat distorted figures because most tourists bound for other destinations have to pass through this city *en route* (airport service or road travel stop-over). This may be due to safety fears or sub-standard communication and transport services. For instance, there is a vast and sacred forest, Chirikuutsi, in Nyanga district, in which the local people of Manyika and Mutasa believe their rainmaking gods and ancestral spirits to reside. This place, among others in the bioregion, is important for cultural rituals, such as rain-asking ceremonies. Hundreds of people, especially whites, are said to have disappeared in this forest (One World News Service, Africa News, 1999). It could also be such stories, whether fact or baseless rumour, that keep some potential visitors away. It should also be borne in mind that bed nights are not reflective of the actual visitor numbers, as one visitor may use a hotel on several nights in a month, thereby increasing the number of bed nights sold. Manicaland Publicity had a total of 9012 visitors in 1996, a figure that is difficult to analyse in conjunction with the total of 158,192 bed nights sold for the region (Zimbabwe Tourism Authority, 1998). It is hard to imagine that very many foreign visitors would bypass the bureau unless they are second time visitors, or they are part of tours organized by local operators.

A general conclusion is that visitor numbers for the EHBR are significant. According to statistics from the Department of National Parks and Wildlife Management (1998), 92,181 tourists visited EHBR out of a national total of 908,323 or 10.1% for the period August 1996 to December 1997. Table 15.1 shows visitor numbers by origin including (and importantly) domestic visitor numbers. However, the statistics do not cover other such vital clues to the nature of visitation as demographics, income, social background, school tours, regional origin and racial origins of the visitors. From personal experience, black people do not visit tourist attractions in any great proportions, be it the Highlands or anywhere else. Although the trend is beginning to change, historically Zimbabwe's blacks have been too economically disadvantaged to afford such luxury.

Though visitor numbers for Nyanga (said to be the most well-known of the three sub-regions of the bioregion) for the same period were not available, the combined figures for the Vumba and the Chimanimani show that domestic visitor numbers, at 49.9% of 33,538 total visitors, are significant and much higher than those for non-Zimbabwean visitors. Trailing behind by a wide margin are visitor numbers from Europe, South Africa and the UK (17.9, 10.7 and 10.2% respectively) though the numbers are still significant. The most surprising category is Africa, in which continent Zimbabwe itself is found. At 4.9%, visitor numbers for Zambia and other African countries are comparatively not significant at all. Research is needed on whether visitor statistics to tourist destinations in other African countries show a similar pattern. Do the high numbers of domestic visitors mean that more and more Zimbabweans are seeking the peace and quiet of the mountain regions? Or, is it that the EHBR, being one of the major tourist attractions in Zimbabwe, is

Table 15.1. 1998 Visitors to the Vumba and the Chimanimani by origin.

	Zimbabwe	S. Africa	Zambia	Rest of Africa	UK	Europe	N. Amer.	S. Amer.	Oceania	Asia	Total
Jan–Mar	3330	383	16	169	599	1080	130	129	123	45	6004
Apr–Jun	6060	979	44	425	740	1188	107	161	188	53	9945
Jul–Sep	3471	1526	110	455	1159	2083	364	185	177	43	9573
Oct–Dec	3880	694	11	427	930	1649	160	127	111	27	8016
Total	16,741	3582	181	1476	3428	6000	761	602	599	168	33,538
% of total	49.90%	10.70%	0.50%	4.40%	10.20%	17.90%	2.30%	1.80%	1.80%	0.50%	100%

Adapted from Department of National Parks and Wildlife Management Head Office (1998).

a prime destination for Zimbabweans unable to afford a holiday outside Zimbabwe? Are holiday seekers from other African countries, few as they are likely to be, choosing destinations out of Africa as shopping tourists (for luxury goods not easily available on the African market)? Or is it just a matter of being unable to afford such a luxury as a holiday given the poverty that most African people face? What do the European and UK visitor numbers suggest – a comfortable level or confirmation of the worst case scenario speculation that international sojourners, with their associated negative impacts, may take over? The worst case scenario presented below suggests the need for policy planning considerations to alleviate negative repercussions of tourism and amenity migration.

Ethno-cultural dynasties of the bioregion

At least six ethno-cultural or tribal historical dynasties have been identified: the Maungwe, the Hwesa, the Tawangwena, the Manyika, the Unyama and the Chikore of Tsangura. How far these remain intact as cultures needs to be the subject of research. According to historians and archaeologists, one of these tribes was responsible for the construction of the Nyanga Stone Complex (Beach, 1995: 31–33). The complex contains evidence of the tribes' ingenuity, primarily reflected in the construction pattern of livestock kraals that were interconnected by tunnels to sleeping houses to guard against stock theft. There is also evidence of irrigation furrows, revealing a superior technology of the time (Beach, 1995).

As for local architecture, the holiday villages of Nyanga, Troutbeck, Cashel, Chimanimani, Chipinge and Juliasdale may contain 'corrupted' African architectural characteristics: round buildings or mixtures of circular and straight walls, finished with thatch roofing, and decorated with a mixture of African and foreign style furnishings. Some lodges, such as Mawenje on a private coffee estate, were designed to blend in with the local flora and fauna (Afrizim.com, 1999), but foreign elements such as *en-suite* bathrooms are still present. These holiday villages, however, also contain typical English-style architecture village dwellings and churches, and the Cape-Dutch style is also not uncommon. This architectural legacy may not be of any global significance; to the appreciating individual however, the village-scape/townscape/farmstead setting in the Eastern Highlands does possess its own unique character.

Historical context

The height of colonial conquest during the late 19th to early 20th century saw the displacement of most indigenous people and the usurpation of their lands by the colonial settlers. The few indigenous inhabitants that remained were pushed to the marginal periphery of the mountain region in order to keep a ready supply of labour for the plantations and for other work, such as the digging of irrigation furrows. As a result, the region's ethno-cultural fabric was seriously and negatively impacted. What tradition there is left may be found in language, customary command and in legends that are not necessarily recorded, but instead have been passed down in oral tradition. It is clear that colonial 'proto-amenity migrants' (see Glorioso, this publication) were not interested in the local culture of the region. If both amenity migration and tourism could revive such lost values, it would have re-established the lost identity of a people who have spent decades trying to get back to who they once were.

In the 1890s, European officials and surveyors moved into the area to survey the potential for European farming, and in 1896, Cecil John Rhodes, on hearing about the beauty of the region, 'bought' 34,800 ha of farmland in the now Nyanga National Park. Though historic records do specifically refer to Rhodes' admiration of the beauty of Nyanga, it is not clear to what extent the Europeans were drawn to the Eastern Highlands for primarily amenity or economic reasons, or for both. What is apparent, however, is that many local indigenous people were displaced as a result of European in-migration. From the Eastern Highlands and other parts of the country, they were relegated to marginal and tsetse fly-infested lands. This provided incentive to remain on white lands as indentured workers (Swaney, 1999: 117). Culture could only survive to a limited extent, with families and clans torn apart, and under the laws and influence of landowners who disregarded it.

In cultures where commerce was not yet developed to any great extent, and in which the amassing of very large acreages of land was not the people's way of life, it is not surprising that it took a long time before it dawned on the people that they had been systematically robbed of their land

Fig. 15.4.   Inyangombe Falls, Nyanga, Eastern Highlands, Zimbabwe.

heritage. When Rhodes took the 34,800 ha for himself, it probably was not an issue with the indigenous people – they probably believed they could still have access to, and some degree of control over it. Unfortunately, for the unsuspecting hosts, the colonialists introduced laws of ownership. After independence in 1980, some of the lands reserved exclusively for white settlers have since been reclaimed for the resettlement of the long time marginalized indigenous population. Although it is unclear whether proto-amenity migration would have increased substantially had it not been for the war of liberation by the indigenous people, it was nevertheless affected by the war. Fearing for their safety and lives, some migrants fled the Eastern Highlands. In fact, the Eastern Highlands is quoted as having been abandoned in larger numbers (than from elsewhere in the country) at the height of the war of liberation, most fleeing to South Africa and Common-wealth countries (Swaney, 1999: 120). However, with a government com-mitted to racial reconciliation after the war of independence, some of those who had fled came back to their mountain havens.

Amenity Migration and Tourism Constructs and Implications for the Eastern Highlands Bioregion

How much amenity migration is occurring in the Eastern Highlands today is not established. There are tourism business proprietors in the region but how far these are strictly business adventurers or amenity-seekers or both, is not known. It can be safely said, however, that the tourists are 'natural amenity tourists' as opposed to 'infrastructure amenity tourists'. To call them eco-tourists, however, is to assume their consciousness of, and care for nature protection and conservation, which they may not have. For the present day, it is therefore safe to speak of tourism in the Eastern Highlands. What evident amenity migration there was occurred during colonial take-over, and it cannot be established whether prior migration was amenity-driven. How-ever, with international trends towards amenity migration and environmen-tal protection and conservation, it would be unwise not to brace for the future dual force of amenity migration and tourism.

Much attention has focused on tourism as an agent of change in moun-tain regions; however, amenity migration is increasingly being recognized as having strong influences on mountain communities and environments in many parts of the world (Price *et al.*, 1997: 249). Yet, as Price *et al.* point out, the difference between these two phenomena is not clear cut and this com-plicates their assessment. Tourists and amenity migrants often target destina-tions for similar reasons, and use the same resources. A person frequenting the same place in the mountains where he or she has a residence may be viewed as a tourist according to some criteria and as an amenity migrant according to other criteria. At the planning level, host communities and gov-ernments are stressed to plan for short time or seasonal visitors, whether amenity migrant or tourist. Adequate planning is essential for peak demand periods for such aspects as water and communication infrastructure as well as superstructure.

Aside from the unclear distinction between tourism and amenity migration, as discussed above, other factors affect policy development. According to Price *et al.* (1997), these include:

- The fact that both phenomena are unevenly distributed over space and time, with effects that are more widely distributed than the phenomena themselves; for example, with respect to demands for resources and the economic costs and benefits at local and national scales.
- The idea that the classification of tourists and amenity migrants fits on to a continuum – with people having a similar culture and/or economic status to that of the indigenous people on one end, and those markedly different in these respects on the other. The newcomers, whatever their calibre or similarity/dissimilarity to the indigenous community, place stress on the local infrastructure and resources, and affect community life and employment opportunities for better or for worse.
- Limited statistics on all aspects of tourism and amenity migration. These statistics also may not be very useful when available. Smith (1995) states that the problems confronting the collection of tourism statistics in general are not incompetence or carelessness among those who collect or report tourism statistics. He suggests that the difficulties arise from the very nature of tourism. Firstly, there is no universally accepted definition of tourism and its statistical concepts. Secondly, tourism, however it is defined, is not seen as an industry in the traditional sense by macro-economists. The addition of the amenity migration construct further complicates the research/statistics compilation effort, as they appear even more difficult to statistically identify, especially as distinct from other 'residents' (Moss, 1999). Further still, the interdisciplinary and trans-industrial nature of tourism and amenity migration, with its complexity of social, environmental and economic aspects, has yet to receive sufficient attention from the many disciplines involved, including anthropology, geography, history, business and political science, or has yet to be dealt with holistically (Moss and Godde, this publication).
- The partial and restricted context in which tourism and amenity migration are viewed: both tourism and amenity migration need to be considered in the broader context of the restructuring of mountain and national economies. It is suggested that tourism and amenity migration in mountain and national economies be considered under the same management umbrella because they overlap and affect each other, and to a great extent, they both affect the host communities in which they occur.

Given the above factors, especially for policy purposes, it is strategic to consider amenity migration and tourism as a single entity. Such recognition is likely to help planning efforts as far as visitor management is concerned, whether the visitor is a long- or short-term sojourner, or whether the visitor decides to settle. The holistic management approach that seems especially appropriate for amenity migration and tourism offers greater promise for more effective management efficiency. Tourism and amenity migration coalesced into one for planning and management purposes in mountain regions such as the Eastern Highlands may pose a greater challenge to traditional tourism management, but this does not negate the probable benefits. With dedicated interdisciplinary effort, it seems to be the best way to harness positive change within the principles of sustainable development. As with any new technique, the initial efforts will be largely experimental but with time, constant review and feedback should help continually to improve the management technique inherent in the amenity migration and tourism entity.

As put forward by Moss (1994) and Dimaculangan (1993), the amenity migration and tourism paradigm is characterized by: (i) increasing motivation for amenity migration and (ii) greater facilitation of mobility. The increase in motivation for amenity migration results from factors such as higher valuing of the natural environment, higher valuing of cultural differentiation, and higher valuing of leisure, learning and spirituality. As characterized by current global trends, international awareness of these values is on the increase and may result in increased amenity migration and tourism to the EHBR. Greater facilitation of mobility is fostered by more discretionary time, more discretionary wealth and, better accessibility through improved and less expensive communications and transportation technology. This last phenomenon promotes greater manipulation of time and space. Migration to the Eastern Highlands occurred before the dawn of sophisticated communication technology, as characterized by the onset of European colonial settlement. However, because of the availability of better information and transport technology in this age, further migration may occur. Awareness of the convenience and comfort offered by these technologies is known not so much by the local people as by people from outside. This may result in less migration particularly, but not necessarily in less tourism by nationals from outside Zimbabwe. Or, it may result in the introduction of these technologies, with the reticulation initiative being spearheaded by foreign nationals through the help of the donor community or loans from international financial institutions.

Scenarios for Future Uncertainty

In intuitive-logical strategic analysis, it is usual practice to develop multiple future scenarios, including a 'worst case' scenario. These scenarios are developed using projected key trends, such as for population, including tourists and migrants, employment and land-use patterns (Beck, 1996; Ringland, 1998). These conditions vary among alternative scenarios developed for discussion, policy and follow-on purposes, to consider the effects of making trade-offs. Among the alternative scenarios may include a worst case and a best case scenario, from the perspective of the objective to be accomplished. For the Eastern Highlands discussion here, only the 'worst case' scenario is developed.

Stakeholders

For our concern here, there are several key internal stakeholders in the Eastern Highlands. The list is by no means exhaustive but includes: the Government-run Parks Administration, Mutare City Council and Nyanga Rural Council, estate owners (this group may be difficult to negotiate with because they want to hold on to their vast estates), rural indigenous people and dissenting tourism/tourism-related business proprietors.

Key external stakeholders include the Zimbabwe Tourism Authority based in Harare, the Forestry Commission and other organizations such as IUCN and WWF.

Strengths and weaknesses of the Eastern Highlands

Strengths
The natural scenic environment, and the moderate climate, with mean temperatures of 22°C, are the prime attractions for tourists and would-be amenity migrants. The mysticism of the region is ideal for seasoned meditators or those who otherwise cherish quiet moments close to nature. The mountains and natural areas offer hiking, fishing, horse riding and golfing opportunities throughout the year. Besides the wide variety of recreational qualities, the waterways also provide aesthetic opportunities. The coffee, tea, forestry and citrus plantations hold the potential for agro-tourism. Historic archaeological sites have been identified, and therefore there is a lot of opportunity to learn about cultural practices and values that may have been lost throughout the ages. Those cultures that survived the colonial onslaught, though they may be few, present an opportunity for those tourists and amenity migrants interested in other cultures. In short, there are natural, cultural, spiritual and mystical values of this region that must be protected and respected. Accommodation in the form of graded hotels, chalets, wilderness cabins, cottages and lodges is available, although competition to get into the cheaper latter four types of accommodation is stiff.

Weaknesses

Amenity migration and tourism are dependent on a number of different land uses and environments that are themselves threatened by amenity migration and tourism or other competing uses such as farming and rural resettlement

Fig. 15.5. Chimanimani Mountains, Eastern Highlands, Zimbabwe.

Fig. 15.6. Tupisi hot springs, 40 miles from Chipinge, Gazaland, in the Eastern Highlands, Zimbabwe.

schemes. Increased competition for land will increase the cost of housing and commercial land. The existing water and waste infrastructure capacity in the region is not adequate to support an increased population. Artificially pumped water holes have actually been reported to go dry (Swaney, 1999: 131). Deeper into the mountain region, water and waste infrastructure are provided by the individual owner on their own property, i.e. private bore-hole wells, traditional wells and septic tanks/soak-aways or pit privies. Some parts of the EHBR are not well connected by public transport, necessitating the use of private transport or the expense of car-hire. The lack of comprehensive national and regional environmental management policies for both the natural amenity and human activities, such as manufacturing and chemical waste disposal, is a threat to successful environmental management in the region.

The inherent inequity in land ownership between white and black may be a cause for the indigenous blacks to take a passive role in environmental amenity protection. The blacks are predominantly landless workers on white estates or rural folk living on subsistence levels. There is no holistic development body to draw the various stakeholders in the region together for participatory dialogue in development efforts. The unavailability of skilled manpower and capital is also a major weakness that needs to be addressed if the dual benefits of amenity migration and tourism are to be realized.

It must be realized that in the long run, what are presently weaknesses or strengths may not necessarily remain so. For instance, too many visitors or migrants may result in the erosion of the natural and cultural amenity. Also, the lack of adequate supporting infrastructure and superstructure may be a strength because visitor numbers and therefore environmental impact, will stay lower than otherwise would have been the case with more development.

Opportunities and threats from the external environment

Because people who are drawn to the Eastern Highlands are attracted by the environment in the first place, environmental standards and growth management initiatives may increase with the rising concern from incoming residents. Unfortunately, to date, this has generally not been typical in other mountain regions (L. Moss, Calgary, 1998, personal communication). Information-based firms may find it increasingly desirable to locate in mountain regions. Their operations are foot-loose and less land-intensive than coffee and tea farming, and because they are moving into the mountains at least in part due to amenity, their proprietors and workers may prove to be good corporate stewards for the environment. If the international interest in agrotourism continues, plantation tours have the potential to disperse tourism from traditional attractions, such as the Victoria Falls. Generally, employment opportunities in the amenity migration and tourism sector and related sectors will increase but the calibre of jobs and levels of remuneration for the indigenous locals may remain the same or decrease.

Potential threats need also to be considered. Amenity migrants are likely to be affluent nationals with different cultural values and norms, and wielding economic power. Land demands and price increases are likely to result in further fragmentation of local culture and potentially displace local people, as has happened elsewhere in the world (see Dimaculangan, 1993). Inasmuch as indigenous populations may be displaced, there is also a likelihood that populations may grow as people from other parts of the country are drawn by the possibility of finding employment. Continued population growth and tourism traffic will place pressure on the carrying capacity of the natural and man-made amenities of this mountain bioregion. Overcrowding may eventually result in some tourists, especially ecotourists, being discouraged from visiting the mountain region. Larger permanent and temporary populations will probably threaten the rural wilderness setting which attracts the tourists in the first place. However, reducing tourist numbers is not necessarily bad because even the so-called ecotourists may be agents of negative impacts on the very environment that they claim to care for. Appropriate amenity migrants may be better off in the long run for the bioregion than hit and run tourists, but the amenity migration phenomenon needs not only the test of time, but careful management and control.

The location of the Eastern Highlands along the border with Mozambique previously was, but is not presently, a major public safety concern. However, the region is a potential route for economic migrants 'border jumping'. This may pose a future problem in terms of public safety and social stratification stress, as some people may choose to be permanent economic migrants in the Eastern Highlands. Already, Mozambican nationals work as labourers on the coffee, tea and lumber plantations.

The Government of Zimbabwe, as the key national actor, has no national policy on the Eastern Highlands as a tourism destination. Neither is it braced for the emerging international trend of increasing amenity migration.

Internal strengths and weaknesses within the Eastern Highlands Bioregion's external opportunities and threats

The major internal weakness for amenity migration and tourism in the Eastern Highlands is the considerable dependence on its amenity resources. The very presence and behaviour of the amenity migrant and tourist poses a significant threat to sustaining both cultural diversity and ecosystem integrity. Breaking down the amenity migration and tourism equation in the event of a downturn, amenity migration is likely to survive because of its nature, i.e. status of permanent resident or citizen. Amenity migration is therefore likely to have a more lasting impression, positive or negative, on the environment and on the cultures of the region. Furthermore, its creation of business grows jobs and incomes. The result is likely to be higher real estate prices, higher taxes and higher commodity prices.

While it may appear a negative impact, the creation of such ventures as agrotourism in the Eastern Highlands may result in the dispersal of tourist pressure from other national attractions such as the Zimbabwe Ruins and the Victoria Falls. The infiltration of foreign customs and norms may also have positive impacts on inhibiting any unfair local customs, such as patriarchal autonomy and other human rights in general.

The following 'worst case' scenario dwells on the likelihood that the internal weaknesses discussed above will have a greater impact than the strengths.

A worst case scenario for the EHBR includes a projection of present key trends and likely future developments: international sojourners with seasonal homes in the area, tourism infrastructure and superstructure development, development on mountain and hillside areas, effects on the culturally different and less affluent local rural people, and environmental degradation and deterioration. International sojourning, with very little national sojourning and seasonal homes, are part of likely future developments. In the existing conditions, tourism development in the EHBR is limited, with such ventures as agrotourism not developed at all. Surviving local cultures are few and their social fabric no longer strong. The following is therefore a more detailed outlook of the worst case scenario: a situation in which international trends in amenity migration have set in.

Within the decades to come, a large proportion of the bioregion's population will predictably be affluent and environment-conscious, international migrants involved in the information sector, education, planning and science. They will earn their incomes both from abroad and from within, spending very little in the region, because they prefer to import goods from overseas. The improvement of information technology and transport technology facilitates this kind of living. Some may be into business-providing services, such as facsimile transmission and photocopying, running holiday villages and operating a local recording studio. Some locals may get jobs as office assistants, but the majority will work as housekeepers, woodcutters and guides. The migrants will promote further technology and transportation development and reticulation in order to pursue their amenity and/or business and other interests. Some migrants may promote protection and revival of cultural heritage norms and values.

As expressed by Glorioso (this publication), the professional calibre of amenity migrants in general may be questionable; they could be the cream or the inept in their countries of origin. They may or may not give the best possible benefits to their new community in terms of professional practice, ethics and attitude, or they may give just enough to maintain a presence. They could also have significant ulterior motives. The hosts may realize when it is too late that they have perpetually lost their land and its amenity heritage to the international sojourners.

Foreign style amenities such as restaurants, hotels and theatres, in the worst case scenario, are likely to take shape throughout the region. Employment will definitely increase in the region, but the jobs offered to the hosts will be menial. However, poor economic migrants coming into the bioregion will also increase, and therefore housing and other services will become inadequate, with shanty villages springing up. The environment will begin to suffer the effects of increased pressure from such activities as hunting, golfing, horse riding, fishing and hiking. The social and cultural fabric of the local people will disintegrate; for instance, more and more women may begin seeking commercial housekeeping jobs at the expense of looking after their children. Young girls may start selling themselves into prostitution in order to afford the visitors' lifestyles. Crime rates will possibly be on the increase because of social pressures and inequities, and also because of unemployment in other parts of the country. There may be an increase in poor economic migrants, with expectations of employment being shattered because of a greater demand than supply of jobs. Animosity may begin to grow toward the migrants and tourists due to competition for limited resources and lack of cultural sensitivity by and towards both locals and immigrants/tourists alike. Increases in the cost of food, clothing and shelter may potentially be blamed on the influx of amenity migrants and tourists. This pattern parallels what has already occurred in the mountain Baguio bioregion of the Philippines (Dimaculangan, 1993).

If significant migration were to occur, the bioregion's infrastructure and superstructure may stretch beyond carrying capacity; in particular, solid and wastewater infrastructure will not be able to cope. To improve the situation, more relatively pristine areas will have to be developed into roads, sewage treatment plants, and airports to raise the comfort level of primarily the amenity and better-off economic migrants, since these are the ones generating income for the country and the bioregion. Foreign exotic species could be imported, threatening biodiversity and resulting in near monocultures. On their individual properties, the migrants may begin to alter the natural environment without adequate self-regulation.

Currently, the hosts' local, regional and national ability to effectively manage amenity migration and tourism is weak. The indigenous nationals involved are not astute enough nor appropriately trained to realize poor advice and action, intentional or otherwise. However, both local and international non-governmental organizations (NGOs) as well as international organizations, such as UNESCO, WWF and IUCN, are beginning to take action to protect the local environmental and cultural amenities. In collaboration with grassroots leaders, the people's capacity to participate in these programmes may improve.

Given the worst case scenario just narrated, with negatives outweighing positives, there is a real need for a pro-active strategic thrust in policy planning in order to counter the negative consequences inherent therein.

Strategic Thrusts in Response

Glorioso, in her study of the Sumava bioregion of the Czech Republic (this publication), cites four strategic thrusts the town of Český Krumlov decided to adapt in order to achieve its sustainable development mission. To counter the worst case scenario and its accompanying effects, one of these four thrusts – the improvement of the citizens' level of global awareness and cultural/environmental appreciation – seems especially significant for the EHBR. Inherent in this thrust are local participation by local people and collaborative alliances between/among the various stakeholders. There is a need to actively pursue this strategic thrust within the Eastern Highlands with the help of the region's administrative centres, Mutare City and the town of Nyanga, and with support and collaborative leadership from the Ministry of Mines, Environment and Tourism headquarters and regional offices. A section on human resources and skills outlined below indicates these requirements for this strategic change to be successful.

Human resources and skills

The key human resources required to implement an effective amenity migration and tourism policy include: amenity migration and tourism researchers; policy analysts and developers; social and cultural scientists; environmental auditors and sustainable development specialists; infrastructure developers and land use planners; mountain region specialists and community and regional planners. Their skills need to be backed up by access to information technology and global communication, especially through global networking.

Cultural sensitivity toward and by the amenity migrants and tourists and professionals from other countries is also essential in order to foster mutual respect and cooperation in the policy development and implementation process. Also, sensitive public participation in consultation with traditional chiefs and the involvement of other identified stakeholders is important. Government commitment and financial support is also vital if the initiatives by the various stakeholders, who constitute the human-resource base, are to be fruitful. Community-based self-help initiatives should also be encouraged and individuals need to be trained for community leadership roles. Champions for community capacity building at a grass root level have to be nurtured. Perhaps the national government, with NGO help, could provide the training.

Trade-offs and Policy Considerations

Trade-offs

Given the aforementioned, it is important that policy considerations take cognizance of the following key trade-offs.

Amenity migrants versus tourists

Fewer appropriate amenity migrants may be better than mass tourists, whose casual coming and going is not conducive to creating a sense of responsibility for the destination. For the amenity migrant, the Eastern Highlands can become home rather than a mere temporary destination. Migrants are more likely to contribute to and participate in community development than the passing tourists. Yet, while amenity migrants may be agents for sustaining and reviving local culture and values, they may pose a threat to the local indigenous people, as they compete for resources.

Population and economic growth versus carrying capacity

Population growth is not easily controlled and can also fuel economic growth. Policies for sustainable tourism and amenity migration should be developed with careful consideration of the limits of EHBR's social and environmental carrying capacity.

Growth versus agricultural/natural land

Amenity migration and tourism growth leads to economic development and job creation in a country with a very high unemployment rate, some 40% (Meldrum, 1997: 79). At the same time, agricultural and natural lands have to be preserved for their direct and indirect contribution to the economy, and to environmental protection and conservation. Policies should adequately address and try to balance this dilemma.

Fees versus access

The prevailing system is a user-pay scheme. However, recently the national government effected a 50% reduction in national park fees (Travel Industry Monitor, 1997: 14). Should policies follow this trend, or should they resort to high-yield amenity migration and tourism, where fees are greater but fewer people are attracted? Lottery systems could be an alternative for keeping tourist and amenity migrant numbers down.

Urbanization versus access to natural amenities

Although the threat of urbanization is not a major concern presently, policies need to be formulated with a long-term vision in order to maintain a balance between built-up and open, pristine areas.

Key policy considerations

Given the above worst case scenario that could well unfold in the world of the Eastern Highlands, the following are major policy implications:

Social problems
This issue involves prostitution and unemployment among the locals, and other negative social factors in the midst of an affluent elite. It may hinder both tourism and amenity migration in the EHBR. The strategic implication is an improvement of the general national economy and more equitable distribution of the wealth generated. This can be done through the creation of training programmes for challenging and satisfying employment prospects for the youth, literacy programmes, and ongoing environmental initiatives involving the illiterate and formally uneducated elders, who nevertheless have important indigenous traditional wisdom. Their sense of pride, belonging and stewardship is vital.

Foreign spending
Stricter customs and excise control could result in more income being spent within the borders of the country. This may entail higher customs duties for goods bought outside but readily available on the local market, but it could also stimulate local production.

Intra-regional cooperation and coordination
To protect the EHBR, Government should work with the local people and chiefs and other leaders of the region. There are cultural, spiritual and mystical values of this region that need to be respected and protected, and the means for achieving this is within these people.

Environmental awareness and preservation
Programmes should be put in place to educate the tourist and amenity migrant of the environmental value of the bioregion, and how they can assist in sustaining it. The establishment of an interpretive centre to provide information on the region through awareness talks, video shows and other dissemination means could prove useful. Too much development should be arrested at an early stage, because it may eventually keep away the tourists and migrants that it is meant to attract. Furthermore, potential environmental impacts must be recognized. Price *et al.* (1997) cite opportunities to test and develop new technologies and strategies in diverse fields such as waste management, water storage and treatment and traffic management.

High yield amenity migration and tourism
In keeping with the concept of tourism carrying capacity, the government should introduce high amenity entrance fees, comparatively higher for

foreign visitors, in order to maintain lower numbers while at the same time generating enough income to maintain local amenities and creating economic opportunities for the locals. In this, local people's involvement is vital but first, their capacity to participate must be ensured. Capacity to participate may be affected by literacy levels and ignorance, but programmes can be tailored to suit needs at different levels. People need to be informed on what amenity migration and tourism can and cannot do for them, both positive and negative, and on the value of environmental and cultural amenity. Involvement can be in environmental conservation initiatives, in business ventures and cultural heritage programmes, whether for culture's sake or for visitor entertainment. Care must be taken not to overly commercialize culture else it loses its value.

Archaeological sites

Although it is good that archaeological sites have been opened for the benefit of the public, the effect in the long run may be the perpetual damage of some sites as well as the loss of some artefacts. Although visitors are not allowed to pick up site relics, it is difficult to keep track of offenders. A policy should therefore be developed to limit visitor numbers. Some sites should be closed to public access, especially if what they depict is similar to other sites in the area. For those sites that are open, they should be closed periodically for scheduled maintenance. Another management option could be opening the sites on a rotational basis, with a well-publicized timetable of which sites are open when. In general, the further opening up of archaeological sites should be discouraged.

Policy recommendations

The Government of Zimbabwe should recognize that tourism and amenity migration could be an important means of achieving positive socio-economic development. Also, the Government needs to become more aware of cultural implications of both tourism and amenity migration. Tourism and amenity migration should be a vehicle for promoting understanding among the visitors and the hosts, and a basis for building friendship founded on appreciation and respect for different cultures and lifestyles (Togbay, 1997). Tourism and amenity migration should not be agents of local cultural destruction or subordination.

There is an urgent need to look much further into amenity migration and tourism development that is based on the principle of sustainability, meaning that the development must be environmentally and ecologically friendly, socially and culturally acceptable, and economically viable.

The needed amenity migration and tourism policy should be reflective of the larger national development philosophy. While the government's goal is to improve the standard of living of its people, development should not be judged merely in terms of material prosperity and income growth (Togbay, 1997). It is important to consider less quantifiable but more meaningful goals, such as happiness, contentment, and spiritual and emotional well-being of the people (Togbay, 1997).

In formulating and implementing national and regional goals and policies, maintaining the Eastern Highlands' natural resources and ecosystem, including its human traditions, value systems and institutions, should be treated as important a priority as economic growth and development, which cannot be compromised. This development philosophy is essentially one of sustainable and equitable development with a human face and should be governments' guiding principle (Togbay, 1997).

Anticipated strategic environment for amenity migration and tourism

Zimbabwe has a ministry that oversees tourism: The Ministry of Mines, Environment and Tourism. The associated tourism aspect of this ministry should make it easier to bring an awareness of the notion of amenity migration on board. Although the government of Zimbabwe is promoting tourism as a major foreign currency earner, it may not be such a good idea for the government to specifically target foreign retirees to locate in the Eastern Highlands in order to generate hard foreign currencies, a strategy being pursued in other countries. Such a strategy may violate the principle of fairness to the local people, leading to a systematic displacement of the local people, as occurred during colonial times. Also, this may cause the government to invest heavily in advanced communication technologies, an exercise whose benefit has not been reasonably assessed, at the expense of other pressing and more important needs of the local people.

Within the country generally, and the Eastern Highlands bioregion in particular, there does not seem to be much awareness of the amenity migration phenomenon, only of tourism. The benefits of amenity migration need to be put forward to the government, since this is the main national actor. Such benefits include a sense of belonging to the bioregion by the amenity migrants, which may develop particularly into a caring attitude toward the environment; and the provision of support funds for environmental initiatives by those professionals without the environmental stewardship know-how. This is not a contradiction to what has just been said above about not specifically targeting foreign retirees: if foreign nationals should migrate to the EHBR, it should be of their own volition rather than through solicitation. In fact, it would be morally wrong and ethically unjust to do so in a country where the majority is landless peasantry. On the flip side to the benefits, the legal right of ownership of 'a piece of the environment' will ultimately shut out the majority poor, be it in reducing land available to them to pursue a decent life or in limiting access to environmentally clean commons. Land available for touristic enjoyment will also likely diminish (Dimaculangan, 1993; Moss, 1994).

On an international level, global economic restructuring appears to be continuing at an unprecedented rate and in which more and more discretionary time and money is leading to more consumerism in all forms. While this may be good for amenity migration and tourism, it is bound to take its toll on the quality of the natural environment as well as on cultural integrity and diversity. Paralleling this, it seems amenity migration and tourism will continue to grow until it levels off, and then start to fall because the prime attractions will have deteriorated. Tourism may suffer a more immediate drop, since amenity migrants are established *in situ* and cannot immediately relocate with ease. Therefore amenity migration may endure after tourism has died.

Conclusions

Amenity migration and tourism in the Eastern Highlands is likely to grow as the Zimbabwean nation grapples with the problems of economic downturn, the need to earn foreign hard currencies for foreign debt repayment, high unemployment rates and accompanying problems.

In order to develop strategies to manipulate future growth positively in amenity migration and tourism to its greatest potential for the Eastern Highlands' communities and environments, it is vital to be able to differentiate between and compare tourists, economic migrants and amenity migrants, and the different groups within these general categories in terms of the nature and magnitude of their diverse impacts, both positive and negative (Price *et al.*, 1997; Moss and Godde, this publication). An understanding of their systemic interaction is essential for the development of strategic policy formulation and integration. Research is needed to understand the ways in which different environmental and cultural resources attract and hold potential migrants and how migrants' and hosts' cultures impact each other. It is also imperative to understand the potential positive and negative gains from these phenomena and to strive to strike a favourable and sustainable long-term near-balance (Price *et al.*, 1997). The critical issues to be addressed in policy formulation are why, how and how much amenity migration and tourism and in what proportion, is desirable and possible. Decision-makers need a clear understanding of the means – physical, fiscal or political – to limit access to the EHBR or to focus on qualitative rather than quantitative growth. Past and current experiences and careful experimentation are vital learning tools in this respect.

Most importantly, the onus is on the Government of Zimbabwe, in consultation with the local government of Mutare/Nyanga and the Eastern Highlands community, to spearhead a policy planning and amenity management initiative, both cultural and environmental. Critical focus must be kept throughout the process on trying to achieve a balance, imperfect as it may be, between and within sustained alpine ecology and culture, human development and the creation of an economic base for the host communities of the Eastern Highlands. In some cases, regeneration may be necessary.

While the ultimate recommendation is to develop policies that treat tourism and amenity migration as an entity, the difference between the two still needs to be understood. Their inter-relationships warrant merging them in policy formulation, but their individual benefits and side-effects still have to be spelt out, so that optimum benefit is obtained from them singly on one hand and together on the other, and without one getting in the way of the other.

Statistics need to be compiled to determine the status of amenity migration and tourism in the Eastern Highlands. It is not clear how many people there are principally for the natural mountain amenity, or for private business, or on government duty, and mixed motives probably play a role. For instance, one might choose to set up a business in the Eastern Highlands because of the mountain and/or cultural amenity. It is also not clear how many are permanent, seasonal or intermittent amenity migrants. Not even the number of second homes in the bioregion is known, whether by migrants or by the indigenous people who have jobs in the city, but return seasonally or intermittently to their rural mountain tribal homeland, which they regard as their true home.

In this age of sustainable development and people's empowerment, the participatory involvement of the local people at a grass root level cannot be over-emphasized. There is need to borrow and to adapt policy and development models from within and from other mountain regions and there is great potential for collaborative alliances and approaches, particularly for obtaining much greater local benefit from amenity migration and tourism.

References

Afrizim.com (1999) Village Inn – Nyanga. 17 May, 1999. http://www.afrizim.com/mawenje.htm.

Beck, G.T.K. (1996) *Amenity Migration to the Okanagon Valley, B. C. and the Implications for Strategic Planning*. Graham T.K. Beck, Calgary, Alberta.

Beach, D.N. (1995) Archaeology and history in Nyanga, Zimbabwe. Department of History, University of Zimbabwe. Paper for presentation to the Tenth Pan African Archaeological Congress. University of Zimbabwe Department of History Seminar Paper No.97, Harare, Zimbabwe.

Button, J. (1988) *A Dictionary of Green Ideas*. Routledge, London.

Department of National Museums and Monuments (1998) Department of National Museums and Monuments Annual Reports. National Museums and Monuments, Harare, Zimbabwe.

Department of National Parks and Wildlife Management (1998) Department of National Parks and Wildlife Management Head Office Statistical Returns. Ministry of Natural Resources, Harare, Zimbabwe.

Dimaculangan [Glorioso], R.S. (1993) Key policy implications for strategic use of amenity resources: a study of longer-term amenity migration, Baguio Bio-region, The Philippines. Unpublished M.Sc. Thesis, INRDM Programme, Asian Institute of Technology, Bangkok, Thailand.

Meldrum, A. (1997) Zimbabwe. In *International Tourism Reports No. 3*. Travel and Tourism Intelligence, U.K., pp. 77–89.

Moss, L.A.G. (1994) Beyond tourism: the amenity migrants. In: Mannermaa, M., Inayatullah, S. and Slaughter, R. (eds) *Chaos in Our Common Futures*. University of Economics, Turku, pp. 121–128.

Moss, L.A.G. (1999) *Policy Issues Brief: Sustaining the Sierra Nevada Bioregion's Integrity under Growing Human Population Pressure*. The Public Policy Institute of Calfornia, San Francisco, California.

OneWorld News Service (1999) 17 May, 1999. HYPERLINK http://www.oneworld. org/news/reports/nov_an3.html;   http://www.oneworld.org/news/reports/nov_ an3.html

Price, M.F., Moss, L.A.G. and Williams, P.W. (1997) Tourism and amenity migration. In: *Mountains of the World, a Global Priority*. Parthenon Press, London and New York, pp. 249–279.

Ringland, G. (1998) *Scenario Planning: Managing for the Future*. John Wiley & Sons Ltd, Chichester.

Smith, S.L.J. (1995) The tourism satellite account: perspectives of Canadian tourism associations and organizations. *Tourism Economics* 1, 225–244.

Swaney, D. (1999) *Zimbabwe, Botswana and Namibia*. Lonely Planet Publications, Victoria, Australia, pp. 113–410.

Tingay, P. (1996) *Traveller's Guide to Zimbabwe*. Struik Publishers, Cape Town, South Africa.

Togbay, S. (1997) Overview of tourism in Bhutan and how it fits into general development plans in Bhutan. *Contours* 7, 21–30.

Travel Industry Monitor (1997) Zimbabwe expects tourism boost. *Travel and Tourism Intelligence* February, 14–15.

Zimbabwe Tourism Authority (1998) Bed nights sold/bed nights available. *Statistical Tables*. Research Development Division, Harare.

Strategy for Future Mountain Tourism

Laurence A.G. Moss[1] and Pamela M. Godde[2]

[1]Laurence Moss & Associates, 2442 Cerrillos Road, PMB 422, Santa Fe, NM, 87505, USA; [2]The Mountain Institute, PO Box 907, Franklin, WV 26807, USA

Introduction

Tourism's continuing rapid global growth is increasingly evident in mountain regions. Authors in this publication (especially Slee *et al.* and Valaoras) along with others recently focusing on the condition of our planet's mountains (see especially Stone, 1992; Denniston, 1995; Luger and Inmann, 1995; Price, 1996; Messerli and Ives, 1997; East *et al.*, 1998; ICIMOD, 1998; Godde, 1999; Mountain Agenda, 1999), indicate that tourism has the potential to contribute simultaneously to the sustainability of mountain regions while satisfying those who visit them. However, experience demonstrates that tourism can also be a considerable threat to the same alpine attributes it relies upon. The idea of sustainability, therefore, is an important one with regard to mountain tourism. And yet, despite the considerable amount of literature on sustainable tourism, there is little understanding that tourism is but one part of other, interconnected phenomena which tourism affects and by which tourism is affected. 'Sustainability' of mountain resources demands that mountain tourism be brought into harmony both with the needs of mountain peoples and the ecosystems they are a part of. By extension, sustainability also demands that we adopt a 'systemic' perspective: the perspective that tourism is not an independent system, but a sub-system of larger systems typically composed of interdependent cultural, economic, environmental, political, social and technological components. One such system is the mountain ecosystem; our focus here. In adopting this ecosystemic perspective, we become better equipped to achieve, in strategic analytical terms, the 'mission' of sustaining the integrity of mountain ecosystems, including their human cultures (Ives *et al.*, 1997; Moss *et al.*, this publication; see particularly Nha Trang and Pensinger, 1994, for relative ecosystemic functioning).

A Strategic Approach to Sustainable Mountain Tourism

Progress made over approximately the past decade in understanding the particular opportunities and issues associated with change and development in mountain regions (see Godde *et al.*, this publication), along with an ecosystemic perspective, sets the stage for more strategic action. The seemingly critical condition of many mountain regions, the difficulty in managing the cause–effect complexity of mountain tourism as part of other systems, and the very limited human and financial resources we can bring to bear on the above mission in even a very optimistic scenario, dictate a strategic approach. A strategic approach leads to the possible within that which is plausible. It is a relatively effective means of analysing and managing complex and highly uncertain conditions, principally through identifying, understanding and manipulating the societal driving forces particular to a given subject, and the key elements in the systems that these forces are composed of. Also fitting the particular needs of ecosystems, this approach espouses the long view of change and its patterning. In perspective and process, a strategic approach is also ecosystemic and, when used with skill, holistic (see Ringland, 1998; Moss *et al.*, this publication).

Within this framework, the use of tourism as one means for sustaining the integrity of mountain ecosystems, and *inter alia*, for mountain tourism itself, appears to be a suitable strategy for achieving the mission during approximately the next decade. The impact of this strategy on the mission, however, may be considerably enhanced if much more were known about one other seemingly quite significant sub-system; mountain amenity migration. In particular, the degree to which it is complementary or conflicting needs early assessment (Price *et al.*, 1997; Glorioso, Moss *et al.* and Tonderayi, this publication).

The strategy is composed of four specific thrusts, or strategic objectives to be reached:

- increase mountain perspective and awareness;
- improve mountain reciprocity;
- reduce mountain degradation; and
- deepen and disseminate mountain knowledge.

Two other candidates for main thrusts of the strategy were considered: use the regional perspective to a considerably greater extent and improve the economic welfare of mountain dwellers. As these are generally being treated here as aspects of the other strategic objectives and key elements, the proposed structure of the strategy seems both appropriate and effective from our present understanding of salient opportunities and issues.

Increase mountain perspective and awareness

In the concluding chapter to *Mountains of the World: a Global Priority* (Messerli and Ives, 1997), Ives *et al.* propose an agenda for obtaining sustainable mountain development in general, and identify six prerequisites for reaching this objective. They begin with the need for a mountain perspective, which provides an understanding of the unique properties of mountain regions, including verticality, limited accessibility and fragility, that in turn determine the necessarily non-conventional approaches to mountains and development therein. Greater use of this perspective will foster a growth in mountain awareness, and thus a more widespread and commonly held essential understanding of the important roles of mountain ecosystems for sustaining life. As Ives, *et al.* point out, while this awareness has seen unprecedented growth since the Rio Earth Summit of 1992, 'more is required' (Messerli and Ives, 1997: 457). Policy and its implementation need to embody a mountain perspective, and when woven into the fabric of strategy, plan, programme, project and allied analyses it becomes a criterion for judging the efficacy of these tools.

Tourism in mountain regions is unlike tourism elsewhere for the same reasons outlined in the more general case above – extreme verticality, limited accessibility and vulnerability of both physical and human environments. Through their Upper Mustang case study, Gurung and deCoursey (this publication) show how limited accessibility and the time necessary for proper infrastructure development within the verticality of mountains demand appropriate policy and planning. The specificities of tourism in mountain regions thus must be clearly understood, and this proposed strategic objective would help ensure this occurs.

Improve mountain reciprocity

Wearing the above mountain viewing glasses also helps clarify the primary role of mountain people in maintaining their surroundings. Ives *et al.* (1997), along with others (e.g. Preston, 1997) propose that one prerequisite is direct compensation by lowland communities for resources extracted from mountains and indirect compensation for the stewardship roles that mountain people typically play in sustaining their environment. This is also a strategic objective for realizing the mission of sustaining mountain ecosystems. Visitors to mountain regions rely upon their natural and human resources not only for the 'tourist experience', but also for their very lives while in the mountains; local water, food, and human hospitality are at the core of mountain tourism. Moreover, these essentials are not limited to mountain visits: they extend to tourists' everyday lives when they return to their homes in other mountain regions or in the lowlands.

Fig. 16.1. A shepherd in Spiti Valley, India, relies on and sustains the mountain environment (photo by Doug Brown).

Yet, as Barkin (this publication) points out, mountain host communities often receive less than they give. In particular, their stewardship, which has over time created and maintained an environment that many may enjoy, is often overlooked or ignored. While the imbalance of returns, and its causes, are reasonably well-known among those involved in this exploitation, few others are aware of it. As a mountain perspective and awareness increases, this ignorance will lessen. However, more direct attention is necessary. Whether the use of mountain resources is for timber, minerals or water extraction, or expanding amenity/recreational activity, such as tourism, far greater involvement of mountain people in the management of their eco-systems and fair compensation for the goods and services they provide are essential.

At the same time, fuller awareness by host communities of both the threats and opportunities that tourism can bring is necessary to help these communities determine if tourism is truly appropriate and desirable, and if so, what a fair compensation may be. Mountain people must recognize that tourism relies upon their stewardship, and that not only should they be paid directly for tourist experiences, accommodation and other services, but they should also be compensated for maintaining the beauty and uniqueness of mountains. The information gap that hinders potential for empowerment by many mountain communities needs special attention, and 'champions' striving to both balance the scales and pass on their skills to local people as swiftly as possible should play a key role.

Reduce mountain degradation

Human activities that degrade mountain ecosystems are probably the greatest obstacle to sustainable mountain development. While Ives *et al.* (1997: 457) refer to this particularly in the context of warfare, the human causes are more varied and complex. Political imperatives of lowland capitals, inappropriate and poorly conceived and managed socio-economic development plans and projects, more profit-focused private and public schemes, including mountain amenity-based activities, and the sum of the decisions of many in-migrants seeking income all contribute to the degradation of mountain environments and their human cultures. Not least of these is unhampered or poorly assessed development of tourism, perhaps most notably in the form of large-scale resorts, as Buckley *et al.* note in Chapter 2. Yet such large-scale tourism development is not alone in degrading mountain environments. Also important is damage caused by aggregation of milder forms of tourism, such as camping and trekking (see Monz and MacLellan *et al.*, this publication) and visitation to particular areas within national parks (see Cochrane and Saffery, this publication).

Although the above activities may bring positive outcomes, such as income to people who need it, reducing or eliminating their negative aspects must be given considerably higher priority in order to reach an acceptable balance. In addition, human response to natural hazards can be greatly improved, particularly in the poorer mountain regions of the world. While such hazards are not particular to mountains, the characteristic of verticality dictates greater frequency and magnitude, and as Hewitt (1997) also points out, lowland catastrophes often originate in the highlands. Reducing both causes of mountain degradation is increasingly crucial as the numbers of mountain visitors as well as new residents grow, especially as worsening conditions generally do not yet appear to be dissuading either visitors or in-migrants (see Price *et al.*, 1997; Glorioso and Moss *et al.*, this publication).

Deepen and disseminate mountain knowledge

Appropriate future mountain tourism will also depend to a significant degree on deeper scientific and humanistic inquiry into the uniqueness of mountain biomes and the reason for sustaining them. There is a need for far greater and early understanding of human movements into and out of mountain regions, and how such migrations affect the mountains and their human communities. This includes understanding the particular role domestic tourism plays *vis-à-vis* international tourism in mountain regions (see especially Cochrane, Saffery and Tonderayi, this publication). Greater understanding of and experimentation with regional, especially a bioregional context for change and development also needs special attention. Not only is this approach supportive of and compatible with maintaining the integrity of ecosystems, but affordable technology has become available to proceed with it in force (Moss *et al.*, this publication). Importantly, this must also influence how information is collected and used; based more on the territory of natural systems, as well as political jurisdictions. Greater correspondence between the two constructs, with political–economic decision making better reflecting the reality of our biosphere, can now be accomplished. Let us integrate it into the process of deepening and disseminating knowledge about mountain regions, particularly in implementing our tourism strategy.

A much larger part of this knowledge can and should now be obtained more strategically, as one outcome of implementing the proposed strategy – through learning by doing. More emphasis should be placed on gaining this knowledge from experimentation; from shifting to greater action to solve tourism problems while realizing its potential benefits.

This is not to say that we should cease other, especially more scholarly inquiry that may contribute to sustaining mountain ecosystems and their diverse cultures. Such activities should also be supported. In particular, academia should be encouraged to give substantially more attention to the tourism phenomenon as a systemic whole. There is first a need to move beyond its too common preoccupation, typical of business management and hospitality and recreation faculties, with the marketing of destinations and accommodation of tourists after their arrival. In this context academics, and others so involved, should progress beyond description of the interactions between the various participants in tourism and of its impacts on physical, societal and cultural environments to more rigorous analyses.

Equally valuable is improving the dissemination of knowledge beyond its current concentration in academic circles and among individual practitioners. Better organization of the considerable amount of existing knowledge, along with the new, is also essential for greater accessibility and use. As the Mountain Forum's electronic conference (Godde, 1999), and similar communication and organizational means demonstrate, there is strong reason to be optimistic about networks and their new tools, like the internet. This is especially the case for netweaving through the three layers of social fabric: globalization/localization, centralization/decentralization, and standardization/diversification (Stevenson, 1998). Used wisely, these emerging means will allow a breaking through of the present mechanistic and expensive hierarchies that dominate communication, constraining information access and use.

Tactical Building Blocks for Sustainable Mountain Tourism

Seven key elements have been identified as strategically the most likely building blocks of new mountain tourism action plans, programmes and projects for pursuing the four strategic objectives. In addition, these elements also appear to be issues needing priority attention, if the most is to be made of mountain tourism's potential. The specific applicability of any or all of these key elements, as with the four strategic objectives, will vary according to the characteristics of particular local or regional mountain conditions and the problem, opportunity, decision or policy being considered. Further, this list of key elements may not be complete, but rather represents our present best effort. Other key elements may be identified through future research and action. The key elements are:

- comprehending and utilizing cultural and social attributes;
- empowering mountain communities;
- understanding and harnessing the potential of 'community';
- collaboration among key stakeholders;
- knowing the capability for sustainable tourism;
- integrating cultural and eco-tourism; and
- using effective networks and other organizations.

Comprehending and utilizing cultural and social attributes

There is a need for deeper understanding of the cultures and societies of mountain people, and how their similarities and differences dictate or influence economies, politics, institutions, natural environments and guided change. Moreover, we need to harness these attributes in a manner that works to enhance human and biophysical symbiosis. Consequently, it is first necessary to have a better understanding of the functional relationships between the cultural and social realms of mountain peoples in the context of the four strategic objectives. This will require moving beyond the present preoccupation with protecting and 'preserving' material culture, especially the bricks and mortar of artefacts, to emphasize understanding and facilitating the continuity of the living cultural traditions of mountain peoples. As Pfister recognizes in this publication, the understanding of the non-material culture of mountain peoples, as embodied in their knowledge, norms, values and ideals, is a cornerstone for building responsible mountain tourism. In this sense, mountain tourism that is truly 'sustainable' must not be restricted to the biophysical and human-built environments; it must be sensitively moulded according to the ways of life and belief systems of local people.

This imperative will be quite difficult to achieve, as cultural change is normal and social engineering is to be avoided. Respect for those living these traditions and wishing to continue doing is fundamental, not only as a human right, but also for sustaining mountain ecosystems. The core of this action is fostering superior comprehension of the past and potential impacts of external change and development forces on local living cultures, and assisting with strategy to manipulate these externalities to the benefit of mountain peoples. But central to such action must be the awareness and decision of the local community, which takes us to the following key element.

Empowering mountain communities

There is a need significantly to expand the political and economic power of mountain communities, as well as marginalized members within these communities, such as women (see Lama, this publication), in order to eliminate their peripheral status (Ives, 1997) and obtain a balance in reciprocity, especially in relation to the benefits accruing from mountain resources. This key element may be best approached through the twin aims of political self-determination and local control of resources. Manipulating the tourism industry to facilitate these aims should be pursued aggressively considering the degree of marginalization of mountain people (Ives *et al.*, 1997; Price *et al.*, 1997).

Private and public development focused principally on material profit have been identified as the main reasons of marginalization. However, it also results from seemingly more beneficial action. As both Barkin and Valaoras suggest in this publication, through the establishment of protected

Fig. 16.2. Empowering mountain communities includes expanding the political and economic power of marginalized members. Here, the women's group in Dhunche (Langtang National Park), Nepal pose after participating in a training session for institutional strengthening (photo by Wendy Brewer Lama).

areas in mountain regions by predominantly lowland policy-makers, non-governmental organizations (NGOs), tourism operators and environmentalists who do not share a mountain perspective, mountain peoples are often denied access to resources upon which they have historically relied for spiritual and material survival. Although these people are often eager to help conserve their environment, this marginalization creates hardships for them, often leading to the loss of traditional economic activities and out-migration in search of employment. Moreover, it weakens or destroys the mountains' traditional stewards.

Understanding and harnessing the potential of 'community'

Complementing particularly the need to address community empowerment is the need to understand and harness attitudes and behaviours associated with 'community' affinity and corresponding motivations of both mountain dwellers and visitors. Many tourism-centred projects, especially in less economically developed and integrated mountain regions, rely considerably on attachment to local place. Here we use 'local' to also refer to bioregional affinity. Generally speaking, it seems that the stronger the sense of this 'place-based' community that people have, the greater their motivations to sustain their place's natural and human built environment, particularly if community members understand how and to what extent they are a part of this environment (Moss et al. in Godde, 1999).

This place-based sense of community appears to be stronger in isolated mountain regions, and to be an essential component of sustainable mountain ecosystems, due to the stewardship roles, cooperation and collaboration it can generate among people in extreme environments and in limited spaces. However, such place-based attributes can no longer be generally assumed in an integrating, global economy based on information and communications technology, nor specifically as this technology penetrates the mountains bringing with it its modern and post-industrial traits. Seemingly, through this trend the significance of local place and independent cultural referencing appear to be waning as a sense of 'interest-based' community grows. Communities of interest are based on socio-economic and political bonds that are a-spatial, transcending locality. This is not to say that non-place community will or must replace place-based community. One factor is that the appeal of place-community is still strongly acclaimed, even among the more information and communications driven societies, such as Germany, the UK and the USA.

If the attributes of 'community' are to be sustained and used for realizing the mission, it is essential to understand it better, along with its potentials and its limits. In particular, we should learn considerably more about interest-based community and the emerging relationship of the place and interest-based reference systems in mountain regions, especially as it affects mountain tourism (Duane, 1999; Moss, 1999). This appears to be an important factor in enabling the next element: collaboration among key stakeholders.

Collaboration among key stakeholders

It is difficult to overstate the importance of understanding, creating and using relationships among all stakeholders in mountain tourism for sustaining mountain ecosystems. This role is heavily emphasized in the recent literature on tourism and amenity migration (Godde, 1999; Moss, 1999; Mountain Agenda, 1999; Moss *et al.*, this publication). Communication, cooperation and moving beyond these to collaboration among stakeholders is a fundamental ingredient in sustained mountain ecosystems and a dependent mountain tourism. As Saffery suggests in Chapter 12, the development of tourism in mountain regions can often take the form of a race, in which the heat of competition negates any cooperative efforts that must exist for sustainable tourism to prevail.

In addition to fostering more mutually beneficial relations among all stakeholder groups, important for appropriate mountain tourism, is giving in-depth attention to existing and potential interrelationships between three key groups of stakeholders: local people, tourists and new migrants coming up into mountain regions, i.e. the amenity migrants and those who follow principally to improve their economic condition (see Moss, 1994a; Price *et al.*, 1997; Glorioso, this publication). We need to give significantly more attention to the existing and potential supportive web of interaction between those arriving and those leaving, or considering leaving, their mountain homes; how to foster collaboration for win–win outcomes. For example, local job training for employment generated by tourism and amenity migration, especially for potential income-motivated migrants, both those considering leaving and those arriving. More strategically, there is the need for policy and programmes that encourage the types of tourists and amenity migrants that will generate employment appropriate to sustaining a locale's ecosystem.

Knowing the capability for sustainable tourism

There is a critical need to ascertain the specific capability of a mountain bioregion, or a more local area and its symbiotic human community, such as a smaller watershed, riparian area or forest, to sustainably support or absorb the growing number of peoples interested in visiting and residing within it. As Groth (1999) points out, first should come the question, is tourism at all feasible as an instrument of sustainable development in a locale.

Fig. 16.3. Floating the Vltava River through historic Český Krumlov, Czech Republic, exemplifies the need for integrating cultural tourism and ecotourism (photo by L.A.G. Moss, June 1999).

Moving beyond the relatively simplistic concept of carrying capacity, this would include the more specific application of constructs and analytical tools such as 'ecological footprinting' (Wackernagel and Rees, 1996). Important to this key element is moving away from planning and engineering standards, to the formulation and use of indicators of sustainability for analysis, monitoring, assessment and strategy or plan formulation (see Monz, this publication). Local people should play a significant role in the design and use of these indicators (Hardi and Zdan, 1997; Moss *et al.*, this publication).

Integrating cultural and ecotourism

Expanding our understanding of mountain tourism beyond its economic dimensions to understanding it both as a whole system and part of larger systems leads to a more accurate view of its interactions with, and effects on, mountain ecosystems and their human communities. Such a shift entails intellectually and functionally integrating ecotourism and cultural tourism in

Fig. 16.4.   Young hand drummers of the St'at'imc Nation maintaining a local tradition. Lillooet, BC, Canada, June 1999 (photo by L.A.G. Moss, June 1999).

mountain regions, in contrast to their characteristic separation by policy-makers, academics and to a lesser extent, practitioners. In comparing mountains to other biomes, the dominant characteristic of mountain environments and their human communities as highly interdependent sub-systems demands that tourism in the mountains, in particular, must recognize a more symbiotic relationship between ecosystems and human cultures.

Using effective networks and other organizations

There is a general need to integrate better, and at times to institutionalize, concern for mountain tourism within organizations that can most effectively advance the achievement of sustainable mountain tourism. This may include local, regional, national, and international political bodies; including business enterprises and governmental and voluntary organizations. A crucial question is how not-for-profit, especially local community-based organizations, and public agencies should allocate their very limited resources (time, skilled people and money) among these. Particular attention at this time should be placed on formulating tactics for the best use of newer, less hierarchical and mechanistic organizations, especially networks and their comparatively low-cost electronic communications tools. There is no single formula, but rather the potentials for this realm appear to offer particularly higher and more equitable returns to limited resources.

Attention should also be given to influencing existing institutions that are especially concerned with tourism within countries and internationally, such as the World Tourism Organization (WTO), Pacific Asia Travel Association (PATA) and the Ecumenical Coalition on Third World Tourism. Further, there is a need to integrate programmes specific to mountain tourism into the work of organizations that emphasize maintaining culture and environment. Such organizations might include the Food and Agriculture Organization (FAO), The World Conservation Union (IUCN), the UN Environment Programme (UNEP), the UN Educational, Scientific and Cultural Organization (UNESCO), the World Wide Fund for Nature (WWF). A mountain tourism focus should also be pursued within innovative and sympathetic units and programmes of others key stakeholders in guided change, particularly bilateral aid agencies, the UN Development Programme (UNDP), the World Bank, the regional international banks, and the Global Environment Facility (GEF).

Future Uncertainties

A strategy that incorporates the main thrusts and elements described above promises to be a superior one for manipulating the complex and highly unpredictable phenomenon of tourism in mountain regions. In particular it offers the needed long-term and ecosystemic framework, focus on external forces and factors and management of high uncertainty. It also fosters the formulation of more resource-conserving and effective strategies and their outcomes. However, while advances are made with the above suggested action, a strategic approach also requires that we must recognize and be responsive to other plausible scenarios for the future of mountain tourism. Given our contemporary strategic environment, which is likely to continue to be rapidly changing and unpredictable, the early concerns in the tourism literature for its vulnerability still seems wise. Despite tourism's remarkable growth and spread to date in mountains around the world, it is necessary to seriously consider that this pattern may not continue. Rather it may decline or even disappear at local or regional scales due to:

1. The depletion or severe degradation of the mountain attributes which attract the tourist to specific locales (Denniston, 1995; Zimmermann, 1995, 1998; Price *et al.*, 1997; Moss *et al.*, this volume). Or more generally this may result from the partial or total failure of our strategy, natural disasters beyond the ability of humans to influence significantly, or global climate change (Hewitt, 1997; Price and Barry, 1997; Buckley *et al.*, this publication);

2. The ascendancy of more socio-economically or technologically evolved and/or more enticing competitors for the same attributes that attract the tourist, such as amenity migration or virtual travel (Moss, 1994a,b). The mass marketing of virtual reality technology in which the 'traveller' can be immersed in a desired place through holographic representation is about 5 years in the future for at least the more affluent economies;

3. Significant shifts from societal values that presently promote mountain tourism, such as a reversal in highly valuing ecotourism, and the growing attraction of artificial environments, such as the theme park, and urban cultural experiences (Judd and Fainstein, 1999);

4. Marked increases in the cost of critical support systems, such as transportation due especially to fuel prices, or a considerable decrease in discretionary time and /or income, for example from significant regional or global inflation and economic depression; and

5. Various combinations of the above factors.

We are faced with growing complexity and uncertainty, both generally and in the specific case of human pressures on mountain ecosystems. This suggests that a paradigm that better deals with this condition and assists in moving towards sustainable mountain development more effectively and strategically is necessary. The tried and not so true must be considerably improved upon, and so the strategic and ecological approach outlined here should become a priority. There is one reasonable certainty in the foreseeable future: if we fail to develop tourism that sustains the environmental and cultural attributes of the mountains, we will be adding to the potential of their degradation, perhaps critically and with this, the likely demise or severe curtailment of mountain tourism and the potential benefits it can bring to the mountain regions of the world.

References

Denniston, D. (1995) High priorities: conserving mountain ecosystems and cultures. World Watch Paper 123, Washington, DC, World Watch Institute.

Duane, T. (1999) Community participation in ecosystem management. *Ecology Law Quarterly* 24, 771–797.

East, P., Luger, K. and Inmann, K. (eds) (1998) *Sustainability in Mountain Tourism: Perspectives for the Himalayan Countries.* Book Faith India, Delhi and Studienverlag, Innsbruck.

Godde, P. (ed.) (1999) Community-based mountain tourism: practices for linking conservation with enterprise. Summary report of the Mountain Forum e-conference, April, May 1998. The Mountain Institute, Franklin, West Virginia.

Groth, A. (1999) Padare and UN Commission for Sustainable Development. *Contours* 9, 6–7.

Hardi, P. and Zdan, T. (eds) (1997) *Assessing Sustainable Development: Principles in Practice.* International Institute for Sustainable Development, Winnipeg, p. 166.

Hewitt, K. (1997) Risk and disasters in mountain lands. In: Messerli, B. and Ives, J.D. (eds) *Mountains of the World: a Global Priority.* Parthenon Press, London and New York, pp. 371–408.

ICIMOD (1998) Environment, culture, economy and tourism: dilemmas in the Hindu Kush – Himalayas. In: *Issues in Mountain Development*. ICIMOD, Kathmandu, Nepal.

Ives, J.D. (1997) Comparative inequalities – mountain communities and mountain families. In: Messerli, B. and Ives, J.D. (eds) *Mountains of the World: a Global Priority*. Parthenon Press, London and New York, pp. 61–84.

Ives, J.D., Messerli, B. and Rhoades, R.E. (1997) Agenda for sustainable mountain development. In: Messerli, B. and Ives, J.D. (eds) *Mountains of the World: a Global Priority*. Parthenon Press, London and New York, pp. 455–466.

Judd, D.R. and Fainstein, S.S. (eds) (1999) *The Tourist City*. York University Press, New Haven.

Luger, K. and Inmann, K. (eds) (1995) *Verreiste Berge*. Studienverlag, Innsbruck.

Messerli, B. and Ives, J.D. (eds) (1997) *Mountains of the World: a Global Priority*. Parthenon Press, London and New York.

Moss, L.A.G. (1994a) Beyond tourism: the amenity migrants. In: Mannermaa, M., Inayyatullah, S. and Slaughter, R. (eds) *Coherence and Chaos in Our Uncommon Futures: Visions, Means, Actions*. Finland Futures Research Centre, Turku School of Economics and Business Administration, Turku, pp. 121–127.

Moss, L.A.G. (1994b), International art collecting, tourism, and a tribal region in Indonesia. In: Taylor, P.M. (ed.) *Fragile Traditions, Indonesial Art in Jeopardy*. University of Hawaii Press, Honolulu, pp. 91–121.

Moss, L.A.G. (1999) Policy Issues brief: sustaining the Sierra Nevada bioregion's integrity under growing human population pressure. Public Policy Institute of California, San Francisco, and http://www.mountin forum.com.

Mountain Agenda (1999) *Mountains of the World: Tourism and Sustainable Mountain Development*. Mountain Agenda, Bern.

Nha Trang, C.H.T.N. and Pensinger, W.L. (1994) The Moon of Hoa Binh. Autopoy Foundation and http: //www.peaknet.org/webpages/autopoy/index.html, Bangkok.

Preston, L. (ed.) (1997) *Investing in Mountains: Innovative Mechanisms and Promising Examples for Financing Conservation and Sustainable Development*. The Mountain Institute, Franklin, West Virginia.

Price, M.F. (ed.) (1996) *People and Tourism in Fragile Environments*. John Wiley & Sons, Chichester.

Price, M.F. and Barry, R.G. (1997) Climate change. In: Messerli, B. and Ives, J.D. (eds) *Mountains of the World: a Global Priority*. Parthenon Press, London and New York, pp. 409–445.

Price, M.F., Moss, L.A.G. and Williams, P.W. (1997) Tourism and amenity migration. In: Messerli, B and Ives, J.D. (eds) *Mountains of the World: a Global Priority*. Parthenon Press, London and New York, pp. 249–280.

Ringland, G. (1998) *Scenario Planning: Managing for the Future*. John Wiley & Sons, Chichester.

Stevenson, T. (1998) Netweaving alternative futures, information technocracy or communicative community? *Futures* 30, 189–198.

Stone, P.B. (ed.) (1992) *The State of the World's Mountains, a Global Report*. Zed Books, London and New Jersey.

Wackernagel, M. and Rees, W.E. (1996) *Our Ecological Footprint: Reducing Human Impact on the Earth*. New Society Publishers, Philadelphia.

Zimmermann, F. (1995) The Alpine region: regional restructuring opportunities and constraints in a fragile environment. In: Montanari, A. and Williams, A.M (eds) *European Tourism. Regions, Spaces and Restructuring.* John Wiley & Sons, Chichester, New York, pp. 19–40.

Zimmermann, F. (1998) Austria: contrasting tourist seasons and contrasting regions. In: Williams, A.M. and Shaw, G. (eds) *Tourism and Economic Development. European Experiences*, 3rd edn. John Wiley & Sons, Chichester, New York, pp. 175–197.

Index